WITHDRAWN
UTSA LIBRARIES

RENEWALS 458-4574
DATE DUE

YO-BSE-655

THE MANICHAEAN BODY

BODY

In Discipline and Ritual

Jason David BeDuhn

The Johns Hopkins University Press
Baltimore & London

©2000 The Johns Hopkins University Press
All rights reserved. Published 2000
Printed in the United States of America on acid-free paper
2 4 6 8 9 7 5 3 1

The Johns Hopkins University Press
2715 North Charles Street
Baltimore, Maryland 21218-4363
www.press.jhu.edu

Library of Congress Cataloging-in-Publication Data will be found at the end
of this book.
A catalog record for this book is available from the British Library.

ISBN 0-8018-6270-1

Library
University of Texas
at San Antonio

To Richard Frye and Kurt Rudolph
for opening the door

CONTENTS

PLATES FOLLOW PAGE 162

PREFACE

The preponderate orientation of the history of religions towards "ideology" . . . should recede in favor of a greater emphasis on the practical field of the cultus. . . . Religious communities are chiefly cultic communities. . . . It is from practice that mythology derives its religious significance; otherwise, it is only literature.
—Kurt Rudolph

We are in danger of losing the Manichaeans. The adherents of this extinct world religion have been brought before our eyes again only in this century, in the form of the lacunous utterances of their tattered books and the faded images of their faces on scraps of a once-accomplished art. This is all that remains of one of the major forces in religious history, a world religion on a scale that rivaled the more familiar members of that elite category: Buddhism, Christianity, and Islam. Beginning in third-century C.E. Mesopotamia in the proclamation of Mani, or Mani*h*ayya (Latinized as Manichaeus, from which we get the modern designation of the religion), it quickly spread throughout the Roman and Persian empires, and within four centuries had planted communities from Spain to China. In each region, it competed with and influenced its religious rivals, leaving a lasting mark on the world's religious inheritance. But failure to gain significant and sustained political backing, relentless persecution, and other factors still not fully understood brought the Manichaean world crashing down. One by one, Manichaean communities died out, disappearing from Europe by early mediaeval times, driven from the

Near East and Central Asia in the tenth and eleventh centuries, and finally fading away in southeastern China sometime after the fourteenth century. Their leadership slaughtered, their books burned, their temples confiscated, it seemed as though history would forget the Manichaeans. But the modern passion for history has taken long strides toward retrieving the Manichaean story, and some of the best minds in the historical study of religions have devoted energy in the last century to reconstructing and understanding the religion of the Manichaeans.

Nevertheless, in the attempt to recover this lost world, to make it speak to the present, we are in danger of all too quickly consigning the Manichaeans to a more permanent oblivion. Our well-meaning attempt to make sense of an alien tradition threatens to entomb it in the role of perpetual handmaiden to our interpretive philosophies, and to the living religions which, as shapers of those philosophies, have found yet another way to bury the heretics. We have been too quick to enshrine the Manichaean tradition as an -ism, comfortably nested in a web of interpretation that locates Manichaeism in its relation to other, better-known dualisms, asceticisms, gnosticisms, mysticisms, and syncretisms. Dissected and dispersed in this way, Manichaeism evaporates into a curious assemblage of doctrinal trivia.

The consequence of the approach that has dominated research into Manichaeism in the past can be seen in the most accessible modern scholarship on the subject where, after close attention has been lavished on the details of Manichaean mythology and on imagining the implications of the religion's dualistic axioms, practice often is relegated to a brief afterthought. Manichaean ideology is fascinating, and one may not notice the neglect of ritual until it is realized that these modern treatments of Manichaeism provide no account of how a Manichaean actually attains salvation. Instead, salvation seems to be a given, by virtue merely of being a Manichaean.[1] This gaping hole in the reconstruction of the religion at times is hypostasized into what I call the "gnostic interpretation" of the religion: the claim that Mani's religion is a body of knowledge that, simply by being known, accomplishes salvation.[2] This understanding of Manichaeism is inaccurate, and fails to explain the Manichaeans of history.

My ambitious goal is to "save" the Manichaeans for history by recovering how they proposed to save themselves. I intend to focus on the program by which individuals and collectivities undertook to be Manichaeans in ancient and mediaeval societies that largely opposed such a lifestyle. In other words, I am talking about what it was to be a Manichaean, what identifying character-istics isolated a Manichaean from any other person in his or her society. The institutions of the Manichaean tradition promoted certain indices of mem-bership, which the tradition classified as markers of salvational aptitude. De-pending on the society, some of these indices would set the Manichaean apart from the general population; others would not. The Manichaean tradition put forward a total package of such behaviors, enforced it with sanctions, and pro-moted it with rationales. The study here reconstructs and analyzes the disci-plinary and ritual complex that every day required an affirmation of allegiance to the Manichaean salvational project.

In the following pages, I reconstruct the Manichaean disciplinary and ritual complex as a system, and present it as best as I am able to a modern audience. My undertaking involves two basic tasks: (1) offering a translation or re-description of Manichaean systems of practice along with their autointerpre-tation, that is, the questions about the practices characteristic of *their* own cul-ture and historical moment; (2) furthering the re-placement of these practices and rationales into our arena of historical comprehension by answering ques-tions about them characteristic of *our* own culture and historical moment. One might characterize these two steps as analogous to literal and paraphras-tic translation. I consider this undertaking, in both of its aspects, to be a *his-toricist* project.

In the process of discussing Manichaean practices and the discourses that supported those practices, I necessarily address certain well-known positions in the fields that constitute the human sciences (traditionally divided between the humanities and the social sciences). Although the more theoretical dis-cussions of this book are in service of my limited historical project, they un-doubtedly impact on broader issues in the historical study of human society and culture. I have tried to avoid the common pitfall of reinventing the wheel, and it is my assertion that the methods employed here are not new. I am by practice an eclecticist, and have little interest in drawing the many methods I find useful into a grand unified theory. I feel that it is necessary, however, to heighten attention to certain limitations of history and of interpretation that to date have not been given due consideration. For this purpose, I appeal from time to time to certain basic premises based in the pragmatist tradition as ex-emplified in the work of George Herbert Mead, including his account of the self, of communication, and of human apprehension of reality past and pres-ent. Mead's pragmatism has had a decisive, often uncredited, impact on subsequent theory in the human sciences, including language theory, the sociology of knowledge, and the analysis of self-forming discourses and practices. I have employed these developments of Mead as well.

The pragmatist understanding of the social character of the self, and the process by which the self is formed in the human individual (set forth in Mead's *Mind, Self, and Society* [1934]), offers the best framework within which to attempt to translate the self-forming goals of Manichaean discourse and practice. Michel Foucault's often eloquent permutation of this tradition is familiar to most of the potential readers of this book, and so supplies convenient language and models with which to convey the Manichaean project of training the body, forming the self, and conducting the institutionally sanctioned work of the religion. Foucault has been, and can be, criticized for a number of weaknesses and contradictions in the body of his work, foremost, his neglect of the pragmatist roots of his own questions and modes of analysis. Nevertheless, I find some of his constructs heuristically useful to the present undertaking for three reasons. First, the present study, like much of Foucault's work, is a project of "counter-memory," of retrieving from the past suppressed options of human embodiment "in order both to excavate alternative possibilities and to display the contingency of our identity to us." Second, this study, like Foucault's work, focuses on the analysis of normative systems, of past worlds that were intended and promoted, leaving aside an assessment of how successfully they were implemented at individual moments or in individual lives. Third, this study attempts to effect a translation of Manichaean discourse into modern academic categories, and so needs a compelling modern discourse to which it can be wedded with a minimum amount of violence to its own ways of speaking. Whatever else one may say about Foucault, he has produced an engaging language with which to discuss issues of human embodiment.

My effort to draw this project out of the available sources also requires a workable language theory that permits us to capture just how Manichaean texts use language. In this case, the pragmatist account of communication lies scattered throughout Mead's publications, but has been successfully taken up and significantly furthered by the work of J. L. Austin and Quentin Skinner. Once again, the familiarity of the latter two authors provides an added value to the use of their language and models within my study. Skinner's historicist application of Austin's speech-act theory, however, needs to be clarified in order to guard it from a naive subjectivism, a task I have taken up elsewhere.[3]

Finally, pragmatist phenomenology (worked out by Mead in *The Philoso-phy of the Present* [1932], and in an unfinished manuscript published as essays II, III, IV, and XXX.F of *The Philosophy of the Act* [1938]) permits us to nar-row, if not to bridge, the gap between what Kenneth Pike has called the emic and etic—a gap that constitutes the most basic problem of understanding or explaining a religion, a culture, a society, or the course of history itself. This third contribution of Mead has been taken up in varying degrees by what is of-ten called the "intellectualist" tradition of social anthropology, and in Peter Berger's sociology of knowledge, as well as by Foucault's interest in "power-knowledge." It is my contention that this body of work represents a *tertium quid* between the dominant Weberian and Durkheimian paradigms of inter-pretation. But my immediate concern in this book is only that it succeeds where those approaches fail: to provide access to the Manichaean body in dis-cipline and ritual.

In chapter 1 I lay the groundwork of the approach taken in the rest of the book, explaining why a reconstruction of the normative system of Manichaean practice is the right thing to be doing at this stage of research on the subject, and justifying how I intend to access that normative system from such a great historical and cultural distance. The subsequent chapters apply this ground-work to all of the currently known sources on Manichaean discipline and rit-ual. I hope that it will be considered a virtue, rather than an editorial short-coming, that I allow the sources to speak for themselves as much as possible. I could have summarized much of this material, and directed the reader to the rare books and specialized journals held in a small number of research li-braries where the texts are to be found, mostly translated into languages other than English. Instead, I have chosen to supply the reader with all of the mate-rial upon which I build my analysis. Because I wish to take regional variation into account, these sources are organized linguistically and geographically into three sets: Central (Syriac and Arabic), Western (Coptic, Greek, and Latin), and Eastern (Middle Persian, Parthian, Sogdian, Turkic, and Chinese). The Central set contains only polemical sources, although these quote Mani-chaean texts extensively; the Western and Eastern sets include varying amounts of both insider and outsider material. To this material I bring the fol-lowing questions: Who participated in the daily ritual meal, and how did one prepare to participate? What were the rationales for these preparations? What did participation in the ritual entail? What were the rationales for participation and for the ritual itself?

I conclude my study with two chapters that reflect upon the significance of this data, both for our understanding of Manichaeism and for our interpretation of religious phenomena in general. In chapter 6 I highlight some key implications of my research for unresolved questions concerning Manichaean doctrines and practices, and for the abiding problems of comprehension across cultural and historical boundaries. Last, in chapter 7, I examine modern theories of religious embodiment and discourse in order to show how certain analytical constructs elucidate Manichaean practices while others seem untenable in light of the Manichaean evidence.

Those somewhat familiar with Manichaeism as it has been set forth in Western scholarship over the last century may be surprised to see the juxtaposition of the words "Manichaean" and "body" in the title of this book. What do Manichaeans have to do with bodies? Surely, to be a Manichaean is the antithesis of being a body. As a Manichaean, does one not strive to be free of the body? Is not Manichaeism the quintessential gnostic tradition,[4] opposing spirit to matter, liberation to embodiment? Is it not a classic case of a "Verneinung des Willens zum Leben"?

It is the principal goal of this book to demonstrate the degree to which this popular understanding of Manichaeism is wrong. The interpretation of Manichaeism accepted until now is wrong not in its myriad details, which are well established, but in the general conclusions it draws from those details. Modern scholarship on Manichaeism has been able to draw the wrong conclusions because it has been free to treat Manichaean testimony selectively, and to assemble it into a system that speaks primarily to we moderns, rather than feeling constrained to leave Manichaean testimony in its original assemblage as a system that spoke to the historical Manichaeans. I have done my best to follow the latter route, although, as a modern myself, I have surely fallen off the path a time or two. I hope that any shortcomings in my analysis of specific details, or in my selection of language with which to convey Manichaean reality to the modern world, will not detract from my overall thesis: that to be a Manichaean, to do what it is Manichaeans are expected to do, and to fulfill the salvational goals put forward by Mani, one must first and foremost be a Manichaean body.

ACKNOWLEDGMENTS

I wish, first of all, to acknowledge the two gentlemen-scholars to whom this book is dedicated—Richard N. Frye and Kurt Rudolph—who first directed me along the path to the Manichaeans. As I have traveled that path, I have benefited tremendously from the mentoring and companionship of my colleagues and friends in Europe; and I would like to thank Peter Bryder, Christiane Reck, Werner Sundermann, Aloïs van Tongerloo, and Peter Zieme for their encouragement. The conclusions to which my research has led me had their infancy and slow maturation in the company of the Manichaean Studies Consultation and its successor, the Manichaean Studies Group, both of the Society of Biblical Literature; and I would like to thank all involved in that endeavor, most especially my coconspirator in Mani-mania, Paul Mirecki, for initiating this forum and taking me on as a partner in it.

This book is a reworking of my doctoral dissertation, and so owes a great debt to the assembly of scholars who saw me through that earlier process: Robert F. Campany, Larry Clark, Nancy Demand, Luke T. Johnson, Jan Nattier, and J. Samuel Preus. For substantial help with languages beyond my expertise, I would like to add an extra word of thanks to Larry Clark (Turkic) and Robert Campany (Chinese). I also would like to acknowledge the National Endowment for the Humanities, and the Stewart and Dagmar Riley Fellowship at Indiana University for the financial support that made my dissertation possible.

Finally, a special word of thanks to Zsuzsanna Gulácsi, both for her assistance with interpretations of Manichaean art, and for her constant intellectual and personal companionship through the four years that saw this book take its definitive shape.

NOTE

ON TEXTS AND TRANSLITERATIONS

To prevent the references from becoming too cumbersome, I cite ancient texts by their shortest, most universal designation. A table of texts at the end of the book provides the necessary key to the bibliography identifying the editor and/or translator of the text in question. For those texts that have been edited or translated more than once, I have limited references to the most well-known or accessible version. I do not always follow the existing translations, but from time to time make modifications according to the original. Each of the languages represented in these texts has its own established system of transliteration to which I have adhered when giving an original term. This mixture of systems may appear strange, but it is essential for the philologically inclined segment of the book's readership.

THE MANICHAEAN
BODY

ONE

OUT OF THE PAST

The pasts that succeed one another could never be prophesied
from one another. Nothing is lost, but that which arrives
that is novel gives a continually new past.
—G. H. Mead

How do we undertake the historical study of a dead religion? How do we bridge the gulf between the present, with all that it entails, and the past? What counts as evidence? What constitutes an understanding or an explanation? How do we assess the validity of interpretation? To what analytical goals do we aspire, and which among these goals are actually achievable? These are the methodological questions that must be addressed if we are to bring the Manichaean tradition out of the past of its historical existence and into the present of our historical knowledge.

Five challenges confront the researcher who would delve into the sources available on Manichaeism. First, the surviving material is both meager in extent and fragmentary in condition, leaving many gaps in basic information. Second, the sources derive from widely diverse historical and cultural contexts, making a synchronic synthesis problematic. Third, the Manichaeans themselves practiced a form of doctrinal translation that radically diversified their discourse, with the result that, for example, Chinese sources present a Sinicized Manichaeism very different from the varieties we find in Latin, Greek, Coptic, Middle Iranian, or Turkic materials, all equally accommodating to local cultural norms. Fourth, all of the sources are products of propaganda, with either apologetic or polemical bias. Fifth, the Manichaean religion is extinct, so it is impossible to conduct ethnographic observation to supplement or critique the literary (and pictorial) presentation of the religion.

THE SOURCES

The story of the rediscovery of Manichaeism has been told many times;[1] but perhaps I will be forgiven an abbreviated retelling simply to situate the reader in preparation for the study to follow. Prior to the twentieth century, historical knowledge of Manichaeism depended entirely on the polemical accounts of its enemies. The reassessment of the entire history of Christianity compelled by the Protestant Reformation and the Enlightenment led to the first critical examinations of the most accessible of these sources, the heresiographical writings of Christian church leaders of the fourth to tenth centuries C.E.[2] The nineteenth century brought significant gains in access to sources; many new Patristic texts (Greek and Syriac) came to light from archives of Orthodox institutions in Greece and the Middle East,[3] and Arabic sources heretofore unknown to the European academy revealed even more detailed accounts of the dead religion.[4] A comparison of all these sources produced a rather sketchy general picture of the Manichaeans as a historical curiosity, seen entirely through the eyes of their religious rivals, Christian and Muslim.

This situation changed dramatically with the 1904 announcement by F.W.K. Müller that he had succeeded in deciphering texts brought back from East Turkestan by a German exploratory expedition, and found them to have Manichaean contents. The heap of highly fragmentary Manichaean literature and art eventually retrieved from the region of Turfan by several expeditions remains the largest and most important known source of information on the religion. The Turfan Manichaean texts, written in three different scripts (Manichaean, Sogdian, and Runic) and seven languages (Parthian, Middle Persian, New Persian, Sogdian, Tokharian, Bactrian, and Turkic), include hymns, prayers, poetry, treatises, sermons, parables, liturgical scripts, calendars, documents, letters, glossaries, and painted miniatures. The edition and translation of these materials proceeded apace, hand in hand with the reconstruction of the largely unknown languages in which they were written, through the extraordinary efforts of Müller, F. C. Andreas, W. B. Henning, Albert von Le Coq, E. Waldschmidt, W. Lentz, W. Bang, A. von Gabain, and others. This work ceased abruptly due to World War II, was taken up only sporadically in the 1950s and early 1960s (primarily by Mary Boyce and Jes Asmussen), but returned to a highly productive phase under the gifted leadership of Werner Sundermann (Iranian) and Peter Zieme (Turkic) from the late 1960s up to the present. New discoveries of Manichaean texts continue to be made in the Turfan region to this day.

Shortly after the initial Turfan discoveries, British and French expeditions found Chinese and Turkic Manichaean texts farther to the east at Tun-huang. The Tun-huang Turkic finds are rather meager compared with the four Chinese rolls which have proven to be extraordinarily important and rich sources of information: the *Hymnscroll*, the *Compendium*, the *Treatise (Ts'an Ching)*, and the *Conversion of the Barbarians (Hua Hu Ching)*. Spurred by the existence of Chinese Manichaean texts, the French scholars Édouard Chavannes and Paul Pelliot led the way in sifting through Chinese historical documents for references to the religion, thus adding a new body of material to outsider accounts like those already known in the West.[5] The combination of the Turfan and Tun-huang discoveries permitted the first synthetic studies of Manichaeism based on primary sources, and gave birth to modern Manichaean studies.

It was not long before the nascent field became the beneficiary of another major wellspring: a small collection of Manichaean books came to light in Egypt in 1929. Eventually traced back to an ancient village in the Fayum district, the Medinet Madi library, written in Coptic, contained seven volumes: the *Psalm-Book*, the *Homilies*, the *Chapters* in two volumes *(Kephalaia I* and *Kephalaia II)*, the *Readings (Synaxeis)*, the *Letters*, and the *History*. In the capable hands of H. Ibscher, C. Schmidt, H.-J. Polotsky, C.R.C. Allberry, and A. Böhlig, the fragile books began to yield their secrets and vastly increase our knowledge of Manichaeism, this time from the western region of its remarkable expanse.[6] Tragically, World War II also intervened in this work, this time with devastating results. The *Letters* and *History* volumes vanished after the war. Work on the surviving pieces of the collection, with the sole exception of the efforts of A. Böhlig, came to a complete halt. The laborious process of reconstruction, editing, and translation only resumed in the 1980s. Even the already published portions of the material received almost no attention in the intervening period. Only the French scholar H.-C. Puech, the Belgian J. Ries, and the German A. Böhlig made substantial use of these rich sources to advance the field during that time.

Two more Egyptian discoveries complete the history of the recovery of primary Manichaean documents. A tiny book acquired by the University of Cologne in the 1960s has achieved fame as the *Cologne Mani Codex*, unveiled to the modern world by the erudite and patient labors of A. Henrichs, L. Koenen, and C. Römer (with smaller contributions from a number of others). This Greek book of uncertain provenance recounts the life of Mani and the early years of his religious activity. It has received a great deal of attention as a unique document that seems to open to us the very earliest form of Manichaeism. Then, only a few years ago, a joint Australian-Canadian archaeological expedition working in the Dakhleh Oasis of Egypt uncovered a new cache of Manichaean documents. This rather heterogeneous assortment of material from ancient Kellis is still in the earliest phase of assessment, and has not been available to me in the preparation of this study.

These sources constitute the material of Manichaean studies, and form the basis of my reconstruction and analysis of Manichaean disciplinary and ritual practices. The sources at hand do not permit a strictly synchronic comparison. They testify not only to regional adaptation but also to development over time. Some of the temporal transformations of the Manichaean tradition originated at the center, in the shape of reforms and deliberated decisions. The majority of the changes, however, accrued at the periphery as local Manichaean communities struggled to survive and come to terms with the larger cultures in which they existed. Each regional collection of texts, both primary and polemical, informs us of a local, discrete variety of the world religion. Each is a product of a particular cultural milieu and literary tradition.

APPROACH

The first task of the historian, therefore, is a reconstruction of the normative system, that is, a description of Manichaeism in terms of the explicitly stated functions of its practices. Melford Spiro has expressed this approach well in relation to his own study of Burmese Buddhism. In taking the normative system as a starting point, he says, he is concerned "not with its social or psychological consequences, but with its purpose; and by 'purpose' is meant, not the personal motives which lead to monastic recruitment, but the culturally stipulated end or ends for which monasticism is the culturally prescribed means."[7] In talking about "Manichaeism" as a unitary phenomenon, my task is to establish what in the diverse material output of historical Manichaeism remains unnegotiated in local conditions, to demonstrate how the range of distinctive references used among these several regions reflects a unified Manichaean tradition of practice. An assessment of how each set of sources shows adaptation to the pre-existing culture and ongoing influences of each regional population is a task best left to a series of separate studies with a more comparative agenda, and only can yield concrete results in light of an established set of norms.

Readers somewhat familiar with Manichaean studies may be under the impression that the presentation of the normative system has been the business of the field for quite some time. They are correct to the extent that a great deal of the work has been primarily philological in nature, and so is concerned with translating Manichaean testimony into a comprehensible body of literature, and also in the sense that a harmonized presentation of Manichaean discourse has been a prominent feature of most discussions of Manichaeism. Since the sources from which we can know the lost world of the Manichaeans are mostly textual, the study of Manichaeism has been conducted until now in the mode of intellectual history or the history of ideas. It has seemed least problematic simply to lay Manichaean discourse alongside that of other traditions, and to trace connections, oppositions, and novelties— in short, to see Manichaean talk as part of, and in relation to, the general religious expression of humankind. I do believe that some accurate and valuable conclusions can be and have been reached in this way. But my approach is different, and so I need to make plain that difference and explain why I think it offers a better historical apprehension of the Manichaean tradition.

Certain characteristics of Manichaean discourse make it difficult for the approach that has predominated so far to yield results that make sense of Manichaeism as a religious system. The Manichaean voice is put in the service of themes from outside of its world, and its paltry remnants are overwhelmed by the voluminous resources of traditions that have shaped the interests and concerns of modern researchers more directly. To put it another way, the Manichaean material is made to answer questions the Manichaeans themselves did not ask, and is ignored or misunderstood when it speaks to concerns that we are not conditioned to have. At best, "reasonable" reconstructions of the tradition are offered which fit into larger schemes of categories and trajectories in the history of religions. Manichaeism survives as an -ism, a worldview perhaps, but does not manage to take shape in our understanding as a community of people who actually put into practice a distinctive way of life.

Mani reportedly said:

> The writings, wisdoms, apocalypses, parables and psalms of the earlier
> churches are from all parts reunited in my church to the wisdom which I
> have revealed to you. As a river is joined to another river to form a powerful
> current, just so are the ancient books joined in my writings; and they form
> one great wisdom, such as has not existed in preceding generations.[8]

A Manichaean parable preserved in Sogdian[9] confirms this sentiment, liken-
ing other religions to small bodies of water and the Manichaean faith to a vast
ocean that receives and assimilates all other waters to its own particular flavor.
Reading such words, historians of religion should tremble, because such an attitude as these passages reflect renders any history of ideas problematic in the
extreme.

The term *syncretism* scarcely does justice to a movement so self-consciously absorbent, so openly adaptive as we know the Manichaeans to have
been. Their appropriation of Christian, Zoroastrian, and Buddhist modes of
expression in the respective domains of these rival religions far exceeded simple disguise or rhetorical strategy. The Manichaean mission actively integrated
itself into new cultural domains, and by converting inhabitants already
steeped in the language of a prior faith made it inevitable that such language
carried with it connotations far beyond a simple masking of Manichaean
dogma. To try to hold together a unified Manichaean tradition in the face of
such striking mutability in the sources is a tall order.

When we make a close examination of the sources from which the synthetic versions of Manichaean doctrine have been constructed by modern
scholarship, it becomes clear that harmonization has partially effaced the historical and cultural transformations of Manichaeism, and that the clarity of
our doctrinal models relies upon an inordinate number of glosses. It is not just
a matter of linguistically distinct terminology and divergent cultural nuance;
the sources also reveal significant discrepancies in the Manichaean pantheon
and in some of the most basic doctrinal exposition. The neat hierarchies we
have sketched for ourselves do not hold up from text to text; and the logic of
the Manichaean *Listenwissenschaft* defies our expectations of order and consistency.

The fluidity of Manichaean discourse in its historical and cultural transformation threatens to deprive the historian of an identifiable and distinct

Manichaeism. In many cases modern researchers apply the term *Manichaean* to loosely defined sets of ideas or attitudes, and speculate on connections to all sorts of religious movements and groups. In this way they continue the venerable tradition of calling any poorly known, heretical group by this name, a practice common not only in the Christian West, but also in the Islamic Middle East, and in China. In order to respond to this threat, we need to identify the uncompromised core of Manichaean identity, if such exists, and try to see Manichaeism as an actual historical community rather than as a free-floating body of ideas.

The best place to look for a religious community is where it appears engaged in collective action. It was, after all, these practices, far more than any shared ideology, which identified the Manichaean community, set it apart from rival religious traditions, and shaped the public character and self-presentation of the Manichaeans themselves. Since they so readily adapted their doctrinal language to the religious heritage of particular regions, we turn to practices in the hope that these prove more stable in transmission, and more consistently mark the Manichaeans with a distinct identity. This study confirms that Manichaean behavioral codes and ritual practices were more conservatively maintained than Manichaean discourse in general, and that, in addition, a core of that discourse likewise retained consistency by its close relation to practice.

In the study of contemporary religions, an investigation of religious practice has an abundance of sources with which to work, and can always generate new material by direct observation. Because the Manichaean community cannot be observed in this way, it is legitimate to raise questions about the validity of the kind of reconstruction this book offers. Is it possible to "observe" a religious community of the past? How can practice be recovered from text? What is it exactly that we claim to be able to see of that past practice? My answers to these questions will necessarily involve debates over method and theory in the study of religions (and so in the fields of anthropology, sociology, history, and literary studies), and will position the approach taken here relative to the major schools of thought in the humanities and social sciences.

All of the literary sources composed and used by the Manichaeans, and which have survived to find their place in this study, are to some degree apologetic in that they communicate an inside, approving perspective on the Manichaean experience of reality. Since my project is to reconstruct and analyze the normative Manichaean construction of that reality, the apologetic nature of the sources does not constitute a significant problem. The institutions of the Manichaean tradition worked to inculcate an experience of reality that conformed to its norms, and—assuming at least a modicum of success in the project of Manichaean authority—we need to take these constructs seriously. The legitimacy of studying the normative configuration of a tradition stems from a recognition of the authority of the norms, not for the researcher, but for the adherents of the tradition. Continued adherence to a religion such as Manichaeism in the face of strong outside pressures suggests the successful inculcation of norms within the individual, and so a historical impact for those norms.[10] An attempt to recover from the past individual subversive or nonnormative religious expression would encounter a host of difficulties that my project simply avoids.[11] Normative texts inform us of what religious authorities sanctioned, not necessarily what actually happened. Nonetheless, the continued existence and invocation of such norms in large part defined what Manichaeism was historically.

Polemical accounts also can be a valuable source of information, especially in the case of a "lost" tradition such as Manichaeism. To be credible, such sources must be assessed carefully by means of comparison with both normative testimony and the traditions of polemical accusation specific to the region and time. The "litmus test" in the use of such sources must be the ability to find some confirming correlation between the polemical account and the Manichaeans' own testimony, however different the perspective of the two positions. In the case of Manichaean studies, polemical testimony has actually enjoyed a relatively favored status, due to the distinctive set of circumstances that makes the modern Western scholar a direct heir, and hence a member of the family, of Christian anti-Manichaean polemicists of late antiquity. Our inherited, generally positive, evaluation of such authors as Augustine of Hippo and Ephrem Syrus makes some loathe to treat them with the same degree of critical skepticism applied to lesser figures. Polemical characterizations of Manichaeism cast a long shadow, and continue to predispose modern researchers to interpretations consonant with the views of the church leaders. While the data supplied by these ancient anti-Manichaean accounts proves to be fairly reliable, the spin of interpretation placed upon it by those accounts has had a deleterious effect on modern understandings of Manichaeism.

Although historical sources are themselves products of selection and design, and partake of the power relationships of their culture and time, the historian produces a new set of coercive forces upon the material and brings the material into relation with new institutions of power. Thus the polemical or apologetic handling of material in sources is replicated in the work of the historian. Historians can choose to adopt the orientation of a given source, and therefore continue its polemic or apologetic significance. Conversely, historians may reject the tendency of the source and engage in a polemic against it, in this way renegotiating the power relationships of the material. But it is naive to assert that historians can get around the perspectives of their sources to access directly past events themselves, or to release timeless objective facts from the matrix of presentation supplied by the sources.

THE LIMITS OF HISTORY

This book is *historicist* in approach and employs a *pragmatist historiography* in its reconstruction of the Manichaean past. In brief, a historicist approach seeks to understand human action and discourse as events within the context of the time and locale of their occurrence rather than assessing them by standards of reason imported from our own location, or extracting from them such elements as can be productively employed in our own situation. A pragmatist historiography is one that emphasizes the differences between the experience of present events in people's lives and the reconstruction and redescription of past events based upon presently available sources.[12] We can never relive the past as it was experienced; instead, we construct models of the past based on incomplete evidence within the limitations of currently dominant categories of reality. But this does not mean, as some have supposed, that pragmatism champions the subjugation of the past to our own interests, and so engages in a kind of rationalist appropriation of the past. Insofar as it is concerned with history, pragmatism seeks to explain how human behavior made the world we now find before us, while acknowledging that any reconstruction is partial and tenuous. The greatest impact of a pragmatist historiography on the study of religions lies in its recognition and insistence that certain aspects of religious experience are not recoverable in our reconstructions of the past. For this reason, certain kinds of research that may be desirable in regard to present religions simply are not practicable with respect to past religions. For the same reason, particular interpretive approaches will find no justification in the kinds of evidence recoverable from the past, and so will be constrained to remain mere speculation.

History only exists because we in the present encounter relics or traces of events that occurred outside of our own experiences.[13] These traces exist in the present, and we analyze and interpret them in exactly the same way as we do any problematic thing we encounter in the present. Once we realize that the past only exists in the present as relics, we can begin to differentiate that which survives in time from that which does not, that which leaves a trace from that which leaves none. The events of the past, as they were experienced by contemporaneous humans, have ceased to exist, and with them have passed into extinction every element of those events which was not rendered into a trace. We do not restore historical events as they were experienced by those for whom they were the present; we give birth to something else, something new, which exists as a part of our present and did not exist in the prior presents that we now refer to as the past.

As a dead tradition, Manichaeism provides no living institutions, no oral culture, no abiding social arrangements that can be directly observed and analyzed. The artistic and architectural legacy of the Manichaean communities is scant. Instead, the historian must rely mostly upon literary evidence of the Manichaean past. Faced with historical traces of this sort, it takes no deep philosophy to reason out what can and cannot be recovered historically from them. I am relieved of what seems to be the working assumption of many engaged in the human sciences: that the trained observer can see, from the outside, what members of a society cannot see precisely because they are inside it. I am specifically excluded by history from observing anything that is not testified to by the sources; these sources are the products of insiders, the participants of the historical and cultural context that forms the object of my investigation. I can "see" only what they choose to tell; I can in no way instruct them to tell me other things and, of course, the producers of these materials had no idea that they were going to be telling *me* anything.[14] Since direct observation is precluded, I have no base of data except that which is communicated by means of the Manichaeans' own categories of meaning and truth (which is only slightly mitigated by contemporaneous observations from outside the community).

Historians, operating within their own categories of meaning and truth, must work out a translation if the communication embodied in the literary relic is to be anything but gibberish in the present. Translation is always much more than a manipulation of lexicons; it involves plotting systems of reference within a literary corpus and deciphering its codes of composition. Manichaean sources for the most part employ languages for which a non-Manichaean literature also exists.[15] Religious discourse problematizes only a small portion of secular language, so one gains access into Manichaean literature in the first place by the lexicon of nonproblematized terms for objects also recognized outside the tradition (e.g., tables, bread, and robes), as well as actions (such as sitting, fasting, and speaking). With this bridgehead established, the translator can extend the lexicon through the system of relations that exists between the known unproblematized terms and the unknown problematized ones. The correlation of behaviors to terms anchors this process of extension, and must be the final arbiter of meaning. Terms identifying objects that do not exist in our universe of discourse (e.g., particular deities, rituals, and ecclesiastical positions) may also be defined in reference to associated behaviors, since their significance derives from response, and analogous responses do exist in our universe of discourse.

By analyzing, interpreting, and assembling the evidence we have determined to be relevant to our inquiry, we construct a historical account as a redescription, in the present, of the prior present that stands as a past to that evidence. We are able to do this in part because, as Quentin Skinner argues, "for at least certain classes of social actions there can be a unique form of . . . redescription which, by way of recovering the agent's intended illocutionary act, may be capable of explaining at least certain features of the agent's behaviour."[16] What Skinner means here is that certain statements and actions carry a *communicated* intentionality, conventional for the culture within which it occurs, as J. L. Austin first suggested. These conventions that provide references to the collective projects in which people are engaged can be catalogued, their significance determined, and in this way "explanations" can be provided for the statements and acts in question, that is, emplacement in larger discursive and pragmatic systems.[17] The achieved "catalogue of illocution" supplies the rationale invoked in the statement and/or act. These illocutions are recoverable because they are part of a lexicon that is used in composing texts, and partly recoverable in those texts. Such elements of "meaning" can enter historical sources, especially literary ones, whereas motivations, causes, and other parts of "what actually happened" are entirely confined to an unrecoverable, dead past. In identifying illocutionary force, we are working with linguistic rather than psychological terrain, and handling the residue of a communicated signification rather than a personal meaning.[18]

In their exposure to Manichaean discourse, it should be noted, modern researchers do not occupy a qualitatively different position from that of the target audiences of Manichaean proselytism in the past. The latter, too, received a text whose only transmitted meaning was its apparent linguistic sense; their internalizations of meaning worked from the same surface starting points as do ours. Their contact with the text also often came via cross-cultural, translational communication. The Manichaean authorities responsible for such translation even indulged in more radical semantic recontextualization than a good historian ever would allow. This is not to say that some elements are not missing from our exposure. For one thing, discussion of practices are not illustrated for us by enactment, so that the total gestalt of practices and discourses in the inhabited milieu of the past is lost. Considering the specific differences between our situation and that of Auditors in the past, as well as between the widely dispersed Manichaean communities of the past, we cannot draw conclusions about the beliefs per se of Manichaeans. But we can describe and analyze the surfaces of Manichaean speech acts as the common base of "meaning" both in the past and to us in the present. In other words, we can study the presented normative system of Manichaean discourse and practice.

Nonetheless, I am not writing a *manual* of Manichaean practice. Robert Campany has stated that the very enterprise of writing a treatise, rather than a manual, on religious rites "suggests that the rites are a sphere of activity that have become peculiarly problematic and opaque, requiring an effort of interpretation or explanation."[19] The opacity of Manichaean rites derives from the extinction of their practitioners and the necessity of reconstructing their system of performance without the benefit of direct inquiry. Translation in this case requires, as Campany maintains, a shift in the controlling center of discourse: the rites themselves need to be elucidated "instead of being the basis upon which other realms of activity" are elucidated (202). According to Campany,

> theoretical thinking about ritual practice . . . entails giving an account of ritual from a point of view outside ritual, using a language and a framework of understanding that are not derived from the ritual world. . . . For the theorist, ritual can no longer be the place from which to start, for *it has become the problem*; recourse must be had to some more secure foundation. (214)

For this reason, I do employ, in a very limited heuristic capacity, etic models of analysis that help to complete the task of translation, however provisionally.

On the other hand, much of what I do in this study qualifies as what Campany describes as nontheoretical, "statements made from within the realm of ritual," which "take ritual itself as their point of departure" and "use ritual itself as the reference point for explaining or describing other areas of life" (214). I do so because the Manichaean way of life was a ritualized one, embedded in ritual relations and operating with reference to ritual ends. It is precisely the controlling force of ritual in Manichaean identity that is lost by interpretations that treat ritual as something to be explained rather than as itself an explanation for much of what constitutes a religious identity.

Many interpretive theories simply have no applicability to historical materials; they depend on methods of observation and inquiry that are not part of the historian's repertoire. The character of historical sources sets limits to the kind of information available, and hence to the kinds of analyses possible. Any interpretation that depends on the postulate that the historical sources misrepresent a reality that one seeks to discover must bring forward other sources that testify to that purported reality. If no such sources are available, then the reality of the sources that do exist is the only historical reality. We can always speculate about what we think to have been the case in the past, but without the means to either prove or disprove these theories such speculation amounts to idle talk.

EXEGESIS

A fault line runs through the theory and method of the human sciences. The academic field of "religious studies," or the comparative study of religions, is itself divided in this way, depending as it does on theories developed in other fields, such as anthropology, sociology, history, and comparative literature. There are those who contend that the business of the human sciences is to "understand" human populations, their structures and actions, by obtaining an account of what motivates and gives meaning to them. This position is known within the humanities as the hermeneutics of charity, and in the social sciences is identified with the tradition of Max Weber. There are those who insist that the task is rather to "explain," and that to be scientists we must bracket the subjective and look only at external arrangements and interactions. This position is known within the humanities as the hermeneutics of suspicion, and in the social sciences is identified with the tradition of Émile Durkheim. These two positions constitute the dominant stances in the modern academic study of religions.

Another fault line does not run between these approaches, but rather bifurcates either approach along a different axis. For in either of these approaches a choice must be made whether to listen to the self-description of the population being studied or to ignore it in favor of new models provided by academic theory. It is not true, as is so often assumed, that the hermeneutics of charity is inherently allied with emic discourse. Nor is it true that the bracketing of the subjective entailed in the hermeneutics of suspicion must perforce subvert emic categories. This other fault line is the more significant in historical study because of the limitations of historical sources, limitations that constrain the historian's access to information beyond what is presented by the interested parties of the past.

The hermeneutics of charity characteristic of what is called "hermeneutics" proper, the interpretive or *Verstehen* approach, is not the natural ally of the categories of studied communities, as is often assumed, but in many cases opens the door to a "hermeneutics of recovery" that appropriates the other as fodder for modern Western academic theories of human nature. By seeking a "reasonable" account of subjective motivation for the observed behavior of others, the attempt to understand all too easily results in a colonial eisegesis.

It is, of course, all too familiar that the hermeneutics of suspicion, also called the "positivist" or "naturalistic" approach, encompassing various kinds of structuralist, functionalist, and materialist methods of analysis, routinely ignores societies' own accounts in favor of modern Western academic categories. Nonetheless, many supposedly naturalistic studies "cheat" by relying on native categories to supply some of the building blocks for their derivative systems. In this way, indigenous self-description creeps into, but rarely controls, systematic accounts of human society and culture.

The fault line of which I speak, therefore, is what Kenneth Pike identifies as the difference between the *emic* and the *etic*. The divide is not simply over who controls the final account, but includes decisions about the kinds of data to include, the methods of acquiring it, the sources from which categories will derive, and most important, what constitutes "understanding" or "explanation." Pike first introduced the terms *emic* and *etic* to differentiate two modes of analyzing sociocultural systems.[20] Emic analyses work with the categories and rules of the society being studied, while etic analyses work with the categories and rules of the outside observer's society. Marvin Harris has contended that emic and etic accounts are based equally in social facts, and that the difference between them involves only how the base of data is selected and organized.[21]

Historical sources provide only emically selected data. Historians can make a second selection, but only within the parameters of what the sources supply. Historical sources also offer their data in an emically organized way. Historians can reorganize this data according to their own culture's categories and rules, but only by coercing data originally fitted to a different organization. Historians working with multiple sources can argue that the different perspectives of those sources justify a synthetic reordering of their accounts in light of each other; but insofar as the sources stem from the same milieu, or from closely related milieux, emic rules continue to set limits to interpretive felicity. Under these conditions, therefore, etic interpretation itself becomes a problem.

Academic (etic) interpretations properly distinguish themselves from religious (emic) ones by rejecting certain transcendental or supramundane premises of the latter;[22] such premises, outside of the epistemological reach of human research, cannot be integrated into testable hypotheses.[23] Bracketing issues of ultimate truth allows researchers to explore many facets of religious traditions as independent human systems. This is very important work. Unfortunately, many academic interpretations, either implicitly or explicitly, claim to represent the *only* reality present in the given religious tradition (or, even more broadly, in all religions); that is, they position themselves as an "ultimate truth" about the tradition in place of the one held by adherents of the tradition. The consequence of such interpretations with which I am most concerned is that they lose sight of important relations operating within the religious community alongside of the various psychological, economic, political, social, ideological, and cultural forces these theories purport to reveal. A set of practical relations that structure an approved embodiment of the tradition's values, coordinated with a set of rationales that legitimate and interpret the significance of those values, forms an essential component of any religious tradition, and provides much of the day-to-day motivation and reinforcement of adherence to it. Without taking these relations into account, no interpretation can be said to have "made sense" of a religion, or to have revealed the whole "reality" of what it is.[24]

Despite the handicap of dealing with constraining historical sources, "explanatory" or social-scientific approaches to religion do not necessarily entail a refutation of emic models, if the latter are recognized as systems operating beside the ones upon which the social scientist focuses. Unfortunately, the surviving sources simply do not provide the kind of data necessary to formulate a truly social scientific reconstruction of the Manichaean community. Researchers opting for this sort of approach are limited to reconfiguring emic data according to imported etic models, a course of action usually defended on the basis of analogies from contemporary, directly observable societies. Provided we acknowledge some common biological or social basis for all human behavior, we can defend the use of such methods, albeit with extreme caution. They do not necessarily entail a rejection of a community's account of itself.

On the other hand, discourse-based or hermeneutical interpretations of religions necessarily cause some displacement of native self-interpretations. Such interpretations also apply to practices when the latter are viewed as obeying discursive rules or structures. In either case, the hermeneut investigates historical sources for structures or essences of meaning compelling to the modern reader. This method tends to divorce religious discourse from the context of its formation and use, and to treat practice as "expressive," a kind of gestural metaphor. The hermeneutical tradition does not bracket traditional *epistemes,* as cautious explanatory approaches do, but disassembles them in order to import some of their contents into the now dominant *episteme.* Jonathan Z. Smith has called upon students of religion to shift from the appropriation of a culture's rights of interpretation to a study of that culture's own systems of interpretation.[25] Even if we eschew the importation of nonnative "meanings" into our readings of their discourse, we still run the risk of reconfiguring the discursive system according to etic standards of significance, interpreting certain elements of a tradition as its "essence" or "core" which are not recognized as such by adherents to the tradition.

The goal of the so-called hermeneutics of charity is to arrive at a "reasonable" account of the subjective states of historical individuals, such that their words and deeds can be accommodated within our own culturally defined categories of reality. The legitimacy of this approach depends entirely upon what is meant by "reasonable," and how much we make the other conform to our criteria of what counts as valid human reason or emotion. Admittedly, such an account only can be based upon external signs, so the hermeneut must acquire a system by which the signs are to be interpreted. I cannot tell you what Mani thought, but I can tell you some of what he said and did, and that will have to suffice for historical accounts. The insistence that the individual is not understood until his or her conscious intention is grasped closes the door to any historical understanding, and much of contemporary understanding as well. Such naive subjectivism must be countered by a more precise account of how we all, in our everyday social interactions, "understand" one another.[26]

Obviously, it is possible to bridge language barriers. People do successfully communicate across languages, and even learn a certain facility with another's language. How is this accomplished? Words are mere gibberish in isolation. To start to understand the meaning of another language (that is, the function of specific terms), we need points of reference. Even when speaking to another person in our own language, we must bridge idiosyncratic vocabularies and usages with points of reference. So external objects and observable gestures allow us to draw analogies between the foreign or idiosyncratic word and one within our own vocabulary. Commonalities of human actions, gestures, and of the environment are the basis for the rough analogizing that is translation.

So translating discourse into something we understand, or interpreting the actions of another as indicative of intentions and states we recognize, involves analogy, typification, and classification. We match novel phenomena as best we can with something experienced before, and in this way normalize it. The only real issue here is how rough of a match will be satisfactory; and the answer to this question will depend on the purpose to which we want to put our supposed "understanding." It is precisely the systematic and professional character of the human sciences that demands more exacting standards than ordinary daily living, because in a sense we are stopping to take a closer look. The risk is always that the analogy made has been too quick, too cursory, too lenient, and as a consequence we have misunderstood. The misunderstanding may remain latent for a time, but eventually it emerges when we come up against a dead end, conflict, or impossible ramification. The risk, in other words, is that the analogy overwhelms the phenomenon, and that we rest content far short of comprehension.

To bring this back home to historical research in Manichaeism, the risk is that we rest too comfortably in our own cosmos, wrestle novel phenomena too facilely into familiar categories, and do not allow our categories or ourselves to be stretched very far. This problem is widely recognized in academics today, and part of so-called postcolonialism and postmodernism is an effort to decenter our own established categories in order to give others a bigger slice of our cosmos, to really confront others more as they are in their own self-understanding, and not be so quick to give them a subservient place in our systems of order. In the words of Ernest Nagel,

> If the history of anthropological research proves anything, it surely testifies to the errors students commit when they interpret the actions of men in unfamiliar cultures in terms of categories drawn uncritically from their limited personal lives. . . . We may feel assured that if an illiterate and impoverished people revolts against its masters, it does so not because of adherence to some political doctrine but because of economic ills. But this assurance may only be the product of familiarity and a limited imagination; and the sense of penetrating comprehension that we may associate with the assertion, instead of guaranteeing its universal truth, may be only a sign of our provincialism.[27]

I am arguing, therefore, for the replacement of interpretation as it is generally practiced with exegesis. Exegesis is a method of discovering relations among language and referents, and is an essential part of translation. "Exegesis . . . does not constitute the interpretation of the symbol, but one of its extensions," Dan Sperber maintains, and so it delineates truth as a set of relations rather than an ultimate determinant of meaning.[28] A "meaning" is only another sign in the system from which the symbol being interpreted comes. As long as we find the meaning within other parts of the system, we are merely rotating signs in a way similar to that done by those using the system. To say that some element or aspect of experience is the meaning of some other simply points out a relation within the symbolic system. Both social-scientific and hermeneutic approaches, however, try to separate out particular referents as the ultimate meaning of native systems. But, to take a common example, social structure cannot be identified as an "external" interpretation of discursive systems that relate to it because both are part of a set of relations in which elements mutually define, structure, and exegete one another. Rather than employing data from other cultures merely to promote our own beliefs about the world, we should take as our task the organization of such data heuristically, as a function of effective translation of what someone other than ourselves values. To do this, we must keep discourse and practice together, in the relationship by which they function, possess significance, and impact upon history.[29]

It is the method of a pragmatist phenomenology to circumscribe a particular set of knowable actions and responses for which the historical testimony bridges the great emic-etic divide, a set that is both recognized in the statements of participants *and* falls within the parameters of empirical verification (that is, could potentially be verified by the observations of outsiders). In the Manichaean case, we actually have the testimony of outsiders, which in its set of congruences with insider testimony provides a starting point for the historian's more comprehensive effort.[30] The core of the data consists of the most basic procedural description of the rites. The set broadens when we work out the relations between the various actors and actions into regulated systems, including something akin to rules of procedure, hierarchies of ritual rights and responsibilities, structural supports and ramifications of the ritual community, networks of statements and the conditions of their recital, and so on. All of these things can be said to be "there" in the sources, and so to be historical verities. None of them requires an exclusively insider or outsider point of view for their verification or acceptance. What is required are rules of translation that will allow us to speak in etically acceptable language of emically defined realities.

This study, then, proceeds on the basis of the idea that what people take to be true, and the ends they value, have some impact on their behavior. I consider this premise so obvious and self-evident that a protracted defense is unnecessary. We all presuppose this premise in our own daily interactions, and to the best of our knowledge every other human society has done the same. Take the concrete example of an automobile accident. Investigators can buzz all over the site, examine every inch of the car, even do a physical examination of the driver, and have no clue as to the cause, which is only revealed when the subjective experience of the driver is heard. She thought she saw something in the road, swerved to miss it, and struck a tree. It can be shown that nothing was in fact in the road, but a shadow creates the illusion of something there. The shadow did not cause the crash, rather the driver's belief that the shadow was a solid object, and her response to the presence of that solid object, caused the accident. Belief impacts on behavior, sometimes with great force.

There is plenty of room for legitimate debate in more complex cases over the scope of that impact, the sources of beliefs and values, and the system of interface between public codes and private identities. Without in any way claiming to know or recover thoughts held within another's brain, a pragmatist phenomenology looks at publicly discernible actions, relations, and speech acts for how they might elucidate the impact of religious, cultural, or social adherence on the course of human events. In this way, a pragmatist phenomenology is a way of redescribing a religious community, culture, or society so that the actions of its adherents can be understood or explained.

This stance will be controversial among certain supporters of the Durkheimian tradition who find themselves contending that what is *really* going on in a religious community does so despite rather than because of what members believe to be true.[31] Nevertheless, I am willing to defend the position that an event like the immolation of the Branch Davidians at Waco, Texas, cannot be made sense of historically without taking into account what the members of that community said and did to indicate adherence to a particular set of beliefs about themselves, their attackers, the world as a whole, and the kind of action or behavior necessary for salvation as they defined it. Similarly, the behavior of innumerable Manichaeans over the course of more than a thousand years cannot be reduced completely to the local mechanics of social relations. What held true for them historically *as a group* has a high probability of finding its explanation in common norms and rationales promoted by the leaders and institutions of the Manichaean community.[32] On the other hand, a great debt is owed to the Durkheimian and Marxist traditions of interpretation for investigating how social conditions determine consciousness, at least to a certain degree. This point is especially important in the present study because community determination of personal reality is precisely what the Manichaean program of embodiment entails.

My use of the expression "pragmatist phenomenology" must be distinguished from the Husserlian philosophical school known as Phenomenology, and the individualistic phenomenology of the social sciences (that of, for example, Alfred Schutz and Maurice Natanson) which, although influenced by G. H. Mead, is very much in the Weberian tradition. These latter phenomenologists do not claim to offer a method, but rather a "conceptual framework within which social reality may be comprehended,"[33] specifically at the microlevel of intersubjective encounter. The key question is what we are looking at, data-wise, to get a grip on subjective meaning in the action of others. In a historical study, the closest we can get to subjective meaning is an actor's statements and deeds. These statements and deeds, of course, utilize publicly available systems of communication and action. To a certain degree, therefore, an individual's inner states are screened and filtered by the cultural symbols through which they must be communicated. At the same time, however, those very inner states are made up of, and constantly shaped by, the very same cultural symbols.[34] In other words, the constituent parts of the subjective individual are knowable to a large degree from the available data on cultural "meanings." How these meanings are assembled in the individual case will vary, and will be strongly influenced by both biological foundations and personal biography. But the most basic and accessible account of past societies will be the publicly available conventions, from which any biographical study will enunciate the key idiosyncrasies and innovations that characterize the distinct individual of the past. Pragmatist phenomenology, true to the work of G. H. Mead, is a collectivist, rather than an individualist, phenomenology, in search of the "objective" reality of the shared social world rather than the subjective appropriation of that world by particular individuals.

REGIMENS, RITES, AND RATIONALES

The same Sogdian parable text that I cited earlier in this chapter, which likens Manichaeism to an ocean absorbing the ideas of every other religion, goes on to speak of "the daily work of the religion."[35] This "work" is the ongoing liberation of light through the concrete daily rituals of the Manichaean community. Thousands of miles from Sogdiana, North African sources demonstrate the same action-focused attitude. Fortunatus of Hippo insisted that Manichaeans could only be assessed by their behavior, not by their philosophy; Faustus of Milevis argued that the true gospel is simply the *modus vivendi* that Christ explicitly enjoined upon his followers.[36] From Algeria to China, from the third century to the fourteenth, Manichaean exhortation constantly urged both its priests and its laity to labor for this most sacred cause. This was the point of being a Manichaean.

The ascetic discipline that shaped the life of all Manichaeans, but most especially that of the Elect, is directly implicated in the ritual procedures of the community. Participation in the rituals depended upon a proven and visible adherence to a way of life that rendered one into a fit vehicle for the "daily work of the religion." Failure to live up to the code had ramifications both in this life and in the life to come. Fortunately for the lax, regular confession and absolution were institutionalized into the faith. But we would be mistaken to think of this as a voluntary baring of the conscience. The Elect, at least, lived constantly under the scrutiny of the Auditors, whose own salvation depended upon the purity of the Elect they supported. The code, much of which is preserved, demanded nothing short of the heroic, and several Manichaean writers testified to the difficulty of living up to it.[37]

The ritual acts and the ascetic disciplines presuppose one another. In

Manichaean ritual processes the performers constantly reiterated their sanctity, their right—earned by discipline—to play the key role in a cosmic drama. They repeated aloud like some mathematical proof the very conditions that were supposed to make the ritual work; they restated the set of technical facts that were essential to the notion that they were actually performing work and not an empty show. And this same discipline that constituted the condition and the technical criteria of "the work of religion" was organized entirely toward the single telos of the rites themselves. In fact, the discipline should be considered as nothing less than a set of preliminary rites. Manichaean asceticism, then, was not the expression of an emotional or philosophical abhorrence of the body or the world. Rather it was part of a very concrete attempt to do something about the body and the world.

Neither the rituals nor the disciplines made any sense without the other in Manichaeism. Yet together they were not enough to stand alone. They needed a broader contextualizing web within which discipline plus ritual equaled salvation, as Mani and his successors claimed. Participants in the Manichaean life needed an anthropology that made the human body the central arena of a salvational struggle. They needed a metabolic relation between the food that entered the bodies of the Elect and the prayers and hymns that emanated from it. They needed a universe that was wired together to make use of the enormous effort being expended at the human level.[38]

In my research I have followed this same basic logic. Identifying a core of practices across the widely dispersed Manichaean communities, I began to build from that core a more complete picture of what it was to be a Manichaean. For a fundamental practice of the faith, such as the daily ritual meal, we can identify a set of symbols or statements that were intrinsic to its performance; from these we can elicit a set of implicated concepts to which the practice directly referred; finally, we can add those elements of Manichaean discourse that were necessary to hold the acts, statements, and concepts together in the total practice. In this way an examination of Manichaean sources builds out from a few characteristic behaviors to a set of interlocking acts and ideas that constituted the Manichaean religious identity.

Statements that contextualize the central acts of being a Manichaean in a particular cosmos, that describe the relations between the acts and the operations of that cosmos, and that explain the ends to which the acts led constitute the disciplinary and alimentary rationales of Manichaeism, the discourses operating in relation to the distinctly Manichaean practices. Verbal behavior

scripted for performance in the context of practice formed the core of these rationales; so, to a certain degree, the categories I employ correspond to the ancient Greek categories of *dromena* and *legomena*, "things done" and "things
said" in a ritualized context. Each rite of the Manichaeans was conducted in
the context of statements made either during the ritual or as a commentary
upon the ritual. In many cases these statements can be considered ritual acts
in themselves, tools with a specific function directly involved with other ritual
proceedings. As the reader will see, Manichaean sources include statements
about "what actually happens" which the modern researcher would etically
classify as purely discursive, "mental," or interpretive. This first translation of
the Manichaean material, therefore, is not completely successful, but it allows
the first contact upon which future translations can build.

There is much more to the Manichaean tradition than its disciplinary-
ritual core. Commentaries and exhortations concerning the practices, organizing strategies that combined entire complexes of practice together, parables
and sermons that generalized an ethos of belonging and shared enterprise,
polemical and apologetic attempts to bolster cultic boundaries, even hymns
sung as stock pieces between ritual acts—all these occupy an entirely different
level of the picture. Such additional discourse varies from region to region
much more than the separate units of practice and their explicitly implicated
presuppositions. In other words, once we get a certain schematic distance
from the core practices, we begin to see the sort of wide variations produced
both by cultural and historical forces, and by the deliberate missionary strategies of the Manichaean leadership.

Such material, of course, must be studied as well. It informs us of the religious, social, and cultural environment in which Manichaeism developed
and adapted. It also shows us how particular leaders and authors brought
Manichaean responses to the world to bear on philosophical, political, and social issues of their time. It demonstrates to us that Manichaeism could embrace both anticosmic and procosmic attitudes, and could be a home for both
those who wanted to flee their bodies and those who sought to protect and preserve them. Such discourse reflects back on Manichaean ritual and regimen,
but without those practices the discourse evaporates into smoke. For a faith as
syncretistic and adaptive as Manichaeism, doctrinal definitions and boundaries simply do not suffice. Without a sure footing in the practical dimensions
of Manichaean identity, an awareness of the public characteristics and performances that set Manichaeans apart from the world around them, we risk

losing track of Manichaeism as a historical phenomenon just as surely as the Manichaeans themselves have vanished from the face of the earth.

The approach of a pragmatist phenomenology permits me to analyze a total system where the more established traditions of interpretation would engage only parts. A Weberian approach would be interested most in Manichaean rationales, and turn to them to establish the "meaning" of Manichaean practices, the possible reasons that motivated membership in the Manichaean community. A Durkheimian approach would focus most on Manichaean disciplinary regimens as the center of Manichaean identity, where the hidden hand of society most directly shaped the mores of the Manichaean. Neither of these approaches would have much use for Manichaean rites, and that is very much my point in addressing the particulars of Manichaeism to broader questions in the study of religions. A Weberian reading would understand Manichaean rites to be expressive of the truths most clearly articulated in rationales. A Durkheimian reading would explain Manichaean rites as part of the mystifying rationalization of social codes most clearly evident in regimens. Both of these readings have had a distinguished following in Manichaean studies. I consider both to be inadequate because studies of Manichaeism that employ them fail to note the degree to which the Manichaean tradition relies upon ritual as the reference point for explaining, justifying, and applying the other elements of Manichaean doctrine and practice.

This study, then, investigates the most distinctive and fundamental practices of the Manichaean tradition: the daily cultic meal of the Manichaean Elect and the disciplinary regimen it presupposes. One can study the body in relation to any set of rites, of course, since the body is essential to any ritual performance as its agent. What sets the Manichaean meal apart is that it was a ritual performed not only *by* the body, but *in* the body. All of the themes and issues examined in the interpretation of ritual must be applied in this context to the human body not only as ritual agent, but also as ritual space, ritual instrument, and ritual offering. In the chapters that follow, I demonstrate that the food ritual was the focal point of Manichaean community organization, the *raison d'être* of Manichaean discipline, and the key to understanding how normative Manichaeism proposed to produce "souls" liberated from the bonds of contingency by the actions of the very body in which they were imprisoned.

TWO

DISCIPLINARY REGIMENS

Desire is the flood . . . the commandment is the ark.
—The Coptic *Psalm-Book*

THE MANICHAEAN COMMUNITY

Who belonged to the Manichaean community? In other words, how did the
Manichaean tradition define its cultic boundaries and assign ritual roles,
rights, and responsibilities? In order to reconstruct the interactive practices of
the Manichaean community, we must have a grasp of its organizing structure.
With such a long history and wide geographic distribution, the unity of that
community on a large scale must be established, not assumed. Certainly, there
have been dozens of religious groups called "Manichaean" by their enemies
who did not identify themselves as such and who in many cases lacked the
slightest knowledge of Mani and his teachings. On the other hand, many
Manichaean groups found it expedient to mask their identity from their per-
secutors and adopted the appearance of Christians, Buddhists, and Taoists.
Manichaean authorities embraced adaptation to the many cultures of the religion's dispersion, and in their ambition sought to reach the entire world. We
must question, therefore, to what degree this diverse and rapidly mutating phenomenon can be studied as a unified entity.

An investigation of the basis on which such a unity can be established for
Manichaeism begins with the institutions that constituted the context in
which the Manichaean way of life could be led. Even though, as I will show,

specific practices produced individual Manichaeans, those individuals came into existence as part of a pre-existing set of relations, and they learned to speak of themselves in roles others had held before them. The role a new Manichaean assumed fit into a web of relations that gave that role defined rights and responsibilities. The collective body of adherents enforced those rights and responsibilities through mutual scrutiny and education, conducted for the most part through the sanctioned practices and discourses of the normative tradition.

The most fundamental structural characteristic of Manichaeism is its division into two subcommunities or classes of adherent. Sources from every region, both normative and polemical, attest to this division of labor in the Manichaean mission. The set of relations between sacerdotal and lay classes formed the basis for all of the religion's practices. The nomenclature attested for these two classes varies slightly from region to region. Modern scholars have traditionally employed the Latin terms *electus* / *electa* ("chosen, selected"; pl. *electi* / *electae*) and *auditor* ("hearer"; pl. *auditores*) for members of the two orders, and I follow that tradition here. I deliberately employ English forms with cropped endings ("Elect" for both singular and plural, "Auditor" and "Auditors") to maintain gender neutrality, since both men and women held membership in either of these ranks.

The Greek *Cologne Mani Codex* quotes Mani's *Gospel*, in which he declares, "I have chosen the Elect, and I have shown a path to the height to those who ascend according to this truth."[1] Members of this more highly disciplined and ritually privileged elite were also called "the righteous." Ephrem Syrus provides what must have been the original terminology of Mani when he states that "a Manichaean called a righteous one *(zaddiqā)*" is the one who refines the light in the ritual meal.[2] He also attests a distinct feminine form of the title, referring to "those idle women of the party of Mani, those whom they call *zaddiqāthā*," who "sit on account of the bright ones, the sons of the light, 'whom darkness came forth and swallowed.'"[3] The Arabic writer an-Nadim, in his *Fihrist*, likewise gives the original Syriac designation *zaddiqā*,[4] and correctly interprets it as referring to "the righteous" *(saddiqina)*; laypersons, he attests, are known as "hearers" *(sama'ina)*.[5]

In the *Cologne Mani Codex*, Mani experiences a vision of the church he is destined to establish, "prepared and perfected with its teachers and bishops, Elect *(eklektoi)* and Catechumens *(katechoumenoi)*."[6] The latter term, borrowed from the Christian tradition, was employed by Western Manichaeans alongside the more general term "Auditor" or "hearer." In the Coptic *Psalm-Book*, the Elect are referred to as the perfect *(netjēk abal)*,[7] the holy *(m.petouabe)*,[8] as well as the Elect *(n.eklektos, n.sōtp)*;[9] the Auditors are called believers,[10] faithful,[11] and Catechumens.[12] The available Iranian literature describes the community as divided into the two "limbs" of Elect *(wcydg'n)*— also called "the Righteous" (Middle Persian and Parthian *'rd'w'n*) and "the religion bearers" (Parthian *dynd'r'n*, Sogdian *dynd'rt*)—and Auditors (Middle Persian *nywš'g'n*, Parthian *ngwš'g'n*, Sogdian *ngwš'kt*). In Turkic texts, as in the Iranian sources, the Elect are themselves subdivided into two "assemblies" *(eki ančuman)*,[13] male and female. The Auditors, likewise, can be distinguished according to gender in Turkic texts, using Sogdian terminology *(nigošak / nigošakanč)*.[14] The Chinese Manichaica make occasional use of the Iranian terms *dynd'r / dyn'w'r (tien-na-wu)* and *nywš'g'n (nu-sha-yen)* to refer to the respective Elect and Auditor divisions of the religious community.[15] Chinese equivalents appear in the majority of cases, however. One stanza of the *Hymn-scroll* speaks for "we the men of the pure religion, the company of steadfast young women, and all the Auditors";[16] other stanzas distinguish the male electi *(shih-seng fu)* from the female electae *(shih-seng mu)*.[17] The term *t'ing-che*,[18] also used in Chinese to render the Buddhist Sanskrit expression *šravaka*, is applied to the Auditor.[19] The terminology used for the two classes of the Manichaean community is summarized in Table 2.1.

In his polemical writings against his former co-religionists, Augustine repeatedly refers to the religion's division into what he calls in one place its "two professions *(duabus professionibus)*."[20] The roughly contemporaneous Latin *Tebessa Codex* undertakes an exposition and defense of the Manichaean community's two *ordines*.[21] "These two grades *(duabus gradibus)*, established upon one faith in the same church, support each other, and whoever has an abundance of anything shares it with the other: the Elect with the Auditors from their heavenly store . . . and the Auditors with the Elect [from their terrestrial wealth]."[22] The author presents the gospel figures of Martha and Mary (Luke 10:38–42) as models of those who serve and those who choose "the better portion";[23] indeed, "many have been *called*, but few *chosen*."[24] Mani cites the same example in his debate with the Elchasaites as reported by the *Cologne Mani Codex*.[25] The bulk of the *Tebessa Codex* fragments focus on a justification of the Elect's activities as "work," worthy of lay support.

Each degree *(bathmos)* within the Manichaean community has a task "in the yoke of Jesus" appointed to it by Mani.[26] Specific tasks belong to each of

TABLE 2.1. TERMINOLOGY USED TO DISTINGUISH THE TWO MANICHAEAN CLASSES

LANGUAGE	ELECT	AUDITORS
Syriac	zaddiqe ("righteous")	šamuʿe ("hearers")
Arabic	siddiqun ("righteous")	samuʿun ("hearers")
Greek	dikaioi ("righteous")	katechoumenoi ("instructed")
	eklektoi ("chosen")	
Coptic	n.sōtp ("chosen")	n.katechoumenos ("instructed")
Latin	electi ("chosen")	auditores ("hearers")
Middle Persian	ʾrdʾwʾn ("righteous")	nywšʾgʾn ("hearers")
	wcydgʾn ("chosen")	
	dyndʾrʾn ("religion-bearers")	
Parthian	ʾrdʾwʾn ("righteous")	ngwšʾgʾn ("hearers")
	wcydgʾn ("chosen")	
	dyndʾrʾn ("religion-bearers")	
Sogdian	dyndʾrt ("religion-bearers")	ngwšʾkt ("hearers")
Turkic	dindar-lar (dyndʾr and pl. suf.)	nigošak-lar
Chinese	a-lo-huan (ʾrdʾwʾn)	nu-sha-yen (nywšʾgʾn)
	tien-na-wu (dyndʾr/dynʾwʾr)	
	shih-seng ("chosen")	tʾing-che ("hearer")

the two classes of adherent, and each is portrayed pursuing those tasks with avidity, "the Elect their commandments, the Catechumens their [alms], eager for the scriptures and revelations, for the psalms and the hours of prayer."[27] Accordingly, each class will receive a suitable reward in the last judgment: the Elect are transformed into "angels,"[28] the Catechumens are welcomed as citizens of the kingdom of light.[29] In his report, the Arab bibliographer an-Nadim also emphasizes that each order is subject to distinct regimens[30] and can expect different rewards after death.[31]

Despite these distinctions, the two classes form a community, frequently invoked as a unity: "Blessed are the Elect and the Catechumens who keep festival on this day, and fast (r-nēsteue), and pray (shlēl), and give alms (ti-mnt-nae), that they may reign in the new aeon."[32] While Western sources actually speak of a Manichaean "church" (ekklēsia), Eastern sources are replete with references to the "flock," or "family," or "assembly" of the Manichaean community.[33] A Sogdian parable-book edited by Werner Sundermann declares,

"And who[ever] comes . . . to the church of the apostles . . . no one is rejected; but in the order of their laws and precepts it places them in their place, and as many as ever enter into it, they have their place either in Auditorship *(ng'wš'kyh)* (or) in Righteousness *('rt'wyh)*, and they all complete (their) work according to their order, zeal, and power."[34] The characteristic deeds of the Elect and Auditors are described in a Turkic text as complementary responses to the summons of Mani.

> You deigned to command them to recite praises and hymns, to repent evil deeds, and to assemble and bring about "collection" *('mw'rdyšn)*.[35] Mortals with confused minds, hearing this command of yours, caused seas and rivers of virtue to flow, and were born again in the land of the Buddhas *(burxanlar)*. Other simple minds walked on pure roads and brought about "collection." They were born again in the palace of immortality.[36]

Both classes have been enjoined, the passage declares, to recite praises and hymns, repent evil behavior, and assemble for "collection." But from this injunction two kinds of Manichaean emerge. Those who have not achieved complete clarity of thought manage to be stirred (by *hearing* Mani's command, an allusion to Auditor status) to good deeds, "cause seas and rivers of virtue to flow," and are reborn as a reward into what this text characterizes as a "Pure Land" of more fruitful existence. Those who have acquired a clear single-mindedness enter upon a life of purity and actually carry out the act of "collection"; they attain the "palace of immortality."

Duality was as inherent to Manichaean community as it was to Manichaean metaphysics. The division into a strictly regimented, "selected" or "righteous," class and a less restricted support class constituted the basis and prerequisite of Manichaean religious life. Neither pole of the community could obtain salvation without the assistance of the other. This point scarcely need be made with reference to the Auditors; Manichaean literature repeatedly reminded them of their utter dependence on the benevolence of the Elect. On the other hand, some modern scholars have ventured the opinion that *only* the Elect belonged properly to the Manichaean community, and that the Auditors constituted a clientele upon whom the only injunction was support of the Elect. Such a position is not borne out by the sources, which, as will be shown, clearly articulate a regimen for Auditors.

The designation "church" may be applied to Manichaeism legitimately insofar as it refers to an organized, centrally administered institution—for such Manichaeism was, during at least part of its history. Mani apparently instituted a hierarchy through which he could direct the far-flung missionary activity he instigated. We know nothing of the origin and development of this system of administration, but at the time of Mani's death, or very shortly thereafter, it consisted of twelve "teachers" and seventy-two regional directors, with a sizable number of lower-level functionaries. Mani himself was replaced at his death by a successor, and this Manichaean "papacy" persisted at least until the ninth century C.E.

The Manichaean community, then, possessed a definite structure and was governed by a hierarchy of authority. The latter was subject to regional and historical permutations, and deserves more careful study. For our purposes, it is enough to recognize that Manichaeism existed as an institution capable of promoting its aims and enforcing its rules. The normative authorities of Manichaeism carefully distinguished the complementary roles of the work of religion, and encouraged commitment to them through a prolific discourse consisting of sermons, hymns, and instructional tracts. Membership in the Manichaean community meant some degree of conformity to these norms, and obedience to a discipline that defined the Manichaean body.

THE DUAL DISCIPLINARY STRUCTURE OF
THE MANICHAEAN COMMUNITY

How did one maintain membership in the Manichaean community and prepare to participate in its ritual activities? The answer depended upon one's place in the community. The fundamental structural division into Elect and Auditors was reflected in two distinct regimens of discipline, each of which prepared its adherents for their proper role in the community's collective purpose. The behavior of both Elect and Auditors must be appropriate to their functions as agents in Manichaean salvational operations; their bodies must be obedient to the tradition's sanctioned models of religious practice. But the Elect were required to meet more stringent criteria so that their bodies could be not only agents in salvational rituals, but also the instruments and arenas of such rituals. In the same way that modern Western discourse sometimes refers to the ideal products of military training as "fighting machines," Manichaean disciplinary practices were designed to construct "ritual machines."

Normative accounts of the regimen sanctioned by Manichaean authority take the form of catechetical instruction, confession scripts, hymns, and illustrative parables. Polemical testimonies that can be checked against normative models offer especially valuable supplement to our knowledge because they presuppose no prior knowledge of the subject among their readership. The polemicists do show blind spots, however, ignoring aspects of Manichaean discipline that did not contrast significantly with their own.[37]

Most Manichaean sources locate the sanction for their disciplinary regimens in the personal authority of Mani.[38] Ascetic codes form part of the contents of his revelations, which he transmitted through his writings[39] and lectures.[40] The extensive review of Elect precepts in the Sogdian portion of the Bema-handbook M 801 repeatedly cites the words of Mani (in Middle Persian) as sanctions for the specific injunctions. Turkic sources likewise ascribe the origins of the disciplinary code (and hence, by definition, of election) to Mani himself.[41] In the Chinese *Compendium*, Mani declares:

> I shall turn the wheel of the great law and shall explain the scriptures (*ching*), disciplinary rules (*chieh-lü*), and the methods (*fa*) of meditation and wisdom (*ting-hui*) and so forth,[42] as well as the doctrines of the three epochs and the two principles. All the beings, from the realm of light down to the dark paths, will thereby be saved.[43]

Although Augustine reports a similar centrality of Mani for the Manichaeans of North Africa, spokesmen for the latter chose, in their apologetic discourse, to focus on Jesus as the sanctioning authority for the Manichaean way of life. The Manichaean bishop Faustus of Milevis argued that only the Manichaeans adhered to the savior's clear injunctions, and for this reason were solely deserving of the name "Christian."[44] Mani himself invokes the "commandments of the savior" in the *Cologne Mani Codex*.[45]

In the Coptic *Kephalaion 1*, Mani says that the Paraclete revealed to him "the mystery of the Elect, [with their] commandments, [the] mystery of the Catechumens, their helpers, with [their] commandments, the mystery of the sinners with their deeds, and the punishment that lies hidden for them."[46] *Kephalaion 80* reviews the disciplines of both the Elect way of life, here called "righteousness" (*dikaiosynē*), and that of the Auditors. The two disciplines bear parallel structures, but diverge in content. The Elect adhere to the "three seals," while the Auditors fast, pray, and give alms; the Elect share their wisdom and faith with the auditors, while the latter sponsor the entrance of family members into the order of the Elect and construct places for alms-service. Faustus of Milevis defends Manichaean discipline by pointing to its division into different intensities, suited to greater or lesser degrees of ability or commitment.[47]

According to an-Nadim, Mani said:

> He who would enter the religion (al-din) must examine his soul. If he finds that he can subdue lust and covetousness, refrain from eating meats, drinking wine, as well as from marriage,[48] and if he can also avoid (causing) injury to water, fire, trees, and living things, then let him enter the religion. But if he is unable to do all of these things, he shall not enter the religion. If, however, he loves the religion, but is unable to subdue lust and craving, let him seize upon guarding the religion and the Righteous (al-siddiqun), that there may be an offsetting of his unworthy actions, and times in which he devotes himself to work and righteousness, night-time prayer, intercession, and pious humility. That will defend him during his transitory life and at his appointed time, so that his status will be the second status in the life to come.[49]

Here, the Auditors do not even appear to belong to "the religion" proper, but occupy the position of a clientele of the religious class. This initial impression is contradicted, however, by the further details of an-Nadim's account, which demonstrate clear and strict regulations governing the lives of the Auditors.[50] Al-Biruni also shows familiarity with the two disciplinary options of the Manichaean community, ascribing their origin directly to Mani.

> He established laws which are obligatory only for the Righteous (siddiqun), that is, for the saints and ascetics among the Manichaeans, namely to prefer poverty to riches, to suppress cupidity and lust, to abandon the world, to be abstinent in it, continually to fast, and to give alms as much as possible. He forbade them to acquire any property except food for one day and dress for one year; he further forbade sexual intercourse, and ordered them continually to wander about in the world, preaching his doctrines and guiding people into the right path. Other laws he imposed upon the Auditors (samma'un), that is, their followers and adherents who have to do with worldly affairs, namely to give as alms the tenth of their property, to fast during the seventh

part of a life-time, to live in monogamy, to befriend the Righteous, and to re-move everything that troubles or pains them.[51]

In the Manichaean worldview, only the regimens introduced by Mani de-liver order from chaos. "Desire (is) the flood," a Coptic psalmist writes, "the commandment is the ark."[52] Similarly, a Turkic text speaks of "the forces, the feelings, the ideas, the thoughts which are (constantly) bubbling and stirring" within the unreformed person, like an ocean whose surface is stirred by winds blowing first one way, then another.[53] The Chinese *Compendium* asserts that "(If) the method of conduct is true, the fruit will be confirmed in the three palaces:[54] the nature *(hsing)* will be separated from the non-bright, its name will be 'one form' *(i-hsiang)*. In this religion, this is called deliverance *(chieh-t'uo)*."

The Manichaeans reduced their elaborate regulatory codes to a variety of formulas, such as the "Three Seals," "Five Commandments," and "Ten Commandments."[55] Some reductionary formulas fail to distinguish the Manichaeans from their religious rivals. The formula "good thoughts, good words, good deeds" was shared with Zoroastrians, Buddhists, and several other traditions. When in a hagiographical account the teacher Ammo explains the Manichaean discipline to a frontier guardian spirit as "We do not consume meat or wine (and) we stay far from women,"[56] the spirit replies, "Where I rule, there are many like you (already)."[57] The historian can often identify an-tecedent and contemporaneous parallels to the constituent parts of Mani-chaean disciplinary regimens, and Manichaean discourse readily acknowl-edges these similarities. For the Manichaeans, it was the distinctiveness of their total system, both in its structure and in its enunciated aims, that set the Manichaean way apart and demonstrated its divine sanction.

THE THREE SEALS

The Three Seals are well known to modern researchers through the testimony of Augustine of Hippo, who enumerates them as the seal of the mouth, of the hand, and of the breast, respectively. This disciplinary construct is attested in all parts of the Manichaean world.

The Central Manichaean Tradition

An-Nadim in his *Fihrist* informs us that "Mani prescribed ten ordinances for the Auditors, which he followed up with three seals *(thalath hawatim)* and a fast of seven days without fail during every month."[58] His testimony appears to apply the seals to Auditors. Yet the only passage in an-Nadim which can be interpreted as an enumeration of the seals refers exclusively to the Elect: "If he finds that he can subdue lust and covetousness, refrain from eating meats, drinking wine, as well as from marriage, and if he can also avoid (causing) injury to water, fire, trees, and living things, then let him enter the religion."[59] "Entering the religion" here indicates becoming a member of the Elect, as what follows this passage makes clear. It is possible to identify the command to "subdue lust and covetousness" and to "refrain . . . from marriage" as the "seal of the breast," the command to "refrain from eating meats and drinking wine" as the "seal of the mouth," and the command to "avoid injury to water, fire, trees, and living things" as the "seal of the hands." An-Nadim does not explicitly identify these commands with the three seals, however, and Nicholas Sims-Williams argues that they should be identified instead with four of the Five Commandments of the Elect.[60]

The Western Manichaean Tradition

Augustine of Hippo undertakes a comprehensive critique of Manichaean religious discipline in terms of the Three Seals *(tria signacula)* in his first major anti-Manichaean tract, *De moribus manichaeorum* (390 C.E.). His exposition, based upon his own training and experience within the Manichaean community, constitutes the most detailed surviving discussion of this matter. His version significantly expands the contents of the seals by making them rubrics for the sum total of the Elect regimen, a role played in other sources by the Five Commandments. But in Augustine's understanding, the Three Seals were to be defined broadly:

> What are these seals *(signacula)*? The mouth *(os)*, the hand *(manus)*, and the breast *(sinus)*. And what do they signify? That man should be pure and innocent in mouth, hands and breast, we are told. . . . The mouth should be understood as referring to all the senses located in the head, while by the hand is meant every action, and by the breast, every procreative lust.[61]

Of the three, Augustine devotes by far the most attention to the first, the "seal of the mouth." He notes that "you neither eat meat nor drink wine."[62] "You say that some foods are unclean," Augustine adds, and that "flesh is composed of nothing but filth";[63] and he scrutinizes the ideology that undergirds this attitude. In ridiculing their rationales Augustine provides us some indication of approved and disapproved foods among the North African Manichaeans.

> You teach that in grain, beans, herbs, flowers, and fruits some part of God is present. It is said that this is evident from the brightness of their color, the pleasantness of their odor, and the sweetness of their taste, and that decayed substances lack these qualities, which indicates that the goodness has left them. . . . You maintain that the brightness and sheen of oil bespeak a plentiful admixture of goodness, and seek to purify it by taking it into your throat and stomach. . . . Why do you look upon the golden melon as one of God's treasures and not . . . the yolk of an egg? Why does the whiteness of lettuce speak to you of God while the whiteness of milk does not?[64]

The logic here is that what is God-filled and full of goodness is good to eat, but what is devoid of God's characteristics should be avoided. By the implications of Augustine's argument, the North African Manichaeans approved of the consumption of the God-filled grain, beans, herbs, flowers, fruits, melon, and lettuce, but forbade the eating of eggs and milk.[65] He similarly reports their rejection of wine but consumption of vinegar and *caroenum*, although he charges that the latter is simply "cooked wine."[66] Augustine's discussion also suggests a favoritism toward fresh produce among the Manichaeans.[67]

Augustine describes Manichaean discipline as rigid and irrational, saying that "you expel from the number of the Elect a man who, perhaps for the sake of his health and not from cupidity, takes a little meat, whereas, if he were to consume peppered truffles like a glutton, you might, perhaps, rebuke him for immoderation but could not condemn him for violating the seal."[68] On the other hand, "you look upon it as a sin for anyone but the Elect to consume the food brought to the table for that so-called purification of yours," referring to the ritual meal.[69]

Whereas the "seal of the mouth" concerned the ingestion of food, the "seal of the hands" involved its procurement. Augustine informs us with astonishment that "if one were to pluck some leaves or fruit . . . he would undoubtedly be condemned . . . as a corrupter of the seal, if he did this intentionally and not accidentally."[70] Furthermore, "you yourselves do not pluck fruits or pull up vegetables, yet command your Auditors to pick them and bring them to you, and you do this, not so much in order to bestow a benefit on the bringer as to benefit the things themselves which are brought."[71] The sin incurred by the Auditors in the gathering of food is expiated through the offerings they make for the ritual meal.[72] Since the Elect do not eat meat, however, no expiation for this food group is possible.[73]

Augustine makes only a perfunctory effort to analyze the third seal, the "seal of the breast."

> There remains the seal of the breast to which your very questionable chastity pertains. For you do not forbid sexual intercourse, but . . . you forbid marriage in the true sense, which is the only worthy justification for it. No doubt, you will loudly protest against this and hurl reproaches at me, saying that you vehemently commend and laud perfect chastity, but do not prohibit marriage since your Auditors, who are in the second rank (secundus gradus) among you, are not forbidden to have wives.[74]

Augustine acknowledges that the North African Manichaeans do not actually prohibit marriage among Auditors; but from his Catholic point of view, the Manichaean encouragement of birth control is incompatible with marriage in the true sense.

> Is it not you who regard the begetting of children, by which souls are bound up in flesh, to be a more serious sin than sexual intercourse? Is it not you who used to urge us to observe, to the extent that it was possible, the time when a woman after her menstruation is likely to conceive, and to abstain from intercourse at that time in order that a soul might not be entangled in flesh?[75]

Throughout his exposition, Augustine implicitly associates the seals exclusively with the Elect class. He clearly envisions a distinct set of values for Auditors, and does not indicate that they were organized according to a Three Seals scheme.

One also can find explicit references to the Three Seals (shamte n.sphragis) in the Coptic Psalm-Book: "The seal of the mouth for the sign of the Father, the rest of the hands for the sign of the Son, the purity of virginity [for the] sign of the Holy Spirit";[76] "Let us seal our mouth that we may find the

Father, and seal our hands that we may find the Son, and guard our purity that we may find the Holy Spirit."[77] In the latter case, another set of practices is enjoined alongside the seals: "Let us pray, then, my brethren, that we may find the Father, and fast daily, that we may find the Son, and discipline our life that we may find the Holy Spirit."[78] But none of these references provide specifics about the regulations encapsulated by the catch-phrases.[79]

In the Coptic *Kephalaion 80*, Mani, the "Illuminator," instructs his disciples in the Three Seals:

> Know [and] understand that the first righteousness that a person will do to become truly righteous (entails three things), that is that he embraces chastity *(enkrateia)* and purity; and (that) he also acquires for himself the rest [of the] hands, so that he will restrain his hands from the Cross of Light; (and) the third is the purity of the mouth, so that he will purify his mouth from all flesh and blood, and he does not taste . . . wine or liquor at all. This is the first righteousness which a person will do in his body [to be] called righteous amongst men.[80]

Here, *enkrateia* and purity constitute the "seal of the breast," the "rest of the hands" or restraint of them from the "Cross of Light" corresponds to the "seal of the hands," and abstention from meat and wine equate with the "seal of the mouth." Although these three precepts are not explicitly called "seals," their content and structure clearly correspond to Augustine's exposition.

The Greek *Cologne Mani Codex* features allusions to the "rest of the hands" *(anapausis tōn cheirōn)*,[81] or simply the "rest," which we have seen used in Coptic sources for the seal of the hands. Mani states that "with wisdom and skill (I was) going about in their midst, keeping the rest, neither doing wrong, nor inflicting pain,"[82] and "[concerning the] rest, one of the leaders of their law spoke to me, having observed that I did not take vegetables from the garden, but instead asked them as a pious donation."[83] The other two seals do not find mention in the surviving portions of the codex.

The Eastern Manichaean Tradition

Iranian sources also allude to the Three Seals *(sn'n mwhr'n, 'δry t'py)*, although never with the kind of detail Augustine provides. The "Hymn of Praise for the Apostles" preserved in the Bema-handbook M 801 speaks of "all the

pure and holy Elect, who are perfect in the five precepts and the three seals."
We read in M 32, a Parthian hymn to a Manichaean deity: "O perfect seal
(mwhr) which (seals) my hand, mouth and thought!" Similarly, in M 174, the
Elect ideally live "in all wisdom and behavior of righteousness, in the five
good precepts *('ndrz'n)* of virtue, and in the three excellent seals *(mwhr'n)*, in
the five great garments, and in vigilance and zeal."[84] One of the fragments of
the Sogdian *Xuāstuānīft*, the confession-script for Auditors, refers to the "ten
commandments *('δs' cg[š'pt])*, the seven gifts *(ptmydy δβ'r)*, and the three
seals *('δry t'py)*."[85]

One Turkic source says of an unidentified prophet (Jesus or Mani), "He
entrusted the commandments *(čxšapt)* and the seals *(tamga)* to his disciples."[86]
The "Great Hymn to Mani" from the Turkic Manichaean *Pothi-Book* says of
the Elect, "They recognized the transitory religions and, in fear of the three
evil ways, in order to be born again in the highest place, they carried out the
Three Seals *(üč tamga)*."[87] In the ninth section of the *Xuāstuānīft*, the "ten
commandments" of Auditors are theoretically assigned three to the mouth,
three to the heart, three to the hand, and one to the whole self. How this division is supposed to work is not made clear but, at least rhetorically, such a
division applies the Three Seals to the Auditor way of life.[88] The Chinese
Hymnscroll confirms the association of Three Seals with the ten Auditor commandments attested in Arabic and Turkic materials. Two confession formulae—the "Penitence and Confession Prayer Text for Auditors"[89] and the "Penitential Prayer of the *ni-yu-sha*" (= Middle Persian *nywš'g*, "Auditor")[90]—call
the Ten Commandments and the Three Seals "the gates of the religion."

Summation

Julien Ries has produced a pioneering comparison and synthesis of sources on
the Three Seals in his 1977 article, "Commandments de la justice," and has
elaborated his analysis in several subsequent publications, focusing on Western testimonies.[91] Augustine, Ries states, "gives the impression that these three
seals constitute the essentials of Manichaean morality."[92] They form the principal concern of a large block of the Coptic *Kephalaia* (79, 80, 81, 84, 85, 87,
and 93), which Ries characterizes as a "compendium of gnostic morality,"[93]
and "a veritable compendium of gnostic ethics."[94] "The seal of the hands,"
Ries maintains, "is one of the great preoccupations of Manichaean cateche-

sis";[95] and he demonstrates this point convincingly in his study of the *Cologne Mani Codex* narratives.[96]

In Ries's opinion, the seal of the mouth, that is, fasting,[97] "reduces alimentation to strict necessity and orients it towards cosmic salvation."[98] H.-C. Puech likewise imagines that the gist of this rule was "to reduce the existence of the 'Perfect' to an absolute and permanent fast."[99] But the Manichaean sources says little about limiting the quantity of food as the hallmark of the "seal of the mouth"; and Augustine levels the charge of gluttony against the Elect. The purity of food and the timing of its ingestion seem to draw more attention in the Manichaean disciplines. The Elect abstained from meat and wine, and ate only once per day in the evening. Whether this entailed a sharp reduction of food intake remains an open question.

A degree of ambiguity surrounds the application of the Three Seals to the two orders of the Manichaean church. Puech regards the Three Seals to apply in principle to both Elect and Auditor. "The sole difference is that what is imposed strictly upon the first, what is made an obligation to be observed in all its rigor, is only applied to the second in a more lax fashion, being in their case softened and relaxed by the expedient of some concessions."[100] According to Augustine, however, the Three Seals do not apply to Auditors, who may perform the very un-sealed acts of marrying, acquiring food, and eating meat.[101] But Ries uses Coptic sources to supplement Augustine. Through fasting, prayer and alms, Ries insists, the Auditors participate in the three seals: fasting overpowers the body's archons, hence a seal of the breast; prayer to the luminaries relates to the seal of the mouth; the donation of alms justifies the activity of the Auditors, giving them claim to a kind of seal of the hands.[102] Ries's general point is surely correct: the Auditors do possess a *koinōnia* with the Elect on the basis of these activities, and the Three Seals construct can be applied to them rhetorically. Ries's creative interpretation entailing an exact correspondence of specific Auditor acts with the Three Seals, however, may be pushing the point too far. Applications of the Three Seals to the Auditors in Manichaean sources always appear couched in generic terms.

The Three Seals (the order of which varies from source to source) obviously belong to the very core of Manichaean practice; their attestation appears not only over a wide geographic expanse, but repeatedly within each region. They offer one possible construct of Manichaean discipline, especially that of the Elect. Their application to the Auditors is not as well attested, and may

have varied from region to region and century to century. For both Elect and
Auditors, however, Manichaean literature supplies alternative disciplinary
constructs: five and ten commandments, respectively.

The relative terseness of eastern Manichaean references to the Three
Seals may reflect more than the fragmentary state of the sources. The Three
Seals system closely resembles, and may have been assimilated to, the common Zoroastrian and Buddhist division of behavior into body, speech, and
mind. The two organizing systems do not correspond exactly, but are so similar that the Three Seals may have failed to convey a distinctively Manichaean
way of life in the eastern regions.[103] In these areas, the Five Commandments
became the operative paradigm for the regimen of the Elect.

THE FIVE COMMANDMENTS OF THE ELECT

Nicholas Sims-Williams has made a careful analysis of sources referring to the
Five Commandments incumbent upon the Manichaean Elect.[104] He cites
parallel lists found in Coptic,[105] Middle Persian,[106] Sogdian,[107] and Turkic.[108]
Sims-Williams also detects references to the Five Commandments in an-
Nadim's *Fihrist*,[109] and the Chinese *Hymnscroll*.[110] He characterizes these
commandments as "expressed for the most part in positive terms and so comprehensive as to regulate every aspect of daily life."[111] By "positive terms," he
means that the Five Commandments are stated as injunctions toward broad
ideals rather than, as in the case of the ten Auditor commandments, as specific
prohibitions (see Table 2.2).[112]

The Central Manichaean Tradition

In the *Fihrist* passage quoted in the previous section, an-Nadim says that the
Elect are expected to "subdue lust and covetousness, refrain from eating
meats, drinking wine, as well as from marriage, and . . . also avoid (causing) injury to water, fire, trees, and living things."[113] It is possible to see in this summarized code either the Three Seals or the Five Commandments. Sims-
Williams subscribes to the latter view, maintaining that the passage refers to
chastity, poverty, purity of mouth, and noninjury. He argues that the remaining commandment, truth-speaking, is missing because it is not peculiar to the

TABLE 2.2. THE FIVE COMMANDMENTS OF THE ELECT

ARABIC	COPTIC	IRANIAN	TURKIC
[Not to lie]	Not to lie	Truth	To be without sin
Not to injure	Not to kill	Noninjury	To not commit dirty evil deeds
Not to marry	Purity	Religious conduct	To be pure in body
Not to eat meat or drink wine	Not to eat meat	Purity of mouth	To be pure in mouth
Not to covet	Blessed poverty	Blessed poverty	To be the blessed poor

Elect, and so does not distinguish them from Auditors. The import of this passage, he rightly points out, is the distinction between the two religious classes.

The Western Manichaean Tradition

In the Coptic *Psalm-Book,* Bema-psalm 235 speaks of "the honor of the commandment that we lie not, the honor of the commandment that we kill not, the honor of the commandment that we eat no flesh, the honor of the commandment that we make ourselves pure, the honor of the commandment of blessed poverty, the honor of humility and kindliness."[114] This explicit invocation of the Five Commandments appears to be unique in the surviving literature of the Western Manichaean tradition.

The Eastern Manichaean Tradition

The Turkic text TM 169 states the following: "Because of the arrival of the pure, divine Mani Buddha, the Elect came into existence. And he delivered the pure law *(nom)* (to them). He delivered to them one command to abstain from harm (and) five precepts *(čxšapt).*"[115] Unfortunately, the text just quoted becomes both fragmentary and obscure as it proceeds to set out what the precepts entailed. In a Chinese translation of a hymn by Mo-yeh the Teacher, Mani is said to expound "the perfectness of the good law *(shan-fa)* and the five precepts of purity *(ching-chieh).*"[116] Other references to precepts in the *Hymn-scroll* are generic allusions: "accept the precepts of purity," "firmly observe fasting and precepts," "observing the precepts."[117] The Turkic "Great Hymn to Mani" in the unique Manichaean *Pothi-Book* edited by Larry Clark, supplies the complete set of the Five Commandments. The hymn says of Mani's disciples:[118]

> They guarded with minds free from neglectfulness the commands that you issued. . . . . Their compassionate minds increased and guarded (1) the commandment to be without sin *(yazïnčsïzïn ermek čxšapt)*. They escaped from the hell which is ever aflame. Their faithful minds [. . .] and they exerted themselves in the true laws, and guarded (2) the true commandment to not commit dirty evil deeds *(kirlig ayïg kïl[ïnčïg kïlmamak] kir-tü čxšapt)*. They thought about the transitoriness of the body and left house and home. They prepared themselves in the good doctrines and carried out (3) the commandment to be pure in body *(et'öz arïgïn erm[e]k čkšapt)*. They exerted themselves in the pure doctrines by which one escapes from dangerous places, and, in order to be born again in the palace of immortality, they guarded (4) the commandment to be pure in mouth *(agïz arïgïn ermek čxša[p]t)*. They all asked for divine blessing. In order to walk along the blessed [. . .] road, through escape from the terrible samsara *(sansar)*, they carried out (5) the commandment to be the blessed poor *(kutlug cïgayïn e[rme]k čxšapt)*.[119] They recognized the transitory doctrines, and, in fear of the three evil ways, in order to be born again in the highest place, they carried out the three seals.[120]

The Sogdian text M 14 likewise enumerates the Five Commandments *(pnc cxš'pδ)*, here as a subset of what are called the "twelve limbs of the conscious soul" *(myn'ndyy rw'n δw'ts 'nδmyyt)*: truth *(ršty'k)*, noninjury *(pw'zrmy')*, religious conduct *(δyncyhryft)*, purity of mouth *(qwcyzprty')*, and blessed poverty *(frnxwndc δšt'wc)*.

These mere rubrics are defined in greater detail in a confessional text for the Elect, in Sogdian, preserved in M 801. The text builds upon the structure provided by the Five Commandments, subdividing each commandment into two parts and recording extensive regulations applicable to each.[121] The confession-formatted review of their disciplinary code by the Manichaean Elect appears to have formed part of the annual Bema ceremony, for which M 801 also provides appropriate hymns. By systematically examining their possible violation of the rules, and asking for forgiveness for such violations, the Elect reverbalize the entire code and publicly reaffirm their adherence to it. Throughout the performance, the confession recollects the sanction for the rules in the authority of Mani, whose words are cited from scripture not in the vernacular Sogdian, but in the prestige "church language" of Middle Persian.

The rule of noninjury is discussed in two parts. The first prohibits inter-active behavior with the world which produces harm to living things, or even to earth and water.

Non-injury Precept (pw'zrmy'h cxš'pδ): As he taught in the scripture: "He who strives to come to that world of peace should collect his own self *(xwys gryw . . . 'mwrdyd)* from here in the manner of the gods of paradise." But I torment and injure at all times the five elements *(mrd'sp[nd]t)*, the fettered light, which is in the dry and wet earth. If (I permitted) the oppressive body, the tor-turous body, with which I am clothed—on foot or riding, moving forward or backward, going quickly or slowly—to strike or cut; (if I permitted it) on the barren earth—wounded and disrupted, oppressed and trodden—to dig or fill, build or erect; (if I permitted it) to enter into the water, into mud, snow, rain-water or dew to make its way; (if I permitted it) to divide or dismember, to wound or disrupt, the five botanic species or the five animal species, be they wet or dry; if I myself have done it, or have asked someone else to that end; if on my behalf people were struck or fettered, or had to endure abuse and in-sults; (if) I by mounting or dismounting, beating or spurring, have done vio-lence to quadrupeds; if I, planning evil against game, birds, sea-creatures or reptiles creeping on the earth, have wounded their life; if I further [have taken a] bath; [if I] have concocted a remedy or oral medicine from a new piece or an old . . . ; if I myself have rejoiced in my arrogance over the com-bat of armies, over the death of sinners or their destruction, over another's in-jury; if I have been averse to the scribal art, have hated or scorned it, have held (and) done much damage and injury to brush, slate(?), silk or paper; if I have spilled a drop from a water jug, so that it was lost: for all these, forgive![122]

These dictates, banning any kind of movement on the earth or contact with its plants or animals, essentially requires the "idleness" charged by Christian polemicists such as Ephrem and Augustine.

Nevertheless, the Elect did eat, and the second part of the rule of non-injury deals with the role of the Elect as storehouses of the light that they col-lect within themselves through eating.[123] The Elect take on the responsibility of making themselves hospitable abodes for divine forces by overcoming hostile drives within themselves. The disciplines addressed in this part constitute the prerequisite regulation of the body that makes such a role possible, and the out-ward behaviors that manifest either the appropriate adherence or the lack of it.

The *Second Section* concerns itself with the "religion glory" *(dynyy frn)* of living humans *(jw'ndyy mrtxmyy)*, and with the living mentalities *(whmn'n zyndg'n)*, who have established themselves in the Righteous Ones. If I have wounded it in the pleasure of passion; if by me it [. . .] has not been strengthened; if on account of my thoughtlessness a brother living together with me suffers doubt; if in the community of brethren I put forward quarrel and words arousing my comrades to dispute (so that) many people suffer corruption of soul or spiritual decrease—as he taught: "He who sees himself only outwardly, not seeing inwardly, is truly inferior and makes others inferior as well." Herein I need forgiveness![124]

One can see, then, that the Elect is committed to maintaining discipline over both external actions and internal attitudes in order to abide by the commandment of noninjury.

The next commandment, rather vaguely termed "religious behavior"[125] in this text, deals with rules of purity and maintaining the integrity of the sacred state of the Elect body. The confession portrays this set of rules as uniquely problematic, due to the mixed condition of human existence. But all that survives in this fragmentary text are regulations against engaging in agriculture.

In higher and greater measure am I especially errant and sinful against *Religious Conduct (dyncyhryft)*. This *yakša*, the wicked devil, who turns hither and thither, constantly pursuing me, who also herself is mixed into this body, in its spiritual and material limbs, and is clothed with them, has encased her arts in all botanical creation, and in the fleshly body scans for what her concupiscences and passions can provoke. If I with great lewdness have planted or sowed in the earth, in a garden or plot of land, fruit-bearing (plants); (if I) have disputed the time of cultivation when it is necessary (to give) water; (if I) have touched a little on spring mornings the sap, shoots, (or) buds of trees [. . .] or the grain of seed; if I have touched snow, rain or dew; if I have tread upon the earth's womb where something grows or sprouts, so that through me a mixture occurs there; and further if in impurity, filthy [attitude . . .].[126]

A few following pages are very fragmentary and yield little continuous sense. The reader can make out allusions only to dietary rules, suggesting that the rule of "purity of the mouth" is under discussion.[127]

The outline of M 801's treatment of the Five Commandments would appear to be, therefore, (1) [Truth], (2) Noninjury, (3) "Chastity" (here significantly broadened), (4) Purity of Mouth, (5) [Poverty].[128] Just as Augustine's account of the Three Seals assigned the discipline of the Elect in all its detail to the three rubrics of that system, so M 801 distributes its encyclopedic code according to the divisions of the Five Commandments.[129]

Summation

The Five Commandments of the Elect, like the Three Seals, provide rubrics for organizing the detailed precepts of the Manichaean disciplinary regimen. Julien Ries, noting the significant amount of overlap between the two disciplinary constructs, has proposed synthesizing them into a single system, in which the Three Seals are a subset of the Five Commandments.[130] But this perfectly logical move appears to go beyond the Manichaeans' own presentation of these constructs. The two organizing strategies appear to be independent models, each capable of comprehending the entire Elect regimen. Such models should not be hypostasized into rigid and monolithic systems, but seen as vehicles for effectively communicating the specific regulations that define the Elect ethos. Together, their detailed exposition is redundant, but as catchwords invoking the discipline as a whole they codify the markers of the disciplined Manichaean body.

ELECT DISCIPLINE IN GENERAL

Manichaean discourse characterizes the Elect as one "who behaves completely differently from the whole world . . . (who) carries the burden and hard toil, the pain of the religion and the heavy load of the law, (who) grasps constantly in himself that which on the whole earth no one carries or grasps."[131] Several sources provide detailed information about the precepts governing Manichaean Elect without explicitly invoking the Three Seals or the Five Commandments. Many of the regulations in these testimonies correlate or complement those treated under the two organizing schemes, and supplement our understanding of the Elect way of life.

The Central Manichaean Tradition

Al-Biruni says of Mani,

> He absolutely forbade his followers to slaughter animals and to hurt them, to
> hurt the fire, water, and plants. He established laws which are obligatory only
> for the Righteous, that is, for the saints and ascetics among the Manichaeans,
> namely to prefer poverty to riches, to suppress cupidity and lust, to abandon
> the world, to be abstinent in it, continually to fast, and to give alms as much
> as possible. He forbade them to acquire any property except food for one day
> and dress for one year; he further forbade sexual intercourse, and ordered
> them continually to wander about in the world, preaching his doctrines and
> guiding people into the right path.[132]

The injunction to give alms is anomalous in this account, since the Elect are
characterized typically as the recipients of Auditor alms. 'Abd al-Jabbar similarly conflates Elect and Auditor regulations in his account in the *al-Mugni fi
abwab al-tawhid wa-l-'adl*.

> The adepts and the chiefs of the sect have instituted obligations: for example
> not to acquire clothes for more than a year, to procure nourishment from day
> to day, as well as other things which they consider as pious works: prayer,
> alms, oration addressed to God, not to kill, not to lie, not to be avaricious, not
> to fornicate, not to commit larceny, not to do to a living being that which one
> does not want to be done to oneself.[133]

In another work, the *Tathbit Dala'il Nubuwwat Sayyidina Muhammad*, the
same author says of Mani that "he mentions that women, sacrifices *(dhabh)*
and eating meat were forbidden by (Christ) to everybody . . . and that (Christ)
has declared to have nothing in common with Abraham, Aaron, Joshua,
David and all those who approve of the sacrificing of animals, of causing them
pain, of eating meat and of other things."[134] In the same vein, Ephrem Syrus
says that the Manichaean Elect "are unwilling to break bread lest 'they pain
the light which is mixed in it.'"[135]

The Western Manichaean Tradition

A famous pronouncement of Faustus of Milevis claims for the Manichaean Elect the status of true Christians, and draws direct correlations between their way of life and the beatitudes declared by Jesus:

> Do I believe the gospel? You ask me if I believe it, though my obedience to its commands shows that I do. . . . I have left my father, mother, wife, and children, and all else that the gospel requires; and do you ask if I believe the gospel? Perhaps you do not know what is called the gospel. The gospel is nothing else than the preaching and the precept of Christ. I have parted with all gold and silver, and have left off carrying money in my purse; content with daily food, without anxiety for tomorrow, and without solicitude about how I shall be fed, or with what I shall be clothed. And do you ask if I believe the gospel? You see in me the blessings of the gospel; and do you ask if I believe the gospel? You see me poor, meek, a peacemaker, pure in heart, mourning, hungering, thirsting, bearing persecutions and enmity for righteousness' sake. And do you doubt my belief in the gospel?[136]

He contrasts this highly ascetic existence to Jewish practices: "I reject circumcision as disgusting. . . . I reject the observance of Sabbaths as superfluous (*supervacuam*). . . . I reject sacrifice as idolatry. . . . Swine's flesh is not the only flesh I abstain from. . . . I think all flesh unclean."[137]

Augustine understands the remark by Faustus quoted above, to the effect that the Sabbath is "superfluous" to Manichaeans, to relate to the fact that the Manichaeans "observe a sort of partial rest," imitating daily, in Augustine's view, the Jewish prohibition of harvesting and food preparation on the Sabbath.[138] Augustine reports, "Those who are called Auditors among them eat flesh meat, till the soil, and, if they wish, have wives, but those called Elect do none of these things."[139] "And so the Elect themselves perform no labors in the field, pluck no fruit, pick not even a leaf, but expect all these things to be brought for their use by their Auditors."[140] The Elect do not eat fish.[141] Moreover,

> They do not eat meat either, on the grounds that the divine substance has fled from the dead or slain bodies, and what little remains there is of such quality and quantity that it does not merit being purified in the stomachs of the elect. They do not even eat eggs, claiming that they too die when they are broken,

and it is not fitting to feed on any dead bodies. . . . Moreover, they do not use milk for food although it is drawn or milked from the live body of an animal. . . . [T]hey do not drink wine either, claiming that bitterness is a property of the princes of darkness, though they do eat grapes. They do not even drink *mustum*, even the most freshly pressed.[142]

The same sort of scrupulous caution when acting in the world is reflected in the Coptic *Kephalaion 85*, where a disciple says to Mani, "I have heard you, my master, say in the congregation of the church that it is proper for a person to watch his step while he walks on a path, lest he trample the Cross of Light with his foot, and destroy vegetation. Also, it counts first for any creeping creature, lest he trample upon it and kill it with his foot."[143] The concerned disciple goes on to describe a situation in which an Elect is ordered to go out on a mission, and might in the course of his journey violate Mani's precept of non-injury. Mani reassures him that an Elect engaged in spiritual work is forgiven the inevitable harm he or she commits by traveling, but the same steps taken for lustful or self-serving purposes incur grave sin.[144] *Kephalaion 38* describes measures to be taken in response to unsanctioned behavior by the Elect. These misbehaviors are described as the outcome of physiological warfare (*polemos, agōn*) within the body of the Elect, manifesting in characteristic vices. The church hierarchy and the lay "assistants" (*n.boēthos*) censure and encourage such troubled individuals, and attempt to restore them to "health."[145]

The Greek *Cologne Mani Codex* depicts Mani maintaining the "rest of the hands." His Elchasaite peers complain about his avoidance of labor: "[N]either do you take [vegetables] from [the] garden, nor do you carry wood."[146] Mani reports that when he approached water, apparently with the intention to bathe, "[from] the waters [a face] of a man appeared to me, showing with his hand the rest, so that I might not sin and bring trouble to him";[147] and in his refutation of Elchasaite practices, he relates two similar episodes involving Elchasai himself.[148] The *Acts of Archelaus* imply the same restriction on bathing.[149]

The polemicist Alexander of Lycopolis tries to convey what he perceives as the tenor of the Manichaean way of life as follows:

Since it is God's decree that matter shall perish, one has to abstain from eating any animals,[150] and should rather eat vegetables and all the other things that are without feeling. One has to abstain from marriage and love-making and the begetting of children, lest, because of the succession of the race, the power should dwell in matter for a longer time. One should not, by committing suicide, bring about an artificial purification of the stains inflicted upon the power by the admixture of matter. Such are their chief tenets.[151]

Although Alexander fails to specify to whom these rules apply, they clearly represent a review of the disciplines appropriate to the Elect. A Greek abjuration formula contains an anathema targeted at the same sort of disciplines:

> I anathematize those who pollute themselves with their own urine, and do not suffer their filth to be cleansed in water lest, they say, the water be defiled. I anathematize . . . (those who) reject marriage and withhold themselves from the lawful intercourse with women, in order, they say, that they will not produce children and lead souls into the mire of human bodies.[152]

The Eastern Manichaean Tradition

In the Sogdian section of the Bema-handbook M 801, the confessional exposition of the Five Commandments is followed by a series of further disciplinary concerns: the practice of confession itself, the five "gifts," and the "closing" of the five "gates."[153] The five "gifts" are five positive dispositions that the Elect receive as a sacred trust and that are injected into their mental faculties.

> *The Five Divine Gifts:* I am also sinful [against] the five gifts which are bound for the main body of the religion, if I have not accepted them in my five divisions *(ptywdn)*, namely, glory *(frn)*, thought *(sy')*, sense *(m'n)*, consideration *(sm'r)* and reason *(ptbydyh)*. In the first place love, which is the nourisher of all good deeds, as he taught, "Where love is little, all deeds are imperfect." If I have not had love, if hate treads in its place; if, in the place of faith, unfaith; (if, in the place) of striving for perfection, imperfection; (if, in the place) of patience, violence; (if, in the place) of wisdom, folly treads; and if I have not rejected from my self *(gryw)* the fivefold infernal passion, so that it intrudes upon me decrease in many respects; if through me the holy spirit should have been irritated: therein am I a death-deserving sinner![154]

Regulation of the Elect body, therefore, includes not only the policing of external actions, but the cultivation of dispositions and attitudes that are considered gifts to the individual.

Another fivefold regulation concerns control of the senses, which are the gateways of harmful stimuli.

> *The Closing ('nwyj'mndy) of the Five Gates:* Also in the closing of the five gates I was not perfect. As he taught in scripture, "What is the profit of that Righteous One who says 'I possess power in my limbs,' when he is ruined through his eyes, ears and other limbs as well?" Thus, if I (have left open) my eyes to sight, my ears to sound, my nose to smell, my mouth to improper food and ugly speech, and my hands to improper contact and touch; and the de-monic Až, who has built this body and enclosed herself within it, produces in-deed through these five gates constant strife; she brings the inner demons to-gether with the outer ones, between which a portion is destroyed daily; if I thus should have kept my gates open and Až should have provoked all of the desire-affected spiritual demons, so that the soul-treasure *(rw'nyh gr'myy),* the living self *(gryw jywndg),* goes astray from me: for all these things, forgiveness!

The confession describes the closing of the sense-gates as a separation of in-ternal and external forces. It implies that the internal "demons" can be quelled in the absence of external provocation. Their arousal leads to the de-struction of the divine "soul treasure" which is the sacred trust of the Elect. Exactly what form this exercise took cannot be discerned here. The five senses are identified as the "doors" of vice, allowing access into the individual. The adherent is called upon to guard, even "close" the sense organs to the outside world's baneful influence.[155]

The Chinese *Compendium* provides a general characterization of Mani-chaean discipline within the temple *(mānīstān):*

> In the five halls (of the *mānīstān*) the religious assembly dwells together in or-der to zealously practice good deeds *(shan-yeh).* (They) may not erect sepa-rately private habitations, kitchens or storehouses. They fast every day *(mei-rih chai-shih).* With perfect dignity, they wait for alms *(shih)*; if no one prepares alms for them, they may solicit (them) in order to provide (for their needs). They only employ Auditors and do not keep either male or female slaves, or domestic animals of the six kinds, or other objects contrary to the religion.[156]

The Elect way of life effects a total absorption in salvational thought and prac-tice, the *Compendium* explains.

By the "great calamity" *(ta-huan)*[157] they have the disgust (which makes one want) to separate from the body; in the "burning house"[158] they have the prayer (by which) they look to escape. They wear out the body for the sake of the (luminous) nature. (Thus) the holy teaching is firmly established. If they [on the other hand] take what is false to be true, let no one dare to heed their directives. One must discern well, and look for the causes of deliverance.[159]

The author unequivocally avers the centrality of the disciplinary codes to the total set of relations within the Manichaean community:

> If these five grades[160] trust each other, obey all instructions *(chiao)* and commandments *(ming)*, and stand firmly by the prohibitions *(chin)* and precepts *(chieh)*, (this) is termed the road of deliverance *(chieh-t'uo lu)*. If a Teacher is violating the precepts, no one shall accept his instructions and commandments. Even though he is well versed in the seven scriptures and eminently skilled in debate, if he has faults *(ch'ien)* and vices *(wei)*, the five grades will not assist (him). It is like a tree that thrives by its roots: if they are exhausted, the tree withers. If a Righteous One violates the precepts, regard him as dead, expose (him) to public knowledge, and expel (him) from the religion *(fa)*. For although the sea is vast, it does not tolerate corpses for long. (Whoever) protects and screens (him) commits the same breach of precepts.[161]

Authority rests solely upon conduct, and great learning cannot compensate for faults of behavior. Such is the case, at least, in this official statement. According to its account, shunning constitutes the ultimate punishment of those who cannot sustain the discipline.

In the Chinese *Hymnscroll*'s "Praise of the Five Lights," the singer(s) enjoins:

> Firmly observe fasting *(chai)* and precepts *(chieh)*, always guard them carefully; and control your thoughts, regulating them constantly. Day and night think only of the true and correct religion *(fa)*; attend to the weighing *(ch'üan)* and clarifying *(ch'eng)* of the five wondrous bodies *(wu miao-shen)*.[162]

The orders entailed in such an utterance include both external and internal regulation, a discipline encompassing outward and inward dimensions of the self. The second canto elaborates on the theme of intense discipline:

Act according to the precepts *(chieh-hsing)*, respect the protocols *(wei-i)*, practicing fasting *(chai)*, rites *(li)*, reverence *(pai)*, and hymn-singing *(tsan-sung)*. Be always clean and pure in the deeds of body, mouth, and mind; sing and chant the words of law without break or stop. And also practice merciful deeds earnestly; be gentle and amicable, bear humiliations and purify all roots *(ching chu-ken)*. These are the remedies for the bodies of light, which spare pain, fear, and many hardships and afflictions.[163]

The non-Manichaean Chinese intelligentsia display a natural interest in the rules governing Manichaean life, since it was the conduct of these strange people, not their thoughts, which concerned the government and other social authorities. The *Hsin T'ang-shu* reports, "The laws of these (Manichaeans) prescribe that they should eat only in the evening, drink water, eat strong vegetables, and abstain from milk and butter *(tung-lo)*."[164] Hung Mai, in his *I-chien chih*, says, "Those who abide by their ascetic rules eat only one meal which they take in mid-day."[165] Tsung-chien, in the *Shih-men cheng-t'ung*, details prohibitions of (1) contact between male and female Elect, (2) the use of medicine, and (3) the consumption of meat and wine.[166] Another member of the Chinese intelligentsia, Chang Hsi-sheng, converted to a highly Sinicized form of Manichaeism, which he seems to have practiced in total isolation from any co-religionists. In a letter (ca. 1264 C.E.) to his old school companion Huang Chen he sums up the high demand placed upon the individual by the disciplinary regimen of the Elect.

When our teacher Lao-tzu went to the region of the West, he became Mani Buddha. His rules of self-discipline are particularly strict. They allow those who practice it one meal a day, and on fast days they have to remain indoors. . . . Mani's rules on asceticism are strict, and although they are no longer practiced they are still extant and I have made occasional records of them as warning to myself and to posterity.[167]

Summation

However "positive" the rhetoric of the Five Commandments, therefore, gleanings from the many other sources available to us indicate a very detailed and restrictive code of conduct incumbent upon the Manichaean Elect. Every possible action and attitude came under intense scrutiny and careful restriction. Hans Schaeder aptly sums up the modern reaction to such an ethos when he writes, "This ascetic demand, if carried out with full severity, means the renunciation of life altogether. Mani for that reason finds a way out, which is consistent with the thought of his system and yet brings an irreparable break in his ethic. Only the restricted number of the 'Perfect' undertake the ascetic demand in its whole severity."[168] The life entailed in membership among the Manichaean Elect bears little resemblance to "gnostic" notions of salvation by self-recognition; nor does it take the form of an inherent nature manifesting itself through a liberation from constraint. But nor do the disciplines of even the Elect commit their adherent to voluntary suicide. Manichaean discipline imposes constraints, reins in behavior, and molds the body to an imposed model that will make it truly functional for the first time. This constantly regulated life is the Manichaean road to "liberation," although the modern reader may find it perverse to see in such a life any kind of freedom. But the discipline of the Manichaean Elect is not intended as an end in itself; it is, rather, the prerequisite for a liberation yet to be attained.

THE TEN COMMANDMENTS OF THE AUDITORS

A common caricature of Manichaean Auditors proposes that their life is in every respect the opposite of that of the Elect—an existence of total indulgence, sanctioned merely by their benefactions to the latter. This impression derives from Western polemical accounts, especially Augustine of Hippo's self-recriminating reflections on his own life as a Manichaean Auditor, which put the worst face on the Elect-Auditor disciplinary distinction. But a close examination of the evidence demonstrates the untenableness of this image when we are speaking of the religion's own norms. Nicholas Sims-Williams notes that the Auditors "were required to observe . . . ten commandments, expressed wholly in the form of prohibitions, more specific and consequently less restrictive than those enjoined upon the Elect."[169] He collects references to these Ten Commandments in Parthian,[170] Sogdian,[171] Turkic,[172] and Chinese;[173] yet none of these texts, he maintains, provides a complete list. Only an-Nadim supplies such a complete list in his *Fihrist*.[174] A Middle Persian text reconstructed from M 5794.II and M 6062 appears to be an elaborated parallel, but breaks off after three commandments. *Xuāstuānīft* 9A aligns the Ten Commandments, at least in theory, with the Three Seals, but gives no specifics.[175]

Sims-Williams identifies a Sogdian grammar exercise as bearing on this same distribution of commandments among the seals.[176] It is notable that no source from the Western Manichaean tradition mentions the Ten Commandments.

The Central Manichaean Tradition

An-Nadim states:

> Mani prescribed ten ordinances for the auditors, which he followed up with three seals and a fast of seven days without fail during every month.[177] ... The ten ordinances (are): renouncing the worship of idols; renouncing the telling of lies;[178] renouncing avarice; renouncing killing;[179] renouncing adultery; renouncing stealing, the teaching of defects (ta'lim al-'ilal), magic, the holding of two opinions about the faith, neglect and lassitude in action.[180]

Sims-Williams regards this as the only complete list of the Ten Commandments. A pertinent question, therefore, would be: Were the same commandments invoked in all parts of the Manichaean world?

The Eastern Manichaean Tradition

The Turkic Xuāstuānīft does present what would appear to be a full list of Auditor commandments. The sixth section of this confession text for Auditors surveys the "ten kinds of sin," violations of the basic "Ten Commandments" that served as the Auditors' code of behavior.

> If somehow we have lied, and if somehow we have taken a false oath, if somehow we have served as witness for a false person, and if somehow we have falsely accused an innocent person, and if somehow we incited enmity between people by carrying their remarks back and forth, if we have corrupted their minds and understanding, if somehow we have practiced witchcraft, and if somehow we have killed numerous creatures and beings, if somehow we have deceived and tricked, if somehow we have consumed a householder's goods entrusted to us, if somehow we have done things that displease the gods of the Sun and Moon, and if somehow we have sinned and erred in the previous existence or in this existence, whether the existence was as women or

boys, if somehow we have inflicted anger or hatred on so many creatures, (then), Majesty, now we beg to be freed from these ten kinds of sins. Release my sins![181]

This Turkic catalog cannot be harmonized with that of an-Nadim and can scarcely be numbered in such a way as to produce ten commandments; these puzzling features of the passage makes Sims-Williams hesitate to see in the Xuāstuānīft an actual attempt to list the Ten Commandments. But perhaps the Ten Commandments was more of an abstract concept for the Manichaeans, given different contents in different regions.[182] A Middle Persian fragment preserves portions of three Auditor precepts:

> They [do not] kill [animals;] even those who [harm?] them, they shall have mercy so that they do not kill them in the same way as the wicked kill. But dead flesh of any animals, wherever they find it, be it (naturally) dead or slaughtered, they may eat; and whenever they find it, either through trading or as a livelihood or as a present, they may eat. And that is enough for them. This is the first precept (*'ndrz*) for Auditors. And the second precept (is) that they shall not be false, and that they, one towards the other, [shall] not [be] unjust [. . .] and they shall walk (?) in truth. And the Auditor shall love the Auditor in the same way as one loves one's own brother and relatives, for they are children of the Living Family (*n'p zyndg*) and the world of light. And the third precept is that they shall not slander anybody and not be a false witness against anybody of what they have not seen, and not swear an oath upon a lie concerning something and falsehood and [. . .].[183]

Enough of this enumeration survives to show significant similarity of content with the other accounts, but no consistency in the order of commandments. This fact furthers the impression that the details of the Ten Commandments were subject to local permutation. The Chinese evidence for the Ten Commandments of the Auditors amounts to no more than allusions.[184] While confirming the place of the Ten Commandments as a fundamental construct of Auditor conduct, therefore, the Chinese material provides no details to compare with the Arabic, Iranian, and Turkic lists.

Summation

We see, then, that the Ten Commandments construct has a wider circuit as an idea than it has as a definitive list of rules. Not attested at all in the Roman region, the commandments have no definitive form among the Manichaeans further east. The Auditors are more than a clientele; they occupy a distinct section of the Manichaean community with a discipline of their own. The details of that discipline, however, vary from region to region, perhaps in tandem with shifts in emphasis from one culture to another about what were considered hallmarks of virtuous behavior.

AUDITOR DISCIPLINE IN GENERAL

Despite the weakness of the Ten Commandments construct, we have sufficient information on the general tenor of Auditor practice to identify their specific contribution to the Manichaean community.

The Central Manichaean Tradition

Al-Biruni, who had access to Mani's *Šābuhragān*, reports that "(Mani) absolutely forbade his followers to slaughter animals and to hurt them, to hurt the fire, water, and plants." After such a blanket statement, he adds that Mani "imposed upon the *samma'un*, that is, their followers and adherents who have to do with worldly affairs" the obligation "to give as alms the tenth of their property, to fast during the seventh part of a life-time, to live in monogamy, to sponsor the *siddiqun*, and to remove everything that troubles or pains them."[185] 'Abd al-Jabbar conflates Elect and Auditor regulations in his account in the *al-Mugni fi abwab al-tawhid wa-l-'adl*, and at least some of the following should be regarded as incumbent on the latter: "prayer, alms, oration addressed to God, not to kill, not to lie, not to be avaricious, not to fornicate, not to commit larceny, not to do to a living being that which one does not want to be done to oneself."[186]

The Western Manichaean Tradition

The Coptic *Kephalaia* contains the most important surviving discussion of the ideology of auditorship (or catechumenate) in Manichaeism. *Kephalaion 91* enunciates a model of the perfect Auditor, and appeals for adherence to this model through a unique promise of reward, for this is "the Catechumen who is saved in a single body"[187] and not subject to painful transmigration. In the account, an Elect explicitly declares his intention to preach this model to the Catechumens so that they will emulate it.[188] Mani supplies the model in the following words:

> The sign of that perfect Catechumen is this: You find his wife in the house with him being handled by him like a stranger. His house, moreover, is reckoned by him like an inn; and he says, "I dwell in a house for rent for (some) days and months." His family and kinsmen are reckoned by him (as) it is necessary (for) men who are strangers, adhering to him, walking with him in the road, as he [. . .] they will separate from him, and every [possession of] gold and silver and vessels of [value in the] house, they become like loaned items to him; [he] accepts them, and he is served through them, (and) afterwards he gives [them to] their owner. He does not place his trust in them, nor his treasure. He has plucked out his thought from the world; he has placed his [heart] in the holy church. At all times his thought is placed upon God. But that which surpasses all these things is the guardianship *(mntbairaush)* and the care *(leh)* and the love *(agapē)* of the holy ones which exist in him. He guards the church in the manner of [his] house, even more than his house. He places his whole treasure in the Electi and the Electae. For this is that which [the] savior pronounced through the mouth of his apostle: "From today those who have a wife, let them become like those who do not; those who buy as if they do not buy; those who rejoice as if they do not rejoice; those who weep as if they do not weep; those who [find] profit in this world as if they do not take advantage." These are the ones who [. . .] come, the ones who [. . .] were sent; and they were sent because of these perfect Catechumens who are released from this single body, and they go to them, to the height, resembling the Elect in their citizenship. This is the sign of those Catechumens who do not come to a body (again).[189]

Having enunciated an extreme ideal, Mani continues by describing a second class of Auditor.

> There are others, too, embracing chastity *(enkrateia)*, having [kept] every beast from their mouth, being eager for the fast *(nēstia)* and the daily prayer

(shlēl), assisting the church, according to that which reaches their hand, through the alms (mntnae). The potential for evil doing (mntbanieire)[190] is dead in them. [They cause] the movement of their feet to the church more than to their house; their heart is upon it at all times. Their manner of sitting and their manner of arising is in the way of the Elect. They strip all of the things of the world from their heart. [But] that man, the mind that is placed in the holy church [. . .] every hour (?), and his gifts [. . .] and his honor and the presents that give profit [to] his life, he [brings ?] them to the holy church—into these, furthermore, who come in to the church,[191] be they his children or his wife or a kinsman of him. He rejoices over those more, and he loves [them], bestowing all of his treasure upon them. Look, this, therefore, is the sign (meine) and the type (typos) of these Catechumens who do not come to a body (again).[192]

This second portrait seems to correspond to the actual norm promoted in the sermons, catechetical instruction, psalms, and other forms of discourse in the Manichaean tradition. Nevertheless, Mani is aware that many will not live up to these standards, and he holds out the promise of some mitigation of a person's future hardships in accordance with the amount of effort invested in reforming his or her life along the lines Mani suggests.

But concerning all of the remaining Catechumens, I have written down in the *Treasury of Life* the way that they are released, and they are purified, each of them according to his deeds, according to his approach to the church. This is the way that his ascent causes his healing and his purification to approach him. Because of this, indeed, it is fitting for the Catechumen that he pray always for repentance and forgiveness of sins from God and the holy church for his sins, the [first] and the last, so that his deeds will be collected, [the] first and the last, and they will be reckoned to his share.[193]

The Auditor gains a total remission of sins upon admittance to the church, Coptic sources declare, and obtains within the church the means to pardon any new sins which he or she may commit.[194] Whatever new sins accrue to the Auditor "will be released many times over [to him] because of his fast (nēstia) and [his prayer (shlēl) and his] alms ([mn]tnae)."[195] Mani proceeds to lay down the standard discipline for Auditors, "the deeds of the faithful Catechumens," including weekly fasting and daily prayers and alms.[196]

Kephalaion 80 reviews more succinctly the discipline of the Auditors.[197] They follow a twofold discipline, becoming perfect in two "characteristics" *(smat)*.[198]

> The first task of the catechumenate that he does is the fast *(nēstia)*, the prayer *(shlēl)*, and the alms-offering *(mntnae)*. The fast in which he fasts is this: that he fasts on the day of [the Lord *(kyriake)* from] the things of the world. The prayer [is this: that] he prays to the sun and moon, the great [illuminators]. The alms-offering, moreover, is this: that he places it [. . .] in the holy one, and he gives it to them in righteousness. [The] second task of the catechu-menate [that he] does is this: the person will give a child of the church to Righteousness (i.e., the Elect class)—or his kinsman, [or a member] of (his) household, or he redeems one when he finds him in affliction, or when he buys a slave—and he gives him to Righteousness, so that he does all good, this one who gives a gift [to] Righteousness. That Catechumen who [does this] will be in partnership *(koinōnē)* with them.[199]

The text goes on to enumerate a "third occasion" for catechumen merit (may we suspect a redactional seam here?): "The person will build a dwelling place *(ma n.shope)* or he will establish a place *(topos)* so that it will be made for him a share of alms in the holy church."[200] The passage sums up these regulations as "these three great things, these three great alms [which one] gives as a gift *(dōron)* to the [holy] church."[201] For that Auditor who performs these services, "there is a great love and a portion *(taie)* of all gifts *(hmat)* and goods *(agathon)* in the holy church."[202]

In Augustine's eyes, however, Manichaean Auditors lead ordinary lives for the most part. His most succinct characterization of the distinction between Elect and Auditor among the Manichaeans states, "Those who are called Au-ditors among them eat flesh meat, till the soil, and, if they wish, have wives, but those called Elect do none of these things."[203] By highlighting those things the Auditors are allowed, he implicitly tells us more about the Elect than any special characteristics of the Auditors. Thus the fact that Auditors drink foun-tain water, and wear wool and linen[204] scarcely sets them apart from their non-Manichaean peers.

The eating of meat appears most frequently in Augustine as a dividing line between Auditor and Elect.

> You, as a concession, allow your Auditors, as distinct from the priests, to eat animal food, as the Apostle allows, and in certain cases, not marriage in the general sense, which is made solely for the purpose of reproduction, but the indulgence of passion in marriage. . . . You make allowance for your Auditors, because . . . they supply your necessities; but you grant them concession without saying that it is not sinful. For yourselves, you shun contamination with this evil and impurity.[205]

Augustine implies in this passage that the Manichaeans could cite biblical authority for their position. Such authority is made explicit in the following: "You follow Adimantus in saying that Christ made no distinction in food, except in entirely prohibiting the use of animal food to his disciples, while he allowed the laity to eat anything that is eatable; and declared that they were not polluted by what enters into the mouth, but that the unseemly things which come out of the mouth are the things which defile a man."[206] The allowance of meat apparently did not entail permission to butcher, even though Augustine found it contradictory for the Manichaeans "to permit your Auditors to eat meat, yet forbid them to kill animals."[207] The ban on killing did not extend to the most minuscule of creatures, however, since "you who refrain from the killing of animals make an exception of lice, fleas, and bugs."[208] Nonetheless, it is a crime to kill bees.[209]

Augustine asks, "Why do you consider it a greater sin to kill animals than plants when you believe plants to have purer souls than animals?" He answers his rhetorical question with the Manichaean teaching on the subject. "A certain compensation (compensatio) takes place, you say, when some part of what is taken from the fields is brought to the Elect and holy men to be purified";[210] "the injuries your Auditors inflict upon plants are expiated through the fruits which they bring to your church."[211] The logic of the regulation emerges fully in a final statement: "But you say that in order that one be pardoned for the slaughter (of animals), the meat would have to be contributed as food, as is done in the case of fruits and vegetables, but that this is impossible since the Elect do not eat meat, and that, therefore, your Auditors must abstain from the killing of animals."[212] This construct of the ritual process makes meat-eating, even among the Auditors, a potentially fatal indulgence.

Despite differences in the food regulations appropriate to Elect and Auditors, the latter were expected to partially emulate the habitual fasting of the Elect. Augustine indicates that the Auditors fasted on Sundays.[213] He discourages Sunday fasting among Catholics for the express reason that the "detestable" Manichaeans "have selected that day for their Auditors to fast."[214]

Next to food, sex distinguished the Auditors from the Elect. Auditors could marry and otherwise conduct sexual liaisons, as Augustine himself did while a Manichaean. But this allowance did not amount to permission for sexual license; the Manichaean authorities encouraged abstinence or, at the very least, birth control. For Augustine, the Manichaean teaching on sex turned the world on its head. "They take wives, as the law declares, for the procreation of children; but from this erroneous fear of polluting the substance of the deity, their intercourse with their wives is not of a lawful character; and the production of children, which is the proper end of marriage, they seek to avoid."[215] In other words, "though you may not forbid sexual intercourse, you forbid marriage; for the peculiarity of marriage is that it is not merely for the gratification of passion, but, as is written in the contract, for the procreation of children."[216]

Augustine shows deep skepticism of the ideological underpinnings of the Auditor-Elect division. He suggests that the Elect indulge the Auditors' vices only to gain their support, and that in the end the Auditors will be cheated of the rewards they are promised, as absurd as these rewards may be.

> If it is true that a man cannot receive the gospel without giving up everything, why do you delude your Auditors, by allowing them to keep in your service their wives, and children, and households, and houses, and fields? . . . All you promise them is not a resurrection, but a change (revolutionem) to another mortal existence, in which they shall live the life of your Elect, the life you live yourself, and are so much praised for; or if they are worthy of the better, they shall enter into melons and cucumbers, or some foods which will be chewed, that they may be quickly purified by your belches.[217]

On the other hand, Augustine can at times acknowledge the virtuous character of at least the rhetoric of Manichaean practice:

> I was involved in the life of this world, nursing shadowy hopes of a beautiful wife, of the pomp of riches, of empty honors and other pernicious and deadly pleasures. All these things, as you know, I did not cease to desire and hope for when I was their zealous Auditor. I do not attribute this to their teaching, for I confess that they carefully warned me to beware of these things.[218]

It was precisely the fine sound of Manichaean moral discourse that induced him to write *De moribus manichaeorum* in an effort to show that the reality did not match the words.

The Eastern Manichaean Tradition

The Turkic *Xuāstuānīft* scripts a detailed review of the discipline appropriate to the Auditors, which they were to recite and affirm on a regular basis. The theme of nonviolence dominates the text. In the third section, the confessing speakers say:

> Majesty, if at any time somehow we have injured or hurt, unwittingly (or) through malice, the Five Gods, or if we have inflicted (on them) the fourteen kinds of wounds, or if somehow we have pained and grieved the Living Self, the god of food and drink, with the ten serpent-headed fingers (and) the thirty-two teeth, or if somehow we have sinned against the dry and moist earth, against the five kinds of creatures, or against the five kinds of herbs and trees, (then) now, Majesty, we beg to be freed from sin. Release my sins![219]

The Living Self, a central rationale of Manichaean practice, appears here in the collective form of the Five Gods, and is identified by apposition to the divine element in food and drink. Eating itself, therefore, becomes a sinful activity through the pain caused by grasping (with the ten "serpent-headed" fingers) and chewing (with the thirty-two teeth). The passage rounds out the set of potential victims of human existence with the totality of animal and vegetable life, conveniently classified into fivefold typologies. The fifth section of the *Xuāstuānīft* elaborates, first identifying the "five kinds of creatures,"[220] and then reiterating the vow not to harm them.

> Majesty, if at any time somehow we have frightened these five kinds of creatures and beings, whether great or small, if we somehow have scared them, if we somehow have struck them, if we somehow have cut them, if we somehow have caused them pain, if we somehow have caused them grief, if we somehow have killed them, (then) we owe a self to such creatures and beings. Majesty, now we beg to be freed from sin. Release my sins![221]

This theme of nonviolence pervades the *Xuāstuānīft*, and indeed sinfulness is practically equated with harm in this text.

In the fourth section of the *Xuāstuānīft*, we find a relatively abbreviated discussion of disrespect towards the Elect, "who are meritorious and bring redemption." It is not particularly detailed or informative, but does speak to the abiding Manichaean concern with relations between the two classes of adherent. The seventh section treats the opposite problem, that is, trusting false religious authorities, with the result that one "kept fast *(bačag)* erroneously . . . worshiped *(yüküntümüz)* erroneously . . . gave alms *(pušii)* erroneously." Even with good intentions, the text makes clear, such behavior is sinful and requires forgiveness.

The *Xuāstuānīft* confirms Augustine's references to a weekly fast among the Auditors. The reciter affirms, "There is a precept that one should observe *wusanti*[222] like the pure Elect fifty days a year, that one must worship God by keeping a pure fast."[223] This observance appears to be the topic discussed in a bookleaf reconstructed from several fragments by Albert von Le Coq:

> They shall not let (the food and drink for the Elect) be spoiled, or let it be poured out, or let it be mixed. And just as the fast [is kept (?)] in purity, so they shall restrain themselves and keep the fast properly according to [pure (?)] food and pure water. . . . And they shall guard and purify and avert themselves from the shameless knowledge—the pure (Auditors) from women and the women (Auditors) from men. And a [. . .] shall not strike a person [. . .] shall not wound, and shall not kill.[224]

Like their Iranian and Turkish co-religionists, Chinese Manichaean Auditors practiced public recitals of "confession," in which they enumerated the possible infractions of which they might be guilty. The two examples preserved in the *Hymnscroll* take the form of short prayers asking for forgiveness. In the "Penitence and Confession Prayer Text for Auditors," the latter declare their repentance "if we have been neglectful of the seven-fold alms-offering, the Ten Commandments, and the Three Seals—the gates of the religion *(fa)*; and if we have damaged the five-fold 'religion-body,' squandering it constantly; or if we have hewn and chopped the five kinds of grasses and trees; or if we have made to labor or enslaved the five species of animals."[225] In the "Penitential Prayer of the Auditor," the speaker declares:

I now repent whatever were the deeds of my body, mouth, and mind, my greedy, indignant, and foolish behavior; and if I have encouraged the robbers to poison my heart, or not restrained my roots . . . or if I have injured the body of Lushena,[226] as well as the Five Lights;[227] if I have begot a feeling of slight and neglect against the Elect . . . or if I have imperfectly observed the seven alms-offerings, the Ten Commandments, and the Three Seals—the gates of the religion (fa)—I wish my sins to disappear![228]

The moral of a parable from the Middle Persian text M 49 presents the path of the Manichaean Auditor as a sharp contrast to the ordinary, unreformed person, who "gives himself up to hate and protects the kingdom and does agriculture and makes payment(s) and eats flesh and drinks wine and has a wife and child and acquires house and property and accumulates for the body and pays taxes in the kingdom and robs and damages and proceeds with oppression and mercilessness." The potential Manichaean Auditor is advised to "ask for the wisdom and knowledge of the gods" and to "think of the soul (rw'n)." If he does so, "he shall keep away from lewdness and fornication and evil thinking, evil speaking and evil doing; and he shall also keep his hand away from robbery and damage and violence and mercilessness and always keep away from soil and water and fire and trees and plants and wild and tame animals and hurt them (as) little (as possible)."[229] In the Sogdian text M 135 Mani himself speaks as follows:

And now I command you, Auditors, that so long as there is strength in your bodies, you should strive for the salvation of your souls. Bear in mind my orders and [my words], that straight path (wyzryy r'dd) and true mold (rštyy q'rpd) which I have shown to you, namely, the sacred religion. Strive through that mold so that you will join me in the eternal life.[230]

This expectation that the Auditors would not only sponsor the Elect, but also strive for their own salvation, accounts for the large percentage of lay-focused material in the surviving Manichaean literature.

Summation

Manichaean Auditors possess a bad reputation in the history books. Augustine's skepticism concerning the motives of Manichaean church authorities has left a lasting impression on scholarship. The popular image is that Auditors enjoyed maximum indulgence for their vices, provided they kept the Elect well supplied. More careful scholars of the last century have moderated but not broken with this impression. Even an authority like H.-C. Puech—who holds that the "Three Seals" apply, at least in principle, to both Elect and Auditors—thinks that any precepts were applied to Auditors only "in a more lax fashion, being in their case softened and relaxed, accommodated by the expedient of some concessions."[231] Taken broadly, this statement conveys the divergence in discipline recognized even by the Manichaeans themselves. Yet its emphasis and conceptualization of the system echoes anti-Manichaean polemicists such as Augustine more than the self-descriptions of normative Manichaeism. The latter distinguishes distinct regimens, each of which molds a body fit for its particular function in the community.

In addition to requiring of the Auditor a fairly generic morality and specific religious exercises that emulated the more constant regimen of the Elect, the Manichaean community created the circumstances in which the Auditors were constrained to review their deviance from the higher norms, and to demonstrate a public compunction for this deviance. Explicitly in the Manichaean confession texts, and somewhat less emphatically in hymns, Auditors learned and performed narratives about their identity which emphasized a wide gulf between their daily actions and the proper embodiment of a saved soul. Even in such a state, however, they possessed a relationship with the saved which promised their ultimate liberation.

Although there can be no doubt that the Auditors are a second class of adherent in Manichaeism, their moderate (but by no means lax) regimen and dedication to the Elect gives them *koinōnia* with the latter. It takes no great genius to recognize that without the Auditors the Elect could not exist, either logistically (in terms of daily survival), or historically (in terms of the survival of Manichaeism itself). A Coptic text speaks of the Auditors as the refuge of the Church, the only company in which the truly "religious" may find shelter and support in a hostile world. At the same time, the text adds, the Elect are the refuge of the Auditors, the only channel by means of which they may effectively connect with God. The respective disciplines of the two classes of adherent mark them as Manichaeans,[232] distinguish them from both outsiders and each other, and make possible their participation in the salvational rites revealed by God through Mani.

CONCLUSIONS

Normative Manichaean texts describe an approved ethos promulgated by the religion's authoritative institutions; even polemical accounts confirm that a certain number of individuals strove to adhere to those norms. The Manichaean life, then, entails behavior conforming to approved models, models that circumscribe and define what a Manichaean is through a system of discipline. Discipline, according to Michel Foucault,

> is a type of power, a modality for its exercise, comprising a whole set of instruments, techniques, procedures, levels of application, targets; it is a "physics" or an "anatomy" of power, a technology. And it may be taken over either by "specialized" institutions . . . or by institutions that use it as an essential instrument for a particular end . . . or by pre-existing authorities that find in it a means of reinforcing or reorganizing their internal mechanisms of power.[233]

Before examining the Manichaeans' own rationales for their disciplinary regimens and exploring how the disciplined body fits into the larger project of Manichaeism, we should pause to ask: What do these practices in and of themselves do?

They seem to do three things: identify, qualify, and control. They *identify* Manichaeans by marking a Manichaean body, guiding a Manichaean ethos, and circumscribing a Manichaean community. Insofar as the behaviors enjoined by Manichaean disciplinary codes are distinctively Manichaean, adherence to them sets individuals and groups apart from others. Likewise, the behaviors disapproved by those codes are identified as expendable to the Manichaean identity, as obstacles to it, corruptions of it. Manichaean disciplines also *qualify* their adherents for particular rights and specific roles within the community. They construct status for individuals and enable the community to engage in the larger tasks for which the disciplines prepare. Finally, the disciplines *control* by setting standards, mutually enforced, that either admit to or bar from participation in the community's activities. They limit status and roles within the community to those who meet the criteria established by the tradition. They allow assessment of individuals in light of such criteria, and provide justification for the correction or expulsion of those who do not manifest the Manichaean body.

But this conformity was not imposed from a coercive center, nor was it integrated with other ethnic socializing systems. Individuals adopted Manichaean identity voluntarily, often at odds with the values of the larger society and under severe threat of persecution. Conformity arose, then, among a dispersed membership. Adherence was the manifest effect of the total system of regulation that Manichaeans adopted, and involved a "microphysics" of coercions by the Elect toward the Auditors, by the Auditors toward the Elect, by members of each class toward each other, and by individuals toward themselves.[234] Manichaeans formed relations based upon mutual scrutiny enhanced by constant reiteration of the proposed paradigms.[235] The complete code of approvals and disapprovals constitute a model of Manichaean "character" that was manifested in the individual, conformed bodies within the community.

> Discipline "makes" individuals; it is the specific technique of a power that regards individuals both as objects and as instruments of its exercise. It is not a triumphant power, which because of its own excess can pride itself on its omnipotence; it is a modest, suspicious power, which functions as a calculated, but permanent economy.[236]

What makes Foucault's language particularly apt for the Manichaean case, perhaps more so than for the society-wide industrial and juridical reconfigurations of the self in modernity, is the voluntaristic position of those within the Manichaean ranks.

Manichaean disciplinary regimens, like the schemes and institutions studied by Foucault, constitute a normative system. Foucault's way of describing such systems tend to credit their successful implementation. If we are careful to qualify the publicly stated intentions of a discipline, then we can say that, ideally, "he who is subjected to a field of visibility, and who knows it, assumes responsibility for the constraints of power. . . . He becomes the principle of his own subjection."[237] This full realization of the self within the models of the discipline is all the more likely to occur in those situations where even the "gaps," the random and unstructured idiosyncrasies of the individual, are offered up voluntarily to the system; in other words, the individual wants to be subjected, and even is alienated from any personal manifestation that does not conform to the power which is articulating through his or her body.

Given the nature of our sources, we are in no position to talk about the

motivations that moved people to become Manichaeans and to adopt Manichaean discipline; but we can explore the rationales that the tradition itself
produced to justify and explain the distinctively Manichaean way of life. To
say that those who joined the Manichaean church found these rationales compelling would be a pointless circularity, and would set up an image of a fully
individuated self that chooses the disciplines and puts them on like a robe.
Rather, to become a Manichaean meant learning to speak (and hence to
think) along the lines Manichaean discourse provided, and to become embodied as a Manichaean.

> The individual is not to be conceived as a sort of elementary nucleus, a prim-
> itive atom, a multiple and inert material on which power comes to fasten or
> against which it happens to strike, and in so doing subdues or crushes indi-
> viduals. In fact, it is already one of the prime effects of power that certain bod-
> ies, certain gestures, certain discourses, certain desires, come to be identified
> and constituted as individuals. The individual, that is, is not the vis-à-vis of
> power; it is, I believe, one of its prime effects.[238]

Whatever the motivations of individuals within the lives in which they became attracted to, swept up in, or coerced into the Manichaean community—
and no doubt they varied from region to region and from one period to the
next, as well as from person to person—their new identity as Manichaeans
emerged from recognition by their associates that they were successfully implementing the code of physical and vocal behaviors that constituted the sanctioned Manichaean ethos. Being seen to be Manichaeans, they in turn saw as
Manichaeans, and articulated the rationales that emplaced and justified the
Manichaean body.

THREE

DISCIPLINARY RATIONALES

*Those who wish to enter the religion must know that the two
principles of light and darkness are of absolutely distinct
natures. If one does not discern this, how can one put
the religion into practice?*
—The Chinese *Compendium*

Why were the rules for the conduct of Manichaean life and for qualification
of ritual participation considered necessary and efficacious? In other words,
what were the rationales for Manichaean disciplinary regimens? Why alter the
body's natural, given predispositions at all? Why adopt an ethos different from
that of the larger society? Most important, why differentiate between Elect and
Auditor codes of behavior? What did the Manichaeans offer as an explanation
for their own conduct?

Rationales are the enunciated concepts and convictions associated with
particular human actions. They form part of an individual's performative
repertoire. In unsolicited contexts, they emerge as statements integral to formalized behavior; but they can also be solicited by direct questioning, which
reveals their latent presence in the mind of the individual, in the covert discourse carried on within. Ethological systems, such as Manichaeism, inculcate
rationales in their adherents in conjunction with the promotion of approved
behaviors. No individual internalizes these systems in perfect conformity to
the models proposed by normative traditions; each person possesses a unique

set of rationales. In this study, however, we are concerned precisely with the normative models, not their realization in individual life histories.

Rationales not only include representations of motivation, which those who adhere to them describe as causal forces and which may be offered in response to inquiries concerning why a particular action is performed, but also involve schematizations of the objects involved in an action as well as of the universe in which the action occurs. The latter constructs serve to answer inquiries about how an action does what is claimed for it, and provide adherents with a broader context in which their behaviors appear as reasonable methods. I use the word *method* deliberately because the kinds of actions we are looking at are associated by their practitioners with particular goals. According to the stated claims of the tradition, Manichaean rituals do work and produce results. Manichaean discipline serves as ritual preparation of the individual's body, as well as a response to the particular universe in which that ritual operates.

Manichaean literature employs a full spectrum of compositional forms, including metaphor, simile, and hyperbole. These literary devices contribute to the characterization of a universe which, however, is not itself a metaphor or poetic representation. If, from the perspective of the present, Manichaean ascetic discourse reflects a distinctive "mood" or expresses a special "attitude," such characterizations are merely aesthetic translations of what the primary sources convey as sets of relations between the speaking voice of the text and the cosmic arrangements in which it is implicated. It is possible to interpret this described universe with a hermeneutic that takes it as metaphor or conceit, a "what if" cosmos that expresses psychological states or communicates compelling images. But the significance of the Manichaean universe—in the sense of why it is there in the first place or what its function is for those who describe it—lies in its relation to the practices that presuppose it. Any given ritual requires for its effectiveness a specific configuration of the universe. Likewise, the codes that guide preparation for ritual performance rely on a particular structure in nature in order to accomplish their task. Such a universe must really exist; it must be there literally. If the features of the universe on which Manichaean discipline or ritual depend for their effectiveness are merely poetic devices, or metaphorical expressions for another real universe whose features are other than those associated with disciplinary or ritual behavior, Manichaean practices would be mere performance, a kind of make-believe game, not real action at all.

Augustine highlights the literal character of Manichaean discourse in three key passages of his anti-Manichaica, which leave little room for modern historians to interpret Manichaean rationales metaphorically. In his *Contra Faustum*, Augustine says to his opponent, "You like to praise Manichaeus for nothing so much as for speaking to you the simple naked truth *(veritatem nudam et propriam)* without the guise of figures *(remotis figurarum integumentis)*."[1] Later in the same work, he elaborates on this point:

> You boast of Manichaeus as having come last, not to use figures, but to explain them. His expositions throw light on ancient figures, and leave no problem unsolved. This idea is supported by the assertion that the ancient figures . . . had in view the coming of Manichaeus, by whom they were all to be explained; while he, knowing that no one is to follow him, makes use of a style free from all ambiguous allegorical expressions.[2]

Mani himself provides the interpretive key to the discourses of prior religions; there is no need to interpret the interpretation. This hyperliteralist norm may have been mitigated in practice by the equally normative principle of cultural accommodation that governed Manichaean proselytism. Nonetheless, the underlying narratives and descriptions that served as rationales for Manichaean practices were not negotiable in this process.

> The Manichaeans, when they abandon their own figures of imagination, cease to be Manichaeans. For this is the chief and special point in their praises of Manichaeus, that the divine mysteries which were taught figuratively in books from ancient times were kept for Manichaeus, who was to come last to solve and demonstrate; and so after him no other teacher will come from God, for he has said nothing in allegories or figures, but has explained ancient sayings of that kind, and has himself taught in plain, simple terms. They have no interpretations to fall back on, therefore, when they hear these words of their founder.[3]

Accepting such characterizations of Manichaean discourse at face value entails certain adjustments on the part of the modern historian trying to reconstruct and understand the Manichaean religion. It follows that, in examining this material, we need not search for the supposed hidden meanings of Manichaean practices as mere signifiers of doctrines, or of the images in

Manichaean discourse as expressions of a more literal truth to be found elsewhere than in the cosmos they purport to describe. Instead, Manichaean cosmological and anthropological discourse supply overtly the natural laws, relevant data, and technical instruction necessary for the performance of particular acts.

EXTERNAL RATIONALES

Manichaean accounts explain and justify their disciplinary regimens in part by referring to cosmogony and cosmology, that is, to basic facts about the universe in which Manichaeans live and act. Rationales for Manichaean discipline are predicated on a property shared by all objects of potential contact, most commonly referred as the Living Self or Living Soul (Middle Persian *gryw zyndg*; Coptic *t.psychē etanh*), but also known under a variety of guises (e.g., the Cross of Light, the Five Elements, the Soul, the Youth, the Vulnerable Jesus). The presence of this entity, which Jes Asmussen has aptly called "the most fundamental concept of Manichaeism,"[4] dictates care and restraint on the part of the Manichaean. Mani tells his listeners that there are "three great mighty things" by which people may find life: join the Manichaean community, receive the initiating right hand, and, "act with restraint and charity to the Cross of Light, which grieves in the totality, being present in what is visible and what is not visible."[5]

The presence of the Living Self throughout the world results from a primordial mixture of it with a contrary substance. Modern studies of Manichaean doctrine usually dwell at great length on the details of various narratives regarding the origin of this mixture. These narratives, however, can be harmonized into a single account only by doing violence to their individual integrity. Their variance across time and from one region to the next reflects the adaptation of Manichaean discourse to different cultures and indigenous religious traditions. The centers of Manichaean authority apparently exercised little control over the permutations of the cosmogonic myth, either from inability or disinterest. A universally consistent account would have had no particular advantage in a period when communication across large distances was irregular, and perhaps certain disadvantages relative to local versions better adapted to the culture of their particular regions. In short, the details of Manichaean cosmogony were negotiable in the process of Manichaean proselytization, but its cosmological consequences and practical ramifications were not.

In its scriptures, sermons, hymns, and other means of discourse, the Manichaean tradition invokes the myth of a primordial combat between good and evil, and summons members of the community to "remember" it. The consequence of this remembrance is a recognition of the presence of the Living Self both within the individual, and throughout the material world. Whatever the details of the particular version of the myth, the events it describes produce a characterization of the condition of the present universe which is shared by the other versions—namely, a condition of mixture of light in the form of the Living Self with darkness. Manichaean cosmogony includes an account of the primordial battle, its unfortunate consequences, and subsequent attempts by the forces of both good and evil to master the situation and control the fate of the universe. The universe exists in an interim state, between the worlds of light and darkness as well as between the prior and ultimate ages when a strict separation of the two worlds obtains. Individual Manichaeans learn their true relation to these forces, their role in the ongoing conflict, and what that role requires in terms of interaction with the structures of the universe.

The Central Manichaean Tradition

The hallmark of the Elect, an-Nadim tells us, is that he or she "refrains from eating meats, drinking wine, as well as from marriage," and also "avoids injury to water, fire, trees, and living things."[6] Why would people be so concerned with harming everything around them? According to Ephrem Syrus, "those idle women of the party of Mani," the female Elect, "sit on account of the bright ones *(ziwane)*, the sons of light, whom darkness came forth and swallowed."[7] The presence of these sparks of divine light makes ordinary behavior in the world sinful, action taken literally against God and, paradoxically, against oneself. In Theodore bar Konai's extracts from Manichaean literature, one reads that Jesus appeared to Adam and "showed him the fathers in the heights and his own self exposed to all, (to) the teeth of panthers, the teeth of elephants, devoured by the devourers, consumed by the consumers, eaten by the dogs, mingled with and imprisoned in everything that exists, shackled in the stench of darkness."[8] This revelation introduces Adam, and in the person of Adam all Manichaeans, to the concept of the Living Self, the divine substance inherent in all of nature as well as human bodies. As in the other regional varieties of Manichaeism, the Syriac and Arabic sources refer to this divine substance at times as a single entity and, in other instances, as a collective of five elements.

The opposing universes of light and darkness came into contact and conflict when the world of darkness, led by Satan, launched an assault on the world of light. The Father of Greatness set in motion acts of self-defense designed to repulse and incapacitate the enemy. "The Father of Greatness called forth the Mother of Life; the Mother of Life called forth Primordial Man; and the Primordial Man called forth his five sons, like a man girding himself for combat."[9]

> Thereupon the Primordial Devil *(Iblis al-Qadim)* repaired to his five principles, which are the smoke *(samm)*, flame *(hariq)*, obscurity *(duhan)*, pestilential wind *(samum)*, and clouds *(dabab)*, arming himself with them and making them a protection for him. Upon his coming into contact with the Primordial Man, they joined in battle for a long time. The Primordial Devil mastered the Primordial Man and took a swallow from his light, which he surrounded with his principles and ingredients.[10]

Ephrem makes special note of the materialistic character of the principles involved in Manichaean cosmogony. Thus, when darkness came into contact with elements of light, "the primitive darkness not merely 'seized' that primitive light, but also 'felt, touched, ate, sucked, tasted, and swallowed it.'"[11] Likewise, "the primal darkness . . . on account of its (greedy) hunger, harmed the light which it 'passionately desired and ate, and sucked in, and swallowed, and imprisoned in its midst, and mixed in its limbs.'"[12]

The result of this primordial contact is a mixture of two opposite substances from which everything in existence derives. The "five luminous ones whom they term *ziwane*"[13] become entangled in the evil substance sometimes referred to as *hylē*.[14] Even in every "creeping thing . . . there is mixed in it some of the good nature *(kyana)* which is scattered through everything."[15] As a consequence, the Manichaean Elect "are unwilling to break bread lest 'they pain the Light which is mixed in it.'"[16] Al-Biruni quotes a statement of Mani which characterizes the relationship between the two natures as that between the animate and the inanimate.[17] Similarly, an-Nadim quotes Mani as saying, "The zephyr is the life of the world."[18] Ephrem's sources show an equal readiness to treat the two in moral terms, such that "everything which injures is from the evil, just as everything which helps is from the good,"[19] or in terms of beauty and ugliness.[20]

Although this mixture is depicted as a stratagem for the victory of good, it definitely entails negative consequences. "When they had consumed them, the five light gods lost their reason. Through the poison of the sons of darkness they became like unto a man who has been bitten by a mad dog or a snake."[21] In more specific terms, an-Nadim quotes Mani:

> When the Primordial Devil was entangled with the Primordial Man in battle, the five ingredients of Light were mixed with the five ingredients of darkness. The smoke mingled with zephyr, from which there was this mixed zephyr. What there was in it of delight and quieting for souls and the life of animals was from the zephyr, whereas what there was in it of perdition and disease was from the smoke. The flame mixed with the fire, and what there was in them of burnings, perdition, and corruption was from the flame, while what was in them of light and illumination was from the fire. The light mixed with the darkness, and what there was in them of such dense bodies as gold, silver, and their like, and also what there was in them of purity, beauty, cleanliness, and usefulness, was from the light. What there was in them of filth, grime, gross-ness, and harshness was from the darkness. The pestilential wind mixed with the (good) wind, and what there was in them of usefulness and delight was from the (good) wind, whereas what there was in them of grief, blinding, and injury was from the pestilential wind. The clouds mixed with the water, from which there was this water. Whatever was in it of purity, sweetness, and deli-cacy for the soul was from the water, while what was in it of suffocating, stran-gling, perdition, and corruption was from the clouds.[22]

The whole history of the cosmos unfolds from this primordial mixture, as good and evil continue to struggle—good to liberate that portion of itself mixed with evil, and evil to retain control of it.

An-Nadim's sources conflict in a number of details concerning the early history of this struggle, and the divine players involved; some of the testimony he quotes conforms to the lengthy account in Theodore bar Konai, other por-tions diverge. That which is presented as an orderly, synthetic cosmogonic nar-rative in most twentieth-century scholarship on Manichaeism stands in the various sources as a tangled collection of conflicting accounts, in need of careful literary-historical analysis. All sources agree the world is crafted by the forces of light, although various deities play the role of demiurge according to the different versions.[23] The demiurge and his agents construct the world as a huge machine, distilling light from its unfortunate mixture with evil; each part functions toward this liberative purpose, from the rotation of the sun and moon to the exhalations of trees and plants.[24] An-Nadim quotes Mani directly on this subject:

> Mani said: "Then he created the sun and the moon for sifting out whatever there was of light in the world. The sun sifted out the light which was mixed with the devils of heat, while the moon sifted out the light which was mixed with the devils of cold. This rises up on a column of praise, together with what there are of magnificats, sanctifyings, good words, and deeds of right-eousness." He said: "This is thrust into the sun, then the sun thrusts it to the light above it, in the world of praise, in which world it proceeds to the high-est unsullied light. This action continues until what remains of the light which is bound is only what the sun and moon have been unable to extract. At this point the angel who is bearing up the earths rises up, while the other angel relaxes his hold on the heavens, so that the highest mixes with the low-est and a fire flares up, which blazes among these things, continuing to burn until what is left among them of the light is set free."[25]

The whole cosmos is designed as a machine of liberation, and the Manichaean must conform him- or herself to the role of an efficient cog in that machine in a way that will not damage the product as it passes through the system.

The Western Manichaean Tradition

As in Syriac and Arabic sources, accounts from the Western Manichaean tra-dition describe the Living Self, or the Five Elements, as the weapons or armor of the Primordial Man in his battle with the forces of darkness.[26] When the forces of evil sought to assault the realm of light, Augustine reports, the latter sent forth "some wonderful First Man, who came down from the race of light to war with the race of darkness, armed with his waters against the waters of the enemy, and with his fire against their fire, and with his winds against their winds . . . armed against smoke with air, and against darkness with light."[27]

Moreover, in his letter to Deuterius, Augustine explains that "they say that the good and true God fought with the tribe of darkness and left a part of himself mingled with the prince of darkness, and they assert that this part, spread over the world, defiled and bound, is purified by the food of the Elect and by the sun and moon."[28] The Manichaeans "think that the souls of men as well as of beasts are of the substance of God and are, in fact, pieces of God."[29] They "say that earth, and wood, and stones have sense";[30] such consciousness manifests the divine presence in them, just as brightness does.[31]

Manichaean literature conveys two essential facts about the Living Self: its omnipresence and its suffering. Augustine makes these two points plain:

> They say that this part of the divine nature permeates all things in heaven and earth and under the earth; that it is found in all bodies, dry and moist, in all kinds of flesh, and in all seeds of trees, herbs, men and animals. But they do not say of it, as we say of God, that it is present untrammeled, unpolluted, inviolate, incorruptible, administering and governing all things. On the contrary, they say that it is bound, oppressed, polluted but that it can be released and set free and cleansed not only by the courses of the sun and moon and powers of light, but also by their Elect.[32]

In the Coptic *Kephalaia*, the sun and moon are said to look down upon the Living Self and see that it is "ensnared and set in a great [fetter] above and below, in the tree and in the flesh [. . .] with every oppression. It is being pressed, drawn near to [and] sliced and eaten as it comes up and down, from above below and from below above. It [is] despoiled and moved from body to body."[33] It bears in "apparent silence" the mistreatment of the world, "it is grasped and receives blows from these five fleshes which destroy and strike it."[34] It is on account of this oppressed and abused divine presence that religion comes into being.[35] The Living Self is only apparently mute; Mani had the ears to hear its cries.

The Greek *Cologne Mani Codex* depicts the Living Self as part of Mani's direct experience, even as a child. A tree being harvested tells Mani, "If you keep the [pain] away from us, you will [not perish] with the murderer."[36] On another occasion, Mani sees and hears the human-like suffering of plants: "Alas! Alas! The blood was streaming down from the place cut by the pruning hook which he held in his hands. And they were crying out in a human voice on account of their blows."[37] Mani heeds the warnings of plants and water to practice "the rest" *(anapausis)*,[38] with the result that he lives "neither doing wrong, nor inflicting pain."[39] Mani, as founder of the faith, provides a proto-type of the perfect Manichaean, exemplifying in his life the correct behavior, and explaining through his spiritual experiences the rationale for that behav-ior. In his confrontation with the Elchasaites, Mani also invokes the paradig-matic figure of Elchasai himself.[40] When Elchasai repented of plowing a field because of the ground's vocal objection, he took up an armful of soil, "wept, kissed (it) and placed (it) upon his breast and began to say: 'This is the flesh and blood of my Lord.'"[41]

In its imprisoned form, this divine presence is called the Cross of Light,[42] or even "the vulnerable Jesus" *(Jesus patibilis)*.[43] One passage says of a Mani-chaean deity that "he came because of his son, crucified in the universe, that he might release him and free him and rescue him from affliction."[44] As the offspring of the Primordial Man, it is the "Son of Man" of the gospel ac-counts.[45] But the Manichaeans build biblical images up into a kind of para-doxical pantheism:

> Cornerstone unchanging and unaltering, foundation unshakeable, sheep bound to the tree, treasure hidden in the field, Jesus that hangs to the tree, youth, son of the dew, milk of all trees, sweetness of the fruits, eye of the skies, guard of all treasures, [the one] that bears the universe, joy of all created things, rest of the worlds: my God, you are a marvel to tell. You are within, you are without; you are above, you are below. Near and far, hidden and re-vealed, silent and speaking too: yours is all the glory![46]

Kephalaion 72 clarifies the sometimes confusing diversity of terminology employed in Manichaean literature for the Living Self's many guises:

> Those to which are given the name "rag"—the "rags" are the power that light-ens, that is swallowed, kneaded, and entwined in [the] body of the world, in the archons above. . . . The great deeds of "plucking" and "tearing" which we mention are the living power which is entwined, reaped, cut, swallowed and restrained in the five worlds of the flesh. . . . [The] "elements," which we call by this name, are the [power] which exists in everything below, emerging [in] the wombs of all the earths, gathered and poured out upon all things. The "cross of [light," is] the power of light, that which is bound [. . .] upon the

earth, in the dry and the moist. . . . That which is given the name "the soul [which is] slain, killed, oppressed and dead"—it is the power of the fruits, vegetables and grain, those which are threshed, gathered, cut down, and which feed the worlds of the flesh. . . . For all these names [refer to that which] is a single thing originally . . . but they divided into all these parts in the first war; they established themselves in all these changing forms and these many names. But when they are loosened from all these [. . .] and they are stripped from all these appearances, [and they are] separated from all these names, they will gather [and] become a single form, a single name, unchanging, immoveable forever in the land of their original nature, from which they were sent against the enemy.[47]

The elements are said to weep at their trials and tribulations,[48] and to invigorate and beautify grain;[49] the Elect in their life of wandering are enjoined to avoid treading upon the manifestations of these elements in plant life. "If a person walks upon the ground, he injures the earth; and if he moves his hand, he injures the air; for the air is the soul of humans and living creatures, both fowl, and fish, and creeping thing."[50]

After the initial conflict, the forces of good so order the universe that the divine substance begins to percolate out of the mixture with evil as a matter of course. Evil intervenes, trying to retain possession of its captive. "You maintain in regard to the vulnerable Jesus—who, as you say, is born from the earth, which has conceived by the power of the Holy Spirit—that he hangs in the shape of fruits and vegetables from every tree: so that, besides this pollution, he suffers additional defilement from the flesh of the countless animals that eat the fruit; except, indeed, the small amount that is to be purified by your eating it."[51]

Since, it is said, a limb of God is mixed with the substance of evil in order to restrain it and to suppress any furious outbreaks—these are your own words— the world is made of a mixture of both natures, that is, good and evil. However, the divine part is being purged daily from all parts of the world and returning to its own domain. But as it is exhaled by the earth and rises toward heaven, it enters into plants, their roots being fixed in the ground, and gives fecundity and life to all grass and other vegetation. The animals eat the plants, and if they mate, imprison the divine limb in their flesh, thus diverting it from its rightful course and causing it to become enmeshed in hardship and error. . . . That is why you forbid anyone to give bread, vegetables, or even water . . . to a beggar if he is not a Manichaean, for fear that the part of God which is mixed with these things will be defiled by his sins and thus hindered in its return.[52]

According to Manichaean ways of thinking, Augustine mocks, "the Elect get others to bring their food to them, that they may not be guilty of murder."[53] Even with that precaution, "some of your sect make a point of eating raw vegetables of all kinds," to avoid the harm of preparing or cooking them.[54]

Western Manichaean sources identify the Living Self in the world with the individual soul of the human. According to the *Cologne Mani Codex*, the personal revelations of Mani involved most emphatically a full understanding of this truth "concerning my soul, which exists as the soul of all the worlds, both what it itself is and how it came to be."[55] A Coptic hymnist echoes this understanding when he declares, "The Cross of Light that gives life to the universe, I have known it and believed in it; for it is my beloved soul, which nourishes everyone, at which the blind are offended because they know it not."[56] The speaker's knowledge and belief translate directly into conduct, as the subsequent verse states, "I have not mingled with the intercourse of the flesh, for it is a thing that perishes; thy good fight I have set myself to."[57] Psalm 246 of the Coptic *Psalm-Book* speaks in the voice of the Living Self:

> Since I went forth into the darkness . . . I bear up beneath a burden which is not my own. I am in the midst of my enemies, the beasts surrounding me; the burden which I bear is of the powers and principalities. They burned in their wrath, they rose up against me, they ran to [scatter] me like sheep that have no shepherd. Matter *(hylē)* and her sons divided me up amongst them, they burnt me in their fire, they gave me a bitter likeness. The strangers with whom I mixed, me they know not; they tasted my sweetness, they desired to keep me with them. I was life to them, but they were death to me; I bore up beneath them, they wore me as a garment upon them. I am in everything, I bear the skies, I am the foundation, I support the earths, I am the light that shines forth, that gives joy to souls. I am the life of the world; I am the milk that is in all trees; I am the sweet water that is beneath the sons of Matter . . . as the sphere turns hurrying round, as [the sun receives] the refined part of life.[58]

The divine substance embedded in the world circulates through it by means of transmigration and movements of nature. Humans have an integral place in this system of interconnections, both physically and morally.

They believe that other souls pass into cattle and into everything that is rooted in and supported on the earth. For they are convinced that plants and trees possess sentient life and can feel pain when injured, and therefore that no one can pull or pluck them without torturing them. Therefore, they consider it wrong to clear a field even of thorns. Hence, in their madness they make agriculture, the most innocent of occupations, guilty of multiple murder. On the other hand, they believe that these crimes are forgiven their auditors because the latter offer food of this sort to their elect in order that the divine substance, on being purged in their stomachs, may obtain pardon for those through whose offering it is given to be purged. And so the Elect themselves perform no labors in the field, pluck no fruit, pick not even a leaf, but expect all these things to be brought for their use by their Auditors. . . . They caution their same Auditors, furthermore, when they eat meat, not to kill the animals.[59]

Sinners experience the direct consequences of their violence to life through the process of transmigration. The Greek anti-Manichaean abjuration formulae speak of this belief as a rationale motivating Manichaean disciplines.

And (I anathematize) those who introduce *metempsychosis*, which they call "transfusion" *(metaggismos)*, and those who maintain that grass and plants and water and other things without souls in fact all have them, and think that those who pluck wheat or barley or grass or vegetables are transformed into them in order that they may suffer the same, and that harvesters and bread-makers are accursed.[60]

The *Acts of Archelaus* elaborates this ideology of retribution which undergirds Manichaean practices.

If the soul has been guilty of homicide, it is translated *(metapheretai)* into the bodies of lepers; and if it has been found to have engaged in reaping, it is made to pass into the mute. . . . Moreover, the reapers . . . (are) translated into hay, or beans, or barley, or wheat, or vegetables, in order that in these forms they, in like manner, may be reaped and cut. And again, if anyone eats bread, he must also become bread and be eaten. . . . Moreover, as this body pertains to the archons and to matter *(hylē)*, it is necessary that he who plants a persea should pass through many bodies until that persea is prostrated. And if one builds a house for himself, he will be divided and scattered among all the bodies. If one bathes in water, he freezes *(pessei)* his soul; and if one does not give pious donations *(eusebeiai)* to his Elect, he will be punished in *gehenna*, and will be reincarnated *(metensomatoutai)* into the bodies of Catechumens, until he render many pious donations; and for this reason they offer to the Elect whatever is best in their food. And when they [the Elect] are about to eat bread, they pray first, speaking thus to the bread: "I have neither reaped thee, nor ground, nor pressed thee, nor cast thee into a oven; but another has done these things, and brought to me; I am eating without fault." . . . For, as I remarked to you a little before, if anyone reaps, he will be reaped; and so, too, if anyone casts grain into the mill, he will be cast in himself in like manner, or if he kneads he will be kneaded, or if he bakes he will be baked; and for this reason they are interdicted from doing any such work.[61]

Human action is an integral part of natural processes, and involves the same kinetic energies. The Manichaean injunction to nonviolence and the avoidance of procreation, therefore, rests as much if not more on physical laws of cause and effect, and the forces governing biological processes, than on moral avoidance of causing harm to other beings.[62] The human body itself is a fulcrum of these cosmic forces, and its formation and reproduction repeatedly play out these same conflicts.

The Eastern Manichaean Tradition

Eastern Manichaean hymns express a summons to reflection, and a command to "remember" the primordial conflict that produced the mixed world. In M 33, for example, the performer sings:

> To you I will speak, my captive self *(gryw)*. Remember (your) home. . . . Remember the devouring that imprisoned (you) and ate you in hunger. . . . Remember the many dark vaults which you agitated and set in motion in the depths. Remember the fierce primeval battle and the many fights which you made with the darkness. . . . Remember the trembling, weeping and separation which occurred then when the father ascended to the height.[63]

In this hymn, the singer speaks to a personal captive self, at the same time publicly addressing an audience of adherents. The remembrance to which (by inference) both alike are called is the cosmogonical episode that established the universe in its current condition, and that is the presupposition of the entire Manichaean salvational enterprise. Through such oral vehicles, the Manichaeans established and reiterated an identification of believers, in their most essential selves, with a long history of salvational struggle, and ultimately with a divine ancestor whose descent into the temporal plane initiated the drama that believers were to see reflected in their own lives. The hymn reports a catena not of the deeds of remote gods or heroes, but pointedly of what "you"—the self in all—did. The audience, even amid its earthly tragedy, is heroized.[64]

Despite the catastrophic nature of this cosmogony, some of its aspects provide paradigms for practice. Thus, when the Primordial Man is called out of his fallen unconsciousness, he is told "Collect your limbs! ('mwrd' wxybyy [h]nd'm),"[65] just as ordinary Manichaeans are called upon to carry out the limb collection of their "soul-work." The rescue, ascent, and homecoming of the Primordial Man, told with loving detail, insinuates a similar hope for the adherents. The advantage provided to the latter lies in the fact that they need not labor alone. While they do undertake limb collection, they are themselves "limbs" of the larger Manichaean community, which is itself personified. M 33 continues: "The secret is taught . . . , the Righteous Ones and the Auditors, the limbs of light, become happy."[66]

The adherent-deity identification takes a practical turn in expositions of the cosmogony which focus on correct and incorrect attitudes and responses to the tragedy it entails. The Parthian *Exposition of the Prayer and Invocation of All the Aeons* discusses the differences between "homomorphic" (h'mcyhrg) and non-"homomorphic" light in terms of correct attitude, not predestined natures. Commenting on the doctrinal point that some light is doomed to permanent mixture with darkness, the writer explains that such a fate accrues to those who think "I am what I am blessed to be,"[67] and do not have the ambition to work out their ultimate salvation. The promise of the Primordial Man not to abandon the "five lights" is not directed, our author states, to those who think, "In my case the original mixing with darkness reaches such a grievous degree of damage and oppression that I am unable to be removed and separated from darkness." Rather, the promise applies to those who rightly think, "My mixture is of such a sort that, with the help of the god Ohrmizd (the Primordial Man) and the brethren, I am able to be purified and saved."[68] Manichaeans are instructed to recognize a fundamental identity between the Living Self in the world and their own souls—not a symbolic or moral identification, but a substantial, scientific connection. Human bodies and souls are formed through reproduction from the mixed substance in the plants one's parents consume.[69] If a person fails to reform him- or herself, the cycle is perpetuated, and the Living Self is dispersed anew both in harmful action and in reproduction.[70]

Awareness of the Manichaean teachings about the Living Self, the "words of reality and truth," makes the individual into "one who has eyes to see . . . a wise and kind person."[71] "If there is any wise and kind, blessed and virtuous person, why would he not think about this great power?"[72] Indeed, "all the Buddhas and Arhants in the past have established their wonderful doctrine for the five lights."[73] Ch/U 6814 reports that "in the five kinds of trees and plants they are living," but "they become mindless, dead (things) in the bodies of the five kinds of so-called 'living' creatures."[74] This presence has direct application to the disciplinary codes, as enunciated by the Auditors in their formal confession.

> If at any time somehow we have injured or hurt unwittingly (or) through malice the Five Gods, or if we have inflicted (on them) the fourteen kinds of wounds, or if somehow we have pained and grieved the Living Self, the god of food and drink, with the ten serpent-headed fingers or thirty-two teeth, or if somehow we have sinned against the dry and moist earth, against the five kinds of creatures, or against the five kinds of herbs and against the trees, now, Majesty, we beg to be freed from sin. Forgive my sin![75]

The suffering of the divine elements in the world is a saga of tragic proportions, incurring endless guilt upon its perpetrators. Awareness of this reality makes possible the restraint of action and avoidance of guilt.

The Turfan finds include many other fragments of treatises devoted the subject of the Living Self, including the Middle Persian *Recitation of the Living Self (Gwyšn ʿy Gryw Zyndg)* and the Parthian *Sermon on the Soul (Gyʾn Wyfrʾs)*, both the subject of recent studies by Werner Sundermann. The *Recitation of the Living Self* takes the form of a series of autobiographical utterances by the divine substance itself. In one passage it says, "I am the Living Soul, and the noble son of the revered kingdoms, your kin from the living place and your soul and life."[76] The *Sermon on the Soul*, of which no less than eighteen copies have been identified by Sundermann in the Turfan material, outlines the characteristics of the Five Elements and discusses the importance of proper interaction with them. The treatise explains that without the knowledge it conveys, the "names of the soul," a person will not be able to answer these questions: "Whence have you come, where are you going, what do you want, why have you come, where have you been sent, and what is *your* name?"[77]

The core of the *Sermon on the Soul* describes the manifestation of each of the Five Elements in five natural processes (called *yšnwhr*, "grace"). Thus the first element, called here the *'rd'w fr'w'rdyn*, encompasses living things as water supports fish. "The creatures inhale life *(jywhr)* with their noses through *'rd'w fr'w'rdyn*." The wind element circulates water through evaporation, invigorates plants, and balances temperature. The light element "is living and gives life," fostering the reproductive process, distributing beauty, sight, hearing, speech and movement. The elements are the life of the entire universe, which will collapse upon itself when they are extracted. Awareness of the presence of these elements in the world entails specific obligations on the Manichaean, as the text proceeds to relate. The fundamental basis of these obligations stems from recognizing the essential identity of these natural life processes with one's own sense of self. In the apt words of Werner Sundermann, "Knowledge of the soul is thus at the same time world knowledge and self knowledge."[78]

The elements are not just victims of the world, they are also its very life, without which the world could not exist. "The tenfold sky above and the eightfold earth below exist because of the Five Gods. The blessings and fortunes, the colors and complexions, the selves and the souls, the forces and lights, the origins and roots of all these upon earth are the Five Gods."[79] The Chinese *Hymnscroll* contains a hymn dedicated to the praise of the "five lights" *(wu ming)*, which shows familiarity with the ideas of the *Sermon on the Soul*, and attributes to the elements the life energy of all natural processes.

> *(They are) the wonderful forms of the essence and flower of the world*
> *Who support and hold various things, many heavens and earths*
> *Who are the bodies and lives of all sentient beings*
> *All who see with eyes, and who hear voices with ears*
> *Who can create bodily strength from bones and articulations*
> *And can make all beings and races which grow and feed*

Who speak many languages of different tongues
Who also make many tunes of different notes
Who are also the broad and great light of the mind and knowledge

. . . .

All the wisdom and kindness of the benevolent person
All the language and eloquence of a rhetorician

. . . .

Who also make the world thriving, abundant, and ripe
And are the various shoots of grasses and trees.[80]

Unfortunately, the presence of these "precious treasures" and "bright pearls" in the world harms them.[81] The hymnist calls them "wave-tossed exiles," sunk "in the midst of the dark, deep sea of suffering," and refers to their "painful boils and sores."[82] They are, in fact, "nothing other than the flesh and blood of Jesus."[83] The hymnist asks, "Why have they come from the Father's side into this world?" and declares to the listener, "Know clearly, that they have suffered for no sins of their own."[84]

But awareness of the Living Self is not an abstract knowledge; it has practical consequences. In the Chinese hymn in praise of the "Five Lights," description gives way to exhortation:

Stop all sorts of evil doings
And return to your own originator
Firmly observe the fasting and precepts, always guard them carefully
And control your thoughts, regulating them constantly
Day and night think only of the true and correct doctrine
And attend to the weighing and clarifying of the five wondrous bodies.[85]

And in the second canto:

Be always firm and strong in observing commandments and protocols
Practicing fasting, rites, reverence, and recitation
Be always clean and pure in the deeds of body, mouth, and mind
Sing and chant the words of doctrine without break or stop
And also practice merciful deeds earnestly
Be gentle and amicable, bear humiliations, and purify all roots
These are all the remedies for the bodies of light.[86]

The hymnist punctuates these instructions with dire warnings:

> *If there are people who suffer in the transmigration of hell*
> *In the fire of the kalpa of destruction and eternal confinement*
> *It is really because they do not recognize the five light bodies*
> *And are therefore severed from the country of peace and happiness.*[87]

And in the second canto:

> *Remember and think, when one is trembling to his life's end*
> *Let his reasons be not unjustified before the king of the balance!*[88]

Summation

The secret of life, revealed to Mani and transmitted by the institutions of the Manichaean church, thus dictates a specific response from all those who wish to avoid the dread fate earned by those who proceed thoughtlessly through the world. Manichaean discourse presents the religion's entire disciplinary regimen as a reasonable, indeed requisite, method for adjusting to the natural laws that govern the universe, and particularly to the presence of the five divine elements that constitute the Living Self (see Table 3.1). The truth about the universe, the special knowledge that only Manichaeans possess, is a practical gnosis inseparably associated with specific precepts and codes of behavior. Manichaeans adjust their relations to a sentient life inherent in all things, exchanging a harmful mode of life for a harmless one, one free from retribution (in greater or lesser degree according to one's discipline). By adhering to such a lifestyle, the Manichaean aspires to negotiate the snares and pits of the world of birth-and-death and to attain the world of light.

In laying out an account of the Living Self, we have already come to a point where many believe Manichaean asceticism is fully explained. The divine presence in the world, combined with the opposite dark forces, so problematizes action in the world that Manichaeans resort to an absolute nonaction as the ideal form of embodiment—so the argument goes.[89] In their salvational enterprise, however, Manichaeans not only make themselves innocent of the suffering of the Living Self, but also strive to become the vehicles of its liberation.

Manichaean rationales describe the world, etiologically and phenomeno-

TABLE 3.1. THE FIVE *ZIWANE,* OR ELEMENTS OF LIGHT

ELEMENT	ARABIC	GREEK	COPTIC	LATIN	PARTHIAN	TURKIC	CHINESE
Zephyr/air	nasim	aēr	aēr	aer	'rd'w-fr'w'rdyn	tintura	ch'i
Wind	rih	anemos	tēou	ventus	w'd	yel	feng
Light	nur	phōs	ouaine	lux	rwšn	yaruk	ming
Water	ma'	hudōr	maou	aqua	'b	suv	shui
Fire	nar	pur	sete	ignis	'dwr	ot	huo

logically, as the arena in which the enterprise of salvation is to be conducted, and as the locale of the objects upon which the Manichaean adherent is to act to effect that salvation. The given characteristics of the world are marked and identified in terms of their relevance to this enterprise, and characterized as accessible to the appropriate salvational manipulation. By stressing the pervasiveness and vulnerability of divine substance in the world, Manichaean discourse brings human action upon that world under sharp scrutiny, and problematizes ordinary human behavior. Such a problematization of behavior opens the way for Mani's proposed discipline, and motivates adherence to it. At the same time, the source of the problematization—the sentient living substance affected by human action—is established as the object of religious action, the substance to be redeemed through the ritual operations of the Manichaean community.

INTERNAL RATIONALES

The texts quoted in the previous section already allude to the fact that the substances and energies within the human body possess an intimate relation to those outside of it. In Manichaean discourse, anthropogony is merely the last stage of cosmogony, and anthropology a mirror of cosmology. The narrative about the formation of humans shows the same regional variation as we find in the cosmogony. According to all surviving accounts, however, humans came into existence as instruments of evil, designed to retard cosmic salvation by serving as depositories of captured light. The human body stands at the intersection of good and evil, containing the richest concentrations of both substances, each attempting to gain ascendancy over the other. Human salvation, therefore, is intimately linked with the details of anthropogony and the structures of the human form. It is these latter that must become entirely familiar to the Manichaean adherent, and that must be acted upon on a regular basis. Manichaeism teaches not a neglect of the body but a conquest of it. Just as the forces of light erected the structures of the cosmos to serve as a liberatory machine, so these same forces contained within the human form strive to convert its structures to a salvational purpose.

The Central Manichaean Tradition

The agents of evil construct Adam and Eve from a mixture of good and evil elements. Their intention is that the evil portion of human nature will dominate the good portion, and thus retain the latter in captivity and slavery. Yet the form of human bodies itself reflects a divine model, which the forces of evil are compelled to copy.[90] This dual heritage of the body provides the potential for each individual to awaken his or her divine identity and take control away from the dominance of evil. The agents of the world of light seek to enable this awakening, and their efforts repeat many of the elements of the first rescue of the Primordial Man, thus replaying the cosmogonic process on the anthropogonic scale. Jesus appears in the role of savior, Adam in the role of the paradigmatic Everyman. "He raised him up and made him eat of the tree of life. Then Adam gazed upward and wept, raising his voice powerfully like a lion roaring. He tore his hair, beat (his breast) and said: 'Woe, woe unto him, the sculptor of my body, woe unto him who has shackled my soul, and woe to the rebellious ones who have enslaved me.'"[91]

The mixed heritage and conflicted identity of humans can be expressed as a contrast of the body and the soul.[92] Mani criticized in his own writings more prosomatic views, such as that of Bardaisan, who held that the reproductive process produced liberation for the soul. Al-Biruni quotes from Mani's *Book of Mysteries*: "The partisans of Bardesanes think that the living soul rises and is purified in the carcass, not knowing that the latter is the enemy of the soul, that the carcass prevents the soul from rising, that it is a prison, and a painful punishment to the soul. If this human figure were a real existence, its creator would not let it wear out and suffer injury, and would not have compelled it to reproduce itself by the sperm in the uterus."[93] But the body, even apart from the soul, is not bereft of virtue; its formation upon a divine plan, worked by the forces of evil to their unknowing detriment, gives the body an intrinsic orderliness. Ephrem acknowledges this positive element of Manichaean anthropology, even while suspecting unsavory motives for it.

> For because they saw that this body is well put together, and that its seven senses are arranged in order, and that there is in the heart an instrument for the impulses of the soul, and that there is in the tongue a harp of speech, they were ashamed to speak blasphemy against it in plain terms, and they had recourse to cunning, and divided it into two parts. But they suppose that its nature is from evil, and its workmanship from the archons, and the cause of its arrangement is from wisdom. And she (wisdom) showed an image of her own beauty to the archons, and to the governors, and she deceived them thereby so that when they were stirred up to make (something) in imitation of what they saw, each of them should give from his treasure whatever he had; and that owing to this cause their treasure should be emptied of what they had snatched away.[94]

Moreover, as-Shahrastani reports that light and darkness each contribute from their respective *ajnas* to both the body and soul of humans. In each case, four of the five elements constitute the mixture of the body: from the divine substance, fire, light, wind, and water; from the evil substance, devouring fire, darkness, suffocating wind and fog. Likewise, zephyr from the good and *al-hummama* from the evil roam about the body as motile spirits.[95]

Of course the actual formation of these bodies remains the purview of evil beings, and their technique is so chaotic and perverse that vast differences of character arise between one body and the next.

> They say that there are bodies which are more evil than other bodies, and corporeal frames which are fouler than others, because (some) bodies are fiercer than others, such souls as chance upon perturbed bodies are more perturbed than others who happen to come to gentle bodies . . . because of the evil which was great in those bodies, on that account the souls that are in them make themselves exceedingly hateful . . . the souls cannot remember, "because the pollution of error is (too) great for them, unless sweet floods have come from their home a second time, and lessened the bitterness in which they were dwelling," or else (it must be) that the souls who have been "refined, and have gone up," descend again that they may come to rescue their companions who have been overwhelmed so that they all may rescue all and

go peacefully to their domain; so that as all came to the struggle (together) . . . (so) they might go up from the struggle (together), and not be separated from one another.[96]

Moreover, souls do not always receive the benefit of a human incarnation. Mani, in his *Book of Mysteries* (as reported by al-Biruni) says that "the Apostles knew that the souls are immortal, and that in their migrations they array themselves in every form, that they are shaped in every animal, and are cast in the mold of every figure."[97]

Contact between the two natures in the body produces a negative effect on the divine substance, and "the refined soul which they say is the daughter of the light puts on that darkness in its deeds and . . . in its conduct."[98] "The evil which is mixed in us, as they say, injures us."[99] The internal dynamics of the human body interact with the external forces of both good and evil through action and ingestion. Ephrem Syrus relates that "they assert that evil collects and increases within us from foods."[100] On the other hand, "they say (that) the pleasant taste of foods is due to the light that is mixed in them,"[101] and that "in fruits and in seeds and in fountains there exists evil that kills, but good that gives life [is also] in them for men." Moreover, "the good is in the majority."[102]

The Manichaeans claim that the rules of conduct revealed by Mani effect a revolution within the body, and the successful separation of light from darkness within it. The materialistic conceptions upon which Manichaean disciplines are based perturb people like Ephrem. "Let them tell us: will 'the blameless conduct of freedom' separate this evil, or will drugs and medicinal roots? . . . If (poison), therefore, this small evil which is mingled with us, is not expelled from us by 'blameless conduct,' but by the virtue of drugs, how can 'commandments and laws' separate that mighty and powerful evil which is mixed in souls?"[103] The reformation and training of the body made possible by their disciplinary regimen allow the Elect to aspire even to assisting in the liberation of the Living Self. "Mani (said) that it was possible to restore the one cast like a thing from its domain into 'sin' by means of righteousness and the observance of commandment(s), and (that) although the *ziwane* were mixed with 'sin' in darkness, they could be refined through fasting and prayer."[104]

According to Mani's *Treasury of Life* (following al-Biruni's account), in heavenly existence no marks of differentiation appear in the perfected, divine bodies: "In the country of joy there is neither male nor female, nor are there organs of generation. All are invested with living bodies. Since they have divine bodies, they do not differ from each other in weakness and force, in length and shortness, in figure and looks; they are like similar lamps, which are lighted by the same lamp, and which are nourished by the same material."[105] Manichaean anthropology stays true to its materialistic foundation, and sees salvation not in terms of disembodied spirits, but as a transformed and perfected embodiment.

The Western Manichaean Tradition

The Coptic *Kephalaia* contain numerous expositions by Mani of the origin, structure, and operation of the human body. Adam and Eve, he explains, were molded by the forces of evil from the mixture of light and darkness. Their form was modeled upon that of a divine manifestation that appeared before the evil archons for a brief moment.[106] They were unique concentrations of light, set apart from other living things in strength and beauty.[107] Yet they are deeply conflicted entities, partaking of both good and evil, with the forces of evil aspiring to maintain control over humans through passion, delusion, and reproduction.[108] Since the time of the first couple, the light has been further dispersed and diluted by darkness in the many separate bodies of the human race.[109]

Augustine, quoting one of Mani's writings, provides the following anthropogonic account:

> They say that Adam, the first man, was created by certain of the princes of darkness so that the light might not escape from them. In the Epistle which they call *Fundamental,* Manes has described how the prince of darkness, whom they introduce as the father of the first man, addressed the other princes of darkness, his associates; and how he acted. ". . . It is better, therefore, for you to give up to me the portion of light which you have in your power. Thus I shall make an image of the great one who has appeared so gloriously . . ." From that food he acquired many powers. . . . Then he called to himself his own wife, who came of the same stock as he did, and, as the others had done, he sowed the multitude of evils which he had devoured, and added something of his own thought and power, so that his sense formed and marked out all that he poured forth. His wife received this as well-tilled earth is wont to receive seed, for in her were constructed and knit together the im-

DIAGRAM 3.1: THE PROCESS OF EVIL ANTHROPOGONY				
Sin takes a **divine limb,**		binds it in a **body-part,**		and adds **an evil limb**
Coptic				
MIND	→	BONE	✛	SIN-MIND
THOUGHT	→	NERVE	✛	SIN-THOUGHT
INSIGHT	→	ARTERY	✛	SIN-INSIGHT
INTELLECT	→	FLESH	✛	SIN-INTELLECT
REASONING	→	SKIN	✛	SIN-REASONING
Chinese				
AIR	→	BONE	✛	DARK MIND
WIND	→	NERVE	✛	DARK THOUGHT
LIGHT	→	ARTERY	✛	DARK INSIGHT
WATER	→	FLESH	✛	DARK INTELLECT
FIRE	→	SKIN	✛	DARK REASONING

ages of all the celestial and terrestrial powers, that what was formed should have the likeness of the whole world.[110]

This succinct narrative provides an etiology for the duality of human nature, promotion of human beauty, denigration of human passions, and correlation of the human microcosm to the universal macrocosm. According to *Kephalaion 38*, evil in the person of "sin" constructs the body by systematically binding the captured elements into prison-like anatomical structures (see Diagram 3.1).

He constructed the body. Its [soul he] took from the five shining gods. [He] bound it in the five limbs of the body. He bound mind in bone, thought in nerve, insight in artery, intellect in flesh, reasoning in skin. He established his five powers: his mind upon the mind of the soul, his thought upon the thought of the soul, his insight upon the insight [of] the soul, his intellect upon the intellect of the soul, his reasoning upon the reasoning of the soul. He appointed his five angels and his authorities over the five limbs [of the] soul. . . . (And,) leading it (the soul) always to all bad deeds, to all the sins of desire, to the worship of images, to the dogmas of deceit, they humiliated [it] by the humiliation of slavery. . . . It put on error and forgetfulness. It forgot its essence *(ousia)* and its race *(genos)* and its kinship.[111]

In the *Kephalaia*, Mani also develops a series of correspondences between the human body and the structures of the universe. The human microcosm reflects in its constituent parts every detail of the macrocosm.[112] These correspondences of anatomical parts with signs of the zodiac, particular deities, classes of plants and animals, and camps of demons constitute an elaborate *Listenwissenschaft* in the Coptic sources.[113] Nearly all of these identifications are characterized as means by which evil keeps the body under its sway. Mani tells his disciples:

> Know that there are many powers that exist in this body, who are inhabitants, who are magnates in it. There are 840 myriads of archons as heads in the body of man, scattered (and) established in it, four to a house. The enumeration and numbering of their houses is 210 myriads. The occasion when all these archons come, creeping and walking in the body and meeting each other, they wound and destroy each other.[114]

These conflicts erupt out of the body as "wounds."[115]

In the Latin version of the *Acts of Archelaus*, Mani gives a lurid account of the character of the human body and its reproduction, highlighting the perpetuation of evil's designs in the mindless behavior of ordinary humans.[116] The human body repeats on a microcosmic scale the mixture and conflict evident in the macrocosm. It is, in fact, specially designed as the point of concentration and most secure imprisonment of the divine substance spread throughout the world; so, the Manichaeans "believe that this portion of the good and divine substance which is held mixed and imprisoned in food and drink is more strongly and foully bound in the rest of men, even their own Auditors, but particularly in those who propagate offspring."[117] Within each human body, therefore, a dual process operates. The congenital soul works out its own future, to be realized through ascent or reincarnation, while divine substance identical in kind, but brought into the body through food, is delivered either to exhalation into the heavens or to reimprisonment through reproduction. Parents pass to their offspring both the polluted substance that constitutes the body and the divine element that becomes the soul.[118] Thus the digestive and reproductive systems are intimately interconnected, and the two distinct products of food bear witness to the dual roots of the individual.[119]

But it is illegitimate to understand these two roots, as many modern scholars have, as simply matter and spirit. The especially pernicious character of the human body results, according to the Manichaeans, from an evil motive force that inhabits it. Augustine reports that "you say that all your members and your whole body were formed by the evil mind which you call *hylē*, and that part of this fabricator dwells in the body along with part of your God."[120] So "every living being has two souls, one of the race of light, and the other of the race of darkness."[121] The evil mixed into the whole universe manifests itself in the kind of behavior humans display outside the discipline of the Manichaean faith. "Fornications, adulteries, murders, avarice, and all evil deeds are the fruits of that evil root . . . and in avarice too you may taste that evil root."[122]

Augustine has no problem identifying such behaviors as evil, or in locating the primary reservoir of evil in human beings; but he explains these things by a corruption and fall of humans themselves. The Manichaeans disagree.

> As they will have it, carnal concupiscence, by which the flesh lusts against the spirit, is not an infirmity engendered in us by the corruption of our nature in the first man, but a contrary substance which clings to us in such a way that if we are freed and purged, it can be removed from us. . . . These two souls, or two minds, the one good, the other evil, are in conflict with one another in man, when the flesh lusts against the spirit, and the spirit against the flesh.[123]

Good souls are "compelled to sin by being commingled with evil."[124] Mani, says Augustine, "will not allow sin to be explained except as due to necessity imposed by the contrary evil nature."[125] The Manichaeans can actually speak of a certain type of "soul which they admonish men to flee."[126] Even the good soul can be corrupted by its contact with evil, and lose its divine identity.[127] Augustine reports that Mani wrote of such souls that they would be permanently bound to evil for all time, and that they "deserve to be thus punished, because they allowed themselves to be led away from their original brightness, and became enemies of holy light."[128]

The understanding of natural and physiological processes entailed in Manichaean discourse provides the rationales for Manichaean rules which otherwise appear arbitrary and even contradictory. Augustine complains that

"you are merciful to beasts, believing them to contain the souls of human beings, while you refuse a piece of bread to a hungry beggar."[129] On the one
hand, belief in reincarnation supports a disinclination to harm animals; on the
other, the knowledge that divine substance in food is reimprisoned through reproduction redirects food charity toward the celibate.[130]

> They believe that the divine members of their God are subjected to restraint
> and contamination in these same carnal members of theirs. For they say that
> flesh is unclean . . . they declare that he must be cleansed, and that till this is
> done, as far as it can be done, he undergoes all the passions to which flesh is
> subject . . . it is for his sake, they say, that they abstain from sexual intercourse,
> that he may not be bound more closely in the bondage of the flesh, nor suffer
> more defilement.[131]

For the Elect, simple celibacy ensures that the ingested light will not be
cast again into a body. The Auditors, not expected to follow as strict a regimen,
were still encouraged to avoid reproduction. "And if they make use of marriage, they should, however, avoid conception and birth to prevent the divine
substance, which has entered into them through food, from being bound by
chains of flesh in their offspring. For this is the way, indeed, they believe that
souls come into all flesh, that is, through food and drink."[132]

Western Manichaean sources characterize sins and passions as rebellions
or illnesses; hence the "sinner" is not in the wrong, but wronged by intrusive
drives against which the Manichaean has legitimate grievance, as in the following Coptic psalm:

> The man who has suffered wrong—lo, the protection of the judge, let him
> hasten unto it. He whom grief has killed, he on whom anger has leapt, he for
> whom lust has soiled the whiteness of his clothes, he for whom obduracy stole
> away the sweetness of his heart, he whom folly made mock of and took away
> his wisdom, he for whom the devouring fire allied with his enemies, doing
> him harm, he whom overweening pride deceived and tumbled to the
> ground—lo, the judge has sat down, he calls out the name of him who has
> been wronged. . . . He knows how to forgive him that shall sin and repent. He
> makes reckoning with none that shall come to him and implore him. But the
> double-minded man—him he forgives not.[133]

By personifying the passions, this psalm constructs a scenario in which the individual is a victim of his or her own carnal drives, seeking redress against them in court. As the psalm proceeds, it moves from legal to medical themes; Mani changes from a just judge to a skillful physician. The psalmist encourages, "Let us not hide our sickness from him and leave the cancer in our members, the fair and mighty image of the New Man, so that it destroys it,"[134] and prays, "[May he] wipe away our iniquities, the scars that are branded on our souls."[135]

Mani the physician, with his precise medical analysis of the body, speaks in the *Cologne Mani Codex*, in what has become, since the codex's discovery, the classic statement of Manichaean anthropology:

> This body is defiled and molded from a mold of defilement. You can see how, whenever someone cleanses his food and partakes of that which has just been washed, it appears to us that from it still come blood and bile and gases and shameful excrements and bodily defilement. But if someone were to keep his mouth away from this food for a few days, immediately all these excretions of shame and loathsomeness will be found to be lacking and wanting [in the] body. But if [that one] were to partake [again] of [food, in the] same way they would again abound in the body, so that it is manifest that they flow out from the food itself. But if someone else were to partake of food (which is) washed and cleansed, and partake (also) of that which is unwashed, it is clear that the well-being and the power of the body is recognizably the same.[136]

But because the forces of evil modeled humanity on a divine form, the human body also possesses the structures necessary to function as a salvational machine. The liberating struggles in the larger universe are replayed in exact mimesis within the individual body.[137] By mastering the body, the Manichaean duplicates the victories of light in its battle for control of the cosmos, and establishes anatomical "posts" corresponding to those which govern the universe.[138]

> The Elect who will subdue and humble the visage of his face atop his body, and who will guide it to the good, is like the mystery of the Splendor-holder who rules over the watchtower that is above the zone. The one who will be lord [over] his heart, and humble it, exists in the image of the Great King of

Honor, who humbles the seven heavens. The one who will be lord of his bosom, and humble his desire, exists in the mystery of the Adamas of Light, the one who humbles Matter *(hylē)*. The one who will humble the stomach and be lord of the fire which exists in it, and who will purify the foods that come into him, is likened to the form of the King of Glory, the one who turns the Wheels, sending the life to heaven. The one who will be lord over the rulership *(archontikē)* which is in his feet below, and bind it in the chain of peace, resembles the Porter, the one who humbles in his footprints the abysses below.[139]

Mani's characterization of the body in the *Cologne Mani Codex,* which on first examination appears pessimistic in the extreme, merely sets the stage for his summons to take up the disciplined life of the Manichaean Elect.

Therefore, [make an inspection of] yourselves as to [what] your purity [really is. For it is] impossible to purify your bodies entirely. For each day the body is disturbed and comes to rest through the secretions of sediments from it. So the action comes about without a commandment from the savior. The purity, then, which was spoken about, is that which comes through knowledge, separation of light from darkness and of death from life and of living waters from turbid, so that [you] may know [that] each is [inimical] to the other and [that you may know the true] commandments of the savior, [so that you] may redeem the soul from [annihilation] and destruction. This is in truth the genuine purity.[140]

Mani's rejection here of external rites of purification has been interpreted as indicating a move on his part "from baptism to gnosis," that is, a spiritualization and intellectualization of salvational praxis. Yet even Ludwig Koenen, who coined this phrase in reference to the above passage, acknowledges that "mention of the commandments of the Savior in connection with *gnosis* is remarkable and, in comparison with other gnostics, seems to give the passage a particular Manichaean ring."[141] The extent of, and emphasis on, disciplinary codes in Manichaeism, and their enunciated function precisely to purify and perfect the body of the Elect, suggests that this passage has not been understood fully.

Mani's statement prescribes not a rejection of purificatory action, but a shift in the locale of that action from the external world to the internal physiology of the human, as first surmised by Jorunn Buckley.[142] The body *as a whole* cannot be purified, because it is not a monad separable from the world (at the very least because it must ingest a part of that world to maintain itself). The body is itself a duality, a mixture of good and evil. So the demarcation of purity cannot occur between the body and the world (as in Elchasaite lustrations), but must be drawn within the body between its positive and negative components. "Even as Mani reinterprets his native religion, then, he keeps its orientation towards practice. His revisions do not demand a rejection of cultic means as such; the Electus is not to be an isolated philosopher, devoted to a purely intellectual ideal of knowledge."[143] A discourse locating purificatory processes within the human body has two possible analogues in modern discourse: psychological and physiological. The study of religions, working from a background in humanities, has naturally favored psychological discourse. But the correct translation of the above passage from the *Cologne Mani Codex*, one that retains the relations between what is being said linguistically and the context of its significance for those who composed, copied, read, and heard it, requires the application of a physiological understanding of Mani's point.

Manichaean gnosis, therefore, is a practical knowledge that permits the reconstitution of the defective body by the separation of its antagonistic components. The reformation of the body's congenital defectiveness forms the centerpiece of divine revelation and action. Thus, in Manichaean interpretation, Jesus came in the body so that "he might ransom those enslaved from the powers and set free their limbs from the subjection of the rebels and from the authority of those who keep guard, and through it he might disclose the truth of its own knowledge, and in it open wide the door to those confined within."[144] Although Mani's mission is unique, he undertakes it with the same originally defective "instrument" *(organon)* shared by all humans.[145] His triumph, then, is paradigmatic for all Manichaeans.

However recalcitrant, the body can be trained to good purpose. Thus the Manichaean authority Baraies relates that Mani said, "Just as nowadays a young horse, used by a king, becomes the king's mount through the capability of the horse trainers, so that he might sit upon it in honor and glory and carry out his particular [task], in this same way [the mind possesses the] body, [in order to do the] good."[146] Manichaeans slay a beast within, usually described as a lion.[147] The individual, whose congenital form is the Old Man, is refashioned into the New Man, ruled by the Mind of Light;[148] he or she comes to resemble the divinely fashioned cosmos, and is able to operate synchronously with it.[149]

The Manichaean accomplishes this reordering of the body with the help of the Mind of Light, a divine agent operating in those who join the faith. Once inside the body the Mind of Light sets about his work:

> He releases the [mind of the soul and he frees] it from bone. He frees the [thought of the soul from] nerve, and he binds the thought [of sin in] nerve. He frees the insight of the soul from artery and he binds the insight of sin in artery. [He] releases the intellect of the soul, and frees it from flesh, and he binds the intellect of sin in flesh. He frees the reasoning of the soul from skin, and he binds the reasoning of sin in skin. This is the way in which he releases the limbs of the soul and makes them free from the five limbs of sin. These five limbs of sin, however, which were free, he binds. He sets in order the limbs of the soul, and he forms them and purifies them and constructs them as a New Man, a child [of] righteousness.[150]

This reconstruction of the individual entails the endowment of additional graces (see Diagram 3.2):

> Now when he forms and constructs and purifies the New Man, he brings forth five great living limbs out of the five great limbs, and he places them in the limbs of the new person. He places his [mind], which is love, in the mind of the New Man. The [thought], moreover, which is faith, he places [in] the thought [of the] New [Man], which he purifies. His insight, which [is perfection, he places] in the insight of the New Man. His intellect, which [is] his patience, he places in his intellect. Wisdom, lastly, which is his reasoning, (he places) in the reasoning of the New Man. . . . The New Man rules by his love, faith, perfection, patience and wisdom. His king, moreover, [is the Mind] of Light, the one who is king over the universe.[151]

The Mind of Light, therefore, functions as soldier, builder, and ruler within the Manichaean body.[152]

In addition to the production of a new body and sense of self, Coptic Manichaica discuss various techniques of maintaining the New Man. A psalm testifies to a "closing of the gates" tradition in Egyptian Manichaeism, as in its Iranian variety, in which the senses must be guarded lest they become accessories to the inflammation of passions.

DIAGRAM 3.2: THE PROCESS OF GOOD ANTHROPOGONY				
From body-part,		Mind of Light releases divine limb,		and adds virtue
BONE	→	MIND	✛	LOVE
NERVE	→	THOUGHT	✛	TRUST
ARTERY	→	INSIGHT	✛	CONTENTMENT
FLESH	→	INTELLECT	✛	PATIENCE
SKIN	→	REASONING	✛	WISDOM

Guide my eyes that they look no evil look. Guide my ears that they hear not a [. . .] word. Guide my nostrils that they smell not the stink of lust. Guide my mouth that it utter no slander. Guide for me my hands that they serve not Satan. Guide for me my heart that it do no evil at all. Guide for me my spirit in the midst of the stormy sea. Guide my New Man for it [wears the] mighty image. Guide my feet that they walk not in the way of error. Guide my soul that [. . .] sin.[153]

Similarly, in *Kephalaion 56* Mani speaks of the Mind of Light's conquest of the senses, closing them to evil and opening them to good.[154]

So, now, because of the bolts to the body of the righteous person are in the hands of the Mind of Light within, he is open [to receive] in all that is pleasing to God. He is open [to take] in by his eyes the visions of love [. . .] and righteousness.[155]

Like the commander of a force of occupation, the Mind of Light fortifies the reformed body against further assaults, guarding the body's perimeter like that of an armed camp.

Look, then, at how much the strength and diligence of the Mind of Light is upon all the watchtowers of the body. He stands before his camp. He shuts all the reasonings of the body from the attractions of sin. He limits them, scatters them, removes them by his will.[156]

The crux of the body's dilemma is that it can never completely cut itself off from the influx of evil, as Mani's scientific argument to the Elchasaites makes clear. The senses provide one avenue of access, but eating necessarily affords evil a constant gateway into the body. One might presume that the Manichaeans would attempt to "close" this gate as well, and that the practice of fasting was intended to isolate the body as much as possible from pollution in food.[157] But the sources reveal a more nuanced and complex response on the part of the Manichaeans. The continuation of eating was never in question; its negative consequences were accepted as unavoidable. In *Kephalaion 86*, Mani explains that the relative strength of evil over good mixed in food is more or less random and unpredictable, and in those cases where it dominates, the consumer will experience an increase of disturbances and passions in his or her body. Fasting does weaken the evil "rulership" already in the body by reducing its reinforcement,[158] but the positive products of embodiment, such as meditation and prayer, depend as much on food as do negative ones such as lust and reproduction.[159] *Kephalaion 38* describes potential rebellions within the reordered body, and recommends that those afflicted in this way seek the counsel of their peers, not only superiors, but also the *boēthoi* or lay-assistants.[160] The passage lists among the signs of an eruption of sin antisocial attitudes, such as the desire to be a solitary[161] and hatred of one's brethren.[162]

> That man makes himself an instrument of damage, and he separates from the congregation, and his end comes down to the world. The mind which existed in him scatters from him and goes up to the apostle who had sent it. He is filled with evil spirits and they occupy themselves [with him], drawing him hither and thither, and he himself becomes like the worldly people, for [he] will change and will become like a bird being plucked of his feathers, and will become a man of the earth.[163]

Beside its complex and sophisticated anthropology, Manichaeism also offered the straightforward motivation of reward for keeping its disciplinary regimens. In the Eighteenth Psalm of Thomas of the Coptic *Psalm-Book*, the speaker's initial attempt to buy a way into "the garden" is rebuffed, and yet an offer of admittance is proffered:

> But if you fast with fasting, you will be taken up into the garden; if your eyes do not glance evilly, they will cause you to sit beneath the shadow of the gar-

den; if your mouth speaks truly, they will show you their image; if your hands are pure from [. . .], they will hear the accents of your pleading . . . ; if your heart is firm . . . ; if your feet walk in the path of truth, [they will] make you one of them.[164]

Elsewhere, Mani speaks of the unreformed senses and other rulers of the body as the fourteen heads of a dragon that lives within each person.

> Whoever will recognize them with the dragon, which is the thought of the body, and struggles with it and is victorious and kills it in them . . . [he is called] the holy righteous one, elect, good person. He receives the victory without suffering on the day of his coming forth (from the body).[165]

The successful outcome of this promise is envisioned in the funerary hymns of the Coptic *Psalm-Book*, where the dead person is told, "your prayers and your fasts have become a crown upon your head."[166] The congregation sings of "perfect virginity, prayer, and fasting, the armor of our soul."[167] The apotheosized Elect speaks for him- or herself of "the glorious armor, that which you girded your commandment [. . .] in me through it; I have put it upon my limbs; [I have] fought against my enemies."[168] This is the armor bestowed by "my savior, who has taught me to wear his holy commandments."[169]

Whereas the Elect receive the reward of ascent into heaven upon their death, the less-rigorous lifestyle of the Auditor leads to further reincarnation, but in an improved state corresponding to the merit earned in previous lifetimes of supporting the religion. The Manichaeans measure improvement by the greater rapidity with which they will attain liberation, a goal that can be achieved through more than one channel, much to Augustine's amusement.

> All you promise (the Auditors) is not a resurrection, but a change *(revolutionem)* to another mortal existence, in which they shall live the life of your Elect, the life you live yourself, and are so much praised for; or if they are worthy of the better, they shall enter into melons and cucumbers, or some food which will be chewed, that they may be quickly purified by your belches.[170]

The Eastern Manichaean Tradition

Many Iranian texts narrate the formation of the human body as a prison of divinity in the world. *The Excellent Verses of Salvation* tell the story in the following fashion:

> Až, that wicked mother of all the demons . . . made a disturbance for the help of her own spirit. And she caused this corpse to be made from the impurity of the demons and from the defilement of the fiends, and herself entered into it. Then she formed from the five elements *(mhr'spnd'n)*, the armor of the lord Ohrmizd (i.e., Primordial Man), the good soul *(gy'n 'y xwb)* and bound it within the corpse. She made it like one blind and deaf, senseless and deceived, so that at first it did not know its own origin and family. She made a corpse and prison, and bound the wretched soul [. . .] she bound the soul in the accursed corpse, and made it [hate]ful and wicked, [wrath]ful and malicious. Then [the lord] Ohrmizd took mercy [upon] the souls, and in the [shape] of a human he descended to earth . . . and plainly revealed everything which was and will be. He swiftly made it manifest that this fleshly corpse was not made by the lord Ohrmizd, and neither did he bind the soul. The intelligent, fortunate soul was resurrected; it believed the knowledge *(d'nyšn)* of the good lord Ohrmizd. Each and every commandment and rule, and the seal of virtue, it zealously accepted like a mighty hero. Its corpse of death was removed and it was liberated forever and raised up to paradise, to that realm of the fortunate.[171]

This recital obviously telescopes the events of primordial time into the fate of the individual.[172] If things had happened exactly in this fashion, liberation would have been complete and final at the dawn of time. Instead, the battle raged on in a see-saw fashion described at length elsewhere. By telling the tale in its own way, this hymn draws concrete links between the aspirations of the individual adherent and the paradigmatic events of the anthropogonic myth. Rather than slavishly retelling the entire salvation history, the composer of this hymn took advantage of the hymn form's inherent requirement for abbreviation to put the most positive spin on what is essentially a tragedy. By projecting back into the myth the salvational promise of the Manichaean church, the author of the hymn both reaffirms the identification of the adherent with the entrapped soul-stuff of the myth, and strengthens the paradigmatic value of the tale by making the first soul itself an adherent of the Manichaean *regula fidei*.

The Chinese *Hymnscroll* speaks of the original creation of the human body more in line with what we have seen elsewhere, as the background to the body's current defective state.

> *When the body of flesh was created by the cunning craftsman*
> *It was she, the vain, fallacious, and evil queen of the devils*
> *Who having completed the den and dwelling such as this*
> *Ensnared and arrested the natures of light* (ming-hsing) *and hid herself behind*
> *The merciless fires of hunger become chains and fetters*
> *And man slaughters and hurts all living beings without an end*
> *Eating and swallowing all day long many bodies*
> *But is still not spared from the tortures of birth and death.*[173]

The *Ts'an-ching* relates that, after the forces of light succeeded in constructing the universe as "the hospital where the luminous bodies are cured,"[174] the "demon of desire" retaliated by arranging for the construction of the human body as a prison for the five divine elements, and as "an exact image, point by point of the universe."[175]

> It locked up the five luminous natures in the carnal body where it made a microcosm. Moreover, it helped the thirteen dark, non-luminous forces by imprisoning and enchaining [the five luminous natures] there. Furthermore, it no longer permitted them to be independent. Thus, the demon of desire locked up the pure ether in the fortress of bone; it established dark thought in which it planted a tree of death. Next it locked up the excellent wind in the fortress of nerves; it established dark feeling, in which it planted a tree of death. Next it locked up the force of light in the fortress of veins; it established dark reflection, in which it planted a tree of death. Next it locked up the excellent water in the fortress of flesh; it established dark intellect, in which it planted a tree of death. Next it locked up the excellent fire in the fortress of skin; it established dark reasoning, in which it planted a tree of death.[176]

Each of these trees of death produces negative passions that dominate the body and make it the slave of darkness.

The Five Elements, locked inside the demonically designed human body, become drunk and delirious through their torment. The *Ts'an-ching* analogizes their situation to that of a man suspended upside down inside a cage made of intertwined poisonous snakes that constantly harass him and spit their poison upon him.[177] In the *Hymnscroll* the Manichaean prays, "That I may leave this poisonous fiery sea of my carnal body / In which the uprising waves and boiling ripples never stop for a moment."[178]

> *It is originally the devils' place and the land of the* Luo-ch'a
> *And is also a dense forest, a marsh of weeds and rushes*
> *Where all evil birds and beasts move intermingled*
> *And poisonous insects, lizards and vipers furtively assemble*
> *It is also the embodiment of the evil-doing greedy devil.*
>
> . . . .
>
> *It is also the sprout of the three venoms of mercilessness*
> *And also the fountain of the five poisons of unkindness*
> *All the male and female devils*
> *Appear with the carnal body, the affinity of birth.*
>
> . . . .
>
> *It is also the heart of the ferocious and venomous* Yeh-ch'as
> *And also the thought in the mind of the greedy devil*
> *All the armor and arms of the devilish kings*
> *All the venomous snares of the offensive teachings*
> *It can drown precious things and merchants*
> *And can obscure Sun and Moon, the Buddhas of Light*
> *It is the gateway of all the hells*
> *And the road towards all transmigrations.*
>
> . . . .
>
> *It still causes me trouble and difficulty even now*
> *Cangues, chains, imprisonment, and bonds steadily ensnare me*
> *Making me now as though mad and then as though intoxicated.*
>
> . . . .
>
> *Like the grasses and trees on the great earth, and the stars and planets in the*
> *   heavens*
> *Like the dust and sand on the globe and the drizzling rain on earth*
> *Are the many sins and wrongs I have committed*
> *Which number even a thousand and ten thousand times more.*[179]

Manichaean discourse on the body's congenital condition often takes the form of lamentation, as in the following Sogdian text:

> Who has transformed you into such multiple forms? And who has humiliated you (and) wrapped you in masculine and feminine bodies? Oh light-god, beloved soul *(rw'n)*! Who has blinded you in your light-eye? . . . And has led you into exile from your land of divine glory? And who has bound you, and who has imprisoned you in this dark prison, this forgetfulness, this place without refuge, which is this fleshly body? Oh light-god, beloved soul! Why, and who constrains you in the infernal creation which there spreads sweet poison? And who has handed you over to the devil's slave, who is nourished in this body in which also his great snake resides? And who has made you into the servant of his shameless, dark, voracious fire, his insatiable impudence? Oh light-god, beloved soul! Who has wrenched you from eternal life?[180]

We hear the despairing complaint of the human born into the mixed world that "the stupid clan of the carnal body . . . are damaging my clean and pure body constantly."[181] It is out of this condition that Manichaean disciplines offer a rescue. Alongside such mythopoeic imagery, the body can be discussed in terms that combine physiological observation with analogy.

> Also, this body that exists upon you, see it and reflect upon it thus: that it was made and created entirely and wholly through tricks and delusions, and through deception and deceit. Numerous within (it) are the forces, feelings, ideas, (and) thoughts which are (constantly) bubbling and stirring. Just as they are enchanting, so are they (like) the great Samutri ocean where disturbances and turmoils are numerous. . . . When the wind that is in the east [blows], then it brings those disturbances, turmoils, tumults and tempests toward the west. Also, when the wind blows in a westerly direction, it brings back those commotions and turbulences in an easterly direction.[182]

Manichaeans learned to consider their bodies occupied territory, which must be liberated from the dominion of evil.

Initial persuasion of people to the Auditor role, and subsequent reinforcement of their duties in that role, appear unsurprisingly in the form of prose sermons reminding them of their sinfulness and their need for constant effort toward improvement. The Parthian text M 580, for example, reminds Auditors that they torture the living things of the earth by their own hand, that they "destroy this Living Self from which you have been born,"[183] and which weeps and laments at their behavior. Failure to keep the Manichaean disciplines necessarily entailed harm to the divine presence in the world, as in the Sogdian *Community Confession (S'nk Xw'stw'nyft):*

> Oh God, forgive my sins *(mnst'r ɣyrz')*! Failing am I and sinning, indebted and a debtor—instigated by the greed-breeding, shameless Až, in thoughts, words and deeds, by the looking of the eyes, the hearing of the ears, the speaking of the tongue, the grasping of the hands, the walking of the feet—since at every moment I hurt and injure the five elements *(mrd'spnt)* . . . the Buddhagotra *(pwt'ny kwt'r)* in the dry and wet earth, the five-fold plant beings, the five-fold animal beings.[184]

To escape the natural retribution for such offenses, the Auditor must resort to the saving relationship with the Elect. "You Auditors, who exist in so much sin and offence . . . seek assembly and absolution from the Elect daily [that] they may bestow forgiveness upon you."[185] Good Auditors pay close attention to their own weaknesses.

> They are like [a man who] is healthy and [without pain], who in his whole body is healthy and [without pain] and does not have any other ache or illness. But in some limb he is wounded (with a) small scratch, and he rises up nervously [and] tends to it constantly and ponders when this wound will be healed so that he will be healthy and painless in his whole body.[186]

Dire consequences accrue to the person who lives according to the dictates of the corrupted body, rather than seeking to reform and take control of its processes. The Chinese *Hymnscroll* warns that,

> *When the flesh-body is destroyed, the devil will then come out*
> *But sinful doings have already pained the clean and pure nature*
> *It will suffer every pain wherever it transmigrates*
> *For man's doings in the previous life were unrighteous.*[187]

Everyone faces judgment for the actions of a lifetime: "There are only two things, good and evil deeds / Which follow your Buddha-nature wherever you go or sit."[188]

Only the shameful deeds and the evil doings
Will become burdens on his back after that day of impermanence
Before the King of the Balance all his reasons are unjustifiable
And he goes through transmigration for birth-and-death tortures.[189]

Positive rationales are expressed as often as the more garish negative ones:

These auditors, too, put off the [body] and all filthiness . . . he saves them from those [. . .] and from all wickedness . . . from the hands of *yakšas* [and] evil men . . . they are shown the gate.[190]

We can see, therefore, that the call to discipline is usually linked to a promise of reward; Manichaean mores resonate with self-interest, not self-sacrifice. The Elect, of course, are assured of an ascent into heaven. This certainty is reflected in the "Bögü Khan" text: "We are the pure and clean Elect. We act fully in accordance with the word of God. When we abandon the body, we will go to the land of the gods. Why? (Because) we do not act contrary to the command of God. We face great oppression and difficult trials, and for this reason we will attain to the land of the gods."[191] Yet it is characteristic of Eastern Manichaean sources to extend the promise of heavenly rewards to the Auditors: "[Those who do good] will find the divine hall: these are the fortunate Righteous One and the dutiful Auditor; and this is the piety (*kyrbg*) which is necessary to save the self (*gryw*)."[192] Similarly, M 7 reports that "the righteous Elect and dutiful Auditors will find the hall,"[193] and establishes a *quid pro quo*: "Restrain (your) heart and mind from the turmoil of sin (and) ascend on the road of peace to (your) light-home."[194] M 77 provides another example of an exhortation to Manichaean disciplines couched in terms of their very concrete rationales:

Delight in the earth and the lust of form and the things of the world are like delicious food in which poison has been mixed. Hold back the self (*gryw*) from those snares! The beings who are deceived by the (other) religions are terrified. They do not find escape; they do not know [. . .] and wisdom. In blind habits they go to destruction. Their form has been turned to bondage and ruin forever. They fall into hades (*nrh*) and hell (*dwjx*) from where they do not find escape again. Peace and well-being do not arise there. (But) we— Elect and Auditors—are prepared for happiness: a hall, throne and garland forever and ever. Auditors, too, become immortal!

Manichaean prayers enunciate a desire for divine assistance in their struggle toward perfection. The gods are called upon to "put my self in order *(grywm'n wyn'r'h)*."[195] The extremely fragmentary double-page M 174 contains prayer-scripts[196] that exhibit such concerns. Passages preserved on the verso speak of Auditors striving for piety *(qyrbgyy)*, "so that I may become perfect in love, spirit and body, and through your power, lord, may conquer the three deceitful demons of my soul *(gy'n)*." Hymns express similar sentiments:

> I will keep zeal by day and by night in order to fulfil, O God, your advice *(pnd)* and order *(frm'n)*. Worldly pleasure and the things of the world—which Až has prepared with activity and with much trickery—I have by your advice abandoned. . . . This is the road, this is the secret, this is the great commandment *(cxš'byyd)* and the gate of liberation *(br mwxšyg)*. Perfect (your) will *(qr'h)*, O God, in me![197]

Hymnists appeal, also, to Jesus for restoration and perfection:

> *O broad and kind, dignified and solemn Jesus Buddha!*
> *Pray, show great mercy and forgive my sins*
> *Listen to my words inspired by pain and suffering*
> *Guide me to leave this poisonous fiery sea*
> *Pray give me the fragrant water of emancipation*
> *The twelve precious crowns, the clothes, the fringes*
> *Cleanse my wonderful nature from dust and dirt*
> *Solemnly adorn my purified body, and make it graceful*
> *Pray remove the three winters, which are the three poisonous ties*
> *And the six robbers, which are the six poisonous winds*
> *Send down the springtide of the great religion* (fa) *to prosper the ground of my*
>   *nature* (hsing)
> *And cause the flowers and fruits of the tree of my nature to thrive*
> *Pray pacify the great billows and waves of the fiery sea*
> *The surrounding canopies of the dark cloud and mist*
> *Compel the sun of the great religion to shine universally*
> *And make my heart and nature always bright and pure.*[198]

The individual is described in terms of a possessed being, seeking exorcism of intrusive spirits:

Pray dispel my morbidity and dullness of many kalpas
The Wang-liang[199] *and other devils and spirits*
Grant the medicine of the great religion to heal and restore me quickly
And silence them with the holy spell and drive them from me.[200]

Besides exorcism, the hymnist employs images of assembly to describe the personal correction sought by the Manichaean:

O great king of healing for all manner of ills
O great radiance for all that dwell in the dark
Diligently reassemble all those who are scattered
All who have lost their hearts . . . !
I have already perished now: pray reanimate me
I am already in the darkness: pray enlighten me
The demon king has scattered me in the ten directions
Tempting me to take forms and be sullied by the three forms of existence
Causing me to be dull and drugged, and lose all my senses

. . . .

Ignorance, delusion, and desire have for long ensnared me
Bestow the medicine of the great religion and let me be healed![201]

The benefit of divine aid requires a corresponding effort on the part of the practitioner, who is encouraged to "exert yourself, that you may be constantly vigilant for this one victorious god, *Dīn Qutī,*[202] who has appeared upon you."[203] In M 7, the hymn's audience is told to "burn into every limb fear, precept and prohibition *(trs 'ndrz u prc'r pt'byd pd hrw hnd'm).*"[204] They are to learn about

> all sins—internal and external, thought, spoken, and done—which (cause) harm. Teach the mixing of pious and sinful thought, and separate the one from the other. Understand your seed, the pure word that itself is pilot to the soul *(gy'n)* which is in the body. And, through it, fully know the false word that leads to the dark hell (as) an infernal pilot. . . . Remember the rebirth *('jwn)* and the hard hell where souls are oppressed and wounded in anguish. Keep the spiritual *(rw'nyn)* zeal.[205]

Restructuring the body takes the form of a sort of landscape architecture undertaken in the interior spaces of the body.[206]

The way of life brought by Mani is likened to a medicine that cures the congenital defects of humans at the mercy of their passions. The "Great Hymn to Mani" from the Turkic *Pothi-Book* echoes this theme.

> When they were being poisoned by the passion of greed, and decaying and perishing, you made a dressing for them with the medicine of "collection" (*amwardišn*). Raving with the passion of anger, they were thoughtless; making them understand their own origins, you gathered (*yïgtïngïz*) their thoughts. You separated the mortals in the five states of existence from ignorance; you endowed them with wisdom, you made them bound for *parinirvāna*.[207]

The Mind of Light plays a reformatory role in the Eastern Manichaean tradition, as in the following passage from the Chinese *Hymnscroll*:

> *The King of Mind is clean and pure, and always vigilant*
> *For the believing and comprehending, he increases signs*
> *Whoever there is, advancing and developing firmly*
> *He conducts him into safety on the even road*
> *By him have now been opened my Buddha-natured eyes*
> *And thus they can see the four-placed wonderful dharmakaya*
> *Through him also, my Buddha-natured ears have been enlightened*
> *And can hear the clear and pure voice from the Three Constancies* (san-ch'ang)
> *I therefore, purifying my heart, worship, laud and praise*
> *And, removing all confused thoughts, speak truly*
> *In the immediate past, I had unknowingly committed many iniquities*
> *Now I repent beseechingly so that my sins shall disappear.*[208]

The *Ts'an-ching* describes in methodical detail the operations of the Mind of Light upon the individual. He enters through the ear, and progresses through the body like a conquering king, setting up his throne in the human heart.[209] He liberates each of the Five Elements from their place of imprisonment and establishes them as masters of the body.[210] He adds to them five virtues: compassion, faith, contentment, patience, and wisdom.[211]

As can be seen in the above examples, regimens and rationales frequently appear in inseparable complementarity. Chinese texts make a direct correlation between certain knowledges and practices purportedly consequent upon them.

I tell you, the flocks of light, the good doers
And those who can comprehend the Five Lights (wu ming)
You must always wake and purify the field of your heart
And accomplish the Father's work without respite
Discriminate and select the many forms of nature
Be aware that the light-strength is caught in fetters
And decide to cultivate this right religion
If you can do this, you will quickly be set free
The admirable Mind of Light (Hui-ming) *is the King of Religion*
    (fa wang = Skt. dharmaraja)
And can snatch us from the wrong path to death

. . . .

He refines them in the pure religion, and renders them admirable
Their mind and thought will be dignified and solemn, and their bodies (will
    manifest) the five wonders.[212]

The discipline cultivates virtues within the Elect, and makes them amenable to the all-important relation with the Auditor community.

> The Elect nourishes the Auditor through his wise knowledge. And just as the eyes are loving to the feet, and the hand is loving to the mouth, so is that one likewise. Loving thoughts are suitable to an Elect person. . . . Then they will have the five kinds of signs. The first sign is in its mildness like the god Ohrmizd. The second is in its strength like the god Wadziwanta. The third is in its beauty just as the bright Sun God is. The fourth is in its wise knowledge like the type that the death-raising sovereign, the Moon God is. And the fifth, changing form and appearance, is like the beloved daughter of the exalted divine king-of-kings, the god Azrua, the flashing lightning-goddess.[213]

These "signs of the Mind of Light" are manifest to the Auditors, "who come and make obeisance and give praise and honor to it, and they know what it is and are witnesses to it in (its) greatness and nobility."[214] The Eastern Manichaeans developed an elaborate catalogue of these signs constituting true Elect embodiment, as found in the *Sermon on the Light Nous* and its Chinese translation, the *Ts'an-ching*.

Putting one's self in order and restraining one's self from sin are not merely mental exercises. Manichaean disciplinary regimens are physical, and necessarily entail the training of the body. It needs to be emphasized that Manichaeans were every bit as concerned with their bodies as with their "souls." One could say, in fact, that the salvation of the Manichaean soul absolutely necessitated a concern with the body—and not solely in negative terms. Manichaeans prayed to the heavenly powers for the health and security of their bodies: "Bright Mani, lord of fair name, life-giver, guard me in body; Jesus, lord, save my soul."[215] Similarly, the blessing of M 74.V.7ff. says, "May the angels protect you, may the spirits give you peace; may you be whole in body, and become saved in soul." And in M 801 a psalmist beseeches Mani, "protect my body *(tn)* and save my soul *(rw'n)*; grant my pious wish, the eternal light paradise."[216]

The surviving Chinese texts enunciate the ideals toward which the Manichaean strives, the final conditions of the perfected self, when "The devilish races will be eternally put into the dark prison / And the Buddha-gotra will leap for joy and return to the realm of Light / All recovering their original bodies, wonderful, dignified, and solemn / And wearing robes and crowns, and being eternally happy."[217] The *Ts'an-ching* states explicitly the rewards of adherence to the "correct religion":

> If there is a person from the pure Elect who is of the type who assures the prosperity of the correct religion without superior, and until the end of life does not fall back, then after that person's death, their Old Man, with the dark, non-luminous force of its mob of soldiers, will fall into hell from which it will never come out. At the same moment, the beneficent light, rousing the pure kindred of its own luminous army, will go completely straight into the world of light; definitively, [this master] will no longer be in fear and receives joy perpetually.[218]

Hymns refer repeatedly to healthy, strong, and beautiful bodies; apparently, however, these are attained only in heaven, where

> *The solemn countenances of the saintly masses are very strange and unique*
> *Light shines on them, and their bodies become splendid and transparent*
> *Compared with the brightness of a hundred or thousand suns and moons*
> *The radiance from the hair-tips of those saints is even stronger*
> *Within and without there is light but no dark shadow*
> *These wonderful bodies eternally glisten in a thousand or myriad ways*

Traveling on the triumphant, famous soil of diamond
They are not so heavy as a feather or a grain of corn.[219]

The hymnist portrays heavenly embodiment in explicit contrast to the pains
and limits of earthly existence:

The bodies of the saintly masses are light, always clean and pure
Their hands and feet, limbs and joints are free from paralysis
While they are not creating the active works of birth and death
How can it be said they have fatigue and exhaustion?
Those saints are pure, humble, and always happy in body
Their frames (chih-t'i) of diamond (chin-kang = Skt. vajra) require no sleep
Since they have neither dream and whim, nor nightmare
How can it be said they have fear and dread?
The saintly masses are always enlightened and with wonderful kindness
Naturally they are not forgetful and short of memory
But all the things and phenomena in the boundless world
They see entirely, as if facing a bright mirror
The minds and thoughts of the saints are all honest and true
Pretension and deceit, vanity and affectation are naturally not theirs
Of their bodies, mouths, and minds, the deeds are always clean and pure
How can it be said they ever uttered a false saying?[220]

By describing heavenly life as embodied, such publicly performed utterances correlate with Augustine's (albeit polemical) characterization of
Manichaeans as materialists who treat spiritual realities in terms of physical
properties. These properties are to be perfected, not rejected.[221] The *Hymnscroll* is unequivocal in this regard: "From the dim past until now, and to time
for evermore / To say that bodies will be destroyed is not true."[222] Perfection
entails a homogenization of individual selves, an erasure of distinctions, and
an opening to direct interpenetration of experience. "Every thought and reflection obtained and all intentions in mind / Are mutually shown and observed, and no suspicion and misunderstanding exist."[223] The saved are "harmonious in mind,"[224] and "every one of them looks the same without
exceptional appearance."[225] "All natures *(hsing)* and forms are equal; and all
places bear no differences."[226]

But the *Ts'an-ching* also expounds an expansive typology of earthly per-

TABLE 3.2. THE FIVE TREES OF LIFE IN THE PERFECTED BODY OF THE ELECT

(FROM THE *TS'AN-CHING*)

TREE	ROOT	TRUNK	BRANCHES	LEAVES	FRUIT	TASTE	COLOR
Mind	Pity	Joy	Felicity	Praise	Calm	Respect	Steadfastness
Thought	Good faith	Faith	Belief	Vigilance	Application to study	Reading and recitation	Calm joy
Insight	Contentment	Good thought	Imposed rules	Truth in all acts	Truthful speech	Correct discourse on the law	Pleasure in meeting others
Intellect	Endurance of injuries	Absolute calm	Patience	Precepts of discipline	Fasts and hymns	Zeal and patience	Energy
Reasoning	Wisdom	Understanding the two principles	Skill in discussing the law	Skill in public address	Skill in debate	Skill in apologetics	Pleasing rhetoric

fection, a catalogue of virtuous attributes displayed by the Elect attesting to their proper adherence to the disciplines of the faith. The *Ts'an-ching* gives three different accounts of manifestations of perfection, which I can only summarize here. The first identifies the presence of the "religious thought of the beneficent light" in each of the five mentalities (thought, feeling, reflection, intellect, and reasoning) according to the virtue an Elect discourses upon.[227] The second depicts a kind of landscape architecture worked by the Mind of Light upon the individual body, uprooting the five trees of death and replacing them with five trees of life, each possessing good properties (see Table 3.2). Finally, the most elaborate exposition entails twelve trees, each with five characteristics displayed in the perfect Elect (see Table 3.3).[228]

These detailed descriptions of the characteristics of human perfection show the results of the total reordering of the body, the triumph of light over darkness within the individual, and the emergence of a divine self. The cure brought by Mani makes the adherent functional in the context of the Manichaean worldview, that is, in terms of the task that Manichaeism establishes as appropriate to human behavior. The virtues cultivated in the Elect recreate them as microcosmic machines whose distilling function parallels that of the Manichaean macrocosm. In both microcosm and macrocosm, an initial catastrophic condition is reworked and perfected into an instrument in the service of salvation.

CONCLUSIONS

Despite its plethora of varying details, Manichaean discourse maintains a consistent outline of reality in which it locates the human individual. The universal macrocosm and the human microcosm both derive from a primordial mixture of antithetical substances, and both exist as battlegrounds of opposing forces. Mani brings to the world a recognition of this state of affairs, or as one Coptic hymn says, a mirror in which he shows humanity the world. The world he shows is the Manichaean world, mapped in minute detail by the religion's enormous descriptive vocabulary. It is a divinely designed, yet recalcitrant world, wired for salvation, yet disrupted by rebellion. The human body, too, has redemptive potential, but can only realize that potential by overcoming the hegemony of evil within it.

In the *Cologne Mani Codex*, Mani declares that "purity . . . comes through *gnosis*," and for many modern interpreters of Manichaeism such a

TABLE 3.3. THE TWELVE FORMS OF THE BENEFICENT LIGHT IN THE ELECT
(FROM THE *TS'AN-CHING*)

1. AUTHORITY
   a. recognizes transience
   b. remits alms received to the assembly
   c. remains chaste; encourages others to chastity
   d. sticks close to wise masters; avoids foolish ones
   e. does not seek isolation; lives among the adepts
2. WISDOM
   a. praises, loves, and lives among the adepts
   b. is not jealous of greater wisdom in another
   c. is ardent and energetic in conduct and study
   d. constantly studies the rules; encourages others to do so
   e. is careful not to violate precepts; confesses immediately when does
3. VICTORY
   a. is not slanderous, flattering, or cruel; avoids those who are
   b. does not quarrel or grumble; avoids those who do
   c. does not flaunt victory over an opponent
   d. speaks only when questioned, after careful reflection
   e. speaks with conciliation, not contrariness
4. JOY
   a. adheres closely to the precepts and rules
   b. takes only one vestment per year and only one meal per day
   c. studies only one's own faith, not other faiths
   d. is humble, not hateful, toward superiors
   e. does not try to outshine superiors; does not consider oneself superior to inferiors
5. ZEAL
   a. does not like to sleep
   b. constantly reads and recites, gives attention to teachers; excites zeal in others
   c. constantly explains and comments upon the law of purity
   d. recites, copies, and mentally repeats the hymns
   e. keeps the precepts firmly

TABLE 3.3. (*continued*)

6. TRUTH
   a. conforms oneself to correct teaching; gives true explication of it
   b. always thinks in accord with truth, not in accommodation to the world
   c. acts always in accord with truth, whether publicly or privately
   d. does not doubt one's masters
   e. guides and encourages one's colleagues

7. FAITH
   a. believes and does not doubt the two principles
   b. is resolved toward the precepts and rules
   c. does not add or subtract a word from scriptures
   d. empathizes with another's joy and torment
   e. does not report faults or spread bad reports

8. PATIENCE
   a. one's heart is constantly benevolent, never angry
   b. is always joyous, never irritated
   c. one's heart is always without hatred
   d. one's heart is never violent; one's speech is neither coarse nor nasty
   e. endures all torments with joy and without hatred

9. UPRIGHT THOUGHT
   a. is always joyous in upright and pure thought, and not bound by torments
   b. welcomes all questions with respect, and responds with joy
   c. does not defend one's own errors in discussion, or nurture discontent
   d. one's speech and action is in accord; does not search for faults in others
   e. avoids those of heterodox ideas

10. MERITORIOUS ACTION
   a. does not speak harmfully; employs appropriate means of instruction
   b. always speaks amiably; does not make calumnies, or harbor hate
   c. is jealous of neither the great nor the humble
   d. does not assemble a crowd of followers, but privately instructs disciples; stays in a pure habitation, not a sumptuous place
   e. is always instructing and inducing others to practice

(continued)

TABLE 3.3. (*continued*)

---

11. UNIFORMITY OF HEART

    a. conforms completely to instructions on skillful means and rules; does not change any precept or follow one's own opinions

    b. lives with the community, not separately

    c. is in harmony with others; collaborates in the alms-work

    d. receives the offerings of the Auditors, and praises them

    e. avoids excitement, quarrels, etc.; protects one's combined natures

12. PERVASIVE LIGHT

    a. excels in expelling pollution from the heart; does not tolerate covetousness or concupiscence; is unmoved by women's sensuality

    b. avoids partiality toward certain Auditors; does not become attached to particular homes or families; is not stirred up by secular events

    c. does not indulge the body in fine vestments, bedding, food and drink, broths and remedies, birds and horses, carts and mounts

    d. constantly meditates on death and impermanence

    e. is personally affable and calm

---

statement confirms the traditional association of the religion with Christian Gnosticism.[229] Moreover, the assumption goes, since salvation by means of gnosis operates at the level of the intellect, all external practices are reduced to mere expressions of that which is known. Julien Ries, for example, finds in *Kephalaion 101* a "gnostic interpretation" of salvation, reacting against the ritualism of the Elchasaites and consequently centered on a spiritual hearing of a divine summons, rather than on a physical ritual. "In other words, salvation does not come from a baptism ritual, but from a gnostic message."[230] Ludwig Koenen, too, sees Mani's separation from the Elchasaites as portrayed in the *Cologne Mani Codex* as a gnostic revolution, abandoning the Elchasaite rites of baptism for a purely spiritual baptism brought about through divine knowledge.[231] But Jorunn Buckley has raised some serious challenges to this interpretation of the Manichaean system,[232] objections borne out by the data assembled in this chapter and the previous one.

    Mani did produce a system of knowledge. Manichaeism can in this sense be justifiably called a kind of gnosis, and it is right to talk about what it is Manichaeans are supposed to know about themselves and their world. The formation of a normative Manichaean body necessitates the production of a body of knowledge. In the words of Foucault, "In becoming the target for new mechanisms of power, the body is offered up to new forms of knowledge."[233]

But in more closely defining the distinctively Manichaean gnosis, it is essential to take into account the context of that term's use in Manichaean materials. In the *Cologne Mani Codex* Mani refers to gnosis in the course of a debate about techniques of purity, in other words, an argument over who knows better what to do. He argues that baptismal washings of bodies and of food fail to purify these objects because their respective impurity exists *within* them, due to their mixed nature, and not as some sort of external accretion.[234] Mani does not conclude, as has been suggested, that the body is therefore a hopeless case. Rather, he declares that "genuine purity" comes through separation of the two opposing forces within the body.

How are we to understand this language? A substantial body of material, excerpted at length in this and the previous chapter, points to a realignment and training of the body, a set of disciplinary practices that replace the chaotic and impure body with a Manichaean body perfectly functional for the tasks the tradition assigns to it. The *Sermon on the Light Nous*, which survives in Middle Iranian, Turkic, Chinese *(Ts'an-ching)*, and Coptic *(Kephalaion 38)* versions, describes the triumphal reformation of the body by the forces of light as the total separation of the two substances, the subjugation of impure and evil forces within, and the manifestation in the bodies of the Elect of the signs of success and perfection. The practical gnosis of Manichaeism, then, is a matter of "discernment," exactly the mental quality essential to becoming a Manichaean according to the Chinese *Compendium*, for without it, "how can one put the religion into practice?"[235]

Manichaeans are taught to discern the divine in the world, and hence to problematize their interaction with it. Julien Ries correctly surmises about the Living Self that "it is the fundamental, ineffable mystery communicated to initiates: the mystery of the light held prisoner in matter, the mystery of the soul of the world, which implicates the attitude of man in its regard. It is upon this mystery that the doctrine of the three *signacula* is grafted."[236] Ries's work has been instrumental in refocusing the attention of researchers on the ideological motives behind Manichaean practice. Yet his characterization of the discipline of the Three Seals as "grafted" upon the idea of a world soul, or Living Self, implies an ad hoc, arbitrary association of practice to doctrine, perhaps as merely a dramatic vehicle for expressing the truth about the world. On the contrary, practice and doctrine are intrinsically interconnected in the Manichaean tradition, part of a seamless whole. Discipline actually works by forming a body of knowledge about individuals and their locale in an interactive cosmos, rather than by inflicting upon individuals some arbitrary external display of power.[237] We must be careful not to relegate Manichaean disciplinary regimens to the role of discursive parades; at the same time, we should avoid the opposite temptation to regard the rationales as ideological window-dressing for behavioral norms. The two emerge and are reproduced together. Power "cannot but evolve, organise and put into circulation a knowledge" which is a principal means of its articulation and realization in the individual.[238]

Hans Schaeder was perhaps the first to give due weight to the way Manichaean disciplinary regimens and rationales work together to produce the distinctly Manichaean ethos, and we would do well to return to his insight on this point.

> If the sole meaning of the world and of its existence is the liberation of the light, it follows that active effort in the sense of light-liberation is the sole norm of action. Thereby is required strict abstention from every act which means injury or destruction to the light-possessing bodies, hence especially from the killing of every sort of living being—not only men and animals, but also plants—as well as from every abuse of the pure elements, the water, fire, and air, finally and above all the cessation of all acts which lead to the prolongation of the constraint of the light, hence above all procreation.[239]

Manichaean disciplines are not emotional reactions to an evil world, or expressions of empathy with divine suffering, but are practical consequences of perceived realities.

> In one sense, Mani shows the ultimate conclusion from the striving for a—in the strongest sense—*unified* world-view, which not only says what is, but in the closest connection with it, what is to be done. World meaning and ethic are brought into the closest conceivable relationship. The viewpoint which allows the meaning of the world and of human existence to be comprehended *uno intuitu* should, at the same time, enable a factually grounded overview of the consequences produced for moral behavior from the nature of things. This is, however, nothing other than the endeavor towards a self-supporting foundation, or towards a *rationalization of the ethic*. The moral precepts become no more derived from the unexamined decree of the irrational divine

will, but from the accurate insight into the nature of things. Their source is now thus no more faith, but metaphysics. Mani presents the principal demands of his ethic, ἄσκησις and ἐγκράτεια, as direct deductions from the human constitution, the bondage of divine power in the dark bodies.[240]

The reluctance of many scholars to accept the scientific character of Manichaean rationales may be due in part to a perception that the consequent ethic, in its ideal form, is impractical and so, in a very concrete sense, irrational. Schaeder echoes this sentiment.

> Mani must naturally relax this practically unworkable ethic, of which strict observance would have permitted only the sole possibility of voluntary starvation, and he did so, in that he introduced a double ethic: a more severe observance for the small circle of the "elect," a lighter one for the "hearers."[241]

But the introduction of a double ethic does not solve the problem. Even with the expedient of the exempted Auditors, the Manichaean Elect did not fast themselves to death as a Jain or a Cathar might do.

To what end, then, are Manichaean disciplinary regimens directed? Several scholars have maintained that ascesis in itself is salvational in Manichaeism.[242] This should already set it apart from religions of gnosis which, by definition, do not entail a mandatory praxis. Approved models of embodiment that they necessarily enunciate involve the manifestation of the recognition gnosis brings; and this manifestation is most characteristically one of detachment from the body and its drives.[243] But Manichaean disciplinary rationales describe the regimens as a process by which the Manichaean self emerges from entanglement with contrary forces within the body; they characterize Manichaean ascesis as a transformation of the body, rendering it into a controlled and functional device within which further purificatory operations may occur. Not a departure from or abandonment of the body, but a conquest of it is at stake in Manichaean practice. We must look, therefore, for alternative models to suitably comprehend the role ascetic disciplines play in the Manichaean ethos.

Émile Durkheim first proposed that ascetic systems derive from an expansion and elaboration of the "negative rites" by which individuals prepare themselves for contact with the sacred in "positive rites."[244] According to Durkheim,

> A man cannot enter into intimate relations with sacred things except after rid-
> ding himself of all that is profane in him. . . . So the negative cult is in one
> sense a means in view of an end: it is a condition of access to the positive cult.
> It does not confine itself to protecting sacred beings from vulgar contact: it
> acts upon the worshiper himself and modifies his condition positively. The
> man who has submitted himself to its prescribed interdictions is not the same
> afterwards as he was before. . . . So the negative rites confer efficient powers
> just as well as the positive ones. (348)

By sacralizing all vegetable food, the Manichaeans create circumstances in
which the Elect who are to consume it must remain perpetually pure; their
preparation for contact with the sacred must be constant, and so the "negative
rites" become a way of life. The temporary suspension of profane labor associated with the performance of rites (345–46) becomes a life-long "rest of the
hands." Once ensconced in the sacred sphere, contact with any profaning substance must be strictly avoided (342), hence the prohibition on the consumption of "dead" meat or "polluting" wine.

Interdiction of specific acts and contacts, fasting, and abstention from sex
can be found in any number of religions as steps toward the sanctification of
individuals prior to ritual engagement. A population can arrange such codes
of behavior into a systematic asceticism by what Durkheim calls "a hypertro-
phy of the negative cult," in which the means of sacralizing the body "develop
in such a way as to become the basis of a veritable scheme of life" (350). In
Durkheim's model, asceticism is not a *sui generis* phenomenon that requires
explanation in its own right.

> Asceticism is not a rare, exceptional and nearly abnormal fruit of the religious
> life, as some have supposed it to be; on the contrary, it is one of the essential
> elements. Every religion contains it, at least in germ, for there are none in
> which a system of interdicts is not found. The only difference in this regard
> which there may be between cults is that this germ is more or less developed
> in different ones. (351)

The expansion of the "negative cult" into a thorough ascesis in Manichaeism
corresponds to that religion's extension of the sacred from a localized sphere
to a universal presence. The sacred and the profane make contact at every possible point, and cannot be circumscribed from one another. This forms the rationale for Manichaean disciplines.

The concepts and narratives assembled in this chapter describe a reality in which the specific disciplines of Manichaean ascesis appear reasonable and potentially effective. Detailed catalogues of the constituent parts of the body, its various forces and products, provide objects upon which Manichaeans can act, and supply identifications for points upon which they can focus their attention. Without such practical application, this vast and meticulous literature finds no justification, and can only be seen as verbiage run amok. But by marking particular traits, acts, or sensations as problematic, such discourse directs the adherent to their reformation or eradication. The methodical application of these guidelines, if carried through in every detail, would produce a body that manifests only approved traits, a Manichaean body prepared for its sacred function in the universe.

In the world proposed by Manichaean discourse, the separation of good from evil, light from darkness, and life from death emerges as the fundamental crisis of practice. The key passage in the *Cologne Mani Codex* spells out the anthropological analysis that undergirds Manichaean ascetic disciplinary regimens. Evil and impurity cannot be kept outside the body no matter how extreme the ascetic regimen. As Jorunn Buckley first suggested, the Manichaean response entails a retreat from the insurmountable challenge of sacralizing space in the world to the more circumscribed and hence more manageable arena of the body.[245] Reducing all other contact with the world to nil, the Manichaean Elect compresses his or her engagement with the world to the single point of ingestion. The problem of mixture and embodiment must be resolved here and nowhere else.

The human body becomes the space that Manichaeans undertake to sacralize by a systematic identification, separation, and respective suppression or enhancement of traits belonging to the two substances. The Manichaean Elect not only prepares to be the agent of a continual ritual activity, but also the locale, the sacred space, of that practice.[246] Manichaean disciplinary regimens, therefore, incorporate not only means of personal purification, but also techniques of exorcizing, demarcating, and sealing a holy site. Within the sacred space of their corrected and perfected bodies, the Elect conduct the principal salvational rite of the Manichaean tradition: the daily ritual meal. The divine substance, the Living Self, that the whole world tramples on and profanes in ordinary life, finds in the disciplined bodies of the Elect the properly prepared temple where it can be offered and returned to its heavenly home.

FOUR

ALIMENTARY RITES

*Today I am attending the vegetarian gatherings of the
Religion of Light.*
—Lu Yu, *Lao-hsueh yen pi-chi*

What did one do in a Manichaean ritual? This question presents the greatest
challenge to the historian and marks the point where the limitations of history
are most acute. Here more than at any other point of this study, the convenient division between rite and rationale becomes an obstacle. For consistency,
I must leave to the next chapter (where alimentary *rationales* are discussed) all
of the discourse which for the Manichaeans was nothing more than an objective description of what went on within the bodies of the Elect, and must retain within this chapter (whose subject is alimentary *rites*) only the exterior
acts that meet etic criteria of observableness. This division reduces the data
on the rites considerably; for the Manichaeans, apparently, the internal phase
of the rite, the metabolism of salvation, attracted the most comment and attention.

Both normative and polemical sources tend to focus on the alms-service
of the Auditors and the ideology of metabolic salvation that made that service
obligatory. Polemical sources critique the latter as absurd, and describe the
alms-service as exploitive and hypocritical. Very little is said in such accounts
about the meal ritual itself, either because very little was actually known about
its details among non-Manichaeans or because it was, plain and simply, a

meal. Like the polemical accounts, Manichaean prose sources focus attention on the physics of metabolic salvation and the alms-service of the Auditors. In this case we seem to be dealing with a literature used primarily to promote the practice among the Auditors. Fortunately, the Manichaean material also includes texts employed in the performance of the ritual meal, outlines of ceremonies that incorporate the meal within their structure, and other tantalizing fragments that hold out some promise of allowing a working reconstruction of this daily operation of the Manichaean salvational system.

THE ALMS-SERVICE OF THE AUDITORS

Auditors are the "collectors" of the Manichaean salvational project, and the "helpers" or "assistants" of the Elect in the latter's ritual function in the Manichaean cosmos.[1] Upon first encountering the command and encouragement to give alms, we might think of generic charity. But the Manichaean tradition defines alms specifically as food offerings given to the Elect for the purpose of the daily ritual meal. The alms-service, then, operates as a preliminary phase of the meal and was formalized as part of the Manichaean alimentary rites.

The Central Manichaean Tradition

Al-Biruni identifies among the obligations of Auditors "to give as alms (*al-tasadduq*) the tenth of their property" and "to sponsor the Elect."[2] It is puzzling that more detailed references to the alms-service, or indeed to the ritual meal, are lacking in the Arabic sources. I have no ready answer to explain this fact, since both al-Biruni and especially an-Nadim furnish very explicit details of other cultic practices among the Manichaeans. It should be noted, however, that neither of these two giants of Arabic literature claimed to derive their knowledge of Manichaeism from first-hand observation. Rather, they both worked from Manichaean literature that they had at their disposal. Perhaps alimentary texts were lacking among their resources; or perhaps they, like some modern researchers, read what they had before them in terms of their own religious heritage, and so overlooked the centrality that a meal could take in religious practice. Islam has its own alms-service, an expectation to distribute a portion of one's wealth to the needy. An-Nadim and al-Biruni appear to have construed the Manichaean alms-service as directly analogous to the Muslim practice. Among the canonical letters of the Manichaean community cited by an-Nadim, no less than seven address matters related to the alms-service.[3]

The Western Manichaean Tradition

One of the sources employed in the *Cologne Mani Codex* portrays Mani attempting to institute an incipient alms-service while still living with the Elchasaites: "One of the leaders of their law spoke to me, having observed that I did not take vegetables from the garden, but instead asked them as a pious donation *(eusebeia)*, saying to me, 'Why did you not take vegetables from the garden, but instead ask (them of) me as a donation?'"[4] Later in the codex Mani envisions his future church, "with its teachers and bishops, Elect and Catechumens, with the tables *(trapezai)*, pious donations *(eusebeiai)*, and greatest helpers *(boēthoi)*."[5] Mani appeals to the paradigmatic example of Jesus and his disciples for accepting the alimentary hospitality of laypeople.[6] Episodes from Mani's early missionary work show the solidification of the alms institution. In one instance, when Mani heals a girl, her father offers Mani any reward he chooses. "[I] said to him, 'Nothing of your possessions [of] gold and silver do I [desire].' I accepted from him only [the] daily [food for] the brethren [who were with] me."[7] A fragmentary section that seems to deal with the foundations of prayer, fasting, and alms includes the following passage: "[When] the hour [approached] for the fast to be ended, [he told us to seek] donations *(euse[beiai])* outside of the house. But I [said unto] him: 'Why is our [table not] attended to?'"[8] In all these episodes of the *Cologne Mani Codex*, the alms-service receives its sanctioning etiology in the life of the religion's founder, not only for its existence, but even for its particular form.[9]

The "Elect and Catechumens" along with the "tables" and "pious donations" constitute the core *realia* of the Manichaean community,[10] and the word "table" is found throughout Manichaean literature as a technical term for the ritual meal. We read in the fifteenth Coptic "Thomas" psalm:

> [A] table *(trapeza)* has been set in the house, a table was set in [the house for] souls that they might not wander, that they might not wander, [that] souls might not be wiped out and destroyed in the world, whose desire is great. . . . O man in whose hands is the richness, why wilt thou slumber in this sleep? Wherefore wilt thou not divide for thyself the night into three parts and sleep

for one, and watch for one, and ruminate *(setbe)* with the rumination of the living for one?[11]

These three activities would seem to comprise, in reverse chronological order, a night's activities for the Elect, with the rumination, or "chewing," occurring in the evening, followed by "watching," and then a necessary rest. The Coptic *Homilies* contains a prophecy of a future golden age for the faith which likewise gives considerable attention to the table and the alms. "They will come and find the scriptures written, [and] the books adorned. They will find the table *(trape[za])* [and] those who prepare it *(netchorch mmas)*.[12] The speaker celebrates the end of war and the reign of the Manichaean church. "Behold, the dogmas have been smitten and destroyed. Behold, the alms-offering *(mntnae)* has been appointed, and those who [prepare] it *(net[chorch m]mas)*. Behold, the fountain has been dug and the good tree planted in it."[13]

A Coptic *Kephalaion*, in language reminiscent of that of al-Biruni quoted in an earlier chapter, distinguishes the Auditor from the Elect by the former's lesser aptitude to keep discipline, and directs attention to the Auditor's supporting role in the faith. "They who have not the strength [to fast] daily should make their fast [on] the Lord's day. They also participate *(koinone)* [in the works] and the fasting of the holy ones by their faith and their alms."[14] This Sunday fast of the Auditors is also attested by Augustine, and seems to be connected to the Pauline injunction to "set something aside" on Sunday for the "saints."[15] According to the author of the fifteenth "Thomas" psalm of the Coptic *Psalm-Book*, "Salome built a tower upon the rock of truth and mercy. . . . The floor of the house is truth, the beams of the roof are alms."[16] Alms-service constitutes an essential activity of the Auditor, one performed "in all the days of the year."[17]

> The first task of the catechumenate that he does is the fast *(nēstia)*, the prayer *(shlēl)*, and the alms-offering *(mntnae)*. . . . The alms-offering, moreover, is this: that he places it [. . .] in the holy one, and he gives it to them in righteousness. . . . That Catechumen who [does this] will be in partnership *(koinonē)* with them.[18]

Kephalaion 91 refers to the superior Auditors, who "assist the church, according to that which reaches their hand, through the alms-offering *(mntnae)*"; the alms are "his gifts and . . . his honor and the presents that give profit [to] his life."[19]

The *Tebessa Codex*, a highly fragmentary Latin Manichaean treatise of the late fourth or early fifth century C.E., offers an extended biblical justification for the alms-service relation between the Elect and Auditors. The author focuses on the complementarity of the two *ordines* of the Manichaean community, and the distinctive kinds of work performed by each. The Mary and Martha story from Luke 10, also cited by Mani in the *Cologne Mani Codex*, appears in this context, as does the advice to "make friends for yourself of the unrighteous mammon" from Luke 16:9. The *Tebessa Codex* also identifies the alms-service with the "collection for the saints" Paul was so concerned with in his letters.

Augustine, himself a former Manichaean and writing in the same milieu as the author of the *Tebessa Codex*, charges that "you make allowance for your Auditors, because . . . they supply you with necessaries."[20] "You yourselves do not pluck fruits or pull up vegetables, yet command your Auditors to pick them and bring them to you, and you do this, not so much in order to bestow a benefit on the bringer as to benefit the things themselves which are brought."[21] So Augustine provides testimony that the alms were dedicated for the liberating ritual meal. He recognizes that the alms-service and ritual meal form a system for which the Manichaeans themselves provide several rationales.

> They believe that these crimes are forgiven their Auditors because the latter offer food of this sort to their Elect in order that the divine substance, on being purged in their stomachs, may obtain pardon for those through whose offering it is given to be purged. And so the Elect themselves perform no labors . . . but expect all these things to be brought for their use by their Auditors.[22]

Augustine's observations reflect parallels between the alms of the Manichaeans and the first-fruits sacrifices of traditional Mediterranean religions. "A certain compensation (*compensatio*) takes place, you say, when some part of what is taken from the fields is brought to the Elect and holy men to be purified";[23] "the injuries your Auditors inflict upon plants are expiated (*expiari*) through the fruits which they bring to the church."[24]

Augustine provides details about the content of the offerings. He refers to "grain, beans, herbs, flowers, and fruits" as a typical variety of foods considered appropriate; oil, melons, and lettuce also belong to this list.[25] The ritual meal was vegetarian, and meat did not form part of the offerings. Augustine shows how this prohibition ramifies into the larger disciplinary codes of the Manichaean community: "You say that in order that one be pardoned for the slaughter (of animals), the meat would have to be contributed as food, as is done in the case of fruits and vegetables, but that this is impossible since the Elect do not eat meat, and that, therefore, your Auditors must abstain from the killing of animals."[26]

The act of making an alms-offering was formalized into a ritual whose details are provided among Western sources only by the polemical account of an Egyptian ecclesiastical letter (Pap. Rylands 469),[27] the contents of which were later incorporated into Hegemonius's Acts of Archelaus and into Cyril of Jerusalem's sixth catechetical lecture. In the Acts of Archelaus version, the Manichaean apostate Turbo reports as follows:

> And when they are about to eat bread, they pray first, speaking thus to the bread: "I have neither reaped thee, nor ground, nor pressed thee, nor cast thee into a oven; but another has done these things, and brought to me; I am eating without fault." And when he has uttered these things to himself, he says to the Catechumen, "I have prayed for thee"; and thus that person departs.

Unfortunately, the setting of Elect-Auditor interaction provided by this account is not explicitly stated in Pap. Rylands 469. The latter only gives the contents of the Manichaean invocation, the so-called Apology to the Bread, which the author claims to derive from a Manichaean document.[28] A comparison of the three versions shows a pattern of expansion that adds an element of hypocrisy to the setting (Hegemonius) or to the words of the prayer itself (Cyril). (An exact comparison of the three versions is provided in Table 4.1.)

Hegemonius adds the setting to accentuate the hypocrisy of the situation. When the Elect has finished an "Apology" that markedly declares the innocence of the Elect, not the Auditor, the Elect says to the Auditor, "I have prayed for thee." Cyril follows Hegemonius's example by having the Elect tell the donor to "stand off a little," so that he will not hear the content of the prayer, to which Cyril adds actual curses upon the donor.[29] Since the specific setting of the prayer is lacking in Pap. Rylands 469, we cannot be certain that the "Apology to the Bread," even in its authentic form, was recited in the alms-service ceremony. But the setting of some sort of exchange between the donor and the Elect supplied by Hegemonius and Cyril probably builds on the known facts of such a ceremony.

Augustine similarly alludes to assemblies where prayers were performed

TABLE 4.1. THE "APOLOGY TO THE BREAD"

PAPYRUS RYLANDS 469	HEGEMONIUS	CYRIL
		"I did not make you. I did not sow you; may he be sown who sowed you.
[. . .]	"I have neither reaped thee,	I did not reap you . . . ; let him be reaped who reaped you
". . . no]r [cast] into an ove[n].	nor cast into an oven.	I did not bake you; may he be baked who baked you."
[Anoth]er has bro[ught this] to me.	But another has done these things, and brought to me.	
[I] am eating without fa[ult]."	I am eating without fault."	
	And when he has uttered these things to himself, he says to the catechumen, "I have prayed for you." And thus the person departs.	

by Auditors and Elect together, and as in the account of the *Acts of Archelaus* insists that the ritual meal itself was taken out of the sight of the Auditors.[30] Yet he does not specifically say that these two rites formed a sequence in his experience. Elsewhere, he refers to ritual acts that seem to fit the alms-service setting, in which "the Auditors kneel before the Elect that they may lay a hand on the suppliant, and this is done not only toward their priests or bishops or deacons, but toward any of the Elect."[31]

The alms-service for the ritual meal appropriates the place of the sacrificial systems of prior faiths.[32] In *Kephalaion* 87 Mani enunciates a sharp distinction between the alms-offering practices of other religions and the unique institution of the Manichaean church.

All of these alms that are given in the world because of the name of God by every dogma whatsoever in his name—the ones that their Catechumens give because of the name of God—every place to which they will bring these alms they lead them to an affliction and a hardship and a wickedness. [There is no] rest or open gate through which they come out and find occasion to go up to God, even though they are given because of his name, except only in the holy church, the one in which the commandments of the alms-service are placed.[33]

"Now the holy church," Mani adds, "exists in two *prosōpoi*: the brothers and the sisters."[34] In other words, the Manichaean ethos reduces all of the various sacrificial and donative offerings found among other religions to the simple mediation of the Elect; only in this dually personified institution can offerings work to salvational effect.

The Eastern Manichaean Tradition

The term *rw'ng'n* is used in the Iranian Manichaica to identify the entire category of practices centered upon Auditor support of the Elect in general, and the alms-service in particular.[35] The word's connotations must be ferreted out, since etymologically it means simply "involving the soul *(rw'n).*"[36] W. B. Henning has identified the term with the institution of funds dedicated for the performance of religious rituals *pād ruvān*, "for the soul" of the donor or someone named by the donor, in Sasanian inscriptions and Zoroastrian literature,[37] since studied in detail by Mary Boyce.[38] According to Chr. Bartholomae, one could set aside donations for the maintenance of a perpetual fire, or "on account of the soul" *(ruvān rāδ)* for the recitation of litanies *(yazišn)* for the "Seelenheil" of the living or the "Seelengedachtnis" of the dead.[39] Several Manichaean texts employ the same terminology with respect to the alms-service.[40]

In the Parthian ecclesiastical letter M 5815, a Manichaean leader urges his readers to "strive as much as you are able with the Auditors, so that when I send brethren they may find reception *(p'dgr'w).*"[41] "Reception" here would include all of the hospitality necessary for itinerant missionaries bound by their discipline not to procure for themselves. So, in the Middle Persian historical account preserved in M 2, Mani sends off the first mission to Khurasan with the words, "Blessed be this religion; may it be advanced in greatness through teachers, Auditors, and 'soul-work' *(rw'ng'n).*"[42] In the Sogdian version of this narrative, Mani predicts to Mar Ammo that "many Auditors will be as workers and helpers in these holy places, and many gifts *(δb'r)* and 'soul-work' *(rw'nk'n)* from these places will be purified."[43]

The alms constituted a "daily gift" *(ptmydy db'r)*, according to a fragment of the Sogdian version of the *Xuāstuānīft*, which, the Auditor adds, "it was my duty to offer to the religious chief *(dyns'r)*."[44] The eleventh section of the more complete Turkic *Xuāstuānīft* phrases the rule in slightly different terms:

> And there is a rule that one should offer the seven kinds of alms *(pušii)* to the pure religion. And if the five gods and the angels who gather their light (and) the gods Xroštag and Padvaxtag were to bring to us the light of the five gods which goes to God and is liberated, (then) there is a rule that we should form and fashion superior things (of this light) and bring them into the religion.[45]

The reference to the "seven kinds of alms" *(yiti türlüg pušii)* could imply the seven days of the week, and hence a daily contribution.[46] The food alms appear here in their identity as fragments of the Primordial Man's five children, the elements embedded in the world. In the natural course of things, some of these fragments pass into the hands of the Auditors in the form of food; in such cases, the Auditors are obligated to offer some of the food to the Elect.

The edict of Bögü Khan foundational for Manichaeism as the Uygur state religion, recorded in TM 276, prominently features "soul-work," undoubtedly the Turkic translation of *rw'ng'n(k'r)*; it also possesses an apparent reference to the "soul-meal," which was the primary focus of such work.

> And for the leaders and the common people he proclaimed a good decree thus: ". . . I am come and have sat myself upon my throne and commanded you: if the Elect [. . .] to you, and if they urge you *(lit:* cause you to hurry) to the soul-meal *(özüt aš)*, and if they urge and exhort to [. . .], walk according to their words and advice, and with a loving disposition honor, respect and serve [. . .]."[47]

We note that the Auditors are urged *to* the meal, not to partake of it.[48] The text proceeds to report,

> Since then they have striven uninterruptedly for the soul-work *(özütlüg iš)* and good deeds. And the blessed, fortunate Khan constantly admonishes that entire people to do good works, and urges them on and makes them exert themselves. And the divine Khan further [. . .] so (and) established the doc-

trine and law. And he placed one man as head of each ten men and made him the "Rouser" *(tavratgučï)* for good works and soul-work *(özüt[lüg] iš)*.[49]

Turkic sources contain a profusion of commands and encouragement to the Auditors regarding the alms-service. "One should present the good, pure Elect with pure nourishment and pure drink," one passage enjoins straightforwardly.[50]

Hymns and prayers rouse the Auditors to their duty of supporting the Elect, whipping up fervor for the task at hand like a company pep-talk or a political rally: "Let us give pure alms *(arïg buši berälim)*, O light soul! Let us worship with pure alms *(arïg bušin tapïnalïm)*, O light soul!"[51] The Chinese *Hymnscroll* likewise enjoins Auditors to "give alms *(pu-shih)*, practice fasting, read and study industriously."[52] The Chinese translator of these originally Middle Iranian hymns sometimes refers to the offerings as *kung*, the standard Chinese rendition of Buddhist Sanskrit *dāna* for donations to Buddhist monks.[53] A prayer designated for weekly recital invokes blessings upon "all the faithful, alms-presenting men and women, who have entered into a covenant with this correct religion, entrusting themselves to the gate of liberation of the Venerable One of Light."[54] In the concluding fragment of the "Parable of Brama the Astrologer," the voice of a deceased Auditor speaks of "those alms which I gave . . . the good deeds which I accomplished."[55] Jesus is cited as an authority who "gave the name 'good-minded' to faithful people who give alms and who seek out their souls."[56] The same text goes on to advise: "Give alms to the extremely distressed Elect. . . . And believe the following single-mindedly: that the reward of your one piece of bread and your one cup of water is immediate and not delayed at all."[57]

The Auditors set aside food for the alms-service during their own weekly fast, during which they refrained not only from food, but also from sex and violence.[58] The material support of the "soul-work" is the topic of a Middle Persian passage: "In the Mesenian Epistle concerning two bodies, (Mani) says: We and you (pl.) remember our own place and strive to go (there). This wisdom which you received with one mind truly endures. With one year's clothes *('yw s'rg pymwcn)* and the meal and banquet of one day *(nhwyn 'wd swr 'yg 'yw rwcg)* [. . .]."[59] The passage, despite its fragmentariness, refers to the yearly clothing and daily food allowances of the Elect. The Auditors also were to cultivate a positive attitude toward the Elect who were to be the recipients of their alms: "(They) shall refer to [the Elect as] 'their souls are good' (*özütın edgü*). And they shall serve pure food and pure drink to the good-deeded, pure Elect. And they shall not speak with the tongue that (the Elect) have diseases, or lies, or sins, or transgressions."[60] If one observed and believed that an Elect had these defects, one could not give that Elect alms with a clear conscience; and to speak the idea to others would be to promote an environment in which the Elect would literally starve to death, since no one would provide him or her with offerings.

The *Xuāstuānīft* confession envisions an obstruction of the Living Self, the "light of the five gods," on its way to liberation as the gravest of sins, as the eleventh section states:

> If we have been unable to give fully the seven kinds of alms to the religion, either because of poverty, or because we are too miserly to give alms, if we have bound to house and household goods the light of the five gods, which goes to God and is liberated, if we have given (this light) to evil-deeded persons or to evil beings or creatures, if we have poured out or scattered (this light), if we have sent the light of God to an evil place, (then), Majesty, now we beg to be freed from sin. Release my sins![61]

The text does not inform us of what was considered the "full extent" one should offer as alms, but does suggest that poverty did not abrogate one's responsibility.[62] The Manichaean authorities had a keen and understandable interest in maintaining a monopoly on the alms-exchange, as in T II D 178.II,[63] where we read: "False preachers who are errant and confused . . . also hold the name Elect and take alms (*buši*) through deception and fraud. They themselves will go to hell and take the donor along with them."[64] Likewise, the seventh section of the *Xuāstuānīft* warns against trusting false religious authorities, with the result that "we kept fast (*bačag*) erroneously . . . worshiped (*yüküntümüz*) erroneously . . . gave alms (*pušii*) erroneously." Even with good intentions, the text makes clear, such behavior is sinful and requires forgiveness, showing the mechanical character of this system.

The alms-service is not an exercise in generosity, it is a technical operation that can go awry if attempted with the wrong instruments. The neglect or violation of the alms-service appears prominently in discussions of wrongdoing. The Sogdian text M 549 refers to those who "did much harm and injury

to the 'soul-service' *(rw'nsp'syy)*."[65] A Middle Persian catalog partially preserved in M 177, recto, includes among a list of bad occurrences, "eighth:
'soul-work' is not purified *(rw'ng'n ny p'cyhyd)*."

The verso of M 177, on the other hand, contains an example of the correct observance of alms-service, providing crucial details about the formalities
of the donation rite. In this Parthian tale, which is known in several versions
among Iranian Manichaean literature, a woman named Khēbrā grieves over
the premature death of her son Dārawpūhr, and is anxious to know the fate of
his soul.

> And in those days the Beneficent One (Mani) came there. And they per-
> formed "soul-work" before him *(rw'ng'n prw'n hw qyrd)*. And at the food hour
> *('h'r jm'n)* the Beneficent One prayed for that youth in the benediction *(pd
> 'frywn)*. Then he prostrated *(nm'c bwrd)* himself three times. And the "chil-
> dren" (i.e., disciples) asked about it: "Explain to us why you prostrated." And
> he said: "I prostrated to my own father and lord Jesus so that my desire which
> I sought from him and also that prayer which you prayed might be accepted.
> And behold Dāraw's soul *(gy'n)* was led by angels and placed before me (and)
> stood arrayed in the customary apparel of kings." And when Ābōrsām and
> Khēbrā Āōsēg heard, they went. And making obeisance *(pd qft 'hynd)* to the
> Beneficent One, they said, "We [believe] in you lord."

Taking this episode as exemplary of alms-service practice, we can extrapolate
several details. The Auditors "perform soul-work" before the Elect (here, Mani
himself), that is, they place their offerings in his or her presence. But then the
Auditors depart, *prior* to the "food hour"; they are not present at the time the
Elect makes his or her prayer.[66]

Although the above account shows a woman personally making an offering to Mani, other sources point to a strict segregation of men from women in
the alms-service. In a polemical reminiscence, Lu Yu reports the following:

> There are the sons of educated families among their ranks and they will say,
> "Today I am attending the vegetarian gatherings of the Religion of Light." I
> have chided them by saying, "These are demon(-worshipers); why should
> (someone of your standing) keep such company?" They replied, "This is not
> the case. The demon(-worshipers) do not segregate men and women but the

followers of the Religion of Light 'do not permit men and women to come into contact with each other.'[67] If a (male) follower of the Religion of Light is presented with food prepared by a woman, he will not eat it."[68]

The scant remains of the Manichaean art tradition seem to support the existence of such a rule.

Turkic and Chinese sources also provide evidence for the rite of alms donation itself. In the fifth section of the Chinese *Compendium*, one of the officers of the *mānīstān* appears under the Chinese transliteration of the Iranian *rw'ng'n 'sp'sg*, or "soul-work deacon." The Chinese translator glosses this rather blandly as "officer of the month," but then adds the comment that "he is especially occupied with offerings *(kung)* and alms *(shih),*" apparently assigned to manage the delivery of donations. Describing the ideal life of the Elect, the author states, "with perfect dignity, they wait for alms *(shih)*; if no one prepares alms for them, they may solicit them." The following Turkic injunction alludes to a chant of invitation to be uttered by the Auditors in this setting:

> Let us worship the pure, upright Elect, and let us pray. Let us not harm them through heart or mind. But let us choose from among them. Let us give them alms, as much as we can carry. . . . Do not let yourself be deceived by the demon of greed. Let us give them alms and goods. Let us pray *'r' nwydm'* to the white-robed Elect.[69]

The editor of the Chinese *Hymnscroll* explicitly designates two versions of a hymn as "for the collection of offerings *(shou shih-tan),*"[70] although the contents themselves do not provide any information about the corresponding ritual action.

Werner Sundermann has recently brought to light another clue to the rite of alms-offering, in the form of a caption accompanying meal hymns in the Middle Persian fragment M 546. The caption informs us, "These (are) hymns of the gifts for the 'soul-work' *(rw'ng'n)*; when (the Auditors) bring them before the chiefs, (the 'chiefs') sing (them) in a beautiful tune."[71] This caption amounts to, in Sundermann's apt characterization, "liturgical stage directory" for the ceremonial procession of donors with their offerings. Its presence on the verso of this fragment draws attention to the formal invocation on the recto side of the same book leaf, where the speaker refers to "the noble gift, full of health," and continues: "Receive it, O Lord, and be happy! Bless them and forgive the sin forever!" Sundermann convincingly identifies these phrases as those the donors direct to the Elect at the moment of bestowing the alms. The text of a hymn follows, which Sundermann believes to be sung by the Auditors. The hymn text that appears after the caption on the verso would be a kind of response by the Elect, as the caption itself implies. With this material, we are able to see that the alms donation rite "was performed in a ceremonial, solemn way."[72]

There is good reason to think that the hymn in stanzas 347–55 of the Chinese *Hymnscroll*, designated "for the conclusion of the daily prayer," corresponds to the last daily Auditor prayer session, performed in the evening, just before the Elects' ritual meal. The first section reads as a benediction over the community.[73] The Chinese editor adds instructions for performance:

> The foregoing should be performed three times, with three obeisances. When those standing have completed the recitation, they conclude with the foregoing stanza. Then the gathered assembly says in unison (the verse) "We who are of superior marks."[74]

The stanza indicated then follows:

> *We who are of superior marks, comprehending the Venerable of Light*
> *Can therefore believe in and accept the clear discourse*
> *Since the Great Saint is the embodiment of good deeds*
> *So may it please him to bestow mercy and make all people joyful.*[75]

The editor then instructs:

> After the "We who are of superior marks" is finished, the assembly is to be silent. The Venerable then recites the *Afuli*-stanza. Next he says the prayer, "The wondrous bodies of radiant light."[76]

Afuli probably represents a transliteration of *āfrīn*, the chanted benedictions of Iranian Manichaeism. The prayer indicated is given as follows:

> *May the wondrous bodies of radiant light quickly be liberated*
> *May those who have acted as donors have their sins dissolved*

All of the Elect and Auditors
Together have glorified their thoughts with this merit
The correct religion will be propagated without hindrance
Eternally, eternally we hope it will be so![77]

We see in this elaborated liturgy, with its instructions and ordered set-pieces, the formalized setting of the prelude to the ritual meal in its distinctively Chinese form.

The materials discovered at Turfan include a small number of paintings from Manichaean books. Three of these miniatures contain features connected with the Manichaean alms-service: MIK III 4974, M 559, and M 6290. These pieces of art have been published and described recently by Zsuzsanna Gulácsi, and my description and characterization of their composition has been developed in consultation with her.[78]

The miniature of MIK III 4974 is part of a highly ornate page featuring elaborate border decoration on three sides, and a consequently compressed text of eleven lines in two columns (see Plate 1). On the viewer's left, two white-robed Elect kneel on a common carpet. Two Auditors composed on a much smaller scale kneel, facing the Elect on a common carpet on the viewer's right. The clothing of the Auditors identifies them as male; although the facial features of the two Elect are no longer discernible, the visibility of their locks of hair conforms to the standard depiction of males. The scene shows, therefore, a moment (ideal or real) of contact between male Elect and male Auditors.

A tripodal bowl containing food appears on the left side of the painting, closest to the viewer. It is positioned exactly at the line between the outer and inner left vertical quarters of the painting, hence in front of and between the two Elect. The Auditors occupy the space directly to the right of the bowl facing toward it. The two Auditors and one of the Elect clasp their hands within the sleeves of their garments. The inner Electus, however, holds out one hand at the exact horizontal midline of the painting, crossing over into the right inner quarter, directly over the head of the inner Auditor. He holds this hand in a distinctive gesture, or *mudra*, formed by the joining of the thumb and forefinger with the palm turned upwards.

In the upper-right corner of the miniature, a very large hand reaches down from outside the field. It is placed in the topmost horizontal quarter, positioned exactly at the line between the outer and inner right vertical quarters of the painting, hence above and between the two Auditors; this positioning shows a calculation mirroring that of the bowl of offerings. This hand is formed into the exact same *mudra* as that of the Electus, but with the palm turned downward. By means of its joined thumb and forefinger, it holds the top of an object or design. The latter consists of a circle with a central point, resembling a solar disc. It possesses a base or appendage beneath it, drawn in the form of a crescent moon, the horns of which project downwards, in the waning phase. Some marks can be seen where elements surrounding this object once appeared. But the painted surface has been rubbed away, and nothing definite can be said about them.[79]

This miniature, by the economy of its representation and the symmetry of its placement, communicates a great deal of information. The hierarchical scaling of the Auditors (smallest), Elect (larger), and hand (largest) distinguishes the relative sacrality of the figures; the same hierarchy is reflected in the relative positioning of the Auditors (bottom), Elect (middle), and hand (top). The carpets of the two Manichaean orders appear to touch at one corner, while the offering bowl and the divine hand are carefully isolated in their respective corners. The latter two form one conjunction of significance due to their similar treatment; the divine hand and that of the Electus form another conjunction due to their shared mirror-image *mudra*. The divine hand seems to pluck the object from the hand of the Electus; at the same time, the hand of the Electus is positioned directly above the head of the inner Auditor, and between that Auditor and the object being taken up to heaven.[80] Gulácsi has identified these correlations as a symbolic communication of the "work of the religion," that is, the transmission of the divine substance from the food offered by the Auditors, through the Elect and the "light ships" of the moon and sun, to heaven.[81]

M 559 preserves part of another alms-offering scene (see Plate 2A). On the right kneels a Manichaean Electa, with head characteristically covered so that no hair shows. She clasps what appears to be a book to her breast. Since the fragment is torn along this figure's right side, the miniature possibly contained originally the figure of a second Electa. On the left, two female Auditors kneel facing the Electa, each bearing a golden fluted bowl filled with flatbread. Just as in MIK III 4974, therefore, this painting depicts an encounter between Elect and Auditors, in this case female to female, as in the prior case male to male. Between the Auditrices and the Electa stands a small portable table, bearing an item that Jorinde Ebert identifies as "a kind of chest or a thick book."[82] In contrast to the miniature of MIK III 4974, in which the Elect appear much larger than the donors, M 559 depicts the donors somewhat larger than the Electa.

An uncolored outline sketch preserved in M 6290 offers us a third glimpse into the alms-service (see Plate 2B). In this instance, we see ten figures (apparently all male) assembled in two rows, representing many different statuses and roles from the Manichaean community within the Uygur kingdom. At least two individuals, at what is arguably the center of the original (now highly fragmentary) composition, are dressed as Elect. Most of the other individuals visible on the fragment appear to be Auditors. Two of these Auditors, standing directly behind the two Elect, carry platters. The most completely preserved platter holds the typical Manichaean *nan* bread, with twisted crescent edging (not enough of the second platter is preserved to determine what it contained). We would appear to be observing either the alms-service, or the serving of the food within the meal ritual itself.[83]

At a bare minimum, one can say that the first two, and perhaps all three, miniatures depict the fundamental act of the alms-service. Gender segregation appears to be the rule. The portable table in M 559 possibly was to receive the offerings carried by the donors. The divine presence in MIK III 4974 indicates the communication between the heavenly and mundane worlds accomplished by means of the offerings. By depicting Auditors, Elect, food, and heavenly hand, the artist has placed within the scene the principle participants in the rite, and dramatized by careful arrangement the mutual associations and exchanges that bind them all together. The act of alms-service was, therefore, important enough in the life of the Manichaean community to be depicted often, and so be attested three times in the surviving art fragments, more than any other event within the community.[84]

Summation

When Bögü Khan encourages Auditor attendance at the meal, he reinforces the system of support intrinsic to the Manichaean church organization. This sacred economy is attested in both normative and polemical sources throughout the Manichaean world. The Auditors procure the vegetarian elements of the meal, bring them to the local meeting place, and place them at the disposal of the Elect. This daily project is the "soul-work" (Iranian *rw'ng'n*; Turkic *özütlüg iš*) of the Manichaean Auditor. In Greek and Coptic sources, alms-offering forms a triad with fasting and prayer as the pillars of Auditor practice.[85] Both the Turkic *Monastery Scroll* and the Chinese *Compendium* show an institutionalization of this supply system with a designated person in charge of coordinating the offerings and ensuring a daily supply.[86]

Although some sources suggest that Auditors delivered foods to the ritual locale at their convenience throughout the day, and did not remain for the ceremony (e.g., M 177), the majority of evidence points to the presence of Auditors just before the meal itself, at the time corresponding to their last obligatory prayer period of the day. As we have seen, Bögü Khan urges their attendance; Chinese polemical accounts also depict them going to the meal. Both Latin and Iranian sources refer to benedictions made by the Elect upon the Auditors when the latter present the food. In M 580 the Auditors are advised to "Seek assembly and absolution from the Elect daily [that] they may bestow forgiveness upon you."[87] The Turfan miniature MIK III 4974 shows such a direct face-to-face offering, with the bowl of alms prominently placed between two Elect and two Auditors. In the late, established Manichaean monasticism of Central Asia attested by the *Monastery Scroll*, most alms were supplied by the monastery's agricultural holdings. The personal mediation of alms was retained, however, in the case of certain officials, who, we are told, were to receive food from the monastery stores to offer to the Elect.[88]

By the terms employed and the structures emplaced, the Manichaeans appear to have drawn on pre-existing systems of sacred beneficences in the respective regions of their dissemination. The donatives of Greek temple service (*eusebeia*), the liturgical sponsorships of Zoroastrian practice (*rw'ng'n*), and the alms of Buddhist mendicancy (*kung*) are each assimilated by the Manichaeans arriving in the regions of their respective cultural dominance. This adaptive program is implicit in Mani's critical comparison of these antecedent institutions to his own in *Kephalaion 87*. Faustus voices the same sentiment in declaring himself, and other Elect like him, to be the Manichaean alternative to the "altars, shrines, images, sacrifices, and incense" of the pagans.[89] In the Manichaean ritual system, the Elect are "the rational temple of God," their well-trained psychic apparatus "the true altar," and their post-meal hymns and prayers "the true way . . . of offering sacrifices."[90]

THE RITUAL MEAL OF THE ELECT

Like the fossilized impression of some ancient sea creature left in the primordial mud now turned to stone, the Manichaean ritual meal is attested by everything surrounding it, pressing upon it, leading to it. We can discern its external contours, but for its internal arrangement we find little more than a void, where rich detail must once have flourished. The Central Manichaean tradition is particularly frustrating in its silence on this subject. Nevertheless, the remarkable consistency of features exhibited in the Western and Eastern sources on the meal provides a kind of indirect testimony to what is missing from our direct view.

The Central Manichaean Tradition

Ephrem Syrus identifies the Manichaean Elect, the *zaddiqa* and *zaddiqatha*, specifically as those who refine the divine light by means of their digestion.[91] This is their primary mission as Manichaean practitioners, an obligation Ephrem dismisses as impossible:

> They also actually proclaim a refining and cleansing of all rivers and sources and fountains, when between them all they cannot refine the water of a single spring! And so look at everything, at fruits and produce and crops and vegetables and fishes and birds—how many can eat of all these that are in all quarters, both by sea and land?[92]

Rather than detail the ritual meal, however, Ephrem offers only oblique references to it. Although the Elect keep a very strict regimen to qualify for their digestive task, "not even willing to break bread lest they pain the light which is mixed with it,"[93] nevertheless "with their teeth they cause it to suffer much more when they eat it, and with their bellies when they confine it there."[94] Ephrem ridicules the gross materialism of such notions, and points to medical concerns that are necessarily entailed in such an odd notion of salvation, such as "cold phlegm, which is over the food—the great enemy of the school of Mani, for it wishes by its coldness to restrain the refining, lest it should be released, and go forth thence."[95]

Ephrem also makes several references to hymns and prayers in connection with the refining of light entailed in the meal. According to the

Manichaeans, the divine elements trapped in the world are "refined by prayer,"[96] for at the end of the metabolic process, they maintain, "this refining . . . goes out of the mouth."[97] Ephrem argues that "there is no evidence that it is refined by prayer as they say,"[98] but his opponents, real or imagined, reply that "the mouth is not aware of the light because it has been rarified and refined."[99] The content of this odd debate makes it clear that eating and praying in general are not at issue, but specifically the process of the ritual meal with its accompanying hymns and prayers.

Islamic writers mention the alms-service of the Auditors, but are strangely silent about the ritual meal itself. Concerning the Elect receiving alms, al-Biruni says that Mani "forbade them to acquire any property except food for one day and dress for one year."[100] 'Abd al-Jabbar reports similarly in the *al-Mugni fi abwab al-tawhid wa-l-'adl*: "The adepts and the chiefs of the sect have instituted obligations: for example not to acquire clothes for more than a year, to procure nourishment from day to day, as well as other things which they consider as pious works."[101]

Yet al-Biruni indirectly provides crucial information about the timing of the meal and its placement in the daily ritual routine of the Elect. In his *'Ifrādu l-maqāli fī 'amri z-zilāl*, al-Biruni outlines the schedule of prayers followed by the Elect and Auditors.[102] Since we know from other sources that the meal was conducted after sundown, we note with interest that al-Biruni places an Elect prayer of twenty-five prostrations *(rak'āt)* at this time, with a corresponding prayer incumbent on the Auditors. Prayer times for both Elect and Auditors are typically spaced apart by several hours, but in the case of the Elect evening prayer it is followed one half-hour later by another prayer of twenty-five prostrations. Since the next Elect prayer session is three hours later, these closely sequenced prayers must be those of the ritual meal, and presumably mark its beginning and its conclusion.[103] A similar framing of a meal by benedictory prayers is observed in Zoroastrianism to this day.[104]

The Western Manichaean Tradition

In Mani's confrontation with the Elchasaites as portrayed in the *Cologne Mani Codex*, an incipient form of the special food practices of Manichaeism plays a prominent role. In addition to questioning his expectation of pious donations *(eusebeiai)*, his opponents complain:

[He] wishes to go to the gentiles and eat [Greek] bread, for we [have heard him saying], "It is necessary to partake of [Greek] bread." Likewise, he says it follows to partake of drink, bread, vegetables, and fruit (which) our fathers and teachers enjoined (us) not to eat.[105]

They appeal to Mani's father, Pattikios, to correct his son:

Your son has turned aside from our law and wishes to go to the world. Wheat bread and fruit and vegetables [which] we [exclude] and do [not] eat, [all] these things he does not follow [and] says it is necessary [to overturn] these things. [He] makes of no avail [the washing] in the way it is practiced [by us]. And he wishes to eat [Greek] bread.[106]

But Mani, while admitting the charges, defends his position as sanctioned by the authority of Jesus.

In no way would I [destroy the] commandments of the Savior. But if you [reproach] me [on account of wheat] bread, because I have said, "It is necessary to eat of it," this the Savior has done; as it is written, that when he had blessed and shared with his disciples, "over bread he said a blessing and gave (it) to them." Was not that bread from wheat? It points out that he reclined to eat with tax collectors and idolaters. Likewise, he also reclined to eat in the house of Martha and Mary on the occasion when Martha said to him: "[Lord], do you not care for [me] so as to tell my [sister to] help [me]?," the Savior said [to] her: "Mary has chosen the [good] portion and it will not be taken away from her." Consider, moreover, how even the disciples of the Savior ate bread from women and idolaters and did not separate bread from bread, nor vegetable from vegetable; nor did they eat while laboring in the toil and tilling of the land, as you do today. Likewise, when the savior sent his disciples out to preach in [each] place, [neither] mill nor [oven] did [they] carry [with] them, but [made haste], taking one [garment . . .].[107]

This detailed argument, ensconced in the centerpiece of the *Cologne Mani Codex* (the break with the Elchasaites, on pages 80–106), provides both a biblical etiology and a foundation in Mani's own hagiography for the Manichaean ritual meal and the alms-service on which it depends.[108]

It is difficult to decide where the alms-service rite ends and the ritual meal begins; they were, essentially, two phases of the same ceremony. The ritual meal proper begins only after the formal delivery of the alms, and the dismissal of the Auditors. Augustine makes it clear that as a Manichaean Auditor he never observed the meal directly. In reply to the Manichaean Fortunatus, he says:

> But you know that I was not one of your Elect, but an Auditor. Hence—since you have asked—while I was present at your prayers . . . , what you who are Elect do among yourselves, I have no means of knowing. For I have often heard from you that you receive the eucharist; but the time of receiving was concealed from me.[109]

The "eucharist" to which Augustine refers undoubtedly represents the daily ritual meal of the Elect, and none of his comments about the meal are given in terms of direct observation.[110]

As Augustine suggests, some sort of intercessory prayers on the part of the Elect were involved in the meal, but it is difficult to distinguish prayers said in the presence of the Auditors from those said privately over the meal. This difficulty impacts upon our interpretation of the Apology to the Bread, as well as to other prayer texts. In a narrative of Mani's imprisonment and death contained in the Coptic *Homilies* collection, Mani himself, in an act that doubtless was paradigmatic for the community, requests bread and salt and prays over them.[111] In *Kephalaion 115* Mani affirms the performance of an "entreaty" *(tōbh)* during the rite by the Elect in response to an individual who makes "the alms-offering and the memorial" on behalf of a deceased person. "The holy ones entreat for him a sin-*tōbh* in the *tōbh* and the memorial which they make for him in the holy church."[112] The success of this entreaty, Mani informs the Auditor to whom he is speaking, depends upon its association with "the alms-offering that you give and the cup of water [that you offer]."[113] Augustine understands the prayers conducted in connection with the meal to involve the absolution of the donor's sins. He speaks of the "one wound your Auditor has been guilty of inflicting in pulling them, of which you will no doubt consent to absolve him."[114] Such an act of absolution occurs already when the Auditors make their offering,[115] however, and the Elect may have turned their meditations to other concerns during and after the meal itself.

In fact, Augustine refers to prayers and psalms acting upon the food which the Elect have eaten, and so presumably as ritual acts during or after the

meal.[116] In *Kephalaion 85* Mani gives food for thought in speaking of the unavoidable pain inflicted upon food, even in the ritual meal by the chewing of
the Elect. Consequently, it is essential that the latter approach this task in the
correct physical and psychological condition, perhaps meditating on the seriousness of the rite: "Thus (the alms) exist in great distress, and you should be
mindful to eat it. Do not eat it in wantonness nor dissipation nor revelry nor
gluttony. Rather, eat it in great hunger, and drink it in great thirst, and take
care of your body with it."[117]

The core of the meal is, of course, simply eating, as the Elect undertake
to purify a food offering "by taking it into your throat and stomach."[118] As far as
Augustine is concerned, the rest of the ritual takes place in the "private labo-
ratory" *(praelio confractum)* of the Elect's digestion, "where your God may be
healed of his wound."[119] He notes that "some of your sect make a point of eating raw vegetables of all kinds."[120] Furthermore, he says, "you look upon it as
a sin for anyone but the Elect to consume the food brought to the table for
that so-called purification of yours."[121] For this reason, "those under your discipline" must consume all of the remains of the meal so that nothing goes to
waste.[122]

In the *Acts of Archelaus* the apostate Turbo provides what he claims to be
details of the conclusion of the meal. He quotes Mani's instructions as follows:
"When you cease eating, pray and put upon your head an olive, exorcized by
many names for the reinforcement of this faith."[123] If this passage merits any
confidence, one should probably emend "olive" to "olive oil."

Whereas Eastern Manichaean sources include several examples of clearly
identifiable meal hymns, the Western material so far provides little in the
same genre. Perhaps the still-unedited first half of the Coptic *Psalm-Book* will
yield such hymns. In the second half, edited by C.R.C. Allberry, only one
hymn would seem to belong to the meal setting: in one of the "Psalms of the
Wanderers" *(psalmoi sarakōtōn)*, the singer addresses the Living Self (by a
number of epithets), describes the cosmos as prepared to "take thee to the
Light," invokes the Mind of Light and Jesus to "wear me until I purify the
[body(?)] of the First Man," and concludes with the declaration, "Glory to this
alms-offering *(ti.mntnae)* and to them that purify it and to them that save it,
the Catechumens of the faith."[124]

The Eastern Manichaean Tradition

Eastern sources provide the bulk of our information on the ritual meal, fortunately correlating to a large degree with the less complete material from the
West. The Chinese treatise known as *Ts'an-ching*, which is based upon a
Parthian original (the *Sermon on the Light Nous*), refers a number of times to
the proper preparation of the Elect for the ritual meal. The Elect display the
successful cultivation of their bodies as vehicles for the light by, among other
things, the following:

> They are not avaricious. In the place where they are staying, if they receive
> alms, they do not make private use of them, but remit them to the great as-
> sembly. . . . The ordinances of the saints regarding vestment, that one changes
> it a single time per year, and nourishment, that one eats a single time per day,
> they observe with joy. . . . Their uniform heart is in harmony; because of this
> harmony the alms which they receive they make into a meritorious work for
> the use of all. They receive constantly that which the Auditors, with respect,
> may give them as offerings, and praise them with love.[125]

The Chinese *Compendium* states concerning the Elect that "they wait for
alms *(shih)* with perfect dignity."[126] The one daily meal of the Elect appears as
a commonplace of outsider accounts of the Manichaeans. A member of the
Chinese intelligentsia, Chang Hsi-sheng, who was himself an adherent of a
Taoicized Manichaeism (ca. 1264 C.E.), informs a friend that "they allow those
who practice it one meal a day, and on fast days they have to remain indoors."[127] Ch'en Kao, writing in 1351 C.E., states that "(The Manichaeans) adhere to very strict rules of discipline and practice vegetarianism zealously.
They eat one meal a day and at night they pray, chant and perform other rites
of worship seven times."[128] The *Hsin T'ang-shu* reports, "The laws of these
(Manichaeans) prescribe that they should eat only in the evening, drink water,
eat strong vegetables, and abstain from milk and butter."[129]

The story of Khēbrā's "soul-work" intercession with Mani, from M 177
verso, has been discussed above for the light it sheds on the alms-service. But
it also is valuable for its outline of the Manichaean ritual meal.

> And at the food hour *('h'r jm'n)* the Beneficent One prayed *(pdwh'd)* for that
> youth in the benediction *(pd 'frywn)*. Then he prostrated *(nm'c bwrd)* himself

three times. And the "children" (i.e., disciples) asked about it: "Explain to us why you prostrated." And he said: "I prostrated to my own father and lord Jesus so that my desire which I sought from him and also that prayer which you prayed might be accepted."

Dārawpūhr's parents return when they hear that Mani has had a vision, and prostrate themselves *(pd qft 'hynd)* before him; but we cannot be sure this is intended as a part of the ceremony. The Auditors depart prior to the "food hour"; they are not present at the time Mani makes his prayer or eats the food. Mani makes that prayer in the context of an *āfrīn*, a term that in Zoroastrian practice denotes a formalized period of religious oration associated with a food offering. In M 177 we see testimony that personal prayers could be incorporated into the proceedings. Mani's prostrations are noted as out of the ordinary in this story, but his justification for them is of such a kind as to imply a mandate for future imitation. If the supreme religious authority says that he prostrates himself so that his prayers might be accepted, that constitutes a strong impetus to do likewise.

The Turkic *Monastery Scroll* (Zong 8782 T, 82) gives some details about procedures at the ritual meal, as well as lists of provisions for it.[130] The latter include wheat, sesame seed, beans and millet, melons, and onions.[131] The scroll represents a late (ca. tenth century), state-directed consolidation of two *mānīstāns* in Turfan, and instructs as follows:

> The food and provisions of the Elect of the two communities shall not be unequal. One month, one preacher *(xrōxōn)* and one works-supervisor *(iš ayguči)* shall stand and take heed (of affairs), and shall have the food and provisions made perfectly. And in the other month, the other preacher and the other works-supervisor shall stand and take heed, and shall have the food and provisions made perfectly. . . . When the Elect sit down to their table *(xuan)*, the two preachers shall be standing, and shall bring the food and drink in an orderly way to the *iwrkani zmastik.*[132] After that, they shall sit down to their table.[133]

Lay-attendants appear to have participated in the meal in some capacity. The text distinguishes between "deacons" *(espasi)* and "servants" *(oglan)*.

> All the intermediary male deacons *(espasi)* henceforth shall serve the Elect who under no circumstances are to have servants *(oglan)*. Moreover, all of the

intermediary servants (oglan) shall be assigned to the iwrkani zmastik, and shall ensure that (the Elect) are served perfectly at their meal.[134]

The meal itself is framed by an activity called the nwyδm', an Iranian loan-word signifying a ritual "invitation."[135]

> When male or female Elect eat at the mānīstān, and when they go to the In-vitation, (the servants) shall bring two pitchers of ice blocks for each and make ice water,[136] and then bring everything to the iwrkani zmastik for the Elect. When the sačrangu (?) Elect go to the Invitation, they shall have the "poured flour" collected (and kept) separately.

When the ritual meal appears as a component in day-long liturgical plans, the procedures are assumed, and the focus is rather on the hymns selected to ac-company the meal on the particular day. The Sogdian text M 114, outlining a day dedicated to a "Body-Soul Rite" (tn gy'n pdk'), gives the following instructions:

> After that, the Mid-day Prayer (nymydcyk 'fryn) should be made, (namely) an Apostle-hymn with (the incipit) "Come hither, happiness." After that occurs the Body-Soul Rite; that is, a sermon about body-soul should first be deliv-ered. When the day draws to a close, have a parable presented, (namely) "The Prince and the Cindāty's son." After that, one should sing the "Body-Soul" (hymn-cycle). Then have a little exegesis follow. When you have ended this arrangement, sit at table (xw'n) [. . .]. Recite the After-Meal Prayer (pš'x'rycyk 'frywn). It consists of the following three hymns: "O light soul ('rw'n), great light self (gryw')"—twice; "Mar Mani, forgive my sins"; (and) "You, Mar Mani, liberate my soul."[137]

The day is structured by two standard caesuras, namely the Mid-day and After-meal prayers or benedictions (āfrīn). These regular daily prayers, and the ritual meal associated with the second of them, stand independently of the Body-Soul Rite per se, which occurs in the afternoon between these two termini. The term "table" (xw'n) appears throughout Iranian sources, as among Western sources, as a name both of a furnishing used in the rite and of the rite itself.[138]

A similar liturgical plan within which the ritual meal stands appears in M 5779, which gives instructions in Sogdian interspersed with the incipits of Persian and Parthian hymns:[139]

recto (?): ". . . from paradise, Mani, the Lord, wants to go. When you go, Lord, (then) save us from birth-death!" "You go, Mani; save me, commander Maitreya!" Twice. *And later:* "You we call, you noble commander with the beautiful name, Mar Mani." "You, Bringer of Light, we praise loudly." *And when the name of the souls is called, finish the hymn (and) stop a little. And then take [. . .] from the Gospel and pay homage to the Apostle and to the Righteous Ones (i.e., the Elect). And the confession (xw'stw'nft) begins. And when it has come to an end,*

{ }

verso (?): *the three hymns (to be sung) are the following:* "Mar Mani, Noble Glory, Beautiful Sight. You, Father, I implore: Forgive my sins!" "Beneficent Mar Mani, O God, answer us!" Twice. "O Mani, vivifier with the noble name, save me, save, forgive my sins!" *And when the words of the Seal Letter have been said, then, facing the Apostle, sing this hymn:* "My Light Father, Mar Mani, ascended to paradise." *And after the Meal (pš'h'ryy) the three hymns (to be sung) are the following:* "Commander with the Beautiful Name, God, Mar Mani. Oh Lord, you go away, lead also me up to paradise." "A messenger came . . ."[140]

The exclusive focus on Mani, and the many allusions to his ascent in these activities point toward the annual Bema ceremony as the occasion of their performance. The after-meal benediction, like that in M 114, consists of three hymns chosen for their suitability to the occasion. The author does not bother to describe or explain the meal.

The hymns suggested for the after-meal benediction (*pš'x'rycyk/pš'h'ryy 'frywn*) by M 114 and M 5779 do not match any of the surviving hymn fragments from Turfan. Among hymns that do survive, some are designated for use at the meal by headlines or captions; unfortunately, these mostly remain unpublished. The Sogdian book-leaf M 134.I, for example, several lines of which have been discussed philologically, bears the headline, "After-meal Invitation" (*pš'x'ryy nwyδm'*). The text on the verso of this fragment gives characteristic remarks concerning the divine substance liberated by the meal.[141]

Other hymns indicate by their contents that they were recited in the context of the meal. The Middle Persian text M 11 refers to *"this* table" (*'yn xw'n*); it consists of benedictions for the meal and various classes of individuals within the religious community.[142] Another Middle Persian hymn, called

the "First Praise" *(nxwst'yn 'st'yšn)* and preserved in M 729.I, includes the
line, "We praise *this* holy table *('yn xw'n ywjdhr)*, the victory of the good-
souled and the woe of the unworthy,"[143] and proceeds to bless the head of the
community and the Elect. To this genre also belongs the Middle Persian text
MIK III 4974, which as noted above is accompanied by a painted portrayal of
the alms-service.

> May [. . .] with good omen and good premonition, and be established over
> the entire holy religion, and over the table *(xw'n)* of Āryāmān-rōshan, and
> over you, praised leader *(s'r'r)*, who stands (as) a banner of the gods of light,
> and over the whole election *(wcydgyh)* of light.

After this opening, the hymn proceeds to invoke the twelve *šhrd'ryft*, a catalog
of virtues identified here with twelve gods of the Manichaean pantheon and
(apparently) twelve ranks within the community. The use of such hymnic cat-
alogs in the setting of the ritual meal connects the rite to the other principal
discourses of the Manichaean tradition: its normative anthropology, its theology, and its ecclesiology.

Other prayers and hymns focus on the ritual acts of the alms-service and
meal, and belong either to the liturgical repertoire of the ritual or to its "ad-
vertisement" in the general discourse of the Manichaean community.[144] An
entire class of hymns, the *Songs of the Living Self (gryw jywndgyg b'š'h'n)*, may
be composed specifically for the ritual meal. In subject matter, they focus on
the divine substance imprisoned in the world, and it is precisely at the meal
that this subject becomes the center of reflection, as other sources attest. References in the hymns to their ritual context include blessing and praising,
weeping, singing, praying, and supplication.[145] The hymns also refer to pres-
ences and arrivals: of the Elect,[146] and of the Living Self itself.[147] There is no
way to determine whether the "we" of the hymns represents the Elect, the Auditors, the whole community, or a choir.

Passages in M 6650, a Parthian catalog of incipits for *Songs of the Living
Self*, reinforce the theory that these hymns were performed in association with
the ritual meal. The singer(s) addresses the "self" *(gryw)* directly, reports that
it has "come" *('gd)* and wishes health *(drwd)* upon it. "Come (is) this bound
self, gathered *('mwštg)* from every direction; from sky and earth-womb and
from all creation."[148] We are told, even more explicitly, "Meritorious and for-

tunate (is) the Auditor who gathers (*'mwrd'h*) the self; well-fortuned and happy (is) the Righteous One who purifies (*pw'c'h*) it."[149] This verse directs attention unambiguously to the alms-economy.

One of the *Songs of the Living Self* seems to be itself a kind of schematic of ritual vocalizations at the meal, identifying other hymns and chants by their incipits:

> You who sing, O Elect, shall find eternal life. Purify the light self so that it in turn will save you. Sing the wonderful song "In health, peace and confidence." "The light-lute (?) of souls" sing happily and sweetly. Blow the happiness-giving trumpet "Gather the souls for salvation." Very joyful are the children of god at this delightful vocal melody. Speak "holy, holy"; call out "amen, amen." Recite "The Light Wisdom"; respond (with) "The Pure Response." "The True Word of Life" releases the captive one from its bondage. With one voice the one who sings and the one who has the response truly praise. Awe, precept and prohibition burn into every limb. Separate [. . .] the pious departed [. . .] light.[150]

As the hymn proceeds, it gives instructions on attitude as well as action:

> Honor the child of the gods as a guest at the divine meal (*'xwrn bg'nyyg*); prepare an inn of kindliness; show a road to the light. Perfect every limb in the five, seven, and twelve. These are the seven bright jewels which (are) truly from the lands of life. By their power live all worlds and every soul-possessing thing.[151]

Although some of its references remain obscure, this passage clearly directs attention to the redemptive exercises made on behalf of the imprisoned divine elements. If the latter find personification here as "the child of the gods," then we should understand the "inn" as the Elect's own body, which processes the elements on their way "to the light." Hence the importance of perfecting every limb. The text continues: "A hall has been found, O righteous Elect and dutiful Auditors. Prepare the self (*gryw*) for purification (*pw'cyšn*), and keep holy this true mystery."[152] The common features of ritual meal discourse, therefore, include references to the cooperative work of the Auditors and the Elect, "the table," the secret presence within the offerings, and the correct attitude with which the Elect should partake of the meal. The same elements appear in the form of confessional formulas, as in the small Bema-handbook M 801, which has been quoted extensively earlier on the disciplinary regimens of the Elect. The statements about the ritual meal in this book likewise take the form of a confession of transgression against the normative performance of the rite by an Elect.

> *The Divine Table (xw'n yzd'n):* Also I have not sat down at the reception of the daily gifts of the divine table with a thankful heart, in thought of God, the Apostle, and humans. Also I have not concentrated on the primordial conflict; and also I have not thought these things: In whose sign do I now stand? What is it that is eaten? For what demons does one habitually eat? Whose flesh and blood is it? For what debt-obligation and for what depository is it that I receive? Further, for what reason do I not exist among the swine, hound or *yakṣa* species? For what reason [do I exist] in [the human species]?

As it stands, this regulation entirely addresses the appropriate mental state of the meal participant. The Elect are expected to meditate on particular themes posed as self-reflective questions. The participant contrasts the sacrality of the meal with profane eating, and relates this sacrality directly to the status and obligation of the Elect—an obligation to which humans, uniquely among beings, are born. The speaker connects the sobriety of the meal to a reality contained in the food, its identity as "flesh and blood." Similarly, M 139.II instructs the Elect at the meal to think as follows: "One's own body, in whose sign is it made or arranged? In whose service does it stand? What is it that it eats?" The answers one is able to give to these inquiries determines whether one is fit to participate in the meal, because on them hinge the success or failure of the redemptive process.

We find a related passage in the Turkic text T II D 173c,1, which at times seems to be answering the questions posed in the Iranian recitations.

> The second thought is this: The consumed food which enters into the body dies. The third thought is this, as one says: My body is a thing that must perform the extensive duty. The food and drink ordained for it must be held in readiness for the appropriate time. What an injury if one does not do it! The fourth thought, it says: Continuous is the struggle with the passions. Why? Because your passions are entirely wonderful tastes to the body. For this reason they become strong. So one must always consume food and drink at the

(right) time, so that the passions shall not become strong and may not do harm to the body. When one sits down at the table *(xw'n)*, one should think these words with the whole mind and take them to heart![153]

Both the Iranian and the Turkic selections propose specific thoughts, almost a dialogue of questions and answers that shape the attitude of the meal participant. The mind is not to wander, or remain fixed on mundane thoughts, but to focus on the task at hand as a difficult and delicately engineered operation. It is crucial to note that the truths and identifications reviewed in the meal meditations do not make the rite a symbol for another reality or another moment in salvation history; rather they reveal the true present character of the food itself and of the body that ingests it, the etiology of that character and of the rite as a response to it.

Two miniatures among the Turfan material appear to depict the meal itself, and so are of extraordinary value to the historian as rare opportunities to "see" the ritual. In my analysis of these works of art, I am once again guided by the observations of Zsuzsanna Gulácsi. Since its first publication, MIK III 4979 has been regarded as a depiction of the annual Bema ceremony, and I see no reason to abandon this interpretation. The outline of the Bema rite preserved in M 5779 shows that it included the ritual meal as a constituent part of the ceremony. Concordantly, MIK III 4979 features food for the meal placed prominently in the center of the image, flanked at the extremes of the image by ranks of seated, male Elect facing toward the center, and framed more closely by a large figure seated upon a raised platform (i.e., a *bēma*) on the left, and three additional Elect facing this figure on the right (see Plate 3).

At the exact axis formed by the horizontal and vertical center lines of the image, a gilded, tripodal bowl contains three layers of garden products arranged in a pyramid, with three cantaloupes visible at the bottom, a layer of what appear to be grapes resting on the cantaloupes, and a green gourd protruding above the grapes.[154] The edge of this bowl is depicted at the eye level of the viewer, whereas everything else in the painting is shown from a perspective slightly above; this treatment is another indication of the centrality, and hence significance, of this object in the painting. Closer to the viewer, a red, ornate table bears a stack of round, white flat-breads (parts of eighteen are visible) which may rest upon a platter.[155] The breads (which are a variety of *nan* still made in the Turfan region) feature a swirled design in its center, and a twisted crescent edging. This crescent-disk conjunction matches that of the halo around the head of the miniature's central figure. At the top of the stack a single bread lacks both the central swirl and the crescent edging; it features instead three circular, red protrusions on three of its four sides, probably intended to represent pomegranate seeds placed atop the bread.[156]

To the left of the bread-bearing table sits a gilded object that Le Coq identifies as the top of a large pitcher, the bottom of which is lost due to a tear in the manuscript.[157] To the right of the table a fluted bowl contains a heap of pale-red and white objects which, because of the damage to this part of the miniature, cannot be identified with certainty.[158] The table, pitcher, and bowl all rest together on an ornate carpet; traces of a fourth object in front of the table can be detected.[159] Thus the table bearing the bread is surrounded by ritual furnishings on all four sides (the bowl of fruit sits directly behind the table, but not on the same carpet as the other objects). The three Manichaean Elect who sit just to the right of these furnishings face them, and are the only figures who can be construed as interacting with them. One appears to read from a book; a second holds a book clasped to his breast; the third figure is mostly missing from the fragment. Although depicted with stereotypical features, these figures apparently represent actual persons, since the name of each is written in red upon his white garments.

MIK III 6257 preserves part of a second possible Bema scene, since it bears some resemblance to MIK III 4979, as first noted by Jorinde Ebert.[160] Once again, the ritual meal features prominently in the scene (see Plate 4A). On the right, a large bowl contains flatbread with the characteristic twisted crescent edging. Just to the left of this arrangement appears a stack of items, perhaps figs, behind which can be seen the base of a podium or *bēma*. To the left of the objects and facing them are two Elect, only the heads of which are preserved.

Summation

The first modern attempt to reconstruct in detail the actual procedure of the Manichaean ritual meal is that of Henri-Charles Puech. Although his results were published in the 1970s, the research on which they depend was conducted mostly in the 1950s, especially in his seminar at the College de France in 1953–54. Puech was forced to rely mostly upon polemical sources, supplemented by a handful of then known Manichaean material (e.g., M 801, M 139.II). His careful, sober, and insightful application of this data produced a basic outline that has stood the test of time. New sources discovered or edited since the time of Puech's researches allow us to confirm many of his suppositions, to place them on a much firmer source basis, and to add important new details. More recently, Nils Arne Pedersen has taken up the subject in a short excursus in his study of the *Sermon on the Great War* from the Coptic *Homilies,* and has made good use of some of those new sources.[161] His reconstruction is in line with my own, and in terms of the procedure of the ritual Pedersen and I only have filled in some details to the basic outline already worked out by Puech.

The meal was conducted daily; testimony on this point is overwhelming. This was, of course, a practical matter since the ritual meal was the only nourishment permitted to the Elect.[162] Only one meal was held each day.[163] At what point in the day was the meal conducted? Although one Chinese polemicist refers to midday, and Augustine suggests midafternoon, most sources specify evening. Yet we cannot assume universal consistency in Manichaean practice. Some regional variation no doubt existed in the exact timing and location of the ritual meal rite, especially in circumstances of persecution.

The formal audience at which the Auditors made their offerings and showed veneration to the Elect appears in Sogdian and Turkic sources under the Iranian name *nwyδm'* ("invitation"). The Auditors were clearly present at this part of the ceremony, and it may have been the occasion for both personal intercession and collective orations. The use of *nwyδm'* in this context highlights parallels between the Manichaean ritual meal and Zoroastrian liturgy. The same term, in its verbal form *(nivaed-),* is the first word of the Zoroastrian *Yasna,* and is repeated at the beginning of the subsequent eighteen verses as a summons to the ceremony.[164] As the Manichaean Elect proceed, following the invitation, to the meal, so the Zoroastrian priest, following the opening invitations of the *Yasna,* proceeds to the *cašni* ("tasting") of consecrated bread. Just as the Manichaean Elect, after the invitation, "sit down at their *xw'n,*"[165] so the Zoroastrian priest, who stands during the first two *ha* of the *Yasna,* sits down to a *xw'n* to perform the *cašni* (see Plates 6A, 6B).[166]

The consumption of the ritual meal by the Elect was preceded by a benediction made by them upon the food. The polemical testimony to an "Apology to the Bread" is supported by normative Manichaean sources that portray Mani praying over bread and salt,[167] and citing the paradigm of Jesus, who "said a blessing over bread and gave (it) to them."[168] If *Papyrus Rylands 469* is to be believed, the content of this prayer included a reminder of the special discipline of restraint that made the Elect capable of acting for the benefit of the elements, rather than to their detriment. In the Iranian text M 177 verso, the offering by the Auditors is definitely set apart from the prayers and psalms made by Mani and his disciples privately at the "food hour." Augustine also insists that he did not observe the meal itself. If these bits of information are complementary attestations to a general practice consistently maintained throughout the Manichaean world, then the "Apology to the Bread" belongs to the same genre as the meal-time meditations found in Iranian and Turkic sources, rather than to the communal liturgy of hymns and prayers that framed the meal.

The Elect partook of the food at a table; indeed the word "table" appears as a euphemism of the whole rite in Greek and Coptic (trapeza) as well as Iranian and Turkic (xw'n) sources. In both the Iranian and Mediterranean cultural contexts, the "table" possessed a clear pedigree as a ritual locale where food products were placed at the disposal of the deity, and from which ritual participants took away a share for consumption. The Monastery Scroll and other sources point to a role for specially appointed Auditors in serving the Elect and making sure that all was in order before, during, and after the meal.[169]

A few texts present the thoughts deemed suitable for the Elect at the meal.[170] While their contents reflect the rationales associated with the ritual meal, and will be discussed in that context in the next chapter, it is important to keep in mind that such texts are not idle jottings, but scripts performed vocally at the meal or promoted for silent reflection at that time. They operate as the normative narration of the ritual acts themselves, declaring the identity of the roles and implements of the rite as they come into action in it.

The ritual was by no means complete when the eating ended. A Greek source mentions a concluding prayer and perhaps alludes to anointing.[171] We find widespread references to after-meal prayers and hymns. Both Coptic and Iranian accounts mention intercessory prayers made at the behest of the lay donors. In some regions, these after-meal activities may have been performed in the company of, or in conjunction with, the Auditors, who may have taken this opportunity to once again venerate the Elect, as the latter now stood imbued with the divine substance liberated from the meal.

It is possible to say a reasonable amount about the chants and hymns performed at the ritual meal. Iranian ritual scripts consistently list three after-meal āfrīns, and a number of both normative and polemical texts describe the divine substance liberated from the consumed food ascending to heaven through the mouths of the Elect in the form of prayers and hymns,[172] an image that requires an after-meal vocal performance. The Iranian *Songs of the Living Self* and the "Praise of the Five Lights" in the Chinese *Hymnscroll* appear to belong to this ritual setting, as their references to both the participants and the divine elements of the meal suggest. There are several additional meal hymns so far unedited whose content may at some future date add more to our understanding of their arrangement and use in the ritual.

The two hymns explicitly designated in the Chinese *Hymnscroll* for "the collection of offerings" are two versions of the well-known list of the "Zwölf Herrschertümer" ("Twelve Authorities, Sovereignties, or Dominions": *šhrd'ryft*).[173] Although the contents of the hymns make no reference to the ritual meal itself, the connection of this type of "Twelve Authorities" recitation with the meal can be confirmed for other regions by complementary evidence. Thus the Parthian fragment M 259c, edited by Enrico Morano, bears the caption, "Finished is [the list of the] light [authorities for the reception of the] meal *(swr)*."[174] The Middle Persian text accompanying an artistic rendering of an alms-offering in the Turfan fragment MIK III 4974 explicitly refers to the meal ("the table"), requests blessing upon the church leader and the Elect (as does the meal hymn in M 729), and, after this opening prayer, continues with a "Twelve Authorities" recitation. This hymn type can be incorporated with other hymn forms in complex compositions.[175] Not all of these variants were necessarily performed at the ritual meal, but this genre especially seems to be associated with it.[176]

At the present state of our knowledge, we cannot be sure of the exact placement and use of these hymns in the procedure of the ritual meal ceremony. Perhaps they were performed as accompaniments to the entrance and exit of food or Elect (the "Invitation"). Perhaps the Auditors performed them while the Elect ate. Some certainly formed part of the Elects' post-meal vocalizations, what Augustine satirically calls their "belching" because of the role they play in sending the divine substance liberated from food up to heaven. In any case, they were sung and heard in close proximity to the conduct of the rite, and the discourse embodied in them formed the immediate context for the participants' reflection upon their activities. In moving from a reconstruction of the meal to an exegesis of it, we must look first to the statements contained in the hymns, chants, and other mealtime recitations, for these constitute the self-interpretation of the Manichaeans of what they thought they were doing in their ritual life.

CONCLUSIONS

The urge to synthesize all these sources is great, but we must be cautious. The depiction of the ritual meal in the Turkic *Monastery Scroll,* for instance, reflects a well-established church institution, with separate halls set aside for particular functions, and a number of payrolled laypersons to assist in the procedure. The North African Manichaeism known to Augustine existed in quite different political and social circumstances, which would have forced adaptations in the ritual's form. The "Twelve Authorities" and other hymns identified as performed at the meal in the Manichaean East do not match hymns known from the West, and may involve regionally distinctive reflections upon the meaning of the rite. The meal itself is the linchpin that transcends regional variation, and the conviction that its performance produces salvational effects underlies the multifarious expression of what happens in it.

The total arrangement, however tentatively reconstructed, bears a striking resemblance to the *Yašt-i-keh* or "Minor Liturgy" of the Zoroastrians, which commonly involves the performance of an offering and consumption of bread, often accompanied by fruit, flowers, and other products of the bountiful earth, constituting an act of worship embracing all creation (see Plates 4B, 5A, 5B). An exemplary account in the Zoroastrian *Arda Viraf Namag* portrays the hero, the "righteous" (*'rd'w*) Viraf ordering the ceremony upon his return from a visionary journey to the afterlife. He makes a preliminary invocation, consecrates the bread, eats a meal, makes another invocation, and performs a set of *āfrīns*. The lay sponsorship of such Zoroastrian ceremonies is termed *rw'ng'n,* which Iranian Manichaeans likewise employed for their own alms-service. The Zoroastrian rite frequently involves benedictions performed on behalf of deceased individuals. That the Manichaean ritual meal involved the same sort of intercessions for the dead is made clear not only in Iranian sources, but with particular clarity in the Coptic *Kephalaion 115.* A further investigation of these parallels is likely, therefore, to produce future clarification of certain performative structures in the Manichaean rite.[177]

Apart from their possible antecedents and emic interpretations, what can the Manichaean alimentary rites be said to do? They clearly establish a relationship of exchange, an economy if you will, between the two constitutive classes of the Manichaean community. This functional aspect has figured prominently in etic interpretation of Manichaean practices. Membership in the community is demarcated by participation in the daily ritual in one of the sanctioned roles associated with it. Ideally, an outsider could identify all of the Manichaeans in a town simply by observing who went to the ritual. It is possible, however, that some Auditors also participated in the rites of other religions. In practice, the boundaries of the Auditor class probably varied considerably in exclusivity of commitment from one region to the next. Yet by being performed daily, the meal offers some prospect of reinforcing community identity through sheer repetition if nothing else. It also serves the integrity of the community by requiring the continuous interaction of the Elect and Auditor classes, and through that interaction a reinforcement of their respective roles.

The meal's frequency also impacts on Manichaean disciplines. First of all, the Elect must maintain a constant adherence to the regimens in order to participate in the daily meal. There can be no question of periods of "standing down" from the discipline between ceremonies. The "negative rites" that prepare the Elect for the meal become a permanent way of life. On the other hand, the daily repetition of the meal effects a certain moderation in Manichaean ascesis. Contrary to the standard models of asceticism, the Manichaean Elect *must* eat, and in fact realize their ultimate purpose in life only inasmuch as they do eat. There can be no solitary vigils, no mortification of the body, no abandonment of the metabolic functions. The Manichaean ascetic cannot destroy the body, but must regulate it, and must return it every day to contact with the world.

Repeated day after day, with mandatory participation, the alms-service and ritual meal occupy the central position of Manichaean religious practice. This ritual complex holds highest status simply by dint of its placement at the intersection of the social webs of time, space, and role put forward by the tradition. It need have no deeper meaning or more compelling mechanisms than what this arbitrary status provides in order to serve as a marker of Manichaean identity. But in fact Manichaeans endow their food ritual with a set of rationales that extend its significance, and make it the governing term in all of Manichaean doctrine and practice, the "reference point for explaining or describing other areas of life."[178] To fully appreciate what is entailed in being Manichaean, we must not stop at the surface acts of the rite, but gaze inside the Manichaean body.

PLATES

PLATE 1. Alms-service of the Auditors: MIK III 4974 recto. (Staatliche Museen zu Berlin — Preußischer Kulturbesitz, Museum für Indische Kunst.)

PLATE 2A. Alms-service of the Auditors: M 559 recto. (Depositum der Berlin-Brandenburgischen Akademie der Wissenschaften in der Staatsbibliothek zu Berlin—Preußischer Kulturbesitz Orientabteilung.)

PLATE 2B. Alms-service of the Auditors: M 6290. (Depositum der Berlin-Brandenburgischen Akademie der Wissenschaften in der Staatsbibliothek zu Berlin—Preußischer Kulturbesitz Orientabteilung.)

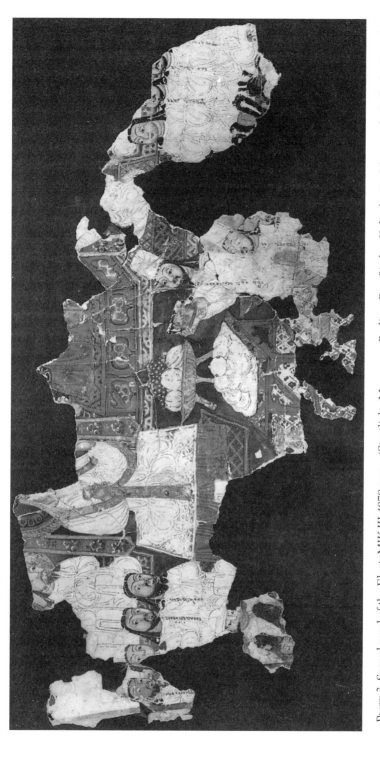

PLATE 3. Sacred meal of the Elect: MIK III 4979 verso. (Staatliche Museen zu Berlin — Preußischer Kulturbesitz, Museum für Indische Kunst.)

PLATE 4A. Sacred meal of the Elect: MIK III 6257. (Staatliche Museen zu Berlin—
Preußischer Kulturbesitz, Museum für Indische Kunst.)

PLATE 4B. A sacred meal ritual conducted by modern Zoroastrian priests, with
laypeople in attendance, comparable to that of the Manichaeans. (Margaret
Oliphant, *The Atlas of the Ancient World* [London: Ebury, 1992], 77.)

PLATE 5A. A sacred meal ritual conducted by modern Zoroastrian priests, with laypeople in attendance, comparable to that of the Manichaeans. (Sven Hartman, *Parsism, the Religion of Zoroaster*, Iconography of Religions 14.4 [Leiden: E. J. Brill, 1980], plate xxxix*a*. Used by permission.)

PLATE 5B. Modern Zoroastrian priests conducting an Afrinagān food ritual without a lay audience. (Hartman, *Parsism*, plate xxxviii*b*. Used by permission.)

PLATE 6A. Modern Zoroastrian priests-in-training standing during the "invitation" at the beginning of the Yasna ceremony, paralleling Manichaean ritual meal procedure. (Hartman, *Parsism*, plate xxxvi*b*. Used by permission.)

PLATE 6B. The ritual leader sits down at the kwan (table) as the Yasna proceeds to the "tasting" portion of the Yasna ceremony, paralleling Manichaean ritual meal procedure. (Hartman, *Parsism*, plate xxxiii*b*. Used by permission.)

FIVE

ALIMENTARY RATIONALES

Purify the light self so that it in turn will save you.
—*Songs of the Living Self*

Why did Manichaeans perform the ritual meal? What was its purpose? What motivated its enactment? These are not the sort of questions one normally asks about eating, whose purpose and motivation would seem to be obvious. But in Manichaean practice, certain acts of eating—in fact, all eating of a particular class of people within the community—were set apart from ordinary eating for sustenance. The ordinary partaking of food was rendered extraordinary by the special status of the holy Elect, and a mundane meal became sacred due to the extraordinary function it served in Manichaean salvational practice.

The transformation of an ordinary meal into a religious act entails the formalization and limitation of the participants, materials, implements, gestures, and vocalizations employed in its performance—in other words, it is a process of ritualization. The previous chapter outlined the distinctively Manichaean manner of ritualizing a meal externally. But ritualization is not limited to external acts; it involves as well the formalization of internal acts, and the careful structuring of the external means by which internal acts are effected. The formalization of thoughts experienced during the ritual, for example, begins with a formalization of speech, so that sanctioned words (and, it is hoped, the normative connotation of those words) in the form of invocations, declarations, chants, and hymns envelope the participant to the exclusion of all intrusive statements. The sacrality of the meal must be marked and constantly reiterated to defend against the incursion of the ordinary; and the participants in the rite must declare to and remind each other and themselves that they are accomplishing something more than the mundane.

The reader will have become aware already of the great difficulty of separating rite from rationale in a discussion of the Manichaean ritual meal. The prayers and hymns associated with the ritual meal, for example, belong structurally to the acts of the ritual, but in their content provide essential contextualizing and rationalizing of the acts within a larger Manichaean universe. Even before we reach a point of discussing explicit rationales, stated in the familiar language of "because" and "so that," we should take special note of the fact that a major part of explaining specific behavior can be accomplished by reference to the world within which the behavior occurs. Since the Manichaean universe is set up in a particular way, certain behaviors will be reasonable and possible, and others irrational or "impossible." The Manichaeans understood the body to operate in a particular fashion, and to be connected with the larger cosmos in concrete, knowable ways. The Manichaean practitioner was able to take advantage of these physiological facts both in the sense of possessing certain knowledge and in the sense of acting upon that knowledge in a salvationally skillful manner.

In asking why the Manichaeans performed the ritual meal, of course, we are also asking why they were Manichaeans at all, practitioners of this ritual tradition rather than some other. To this question, Mani gives a clear and strong answer:

> All of these alms that are given in the world because of the name of God, by every creed whatsoever in his name . . . every place to which they will bring these alms they lead them to affliction and hardship and wickedness. [There is no] rest or open gate through which they come out and find occasion to ascend to God, because of whose name they are given, except only in the holy church, the one in which the commandments of the alms-service are placed. . . . Now the holy church exists in two personas, the brothers and the sisters.[1]

The unique discipline of the Manichaean community makes its ritual practice effective in a way that other ritual traditions are not. Here and elsewhere, the Manichaean tradition explicitly analogizes its practices with contemporaneous systems of sacrificial offerings. But Manichaeans participated in a templeless and altarless tradition. While other religious communities carried their offerings into temples, where their priests burned them on altars, the Manichaeans bore their alms to the Elect, who cooked them in their own stomachs. Consequently, the Manichaeans talked a great deal about what goes on within the body in connection with the digestion of food. As other traditions detail what occurs within temple precincts, generally unobserved by the layperson, so Manichaean discourse dwells upon the unobserved operations of Elect metabolism.

This peculiarly Manichaean discourse poses a great challenge to the modern researcher when it comes to deciding when treatment of rites has ended and discussion of rationales has begun. Because in Manichaeism the body served as not only the actor but also the arena of salvation, religious practice within the faith necessitated a detailed metabolic discourse. The internal activities of the human body form an integral component of the Manichaean ritual meal, without which the external meal is incomplete and ineffective. These activities were controlled and formalized just as are the external acts of the rite, and the discourse concerning them is not to be relegated to a different sphere of meaning. Rather, the bodies of the Manichaean Elect were treated as implements employed in the ritual meal.

Our etic category of alimentary rationales, then, includes all of the statements made in the process of performing the Manichaean ritual meal, and all of the further discourse referenced by those statements. The latter constitute the materials of instruction that the Manichaeans themselves learned as they became Manichaeans, and heard repeated in the periodic lessons, sermons, and exhortations offered by Manichaean authorities. It would be a reasonable historical assumption that the language of Manichaean ritual texts included allusions that would be familiar to the Manichaean who uttered or heard them. On an individual basis, however, one will find varying degrees of competence and literacy among members of the community. I offer a reconstruction not of such individual appropriations of faith, but of the normative rationales organized and promoted by the authoritative institutions of the Manichaean religious community.

Manichaean literature possesses a remarkable variety of ways to express and communicate the information connected with the alms-service and ritual meal, any one of which could serve to organize my own exposition. I have chosen to follow the fourfold analysis, offered to Manichaean Auditors, of *Kephalaion 115*:

Know that the one who brings the alms and the memorial of the person who has come out of the body, brings rest. The entreaty which he makes accomplishes four great victories. First, [he rescues] the Living Soul that is entwined and bound in the whole world, since it is released and cleansed and purified and rescued because of him. Second, he brings rest to the holy church by the alms which he brings for the person who has been released from his body. The [blessed] children of the church rest upon it. . . . The third victory is [that which the donor accomplishes on behalf of] the person who has come out of his body. [It is] an alms for him and a remembrance for his brother or his father or his mother or his son or his daughter or his kinsman who has come out of the body [. . .].[2]

The fourth victory is missing from the fragmentary text, but many other sources agree with what would be our own common-sense guess, that the fourth victory is the one donors gain for themselves. I shall examine in turn these four victories—from the Manichaean point of view things actually effected—as rationales for participation in the Manichaean alms-service and ritual meal.

RESCUE OF THE LIVING SELF

Under the rubric of disciplinary rationales (chapter 3), I introduced the reader to the "Living Self," the divine substance percolating through the world according to Manichaean cosmological discourse. In the disciplinary context, the presence of the Living Self provides a rationale for regulating human action to curtail the harm inflicted upon this very immanent deity. At the same time, the disciplinary regimens are said to correct and perfect the deficient human body, rendering it into an instrument that can actively assist in the liberation of the Living Self from its "mixture" in the universe. The Manichaean Elect perform this latter operation through the ritual meal, and the Auditors, through their alms-service, sponsor this salvational practice. The rescue of the Living Self constitutes the principal purpose the Manichaeans themselves express for performing the ritual meal.

The Central Manichaean Tradition

The one inescapable contact between the human body and the divine substance diffused in the world occurs in eating, in which the individual actually ingests God in the form of food. Ephrem Syrus is aware of the Manichaean view that trees and fields of grain, even the ground itself, exude "light" in a refining process,[3] and that the human body similarly performs as a "refining furnace."[4] The Manichaeans teach that the divine substance is perceivable to the senses, such that "the pleasant taste which is in foods belongs to the light which is mixed in them."[5] But food, like all things, has a mixed character, and its ingestion carries risks to the body's well-being. Ephrem recognizes that Manichaeans employ a medical mode of discourse in their discussion of human metabolism. In those terms, "just as poison becomes excessive in us from nutriment, so they say that 'evil collects and increases in us from foods.'"[6] Nonetheless, Manichaeans held that a properly trained and disciplined body could achieve the status of a liberating machine, so that "the refining furnace which (Darkness) fashioned actually does harm to itself and refines the Light."[7]

By the digestion of food in the bodies of the Elect, "the good is refined little by little and ascends."[8] Ephrem's account is one of the best we have in conveying the Manichaean sense of mission in connection with this work of religion.

> Mani (said) that it was possible to restore the one cast like a thing from its domain into "sin" by means of "righteousness" and the observance of commandment(s), and (that) although the *ziwane* were mixed with "sin" in Darkness, they could be refined through fasting and prayer—that if they were mixed in order to ensnare Darkness with them, now that it has been caught, by all means it becomes necessary (to know) how the sons of Light will return to their domain. . . . For if purification is necessary—what they term "streams of refining"—[. . .] to purify and to refine that which is mixed in the sea and the dry land and in heaven and earth and all that they contain.[9]

Drawing on the terminology of his Manichaean sources, Ephrem directs attention to the role of "righteousness,"[10] that is, the Elect class, made possible by the observance of commandments. Purification itself comes about through their fasting, which prepares and stokes the digestive fires, and prayer, on which the "streams of refining" mount to heaven.[11] An-Nadim also attests the view that the separated light "rises up on a Column of Praise with the prayers, benedictions, pure speech, and pious works."[12]

Ephrem sees a number of inconsistencies in these Manichaean rationales. For one thing, he cannot imagine how the human soul and the soul-stuff extracted from food—which are of identical natures—remain distinguished in the filtration process, so that only the food's light departs for heaven without the soul of the Elect.[13] Moreover, the body's ability to work this effect on food appears to Ephrem as a glaring loophole that evil should certainly have filled.[14] The apparent inability of evil to catch on to how good is taking advantage of the former's somatic creation leaves Ephrem incredulous.

> But if he who framed the body is evil, as they blasphemously say, and . . . if the darkness contrived to frame that body to be a prison-house for the soul that it might not go forth thence, it would not be difficult for him to know from this that the refining furnace which he framed injured him and refines the light. But if it escaped his notice at the beginning he could, now that experience has taught him, destroy his framing and make another body, not one that separates (the light), but one that imprisons; not one that refines, but one that befouls; not one that purifies, but one that defiles; and not one that makes room for the light (to escape), but one that detains the light.[15]

In the face of such arguments, the Manichaeans steadfastly maintain that the body is reformable, the weak link in evil's chain of control. A third and final objection raised by Ephrem concerns the eventual imbalance in the universe between good and evil which would result from a constant departure of the divine substance. Since, "as they say, the number of souls constantly becomes less from day to day because they are 'refined and go up,'" evil should gradually gain greater power in the world.[16] But for this question, too, the Manichaeans of Ephrem's day were ready with an answer. "For in proportion as the good 'is refined and goes up,' so the evil becomes [gross], and goes down," and is, in effect, deactivated.[17] Moreover, "they say that even one part of all these parts [of good] which are mixed at present would be able to conquer the evil."[18]

The Western Manichaean Tradition

Augustine epitomizes the Manichaean salvational discourse in his treatise *De natura boni*:

> They say that this part of the divine nature permeates all things in heaven and earth and under the earth; that it is found in all bodies, dry and moist, in all kinds of flesh, and in all seeds of trees, herbs, men and animals. But they do not say of it, as we say of God, that it is present untrammeled, unpolluted, inviolate, incorruptible, administering and governing all things. On the contrary, they say that it is bound, oppressed, polluted, but that it can be released and set free and cleansed not only by the courses of the sun and moon and powers of light, but also by their Elect.[19]

This dual purgation—by natural forces and by human digestion—is the purpose for the world's existence and the worth of human beings.

> They claim that not only do the powers of God effect this purgation and liberation of good and evil throughout the whole universe and of all its elements, but also that their own Elect achieve the same results by means of the food of which they partake. And they state that the divine substance is intermingled with this food just as it is with the whole universe, and imagine that it is purified in their Elect by the mode of life which the Manichaean Elect live, as if their mode of life were holier and more excellent than that of their Auditors.[20]

( )

> They tell us that the part of the divine nature that is mixed with evil is purified by their Elect, by eating and drinking, no less. For they say it is held bound in all foods, and when these are consumed by the holy Elect who eat and drink them for the refreshment of their bodies, the divine nature is released, sealed and set free.[21]

Although we might be inclined to resist Augustine's rhetoric as a crude caricature of a tradition to which we want to extend a hermeneutic of charity, the Manichaeans' own statements essentially validate Augustine's account. The ideology of food underpinning the Manichaean ritual meal must not be metaphorized or "spiritualized" into a moral discourse merely about the psychological attitudes of the practitioner, or the "mystical" significance of eating. Instead, we must recognize the concrete, materialistic dietetics that the Manichaeans themselves employ to explain the effects of food on the physical and psychological, as well as the spiritual condition of the eater.

The Manichaean battle for the body intensifies whenever food enters into it. The Elect body struggles to rescue and purify the divine element in the food while resisting the rebellion of its own dark forces which are reinforced by the infusion of more evil substance contained in the food. This basic analysis can be expressed in the mythological and psychological accounts seen in some sources, or in the dryly scientific mode displayed in the *Cologne Mani Codex*:

> This body is defiled and molded from a mold of defilement. You can see how, whenever someone cleanses his food and partakes of that which has just been washed, it appears to us that from it still come blood and bile and gases and shameful excrements and bodily defilement. But if someone were to keep his mouth away from this food for a few days, immediately all these excretions of shame and loathsomeness will be found to be lacking and wanting [in the] body. But if [that one] were to partake [again] of [food, in the] same way they would again abound in the body, so that it is manifest that they flow out from the food itself. But if someone else were to partake of food (which is) washed and cleansed, and partake (also) of that which is unwashed, it is clear that the well-being and the power of the body is recognizably the same.[22]

This account of "mixture" removes the issue of purity from an external locale to an internal one. For Manichaeans it is not possible to separate the whole person from contamination, because the person is constituted by both good and evil qualities. Separation, then, must be performed within the individual.

> Therefore, [make an inspection of] yourselves as to [what] your purity [really is. For it is] impossible to purify your bodies entirely. For each day the body is disturbed and comes to rest through the secretions of sediments from it. . . . The purity, then, which was spoken about, is that which comes through knowledge, separation of light from darkness and of death from life and of living waters from turbid, so that [you] may know [that] each is [inimical] to the other and [that you may know the true] commandments of the savior, [so that

you] may redeem the soul from [annihilation] and destruction. This is in truth the genuine purity.[23]

Separation secures the substance of the soul from destruction by clearly demarcating its boundary and contents, and freeing it from association with non-soul, the inimical substance from the other side doomed to return there.

Augustine explicitly identifies a set of biological and physiological facts as the rationale (*rationem*) the Manichaeans cite for the alms-service and ritual meal:

> The divine part is being purified daily from all parts of the world and returning to its own domain. But as it is exhaled from the earth and rises toward heaven, it enters into plants, their roots being fixed in the ground, and gives fecundity and life to all grass and other vegetation. The animals eat the plants, and if they mate, imprison the divine limb in their flesh, thus diverting it from its rightful course and causing it to become enmeshed in hardship and error. But when food prepared from fruits and produce is served to the holy men, that is, to the Manichaeans, whatever in it is excellent and divine is purified by their chastity, prayers, and psalms, and is perfected in every way, so that it can return to its own domain free of all defilement. That is why you forbid anyone to give bread, vegetables, or even water . . . to a beggar if he is not a Manichaean, for fear that the limb of God which is mixed with these things will be defiled by his sins and thus hindered in its return.[24]

The rules governing the handling of food, the prohibition on ordinary food alms to the poor, and the concern that every bit of food offered at the ritual meal be consumed by the Elect[25] make it clear that Manichaean food-economy is not about charity or the cultivation of comensality. Alms within the Manichaean community are literally *korban*, set aside for the altar of sacrifice and forbidden to profane consumption.

The sins of the non-Manichaean which threaten to defile the divine substance in food include, first and foremost, sexual intercourse, which congeals the substance into a soul locked into a new body, since the traducian Manichaeans hold that "all animal souls come from the food of their parents."[26] In the Auditor or the non-Manichaean, sperm is the end-product of the digestive process which has sifted and concentrated food into its constituent good and evil properties. The divine material courses through the human metabolic system; it is for this reason that a properly disciplined body can control its processing and destination. Even in ordinary bodies "the life escapes in the mastication and digestion of the food, so that only a small portion remains in the excrement";[27] that "life" joins with the body as nutriment, and is expended by it as kinetic energy.[28] In the Elect celibacy precludes reimprisonment of the light through reproduction, and the "seal of the hands" maintains innocence from murder.[29] Instead, the ingested light either flows out through the typical activities of the Elect—prayers and psalms—or binds itself to their soul, rising with them to heaven.

Sermons and psalms associated with the observance of the meal focus attention on the hidden, sacred identity within the food. One psalm alludes to a self-interrogation of the meal's partakers, similar to those known from Iranian and Turkic sources: "We also, my beloved, let us separate the word 'Who is this that eats?' (from) 'Who is this that is eaten?' 'Who is this that seeks?' (from) 'Who is this that is sought?'—the sheep that is bound to the tree, for which its shepherd searches."[30] The answer, in Western Manichaeism especially, frequently comes in the form of eucharistic allusions to Christ, "the holy bread of life that is come from the skies, the sweet spring of water that leaps unto life, the true vine, that of the living wine."[31] This profound mystery of the imprisonment of what can be called the vulnerable Jesus, the dispersed soul of all, to whose aid the Elect come in the ritual meal, was a source of great irritation to the Christian polemicists. Augustine treats the idea in several places, always with phrases full of outrage and dripping with sarcasm.

> By your sacrilegious absurdities Christ is not only mingled with heaven and all the stars, but conjoined and combined with the earth and all its productions—a savior no more, but needing to be saved by you, by your chewing and belching him. This foolish custom of making your Auditors bring you food, that your teeth and stomach may be the means of aiding Christ, who is bound up in it, is a consequence of your impious fancies. You declare that Christ is released and liberated in this way—not, however, entirely; for you hold that some tiny particles of no value still remain in the excrement, to be mixed up and compounded again and again in various corporeal forms.[32]

In this way, the Manichaean conception of Christ subjects him "to such polluting contact with all earthly things, with the juices of all vegetables, and with the decay of all flesh, and with the decomposition of all food, in which he is bound up, that one great way, if not the only way, of releasing him, is that men, that is the Elect of the Manichaeans, should succeed in belching their herbs and roots."[33] The "eucharist" becomes for the Manichaeans a daily meal, and requires no transubstantiation to render its elements divine, for they are already the "body and blood" of Christ. For Augustine, of course, such a position is sheer blasphemy.

> It is not any bread and wine that we hold sacred as a natural production, as if Christ were confined in grain or in vines, as the Manichaeans fancy, but what is truly consecrated as a symbol. . . . According to your notion, Christ is confined in everything you eat, and must be released by belching from the additional confinement of your bowels.[34]

Despite its strong tendency toward Christianizing its discourse, Western Manichaeism also retains the more widely attested characterization of the bound divine substance as the Living Self or Living Soul. The edited portion of the Coptic *Psalm-Book* contains one psalm that belongs to the genre known in Iranian Manichaeism as *Songs of the Living Self*. The singer(s) begins by invoking the reforming agents of the body:

> [O] Father, O Mind of Light, come and wear me [until] I have recited the woe of the Son of Man. [My] Lord Jesus, come and wear me until I purify the [body (?)] of the First Man.[35]

The singer than turns to address the alms in their persona as the Living Self:

> You are the two-edged axe with which they cut the bitter root. You are the [. . .] that is in the hand of the Maiden, which was thrust into the heart of the enemy. You are the first ship (?) of the first warrior, wherein they caught the thieves that rebelled. You are the first weapon of the first hero, which was brandished behind the foe that arose. . . . [How great] is your fortitude, O Daughter of Wisdom: for you have not yet wearied, watching over the enemy.[36]

Next, the singer declares that the cosmos is rightly arranged for the success of the liberative process of the ritual, and urges the liberated elements on their way:

For you the ships are waiting on high that they may draw you up and take you to the Light. Behold, the Perfect Man is stretched out [in the middle of] the world, that you may walk in him and receive [your] unfading [garlands]. Behold, the five Porters are spread over the world that your heart may not suffer and that you may cast the burden from off you. [Behold, the] Righteous Ones will illumine you; behold, the forgiveness of sins of the Catechumens of the faith. [Behold], the medicine-chest of the physician will heal your wounds; behold the knowledge and wisdom will put your clothes upon you. [Walk], therefore, in joy, drawn to the Land of Light, sealed with your seal and with your unfading garlands. Walk also in gladness: your sufferings have passed today; behold, the harbor of peace—you have moored in it.[37]

The psalm concludes with a final benediction:

Glory to this alms-offering *(ti.mntnae)*, and to them that purify it, and to them that redeem it, the Catechumens of the Faith.[38]

Given its overarching ethos of disciplined restraint, and the strong impetus to consider the world suffused with a vulnerable divine presence, it would seem that Manichaeism faced a promotional challenge in instituting the alms-service and ritual meal as the heart of religious practice. By teaching the presence of the Living Self in all things, the Manichaean tradition problematizes acts fundamental to human life. Subsistence itself becomes a source of great anxiety, given how the procurement of food runs afoul of the Manichaean concept of the sanctity of all living things, and a potential paradox (not overlooked by anti-Manichaean polemicists) enters into the very relations Manichaean authorities promote. Arthur Vööbus once commented that the system of practice encompassing the alms-service and ritual meal seems "a very peculiar auxiliary device . . . not at all in harmony with (Mani's) consistent line of thinking," focused most of all on an ascetic withdrawal from acting harmfully upon the world.[39] A whole battery of discussions in the Coptic *Kephalaia*, including *Kephalaia* 81, 84, 85, and 93, address this conundrum, providing a unique testimony to Manichaean rationales in action.

In *Kephalaion 84*, an Elect expresses to Mani his concern that, by preaching the alms collection to Auditors, he is inviting harm upon the plants from which the Auditors will obtain their alms. Mani reassures him that encouraging alms collection is not the same as ordinary human behavior toward the world, for the alms-service is "for the release of the soul [. . .] for the mystery [of its] healing; because the Righteous One, who speaks to the need [of] alms, speaks to its healing and its gathering in."[40] Admittedly, "that [alms-]giving will not be able to be saved without toil and pain, because . . . (the Elect) chew as they eat it." Nonetheless, "there is no other mode for the alms than this, because (the Elect) is its gateway to come forth [. . .] from the world."[41]

In *Kephalaion* 93 an Auditor asks, "Do I cause a wound to the alms-offering when I make an offering *(prosphora)* to the holy ones?"[42] Mani reaffirms the sanction of the alms-service by exonerating the Auditors from any sin in the matter. "Do not fear the sin that you do on that day to the alms-offering. For all of that which you do [to] this alms-offering on that day, you do for [its] healing, bearing this alms-offering which you bring to life and rest."[43] The Auditor is likened to a physician who may cure a wound with the very device, for example, a knife, that caused the wound in the first place, but "all that he did to him, he did for good, not for evil."[44] The Elect, unlike ordinary people, eat as part of a divine redemption, not to sustain a sinful lifestyle. "A breadth *(ouastn)* exists for it (the alms-offering) and it is healed in the Elect, in the psalms, [in] prayers, in praises."[45]

The key difference between ordinary profane eating and the Manichaean ritual meal lies in the disciplines kept by the Elect. They undertake "the task of purifying the spiritual gold from the excrement with which it is mixed, and of releasing the divine limbs from their miserable entanglements."[46] The sanctified digestion of the Elect takes up its task where the external world fails due to the hostile efforts of evil, which initiated consumption precisely to reimprison the divine light in the world. In the typical, unreformed individual food goes through a process resulting in particular kinds of products (see Diagram 5.1).

> This food of various kinds that men gather in, as they eat it, it goes into the body; it is scattered to five "births" *(jpo)*. The first birth is this that comes out of the man in the trance *(p.oonsh)*,[47] and it rises up in the mind, and it comes out in all of his limbs without measure.[48] The second is this that comes out of the man in the voice and the word. The third is this that vibrates *(foche)*[49] in power and vigor. The fourth is that which is born in the pleasure of lust in men and women. The fifth is this that is formed, and is constructed in the flesh, and is born and comes out, which is this corporeal birth. This birth that is born is the only one that its parents know: its heart's desire and its thought

DIAGRAM 5.1: THE PRODUCTS OF DIGESTION (FROM *KEPHALAION 104*)

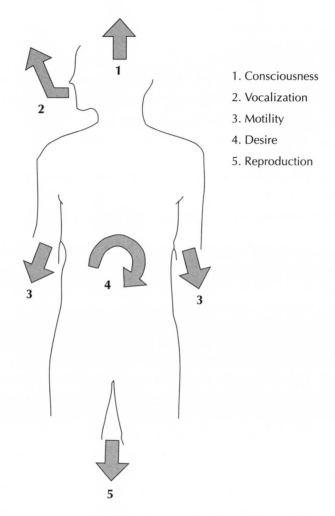

1. Consciousness
2. Vocalization
3. Motility
4. Desire
5. Reproduction

and its love (is) that which they seek after daily, at all times. These other four births, however, they do not perceive, nor do they take pity on them, since they are not revealed to them.[50]

The disciplinary codes of the Elect work on these channels of caloric production, closing some and purifying others. The five commandments effectively shut down the expenditure of kinetic energy in the limbs (noninjury), in the passions (chastity), and in labors for the well-being of the mundane household (poverty), while at the same time training and perfecting the use of the mind (truth) and voice (purity of mouth) for salvational work.

Because other religions offer alms to ordinary people, or even to supposedly sacred individuals who nonetheless do not keep the divinely ordained disciplines of the Manichaean Elect, they doom these alms to profane metabolism, whereas alms offered to the Elect are processed through a perfected metabolism that redeems the divine substance within them. The passage from *Kephalaion 87* quoted at the beginning of this chapter continues as follows:

> Now the holy church exists in two personas, the brothers and the sisters. The time, then, when these alms will reach the holy church, they are saved in it, and become pure and rest in it. They emerge from it and go to the God of truth, because of whose name they are given. The holy church itself, moreover, is the place of rest for all these alms that rest in it. It itself becomes a door to them and a ferrying place to that country of rest.[51]

Because of their disciplined bodies, the Elect are able to transport the liberated particles of the Living Self to their proper home. "This is the way of this alms-offering which passes from the Elect, and they give form to it in many images, and it is purified, and it goes into the country of the living."[52] Once again it is Augustine who, despite his sarcasm, provides crucial testimony about what he himself had been taught concerning the rationales for Manichaean practices:

> I was gradually led to believe such nonsense as that a fig wept when it was plucked, and that the tree which bore it shed tears of mother's milk. But if some sanctified member of the sect were to eat the fig—someone else, of course, would have committed the sin of plucking it—he would digest it and breathe it out again in the form of angels or even as particles of God, retching them up as he groaned in prayer. These particles of the true and supreme God were supposed to be imprisoned in the fruit and could only be released by means of the stomach and teeth of one of the Elect.[53]

Kephalaion 115, quoted at the beginning of this chapter as providing the four alimentary rationales for Auditors, says that the person who donates alms for the ritual meal "[rescues] the Living Soul that is entwined and bound in the

whole world, since it is released and cleansed and purified and rescued because of him."[54] Relatedly, one of the "four great works" accomplished by the
fasting of the Elect is that, "this soul, which comes into him daily in the metabolism (oikonomia) of his food, becomes pristine, and is purified, separated,
and cleansed from the mixture (synkrasis) with the darkness that is mixed in
with it."[55] After outlining the polluting effluents of digestion in the congenitally defective body, Kephalaion 94 relates the more favorable digestion of a
properly governed body:

> That which they gather in reaches them in the metabolism (oikonomia) of
> this soul meal (trophē n.psychikos) [which] comes into the body. At the time
> when they come into the body, and they are purified, and they are cleansed,
> and they are established in their living image which is the New Man, they
> live [. . .] and they attain the Mind of Light, and they are cleansed in their
> image, and they come out pure, holy, and they reach their first rest. The time,
> then, when they reach the Elect, this is the way that they are purified, and
> they go up [to] the land of the living. These, however, that come to [. . .] sin-
> ners, and they pass through them, and they [come out?] in sins, their end will
> be in "transfusion" (metaggismos) and a spirit.[56]

Kephalaion 114 speaks of the "three images existing in the Elect," through
which food passes, sloughing off elements in their appropriate place within
the body, refining a pure core of divine substance (see Diagram 5.2). Mani
concludes this physiological lecture as follows:

> This is [the] way, then, that this living limb [is purified] and it lives, that
> which comes into the body of [the] Righteous One from outside in the me-
> tabolism (oikonomia) of the food of various kinds, in this way. The Living
> Soul becomes pure every day completely; and it traverses these three images.
> It loosens itself from the body which is not its own in the "somatic" (image).
> It loosens itself from the souls which are not its own, these that are mixed with
> it, in the "psychic" (image), which [are] wrath, lust [. . .] and foolishness,
> envy and divisiveness and these other evil knowledges which are not its own.
> But in [the] "pneumatic" image it lives, and it mixes in with [the] patience,
> perfection of the faith, and love which reigns over all of them, which is the
> Virgin of Light, the one that is a raiment to the New Man, the one who is
> called the hour of life. She is the first; she is also the last.[57]

DIAGRAM 5.2: THE DIGESTIVE PROCESS (FROM *KEPHALAION 104*)

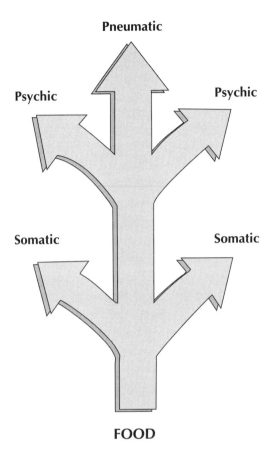

Thus "righteousness," or the Elect, "gather the five to themselves" in the ritual meal, and within the body "they ornament it . . . [and] it is well established."[58] At the end of this process, the purified Living Self emerges from the Elect in their prayers and hymns, as "angels" produced by fast-stoked digestive fires,[59] or as "the sound of all the people who respond" in the assembly of the Elect, which "shall collect and come together . . . is formed and makes a good image, very beautiful and honored," and "ascends to the land of tranquility and peace."[60]

The Eastern Manichaean Tradition

In the Sogdian passage on the "divine meal" from the confession section of the Bema-handbook M 801, the author directs the attention of the Elect to the discursive context within which they should participate in the rite, in the form of confessed neglect of the normative rationales:

> I have not concentrated on the primordial conflict; and also I have not thought these things: In whose sign do I now stand? What is it that is eaten? For what demons does one habitually eat? Whose flesh and blood is this? For what obligation and for what depository is it that I receive?[61]

The surviving Eastern Manichaean literature provides the answer to these questions in the form of narratives of the primordial conflict, descriptions of the divine force within the food, and characterizations of both the corrupted and reformed physiological processes involved in the rite. In M 139.II, a similar set of self-inquiries determines one's fitness to participate in the ritual meal. The reader is warned that "every eater who is not worthy is deprived of his toilsome effort and separated from the light heaven. But the chosen Elect and faithful Auditors who recognize the greatness of the Living Self dwell happily in immortal life in the light paradise." The *Recitation of the Living Self* (*Gwyšn 'yg Gryw Zyndg*) puts into the mouth of the redeemed elements of the alms-service both the paradox and the logic of the Auditors' role in the economy of salvation:

> You buy me like slaves from thieves, and you fear and implore me as (you do) lords. You select me from the world like disciples for the Righteous, and you show me reverence as (you do) masters. You smite and hurt me like enemies, and you save and revive me like friends. But my parents are strong and able to show you manifold gratitude. And as a reward for one fast day, they give to you eternal happiness. And they send gods before you in order to send the share which is yours through me. And the share (is for) the toil and sorrow which you bear and suffer on my account.[62]

The sermon proceeds, still in the voice of the Living Self, to analogize the "soul-work" offering to traditional Zoroastrian rites:

I am the fire that Zarathustra built; and which he bade the righteous to build. . . . From the seven consecrated, sweet-smelling fires, bring to me, the fire, purified fuel. Bring clean firewood and delicate and fragrant incense. Kindle me with knowledge, and give me clean oblation. I am the water to which it is proper to give the water-oblation, so that I may become strong. . . . I am the lamb which [. . .] called to Zarathustra.[63]

The Living Self also speaks in M 42, where it says, "For my sake Zarathustra descended to the Persian realm; he displayed righteousness (and) selected my limbs from the seven-faced lights."[64] Later in the same text another voice says, "Your great battlefield (is) like that of the god Ohrmizd (the Primordial Man), and your collection of treasure (*frg'w 'mwrdyšn*) like that of the chariots of light (the sun and moon); moreover, this Living Self which (is) in flesh and tree you are able to save from Až (the demon of greed)."[65]

Similarly, the *Songs of the Living Self,* which may have been composed specifically for the meal service, focus on the divine substance imprisoned in the world, usually by addressing the Living Self directly. The incipits preserved in the hymn-index M 1 describe it consistently as "light," and variously as "bound,"[66] "captive,"[67] "saved,"[68] "free,"[69] "great,"[70] "beneficent,"[71] "blessed,"[72] and, of course, "living."[73] In three cases the Living Self speaks in the first person.[74] Thirteen hymns listed by M 1 have been identified in surviving fragments.[75] The hymn beginning "To you will I speak, my captive self" is preserved in M 33:

To you I will speak, my captive self, remember your home. . . . Remember the devouring . . . that bit you asunder and devoured you in hunger. . . . Remember the hard primordial battle and the many wars you had with the powers of darkness. . . . Remember the trembling, the weeping, and the grief that you had at that time, when the Father (the Primordial Man) went up on high.[76]

In the process of telling the "self" to remember the cosmogonic myth that stands behind the current condition of the divine in the world, the singer simultaneously implants and evokes the recollection in him- or herself and in the audience who listens to the song. At times the Living Self speaks through the mouth of the hymnist: "I am from the light and from the gods, and I have become an exile, away from them. The enemies fell over me and have led me to the dead. Blessed be—that he be saved—the one who will save my self from distress."[77] In this hymn the singer identifies him- or herself with the Living Self, fallen into earthly existence from a divine heritage. The mythological experience of primordial time and the contemporary experience of the Manichaean are made continuous one with the other. In the context of the daily ritual meal, it enunciates a relation between the portions of the Living Self being liberated in the meal and the self-identities of the participants who come to the aid of their compatriots.

The Chinese *Hymnscroll* likewise contains stanzas dedicated to the themes of the "Living Self" and its redemption through the activities of the community.

> *All the hindered and unhindered bodies and natures* (hsing)
> *Have for long sadly sunk into the sea of birth and death*
> *Their limbs and articulations scattered in the three realms*
> *Pray gather and restore them to soar above the myriad things.*[78]

Despite the positive role of these elements in the world, for which they receive due praise,[79] their presence there is a tragedy, a misfortune to be remedied, not condoned.

> *Know and observe the five great Buddhas of Light*
> *Why have they come from the Father's side into this world?*
> *Know clearly that they have suffered for no sins of their own*
> *And that the good and clever beings will be extracted from the devils' den.*[80]

According to Turkic sources, the "Living Self" is "the god of food and drink."[81] The five divine elements that are the object of salvational action exist within humans both genetically and through ingestion. They provide the essential forces of life, and so their relative abundance or dearth creates different conditions in the body.

> Just as craftsmen cannot work without any materials, so similarly men and women, to the extent that they do not partake of the power of the Five Gods, cannot incite the shameless heat through love of the body at all. Nor will they give birth to sons and daughters. Then, when the power of God becomes (their) food and drink, they will grow and be strong. As a consequence, they will give birth to sons and daughters.[82]

Unfortunately, one cannot consume unadulterated divinity, for it is always mixed with evil substances that stir up the passions.

> That external lust of yours which is mixed with food and drink and thus enters the body, is mixed with the internal lust that is in male and female bodies. Then your lust becomes so powerful that, as fire consumes dry firewood, and also as fish swim in water, as seed and grain spring up in moist ground, just so your lust is that powerful inside the body. Then your lust, from the top of your head to the tips of your toenails [. . .].[83]

Eastern Manichaeans, as those elsewhere, were made acutely aware of the defects of ordinary metabolism, and the crucial role a perfected body could play in the work of religion. "This fire which is in the body," we are told, "devours the external fire which comes in fruit and food, and finds it pleasant."[84] The literature emphasizes the importance of a clear understanding of the processes one initiates in fasting and eating. A Turkic script guides the adherent through a series of reflections on the interaction of body and food to be performed at the meal:

> The second thought is this: The consumed food which enters into the body dies. The third thought is this, as one says: My body is a thing that must perform the extensive duty. The food and drink ordained for it must be held in readiness for the appropriate time. What an injury if one does not do it! The fourth thought, it says: Continuous is the struggle with the passions. Why? Because your passions are entirely wonderful tastes to the body, for this reason they become strong. Thus, just as fire burns dry firewood, so must one always consume food and drink at the (right) time, so that the passions shall not become strong and may not do harm to the body. When one sits down at the table *(xuan,* from Iranian *xw'n)*, one should think these words with the whole mind and take them to heart![85]

The Elect appear to walk a tightrope in their divine service between ordinary consumption and starvation; both their food and their digestive forces possess an ambiguous status in the divine economy, equally amenable to evil and good consequences. Mastery of their metabolism through a careful pattern of fasting and consumption produces the desired salvational effect on the divine substance within their food. So the *mānīstān,* where the ritual meal is performed, can be characterized as "the healing place of the element *(mrd'sp'nd)* gods."[86]

Only a reformed metabolism can redeem the divine substance from food. The Parthian *Discourse on the Living Ones (jydgan sxwn)* warns,

> [The one who] takes merit-food *(pwnw'r)* as much as a big mountain and is able to redeem (it), must eat (it); together, he himself will be saved *(bwxsyd)* and that one, too, will be redeemed who gave the merit-food; and without damage it reaches the abode of the gods. And the one who takes as much merit-food as a grain of mustard and is not able to redeem (it), he better [. . .] and goes (?) [. . .] fire [. . .] who sees (his) own seed by a thousandfold [multiplied(?)]. And that person who [. . .] breaks the precept *(cxš'byd)*, is led in great shame and fear before the righteous [judge], and he [is not able (?)] to turn; and he [. . .] to eat (his) body. And his ear they cut off again [and again]; and his tongue they hack into slices; in the same manner they cut all of (his) [limbs]. And again and again they pour molten copper into his mouth, and give (him) red-hot iron to eat; and they drive an iron nail into (his) ear. And who is able to describe completely the wicked, horrible suffering and hardship that that accursed [and] unbelieving person [who] defiles the pure [religion] experiences? [But] fortunate is that person [who] keeps completely the pure [religion] and precept.[87]

The individual, therefore, must adhere to the ritual role that corresponds to his or her disciplinary status. As specified in one of the *Songs of the Living Self*, these roles are that of the "dutiful and fortunate Auditor who gathers the self," and the "fortunate and happy Righteous One who purifies it."[88]

In his farewell discourse, Mani enjoins his followers to "bear the toil of the Lord, so that you may find reward and pious recompense and eternal life in the highest."[89] One of the duties of this "toil" is "purification of the Living Self" *(p'c[yšn] 'y gryw zyndg)*. In the *Songs of the Living Self*, this purification is celebrated:

> To you will I pray, virtuous god, Living Self, gift from the Father. Blessed, blessed be you, light self; in health ascend to your own home. Delighted power, chosen greatness, strong power, intelligent and wise: all light gods for your sake [. . .] the Elect strive so that you may truly be exalted. . . . This anguish, persecution and hardship which you experience, who is able to teach

it? The merciful illuminator, blessed lord, strong and noble, beneficent Mar
Mani. Always will we bless that divine glory which has shown salvation to you,
light self.[90]

Here, with brief allusion to the suffering described more expansively in M 33,
the Living Self is wished on its way to liberation, with due thanks to Mani who
has made this victory possible.

The Chinese *Hymnscroll*'s "Praise of the Five Lights" is probably a re-
cension of the *Songs of the Living Self*. It contains very similar passages, in
which the singer(s) enjoins:

> Firmly observe fasting *(chai)* and precepts *(chieh)*, always guard them care-
> fully; and control your thoughts, regulating them constantly. Day and night
> think only of the true and correct law; attend to the weighing *(ch'üan)* and
> clarifying *(ch'eng)* of the five wondrous bodies *(wu miao-shen)*.[91]

In its second canto, the "Praise of the Five Lights" makes ideological and practical references to the practice of the ritual meal, in which the "five lights" of
the title are sifted from food in the bodies of the Elect.

> Again I proclaim to you, doers of good deeds, brothers of light, apply your
> minds to think solely on the weighing[92] of the wondrous bodies. Be each of
> you as a courageous and wise ship captain, to ferry across these wave-tossed
> exiles. They are the precious treasure of the Venerable of Light: bear them all
> off the sea with your bodies as ships. Like diligent physicians, cut out their
> painful boils and sores; for they have long suffered, hoping for deliverance
> and protection. Be compassionate, each of you, in receiving the truth, and
> quickly return them to the Lord precisely according to their number. This no-
> ble clan has been wave-tossed for untold years now: quickly dispatch them
> back to their homeland, the place of peace and joy. The upright, correct, and
> radiant ones with all the marks intact: extract *(pa-li)* them soon from the store-
> house of greed and desire; seek out [these] rare treasures in the midst of the
> dark, deep sea of suffering, and quickly lift them up to the King of Nirvana
> and Purity. Pull out the grievously wounded, remove their ulcerous sores;
> wash and bathe [these] bright pearls, remove them from filth. For the law says
> that all wondrous offerings *(kung)* that are received are to be restored in
> proper purity to their original lord. For they are nothing other than the flesh

and blood of Jesus, which may be taken freely by whoever is fit to receive them. But if one should act falsely, with a betraying heart, then Jesus himself would be powerless and there would be no escape.[93]

Here the Elect are "physicians" able to heal the elements, provided that they are "upright and correct . . . with all the marks intact," that is, manifesting the perfect observance of the disciplines. Even in China, we see the identification of the divine elements with the eucharistic "flesh and blood of Jesus." Even more startlingly, this Chinese Manichaean hymn fully confirms the polemical charge of Augustine that Manichaean ideology posits a savior in need of salvation, a portion of God that itself requires the ritual aid of humans.

Some *Songs of the Living Self* welcome the arrival of the divine presence, ripe for liberation, at the ritual meal, for example, "Come are you in health, gods' self, light which shines in the darkness";[94] "Come are you in health, bound self, gathered from every direction."[95] In greeting the Living Self, the meal participants (the "children of truth") are encouraged to "praise the self which is our life," which has come "from the sky and the womb of the earth and from all creation."[96] In one case the welcome, "Come is this saved self, (it is) come to this religion of righteousness," is answered by the Living Self: "Always pray thus, O Elect, so that you purify me, in hearts full of wonder, and lead me to life."[97]

One *Song of the Living Self*, itself containing liturgical instructions discussed in the previous chapter, instructs the community to

> Honor as a guest the gods' child at the divine meal. Prepare the kindly abode; show the road to the light. Make every limb complete in the five, seven and twelve. These are the seven bright jewels which truly are the lands of life. By those powers live every world and all soul-possessing things. They are like a lamp in a house which in the dark shines light. . . . A hall has been found, O righteous Elect and dutiful Auditors. Prepare the self for purification and this true, holy mystery keep.[98]

This text connects the performance of hymns with the acts that liberate the Living Self. A recitation known as "The True Word of Life," we are told, "releases the captive one from its bondage." The narrator says that "You who sing, O Elect, shall find eternal life. Purify the light self so that it in turn will save you."[99] Vocalized prayers and psalms actually constituted the vehicles by which the emancipated light ascended to heaven as the end of the metabolic process. In Pelliot Chinois 3049, a prayer-text associated with the alms service, the speaker appends a prayer for a prayer, so to speak: "Cause this prayer to enter into the palace of the Powerful God! May it be eternally so!" The Powerful God *(Küclüg Täŋri)* is in this context a designation for the Column of Glory, who "'by his own power gathers and bears to the height the lightweight god."

Summation

By sheer bulk alone, the "rescue of the Living Self" dominated Manichaean exposition of the alimentary rites. This rationale shared the same ideological constructs (cosmogony, cosmology, anthropogony, anthropology) as Manichaean disciplinary rationales, and so allowed for a strong coherence of discourse within which the individual Manichaean could operate. Behind its many permutations, including the inconstant identification of the Living Self with "the flesh and blood of Jesus," we can discern the broad contours of what we might call a myth; but it is important to keep in mind the regular juxtaposition of primordial time and present circumstance in the language of these texts. The Manichaean discourse on the Living Self did not provide a symbolic key by which the ritual meal became a mere depiction or representation of something that occurred in mythic time, or was occurring somewhere else in the cosmos. The "myth" of the Primordial Man and the origins of cosmic mixture provided the etiology for the present situation upon which the ritual meal operated. The voice of the Living Self, speaking through the Manichaean hymnists, was not the echo of an ancient commemorated god, but the voice of the immanent deity within the alms-offerings of the ritual meal. By partaking of the offerings the Elect did not symbolically commune with their god, they digested him.

SUPPORT FOR THE ELECT

A second rationale for the alms-service is support of the Elect class within the larger Manichaean community. In certain respects, this dimension of the religious economy is similar to Catholic lay support of the priesthood, those who have embraced a higher order of religious life and serve the community in specialized ways. But the divergent fate of the Elect and Auditors in Manichaean soteriology gives support for the Elect a character more closely analogous to Buddhist lay sponsorship of monks and nuns. In the words of *Kephalaion 115*, the Auditor "brings rest to the holy church by the alms which he brings . . . the [blessed] children of the church rest upon it." Thus, the alms-service can be portrayed as a kind of altruism on behalf of those who wish to devote their full attention to spiritual matters and achieve liberation on the shoulders of the support group. The layperson, both Manichaean and Buddhist, counts upon similar support when it is his or her turn to adopt the higher discipline in a future life.

The Central Manichaean Tradition

While the key Arabic writers on Manichaeism relate portions of the discourse on the Living Self, they appear uniquely oblivious to its ritual connections. Instead, they see the alms-service of the Auditors largely in terms of a support by the "common people" *('amma)* of the religion's "elevated ranks" *(khawass)*.[100] The alms-service is analogized to the Islamic tithe. Al-Biruni reports that Mani required the *samma'un* to sponsor *(muwasat)* the *siddiqun*.[101]

The Western Manichaean Tradition

The Elect could not perform their divinely appointed task of redemption without the support of the Auditors. "The holy church itself does not have a place of rest in all of this world except through the Catechumens who heed it . . . who give rest to it . . . from whom it harvests."[102] Furthermore, the "assembly of Catechumens" *(t.sauhs n.n.katechoumenos)* "receives the holy church, becomes fixed to it, and gives rest to it in all its works and all its pains. It becomes to it a place of rest, since it rests itself in it in every place. The place in which there are no Catechumens, the holy church has no rest in it."[103] The mutuality of this exchange forms the foundation of the entire edifice of Manichaean life and practice. "This is the way, then, of the [holy] church; it becomes a place of rest for the alms of the Catechumens, and the Catechumens on their part become a place of rest for the holy church."[104]

In the Latin *Tebessa Codex*, the anonymous author adduces several passages from the New Testament in support of the partnership of the Auditors with the Elect. "These two levels, founded upon one faith in the same church, support each other, and whoever abounds in anything shares it with another:

the Elect with the Auditors from their own heavenly treasure . . . and the Auditors with the Elect [. . .]."[105] The rich, "who are themselves called disciples of the second order," are commanded to "make friends" of the Elect.[106] The author speaks favorably of those "who were insufficiently strong to ascend to the level of election, dwelling in their own houses; but they assisted the Elect and, receiving them within their own [houses] and residences, furnished whatever they had (that was) needed."[107]

The alms-service of the Auditor allowed the Elect to avoid sinful interaction with the world. This is the point, however pejoratively framed, of the so-called Apology to the Bread. The support of the Auditors made possible the disciplined and perfected life of election, free from sin and leading directly to ascent into heaven.

> For, as I remarked to you a little before, if anyone reaps, he will be reaped; and so, too, if anyone casts grain into the mill, he will be cast in himself in like manner, or if he kneads he will be kneaded, or if he bakes he will be baked; and for this reason they are interdicted from doing any such work. . . . And if a person walks upon the ground, he injures the earth; and if he moves his hand, he injures the air; for the air is the soul of humans and living creatures, both fowl, and fish, and creeping thing.[108]

Freed from such retributions by the sponsorship of the Auditors, the Elect served as a vanguard, demonstrating and implementing the path to salvation so that others might follow in their due time. According to Augustine, "the Elect get others to bring their food to them, that they may not be guilty of murder."[109] The alms-service thus insulated the Elect from an interaction with the world that would, of necessity, entail harm.

The Manichaean tradition cultivated in Auditors a recognition that one benefit to them for sustaining an Elect class, among others, is that the Auditors themselves will be Elect in a future life. Augustine attests to this emphasis: "All you promise (the Auditors) is not a resurrection, but a change (revolutionem) to another mortal existence, in which they shall live the life of your Elect, the life you live yourself, and are so much praised for."[110]

A significant exchange comes in the Coptic Kephalaion 88, when an Auditor insists that when he sees a so-called Righteous One "wrathful, cholic, quarreling with his companion, separated by his own wrath, speaking ugly words," he comes to the conclusion that such an individual "cannot be right-

eous . . . cannot be established in the truth," and therefore is unworthy of support.[111] But Mani criticizes such a facile view of Elect status.

> But you, do not be disturbed in your heart. Know once and for all that they
> are established in a body that is not theirs, enraged against the flesh of sin
> which becomes the other inhabitant in a strange land. . . . Since you have
> known the mystery of the two natures, you have understood that [that] which
> is good and that which is evil dwell in every man. You have understood, fur-
> ther, that the holy ones bear a great burden upon their shoulders. . . . Under-
> stand also . . . the way that you dwell in sin constantly; you make your life in
> food and drink, in the desire for women, gold [and] silver. Your hands are
> loosened constantly to wound the Cross of Light. See, you are established in
> all these sins. The holy ones watch you doing them. Nevertheless, they do not
> reproach them, nor do they hate you, nor do they distance (themselves) from
> you, nor do they say, "As long as he commits sins in this way I will not be a
> teacher to him." But they receive [you] with love and sweetness. They speak
> with [you] in the wisdom of God, teaching you [concerning] your festivities
> and deeds . . . that they are sins. And they bring you all these alms. They say
> to you: "You are our brother. You are our associate, who will walk with us to
> the land of light."[112]

Although some Manichaean discourse urges close scrutiny of the Elect on the
part of the Auditors, the passage quoted above encourages a degree of toler-
ance for the imperfections of the Elect, as a tactful and tactical reinforcement
of the alms-service.

The Eastern Manichaean Tradition

Exhortations and parables stress the partnership of the Elect and Auditors in the
sacred operation of the community. A book preserved in the fragments M 101
and M 911 includes the following parable, written in the abbreviated style indicative of a mnemonic script for oral performance:

> And the Auditor within [the community (?)], (and) the "soul-work" in the re-
> ligion, are like a ship [upon the sea] — the towing-line in the hand of the [tow-
> man] on shore, the sailor [(holding the other end) on the ship]. [The] sea is

the world, the ship is the [Auditor, the sailor is the alms-]service, the tow-man is the [Elect, the towing-line] is wisdom, [the shore is salvation].[113]

Sympathy for the burden carried by the Elect seems to underlie the injunction to Auditors to "give alms to the extremely distressed Elect. Feel (their) pain and suffering."[114] Mani's *Šābuhragān* refers to "the Elect with their helpers *(hy'r'n),*"[115] and to these "helpers of the Elect" Jesus speaks the judgment of Matthew 25, praising their assistance to his disciples.[116] The Auditors appear in Turkic hymns as guardians of the Elect: "Equipped with armor, they stand ready to aid the pure Elect."[117] While we are accustomed to metaphorical descriptions of Elect "armed" with the seals and precepts, one cannot be sure that the armor of the Auditors in this passage is not the literal accouterments of the Uygur warrior class, who by defense of the Uygur realm also protected the Manichaean faith that flourished there.

The Middle Persian text M 8251 bears the title "Precepts for Auditors" *('[n]drz 'y[g] nywš'g['n]);* but far from being a table of rules, this text has the character of an instructional discourse on the importance of unity with the Elect.

> Through the "soul-work" and through friendship they are mixed *('myxsynd)* with them, and with all their heart they strive for friendship, and they are as loving as if they were their kinsfolk. And through these two signs they are bound with them: through the sign of love and through the sign of fear, which they receive from them. And they hold them in honor as one holds one's own master (and) lord, and they fear to transgress their command and to confuse these mysteries and greatnesses that they at all times hear from them. And in the same way they also fear and keep away from wickedness and greediness, [and] with true knowledge they are strongly mixed *('m[yx]t).*[118]

"Mixture" with the Elect offers advantages to the Auditors, and alleviates the conditions of "mixture" with the world.

> (For) in the precept *('ndrz)* and deeds *(kyrdg'n)* they are [still] inferior; because they [are] mixed *(['m]yxt)* with the activity of the world and with the covetousness of Až and with the lust of male and female [and] with pregnancy and birth of [. . .] gold and silver. . . . And because [the Auditors] are

inferior to the Righteous Ones, for that reason transmigration *(wrdyšn)* will be ceaseless until they, in various places, are made suitably free from that evil turning *(dyjwštyy)*. This is because they have not put off the world and its evil as perfectly as the Righteous Ones have put (it) off. For the Righteous Ones have put off the whole world and its covetousness and have become perfect through that one desire for godliness. [And through these] two signs they devotedly stand in one mind, through the sign of love and through the sign of fear, because of which they have put off all covetousness and all transmigration and distress [and] all suffering and destruction from it (the mind?), and are saved without defilement and go and are received and [collected] into that great and praised world [and] into that light of [. . .].[119]

This text's comparison of the Auditors and Elect resembles that found in the Latin *Tebessa Codex*.[120] Both works take pains to emphasize the unity as well as the distinctiveness of the two ranks. In M 8251, both elements of the treatment center on "the signs of love and fear," which mean different things to the two ranks but nevertheless bind them together. While for the Elect the two signs are discussed in general terms of their liberating effect, for the Auditor these same signs have very specific relevance to the latter's devotion (through love) and obedience (through fear) to the Elect.

Summation

H.-C. Puech sees the relationship of support between the Auditor and the Elect as the essential purpose of the Manichaean alms-service. In so many other ways outside the parameters of church membership, the Auditors were made partakers of the Manichaean covenant by this system of support and interaction. "The acts permitted to the Auditors change in meaning completely, turning from evil to good, in the measure to which they are exclusively accomplished in the function, favor and service of the church, oriented not towards oneself . . . but towards the 'Holy Church,' in the direction and to the profit of the Elect, the saints, who incarnate it in their persons."[121] The alms-service established a daily contact between Elect and Auditor, in this way making the latter into an "auxiliary" of the church. Hans Schaeder likewise asserts that "the hearers fulfill a set of cultic observances, but their chief contribution lies in devoted service to the Elect."[122] In the view of Michel Tardieu, the whole purpose of the alms-service was for the Elect to be able to fulfill "their function of prayer and preaching,"[123] and Hans-Joachim Klimkeit characterizes it as the "financial base for the elect."[124] Thus, some of the leading voices in modern Manichaean studies have endorsed this rationale as the most important in understanding the Manichaean ethos, to the neglect of any other purported function.

The reasoning that favors emphasis on support for the Elect as the primary significance of the alms-service is not difficult to fathom. First of all, it is the rationale that best fits an interpretation of Manichaean disciplines as an end in themselves, without an essential relationship to rituals. If the principal practice of Manichaeism was an extreme ascesis that itself produces salvation, it would be only logical to assume that sponsoring that ascesis would be the most important project of the larger Manichaean community. Second, such a rationale possesses ample parallels in other religious traditions, making constructive comparison possible, whereas the rescue of the Living Self does not have such obvious analogies. Third, and perhaps most important, this rationale alone of the many offered by the tradition can be embraced from an etic standpoint. With the unspoken assumption that the salvational goals enunciated as the ultimate purpose of even this rationale are simply erroneous, the researcher can apply various social scientific explanatory models to uncover the true relations involved in Manichaean polity. Interestingly, this interpretation of what the Manichaeans are really up to matches exactly that of Augustine and the other Christian polemicists, who viewed the entire construct of Manichaeism as an elaborate fraud designed to dupe Auditors into sponsoring the idle Elect.

The Auditors did support the Elect in the latter's higher spiritual endeavor; of that there can be no question. But the degree to which this one aspect of the complex relations between the two classes has been exalted in the modern scholarship as the essential operating motivation begs for justification which the sources are unable to supply. The examples cited above attest to the fact that the Manichaeans employed rhetoric of partnership and support as part of larger set of encouraging and morale-reinforcing tropes. But they are insufficient in quantity or in connection to other aspects of Manichaean discourse to be given the primary place among Manichaean alimentary rationales, as some modern scholars have ventured to do. In fact, it would be very easy to redistribute most of the texts cited to the categories "Rescue of the Living Self," and "Merit," in that they depend upon these other rationales to in turn justify lay support of the Elect. Augustine actually says as much when he criticizes the Manichaean use of Matthew 25, since, he says, "by your absurdities, a man will not be received into the kingdom of God for the service of giving food to the saints, but because he has chewed *(manducavit)* them and exhaled *(anhelaret)* them out, or has himself been chewed and exhaled into heaven."[125] If we narrow our field of view to the interpersonal relationship that doubtless arises in the Manichaean alms-economy, we are in danger of relegating a large portion of the larger Manichaean *episteme* to the dustbin. The Elect are valued in the normative tradition primarily as conduits to other processes with which the larger community is concerned, the rescue of the Living Self and merit.[126]

ASSISTANCE TO THE DEAD

According to *Kephalaion 115*, "the one who brings the alms and the memorial of the person who has come out of the body, brings rest." Among the "four victories" accomplished by the alms-service, the third is that which the donor accomplishes "[on behalf of] the person who has come out of his body." For the donor, it gains credit as alms, but it is also "a remembrance for his brother or his father or his mother or his son or his daughter or his kinsman who has come out of the body."[127]

The Western Manichaean Tradition

Given the belief that they would be judged according to their own deeds, and that their behavior remained, to a significant degree, embroiled in sin, Auditors had due cause to worry about their postmortem condition. Were the Elect in a position to aid them, alleviate the penalty for their sins, or assist them to a happier existence? *Kephalaion 115* addresses this concern specifically with reference to offerings made on behalf of deceased individuals. Mani affirms the validity of the intercessory prayers of the Elect,[128] and supplies a primordial antecedent for such practices. The fall and restoration of the Primordial Man provides a direct analogy to the condition of the dead Manichaean who sought to rise from an earthly imprisonment to heaven.

> Know, therefore, from this word that every perfect Elect and every faithful Catechumen who exists in the truth, who stands to pray in faith, who entreats,

who prays in faith, [be it] for himself alone [or] else for another who has been freed from his body, his entreaty and his request [which he asked for] is given to him the way that the entreaty of his fathers was given.[129]

The intercession of an Elect is part of an exchange of assistance that includes the usual alms-support for which the Auditors were responsible.[130] Mani analogizes the situation to a human court, where a criminal's kinsman petitions on his behalf. The wheels of justice are greased, so to speak, by a bit of lucre, which Mani characterizes as "the assistance (*boēthia*) of those whom he petitioned, to give them something so that they might help him," and the malefactor receives pardon.[131]

> Now this is the way that the deed of this man is like (the case of) the one who has been freed from his body. Afterwards a Catechumen or Catechumena or family member of him [comes] and loves him and makes a memorial in the church for him; and the holy one entreats for his sin in the entreaty and memorial which is made for him in the holy church. That soul is released and it emerges from affliction to breadth (*ouastn*). This Living Soul, then, which has been freed because of this other soul, that is, the Living Soul which has been rescued in the name of that person and has been rescued, purified, and established in its original nature (*ousia*), becomes his fellow assistant and entreats for the soul of the one who has been freed from his body. It petitions for mercy for it, and a pardon through the power of light. The way that the breadth [exists] for this Living Soul because of this soul, [this is the way] that the soul finds breadth and becomes free [of that body] and it goes to the land of light.[132]

In other words, the divine element within the alms-offering, essentially identical to the divine element that constitutes the human soul, takes the opportunity of its own salvation through the ritual meal to assist that soul for whom it is offered. "The way that the breadth (*ouastn*) exists for this Living Soul (in the alms-offering) because of this soul (on whose behalf it is offered), [this is the way] that this (latter) soul finds breadth, and it becomes free [of that body] and goes into the land of [light]."[133]

Mani exhorts his listeners with a promise that holds good "as long as [you] give alms and memorials and [. . . for these] souls which come out of their bodies," namely that, "because of [the gift] of the alms-offering which you give and the cup of water [which you offer] to those who are holy, you bring a great good for this Living Soul, the one that has [been bound] in 'transfusion' *(metaggismos)*, [and for the soul for] which you bring a memorial, which you rescue from a thousand afflictions and ten-thousand 'transfusions.'"[134]

The Eastern Manichaean Tradition

With the story of the devoted Manichaean auditor Khēbrā, the Iranian Manichaean community warned against the inappropriateness of mourning the dead and encouraged the more productive response of performing alms-service as a memorial for the dead, so that the Elect could offer intercessory prayers.

> And in those days the Beneficent One came there. And they performed alms-service *(rw'ng'n)* before him. And at the food hour, the Beneficent One prayed for that youth in the benediction *(pd 'frywn)*. Then he prostrated himself three times. And the "children" (i.e., Mani's disciples) asked, "Tell us for what reason you prostrated yourself." And he said, "I prostrated myself to Jesus, my own father and lord for my wish that I sought from him and for a supplication that he would also accept your prayer. And behold, angels led Daraw's soul and placed it before me, standing arrayed in the customary apparel of kings."[135]

Iranian Manichaeism adopted the term *āfrīn* from Zoroastrianism, where it is used for a kind of benediction associated with a food rite. The Zoroastrian *āfrīngān*, rite of the *āfrīn*, is usually performed on behalf of the dead, as a commemorative ceremony thought to assist the departed soul in its afterlife. This parallel is at least suggestive, and a careful investigation of ritual relations between the two religions is warranted.

The Chinese *Hymnscroll* contains a hymn designated for use as a conclusion of "the prayer during offering for the dead."

> The Light-nature of a certain Yi has passed away from his carnal body. His actions and deeds are imperfect, and we fear he may sink into the sea of tortures. We entreat the two great lights, the five-fold law-body, the clean and pure Elect, the great compassionate power: rescue and lift that nature, free it from transmigration, the rough and hard bodies, the various earth-dungeons,

boiling water in caldrons and burning charcoal in furnaces. May all Buddhas have pity on that nature, beget great compassion, and give it emancipation; (may they) conduct it themselves into the world of light, its original birthplace, and the peaceful and happy land. The labor and expenses of the service for merit have been contributed as equal to our above wish.[136]

The last clause of this hymn, with almost legal precision, expresses an expected *quid pro quo* between the "virtuous service" of the rite in which this hymn is performed and the fate of the deceased's soul. The context of this service is not specified. Based on the Coptic and Iranian data, one can propose a setting in the context of the ritual meal. But greater certainty on this point awaits a detailed study of Manichaean funeral practices.

Summation

This rationale for the alms-service, more practical and understandable from an outsider's point of view, seems quite anomalous to the tenor of the Manichaean ethos as it has been understood, where each individual must make account for his or her own action. If it evokes surprise from the modern researcher for that reason, this reaction can also be found among the Manichaeans themselves. The Auditor who addresses Mani in *Kephalaion 115* has his doubts about the practice, "because we have heard from you [that] each receives requital according to his deeds."[137] But Mani affirms that the special bonds between Auditors, Elect, and the divine forces above allow for special intervention. At the same time, the addition of this facet to the ritual meal furthers the process of ritual consolidation remarked upon earlier. The ritual meal also assimilates rites on behalf of the dead, confirming its status as the all-inclusive core of Manichaean religious life.

MERIT FOR THE PARTICIPANT

The Manichaean tradition possessed a concept of religious merit analogous to that of most known religions, whereby an implicit or explicit promise of reward provides a rationale for participation in the religion's system of practice. Although the fourth "victory" is missing from the fragmentary passage on the rationales for the alms-service in *Kephalaion 115*, there is an allusion to merit within the third "victory," where it speaks of an offering being an alms for the donor, as well as a memorial for the dead.[138] The ample amount of testimony to merit connected with Manichaean alimentary rites in other sources would necessitate its inclusion in our discussion here, even if it were not identified as one of the four "victories."

The Central Manichaean Tradition

An-Nadim quotes Mani's advice to the one who is unable to adopt the life of the Elect, "unable to subdue lust and craving," but who still "loves the religion": "Let him seize upon guarding the religion and the Righteous Ones, that there may be an offsetting of his unworthy actions. . . . That will defend him during his transitory life and at his appointed time, so that his status will be the other status (i.e., that of an Elect) in the life to come."[139]

The Western Manichaean Tradition

Mani declares that "every person shall follow after his deeds, whether to life or to death."[140] He describes the fate of the typical Auditor as directly correlated with the latter's alms-service: "They are released, and they are purified, each of them according to his deeds, according to his approach to the church."[141] In fact, a direct analogy is drawn between the path of the perfect Auditor after death and the processing of food in the bodies of the Elect.

> They are purified in the skies, and they are harvested in the manner of a ripe fruit. . . . This is the way of this alms-offering which passes from the Elect, and they give form to it in many images, and it is purified, and it goes into the country of the living. This is the way, moreover, that the souls of the Catechumens are like to it—these who do not come to a body (again).[142]

The Auditor should pray, Mani directs, "so that his deeds will be collected, [the] first and the last, and be reckoned to his share."[143]

> [The] alms will be reckoned [to] his good deeds—the fast that he did, the garment that he gave to them, the holy ones. A daily participation (koinōnia) they also share with them in it, in their fast and their good. These things are counted along with these others, and his deeds are divided into the good,

(and) the other half sins. And yet the sins in which he sins in half of the year are scattered to five parts. Four among them are released to him through [his] patronage of the holy church, through the faith [and the] love of the Elect—one because of this [and] another since he knows the *gnosis*. He separates the light from the darkness. He gives a hymn and a prayer [to the] exalted Illuminator. The rest also of those whom he [sponsors]. Because, then, of these good deeds [that he did, they release] four parts to him . . . [sins] in which he sinned from the day when he became a Catechumen. The remainder (is) a single part, the one that is reckoned to him, and he is wounded on their account. . . . And afterwards he is purified, either above or else below he is purified according to the worth of [his] deeds. And he is cleansed, and he is washed, and he is arranged. And afterwards he is adorned in an image of light, and [he is drawn] up, and he attains the land of rest, so that [the place] where his heart is, his treasure also will be there. If he remains firm, that is, in his catechumenate, he receives requital of his good deeds in this manner. But if he lies and he perverts the truth, then they will count his sins to him completely, and furthermore (both) the first and the last.[144]

Whatever new sins may accrue to the Auditor "will be released many times over [to him] because of his fast *(nēstia)* and [his prayer *(shlēl)* and his] alms-offering *([mn]tnae)*."[145]

We find many statements implying a *quid pro quo* between the deeds of Manichaean adherents and their afterlife. A psalm voices hope for a concrete manifestation of the fruits of the speaker's labors, and requests, "send my alms to meet me,"[146] "give me now the reward of my deeds according to the agreement of my savior."[147] This reward is not a grace, but a payment for services rendered: "Gather all of you, O souls, that [. . .] my alms, and repay me [. . .] the favor which I did for you."[148] "Yoke for me quickly my soaring chariots and my holy fasts, which are my horses; and my prayers to God and my alms. Take me speedily to the Land of the Glorious."[149] The faithful Auditor is assured that each alms-offering made "becomes a comforter before you and causes them to free you from a multitude of obstacles."[150] The Elect also earn merit in this system; that is at least the implication of claims they make about the work they have done. "I have purified you, my God," an Elect declares.[151] "I have purified you, my God, from flesh and blood; do not abandon me in the desert of this world. The Father, the king of the crowns, I have made him pure from [. . .]. This power that supports the universe, I have guarded its freight."[152] In the funeral hymns, the congregation speaks to the deceased, re-assuring him or her that "your wares that you produced, behold they are first before you: some following after you, some overtaking you. Rejoice, therefore, and be glad as you step before the judge."[153] The apotheosized Elect is in-formed that, "your prayers and your fasts have become a crown upon your head."[154]

The alms-service, like any system of merit, implies a corresponding con-cept of demerit, such that "if one does not give pious donations (*eusebeiai*) to his Elect, he will be punished in *gehenna*, and will be translated into the bod-ies of Catechumens, until he render many pious donations; and for this rea-son they offer to the Elect whatever is best in their food."[155] In fact, merit for the Auditor is often characterized as a release of sins rather than the earning of spiritual capital. "They believe that these crimes are forgiven their Auditors be-cause the latter offer food of this sort to their Elect in order that the divine sub-stance, on being purified in their stomachs, may obtain pardon for those through whose offering it is given to be purified."[156] Notice how the rescue of the Living Self constitutes the engine that drives merit in this tradition; merit is predicated on participation in this rescue, which directly offsets harm in-flicted on what is being rescued. "A certain compensation (*compensatio*) takes place, you say, when some part of what is taken from the fields is brought to the Elect and holy men to be purified";[157] "the injuries your Auditors inflict upon plants are expiated through the fruits which they bring to your church."[158]

Augustine reports a more direct form of assistance to the Auditor accom-plished by the alms-service and ritual meal. Those Auditors who "possess greater merit" than those who will be reborn as Elect (a worthy lot them-selves!) "shall enter into melons and cucumbers, or some food which you (Elect) will masticate, that they may be quickly purified by your belching."[159] This is not a case of Augustine's rhetoric running away with him, for he repeats the idea in a later work: "They believe that the souls of their Auditors are re-turned to the Elect, or by a happier short-cut (*compendio*) to the food of their Elect so that, already purified, they would then not have to revert into other bodies."[160] Here once again, the Auditors tap into the system that liberates the Living Self as a source of their own personal salvation.

The Eastern Manichaean Tradition

In the fragmentary remains of his farewell discourse, Mani enjoins his followers to "teach assistance to the religion," to "bear the toil of the Lord, so that
you may find reward and pious recompense and eternal life in the highest."[161]
Eastern Manichaean literature possesses several prose discussions of the relations between Elect and Auditors, focusing primarily on the alms-service, as
well as poetic reinforcements of this discourse. The voice of a deceased Auditor confirms Mani's promise in the concluding fragment of the Turkic "Parable of Brama the Astrologer," when it says, "From those alms which I gave,
from the good deeds which I accomplished, I have found as (their) fruit the
light, divine heaven."[162] Mani's *Šābuhragān* contains a last judgment scene
derived ultimately from Matthew 25, in which Jesus declares to the "helpers
of the Elect," "That which you did to the Elect, that service you did for me.
And I shall give you paradise as a reward."[163] And further on, the idea is reiterated that "he who shall do the will of the gods [and] be a traveling-companion
and helper [of the Elect, and he] too who [is] well-disposed to them [. . .]
shall be [. . .] with the gods in Paradise."

"Soul-work" *(rw'ng'n)* is, by definition, an activity "involving the soul";
but in what way does it involve the soul? On the one hand, this activity collects "soul" *(gryw, gy'n)* from its dispersal in the cosmos and "brings it to religion," so that it can ascend to heaven. On the other hand, the major point of
all this, from the position of the Auditors, is forgiveness of the sins that impinge
upon their own souls *(rw'n)*. One should note that the "soul" of "soul-work" is
rw'n, and not *gy'n* or *gryw*. The texts refer to the right sort of Auditors, those
who do their "soul-work," as "good-souled" *(hw-rw'n)*, and so it can be said that
the work they are doing is upon their own souls. Thus a mundane economic
relation transmutes into part of a discipline focused on the self-formation of its
participants, at the same time providing, within its own *episteme*, a reasonable
means of salvation.

The Parthian text M 6020, identified by headline as the *Discourse on the
Living Ones (jydgan sxwn)*, outlines the basic system of merit associated with
Manichaean alimentary rites.

> And that person who is in the religious community should know how that
> service that he performs for the pure Elect is for the soul *(pd rw'n)*. And he
> should know that fruit which is born from the gift. If (his) whole house were

of gold and pearls and he gave it for the sake of the soul *(rw'n r'd)*, he would not necessarily be pitied. [And if] it were so that he were able to bake as bread the flesh [upon] (his) body, and cut (it) off [with] (his) own hand and give (it) to the Elect [. . .] it is necessary to know what [. . .]. [The one who] takes merit-food *(pwnw'r)* like a big mountain and is able to redeem (it), must eat (it); together, that person will be saved and that one, too, will be redeemed who gave the merit-food; and without damage it reaches the abode of the gods . . . Fortunate is that person [who] keeps completely the pure [religion] and precept [. . .] which not [. . .] not eternally [. . .] makes merit *(pwn qryd)*.

A Turkic exhortation commends the Auditor, who

> shall do good deeds through the power of alms *(buši)*. Moreover, the Messiah Buddha, because of their good hearts, gave the name "good-hearted" to faithful people who give alms and who seek out their souls. . . . And also he spoke thusly, "Whoever suffers and agonizes because of the body, then his reward is the acquisition of death and decay for the body. Whoever sows good seed for his soul *(özüt)*, shall obtain (as) his reward an eternal, immortal self *(öz)* in the land of the gods." . . . Give alms to the extremely impoverished Elect. . . . Also, believe the following single-mindedly: that the reward of your one piece of bread and your one cup of water is immediate and not delayed at all.[164]

Because the condition of the person who eats the offerings means either salvation or damnation for the divine substance in them, Auditors have good reason to scrutinize the behavior of the Elect they support. They are warned that "False preachers who are errant and confused . . . hold the name Elect and take alms *(buši)* through deception and fraud. They themselves will go to hell and take the donor along with them."[165] It is perhaps no coincidence that M 139.I, dealing with the absolution of the Auditors' sins at the hands of the Elect, belongs to the same book as M 139.II, which instructs the Elect in worthiness for the meal.

Parables also are employed to communicate the advantages of alms-service. "[B]y their own 'soul-work' those Auditors are mixed *("myxsynd)* with the holy religion and have the same portion with the Elect Ones. And the Auditor who brings that 'soul-work' to the Elect is just like a poor man who had begotten a pretty daughter."[166] The text continues the parable, recounting how the man gives his daughter to the king, who begets by her a son. There the parable breaks off, and we do not know if it originally made the analogy more explicit.[167] Another parable with a similar theme appears in M 47.II, part of a bilingual book of narratives written in an unusual, "highly condensed" style of composition,[168] which suggests more a set of mnemonic notes than a prose composition. It may have served, therefore, as a script for an oral performance. In the parable, a wealthy man hosts a king and his entourage; a banquet is served, and gifts exchanged. At sundown the satiated host neglects to light the lamps, whereupon the king becomes suspicious of him, and the king's entourage remarks aloud, "This man made a fair banquet and gave gift(s), but did not light the lamp; may he not be contemplating an offence!" The man, stricken with fear, faints. But his servants rush about to save him, lighting a thousand lamps, and saving for him the goodwill of the king. The interpretation of the parable concludes as follows:

> The servants who lit the lamps were friend(s) to (that) man; (likewise) pious deeds are friend(s) to the Auditors. If Auditors are able, as in this parable, to serve the religion with heart(s) (filled) with love, the gods will befriend (them), (and) they will receive victory from the fortune of the religion.[169]

M 1224, widely known as the "Bactrian Fragment" after the studies of Ilya Gershevitch, contains further analogies to explain the benefits that accrue to the Auditor performing "soul-work."

> [Just as, when] one lets [water into] gardens and orchards, thereafter the roots produce fruits and flowers, and just as the grass and water which one gives to sheep and cows produce meat, cheese, milk, and butter, so are the [. . .] gifts which they keep for the pure Elect. An enormous variety of merit *(pwn)* agreeable to the judges, and law-conforming and pious deeds, are all born out of the gifts. When a layman gives gifts, the gifts are accompanied by all the merit, and a single gift produces fruits consisting of merit by the thousands, and he sews up all hells, and keeps the merit forever.[170]

The Chinese *Hymnscroll* echoes these sentiments:

> *All faithful, alms-presenting men and women*
> *Who have entered into a covenant with this correct religion*

Entrusting themselves to the gate of liberation of the Venerable of Light
May they be universally removed from the suffering of birth and death.[171]

According to the "Bactrian Fragment," the fate of an ungenerous person is correspondingly grim:

> Then the soul of the person that has committed evil deeds will [abandon] hope that she (i.e., the soul) may get a hearing before the all-knowing and seeing just judge; and she is abandoned if her former person (i.e., the soul's most recent embodiment) did not make anyone into a holder of supportive and [. . .] maintenance, be it an Elect or a prophet, and (if) he (i.e., the "former person") consigned to perdition the beauty of grain, and did not heed the non-returnability of *karma*.[172]

The negative side of the picture appears likewise in the Chinese *Hymnscroll*:

> *If there are people who suffer in the transmigration of hell*
> *In the fire of the kalpa of destruction and the eternal confinement*
> *It is really because they do not recognize the five Light Bodies*
> *And are therefore severed from the country of peace and happiness.*[173]

Summation

In the merit earned by Auditors through their alms-service we finally find a direct reward beside the selfless rationales of rescuing the Living Self, supporting the Elect, and assisting the dead. Even the most selfish individual could appreciate this rationale and perhaps be motivated to practice. The Manichaean system of lay merit possesses strong analogies to the surviving systems of other religions, especially that of Buddhism. Such analogies should dissuade us from seeing this kind of merit system as an artificial addition to the core faith, or a convenient concession to benighted masses. In some ways, the merit rationale binds the other rationales together and establishes the basic reasoning of individual interest in what otherwise would be an attenuated set of altruistic relations.

The natural question one must ask of any demarcation of an elite class is, What benefit does the whole community receive from the privileged status of a few individuals? Certainly, the Elect were able to devote their attention to their own salvation, and were able to adhere to the restrictive code of behavior upon which that salvation depended, by Auditor sponsorship. Perhaps their privilege also enabled their attention to the Auditors in the form of instruction and exhortation. Perhaps. Melford Spiro found that the latter benefit was not given much emphasis among the Buddhists of Burma, whose two-class polity parallels that of the Manichaeans. Instead, "the primary duty of the monk is to practice a discipline by which he can accelerate his attainment of his own salvation."[174]

> Nor would the layman have it otherwise. . . . This is not to say that the layman does not need the monk; on the contrary, he needs the monk desperately. He needs him, however, so that he (the layman) may serve him, rather than being served by him. For it is primarily by offering *dāna*—food, robes, housing, and so on—to the monk that the layman acquires the merit necessary for *his* salvation. And that is why the layman, from his point of view, holds that the primary function of the monk is to seek his own salvation. For it is only by making offerings to a pious monk, one whose life is devoted to soteriological action, that merit is acquired.[175]

The apparent generosity of supporting the Elect, therefore, may have been seen from the Auditor perspective as not particularly altruistic. Regardless of any personal attention the Elect may or may not have given to Auditors, their presence served a salvational function, almost as an object. Spiro remarks of the Buddhist monk, "His mere existence provides the laymen with what Buddhism terms a 'field of merit,' and this is for the laymen by far the most important attribute of the order."[176]

The identification of interest between the Auditor and the Elect extended to the other rationales as well. Assistance to the dead achieved through the alms-service was intimately connected to this system of merit for the living. It operated on the same principles, and produced the same results for the deceased that the living hoped would be achieved on their behalf when they, too, left the body. The shared aspirations of the living—Auditor and Elect—and the dead also applied to the divine element contained in the offerings themselves. The rescue of the Living Self by the joint altruism of Elect and Auditor amounted to an identification of interest between the human and nonhuman forms of the divine presence in the world.

It has been tempting to the modern interpreter to conclude from this shared identity that the Manichaeans expressed in the voice of the Living Self their own personal alienation and quest for liberation. In this interpretation, eating the ritual meal simply dramatized personal concerns through a public symbolism. But if such an interpretation was true from the Manichaean point of view, they would need to find and employ *another* technique for actually achieving the salvation they desired. The dramatization would be fine in itself, but would not produce salvation. The Manichaeans had no such additional technique. Their salvational enterprise was invested completely in the effectiveness of the ritual meal, which combined in itself the power to produce the multifarious benefits enunciated in Manichaean alimentary rationales.

With this fact in mind, it can be seen that the rescue of the Living Self, even more than the concern with merit, holds center stage in normative Manichaean discourse on the function and purpose of the ritual meal and the alms-service that supports it. The Living Self is the ever-present reference point, whose aid produces merit for the living and the dead, and whose liberation through the disciplined bodies of the Elect is worthy of sponsorship by the Auditors. This element was what set Manichaeism apart from other ancient systems of ritual and merit.

The more difficult question is how the Elect themselves benefited from their service in the ritual meal. Outsiders such as Augustine certainly had the impression that the Manichaean ritual system implied that the Elect did not *need* merit or salvation, that they were in the position to bestow it on others, even on God himself. We have seen a few allusions to the Elect claiming merit for their service. But it would seem that the strongest linkage between Elect salvation and the ritual meal came not through merit, but through the identification of the Elect's self with the Living Self. This subject will be addressed in the following chapter.

CONCLUSIONS

It is only in "the holy church, the one in which the commandments of the alms-service are placed," that sacrificial offerings, composed of the five elements of the Living Self, find "an open gate through which they come out (of the world) and find occasion to go up to God."[177] "Now the holy church," Mani immediately adds, "exists in two personas: the brothers and the sisters," of the Elect order.[178] Patronage *(patronia)* of the Elect places the Auditors in partnership *(koinōnia)* with them, or as Iranian sources say, "mixes" *('myxš-)* the two orders of the community, in the salvational operation of the ritual meal. For the Auditor, alms are "the presents that give profit [to] his life."[179] They generate direct rewards for the donor. The neglect or misappropriation of alms, on the other hand, entails dire consequences. Sanction for the alms-service is adduced not only from the life of Mani, but also from the lives of Jesus, Zarathustra, and the Buddha.[180] Yet these prior revelations have fallen short. Their adherents do not "accomplish the work";[181] only the Manichaean community has established the conditions by which alms-service may produce beneficial results. All antecedent rites are assimilated to the one sacred meal of the Manichaean faith; all prior relations with the divine are reduced to the single medium of the Elect.

The Sogdian text M 139.II declares:

Happy, happy is the one who [. . .] to it, and takes it in reception as gold, and delivers it to its owner in the proper measure and completely; there it does not come to great strife. Guard it with caution, keep it with great firmness; there it is not allowed to be bespattered with dry or moist blood, and thus, on its part, it makes you joyful and happy [. . .] The primordial [. . .] conflict, injury [. . .] remembers the debt with respect to [. . .] days, as it begins, through Až [. . .] one's own body, with whose sign is it arranged or oppressed? In whose service does it stand? And what is it that it eats? For every eater who is not worthy of it will be deprived of his labor and effort and excluded from the light heaven. The chosen Righteous One and the faithful Auditor, (however), who recognize the greatness of the Living Self, will be happy with immortal life in the [light-paradise]. [Beloved brother], purify yourself and hear from me the good [. . .] It is a duty and precept for the wise, that they stand and serve in the religion in this function.

The same reflections on the hidden truth, the secret *persona* of the food offered in the sacred meal, can be found in the Bema-handbook (M 801), the Coptic *Psalm-Book*, the Turkic *Pothi-Book*, and the Chinese *Hymnscroll*. The premise of the Living Self formed the foundation of Manichaean practice. The clear and explicit rationale for Manichaean life was this: given this one fact about the universe, what should one do?

The Manichaean tradition made the observation that it is intrinsic to an ordinary human life to harm other living things in the universe—first and foremost in the procurement of food, but also in sheer destructiveness. For this painful truth, with its implications of retribution, Manichaeism offered the solution of a disciplined class of virtuosi, insulated from mundane entanglements, who undertook the rectification and healing of a damaged existence. The Elect compressed their contact with the world, which is problematic for both its profanity and its sacrality, to the single point of ingestion. Their resolution of the problematized world, therefore, was metabolic. The second class received absolution from the guilt it had incurred in the world by sponsoring these physicians of the cosmos, providing them with the means for their operations, and entering into a partnership with them whose ultimate goal was not only their own liberation, but also salvation for all life. Hence there is a powerful truth in Augustine's quip, that the Manichaeans taught and trained their members to perform these practices, "not so much in order to bestow a benefit on the donors," or on the *receivers*, we might add, "as to benefit the things themselves that are brought."[182]

SIX

THE LIBERATION OF THE
EMBODIED SELF

*It is the essential function of ritual to enable men to do what is
needed and yet not permitted in normal life.*
—Ludwig Koenen

To be a Manichaean was to be a participant in the institution of the alms-service and ritual meal. The Manichaean community cohered through the relations entailed in this institution, and the community's structure dispersed
roles, rights, and responsibilities according to its operation. The codes of behavior sanctioned by Manichaean authority regulated individual action with
explicit reference to the goal of the ritual meal, and defined adherence to
Manichaean identity according to the standards for physical and mental participation in it. Manichaean anthropology and cosmology modeled a universe
that enabled the alms-service and ritual meal to function for salvational effect,
and this ritual system was the central soteriological operation of the religion.

By proposing a specific model of salvational action, a technique claiming
liberative effectiveness, Manichaean discourse sanctioned, promoted, and motivated adherence to a particular set of ritual behavior, a ritual ethos that defined the individual Manichaean and identified the community of the saved.
Like any plan of action, sacred or secular, the Manichaean strategy promised
rewards for conformity, and warned of dire consequences to befall those who
rejected the wisdom of the proposed solution to the human predicament. The

victory obtained through the ritual required participation in an approved capacity, and this requirement in turn created motivational conditions for adherence to the disciplines that qualify participants. The disciplinary and ritual practices, therefore, form a unified system; and their respective rationales overlap and interlock, creating a universe of discourse, or an *episteme*, which includes all of the knowledge necessary for the successful implementation of the Manichaean salvational strategy.

The successful translation and accurate exegesis of the sources examined in this study requires identifying the practical context to which they refer, and correlating that context to an analogous one within our own universe of discourse. Because of disjunctions between the Manichaean world and our own, no cultural correlation can be completely felicitous. But we move closer to bridging the emic-etic gap the more accurately we exegete the set of relations implicated in Manichaean discourse and practice. Manichaeans characterized their practices as "self"-forming, that is, they self-consciously discussed their disciplines and rites in terms of their effects on, and interaction with, the individual identity. Several current etic models of interpretation likewise claim a self-forming function for such practices, although they deny that native participants are aware of this function. From this etic point of view, Manichaean disciplines and rites were really about the formation of socialized selves, the social integration of individuals into the larger Manichaean ethos. According to this interpretation, the "salvation" to which emic discourse refers as the principal rationale for these practices is a false one, an illusory goal in the service of hidden social ends.

But the Manichaean program of self-liberation, of metabolic salvation, was not an enacted metaphor for a truth about human identity; it was not a means by which the Manichaeans signaled to themselves, under the pretext of ritual acts, a knowledge about the human soul; it did not secretly bestow identity upon them as they distractedly undertook a fiction; nor, finally, was it a mistaken hypostasization of spiritual or psychological categories. Instead, Manichaean alimentary rites were practical applications of a science, an experienced and interpreted apprehension of the world. That apprehension determined the *possibilities* of the Manichaean world, structured the *reasonable means* within the limits of those possibilities, and selected the *ends* from those possibilities, obtainable by those means, which human interests necessarily valorized within that world. Manichaean cosmology and anthropology are analogous to our culture's science. Manichaean ritual corresponds not solely to what in our culture might be called "religion," but also to its engineering, medicine, training—in short, to the *practical techniques* we employ to change both the world and ourselves.

THE MANICHAEAN BODY IN ACTION

No one has contributed more to our understanding of Manichaean practices than Henri-Charles Puech and, in more recent years, Julien Ries, and that is the major reason I use them here as the touchstone of the received wisdom in the study of Manichaeism. Both scholars have devoted large portions of their research to reconstructing Manichaean disciplines, rituals (such as the annual Bema festival), and their rationales. The majority of their conclusions have stood the test of time and significantly advanced the field. My own research has confirmed many of their suppositions and conclusions: the chapters on disciplinary regimens and rationales largely covers ground well prepared by Ries in the 1970s and 1980s; the discussion of ritual builds upon the foundation laid by Puech in the 1950s, 1960s and 1970s. Nevertheless, I have come to the conclusion that both Puech and Ries overlook the centrality of ritual in Manichaean religious life, and for this reason give an incomplete picture of the Manichaean ethos. They overemphasize the "spiritual" matters of the Manichaean faith at the expense of the bodily, and the quietist elements of Manichaean practice at the expense of its active manifestations.

Puech contends that Manichaean Auditors were a "marginal element" of the Manichaean community, "still engaged in ignorance and sin."[1] In identifying the Elect as the only true Manichaeans, Puech echoes the claims of Christian polemicists who direct their ire exclusively against the Manichaean sacerdotal class and regard the Auditors as mere pawns. Richard Lim warns, "The strategic decision made by many Catholic writers to drive a wedge between the elect and the hearers and to argue that the former group *alone* constituted the true perverse Manichaean church should not determine historians' efforts at analysis."[2] This study has shown the essential role played by the Auditors in the community, such that there was no "rest" for the Elect in the world without them, there was no metabolic salvation without their alms-service, there was no possibility of the Elect lifestyle without their support.

"Auditors, too, become immortal!" we are told,[3] and certain kinds ostensibly could achieve this goal in a single lifetime, just like the Elect.[4] To be a

Manichaean Auditor required recognition of certain truths about the world which motivate fulfillment of the Auditor's role in the project of salvation. The individual desire to escape sinful existence was presupposed in the system of merit which made service of the Elect worthwhile to the Auditor—not just to escape to another world, but to escape a particular mode of being in this world, to be healed of the physical and psychic sickness that sin is, and to arrive at a healthier, happier existence in this lifetime, too.

Puech maintains that the distinct regimens of the Elect and Auditors relate to one another as rigid and lax forms of the same ethos, as a strict ideal and a form accommodated to the world's realities.[5] The Manichaeans themselves described the two levels of ability implied in the distinct regimens and hierarchized the degree of perfection inherent in each. But they did not characterize the regimens as a single system adhered to with greater or lesser commitment. Puech's terms reflect more closely the sentiments of Augustine than they do those of Mani. Rather, the distinct regimens appear in Manichaeism as separate disciplines, each related to a particular role within the community and making their respective adherent fit for a specific ritual function. Certainly, Auditors learned to admire and respect the superior life of the Elect, but they were not faulted for holding the status of an Auditor, instead they were praised as "good-souled." The self-deprecation involved in some Auditor discourse, such as the confession texts, in fact, was part of a ritual solution to that status which absolved the imperfection and allowed Auditors to accumulate merit even without living up to the disciplines of the Elect. Hence, some distinct advantages accrued to Auditorship.

Puech sees the Manichaean Elect embracing "an ideal of total abstention."[6] He interprets the asceticism of the Elect as a reduction, as far as practicable, of all contact and interaction between themselves and the world.

> Like the macrocosm, the microcosm must sunder the mixture and release the living soul, must restore the original duality. Accordingly, the entire ethic consists in a single commandment: abstain, in order to acquire and preserve purity, a largely negative commandment. . . . [T]he break with matter is here renunciation, withdrawal, removal.[7]

Total fulfillment of such a discipline entails a negation of life itself.[8]

(The Elect) must renounce his body to the point of absolute withdrawal in or-

der to maintain himself in a state of redemption. Ultimately such total abstinence must imply immobility and suicide; a gruesome refusal to move, to
take nourishment, to live, corresponding to the *endura* (of) the medieval
Cathars. . . . But in reality this ideal theory of redemption permitted a certain
alleviation.[9]

The ideal of absolute divorce from the world was mitigated only by the necessity to eat, which is a concession to the body's imperfectibility.[10] According to
Puech, "the ethical ideal would thus have been fully realized, except for the
need of nourishment."[11] But if his reading of the ideal values of the Manichaean community is correct, then surely the Elect, one and all, would be regarded as failing, as falling short of liberation, to the degree that they yielded
to the need to eat. The tradition would need to supply an alternative means of
redemption. Wolfgang Lentz has also claimed, "Even the ideal of starvation as
the only manner of death corresponding to real wisdom lies not far from the
ordinances of the Elect."[12] Samuel Lieu has stated similarly, "Taken to its logical conclusion, strict observance of these Manichaean ethical precepts would
result in starvation and the eventual extinction of the human race."[13] But
Werner Sundermann has taken such a notion to task by pointing out that an
active response, not just a cessation of action, was called forth by conversion to
the Manichaean worldview, such that "the ritual meals of the elect rather than
starvation" were the outcome of the Manichaean ethos, guided in the individual by *gnosis*.[14]

Manichaean ascesis, in all its extremity, derived not from an increased an-
ticosmism relative to contemporaneous traditions, but from a heightened
problematization of the cosmos by the dual sacrality of evil and divine presence. As Puech correctly surmises concerning Manichaean disciplines, "These
prohibitions are based not only on the fact that these occupations create a contact with matter and hence carry a taint, but also on the mythical conception
that they constitute so many assaults upon life, upon the luminous substance
that is mixed with all matter."[15] The latter, although "imprisoned," is the "life"
of the world,[16] its "beauty."[17] But even a recognition of this ideological element
in the motivation for Manichaean self-restraint, which is found in most modern scholarship on Manichaeism, has not brought with it a full acknowledgment of the *active* response entailed in Manichaean ritual alongside of the
more passive response of its disciplines. Manichaeans endeavored not to set
themselves off from the world as something alien to it, but to exercise a heal-

ing operation on that part of the world with which they identify, and to resolve
the cosmos into its proper, separated constituents.

Although the Elect did reduce their interaction with the world to a great
extent, eating was not a shortfall of an ideal ascesis but the productive culmi-
nation of a successful ascesis. The ritual meal became the ultimate arbiter of
salvation, concentrating in itself the whole of Elect contact with the world,
and absorbing into its operation the entire ritual mediation of salvation. Far
from Manichaean discipline aiming to replace consumption, it had its own
end in consumption. A Coptic text says that Auditors are saved by their alms-
service and the Elect by their fasts. These two apparently incongruous activities correlate via their relation to the ritual meal. By the alms-service, Auditors
"collect" and bring in the Living Self. By fasts, the Elect both prepare their
bodies for the meal and, after the meal, process the ingested food toward salvation rather than redispersing it. Fasting produces "angels" from the food,
who ascend to heaven.[18] Manichaean disciplines should be described not as
mortification, but as vivification;[19] Manichaean fasting finds its *raison d'être* in
life, not death.[20]

The fact that the Manichaean Elect engaged in a daily meal around
which was clustered some peculiar rhetoric is not a new discovery. The ritual
meal is referred to obliquely in nearly every modern book-length work on
Manichaeism.[21] Puech composed one of the earliest and most accurate of
modern accounts of the Manichaean ritual meal, and of Manichaean rationales for it. He recognizes the role played by the Elect in liberating the divine
substance in the world. "Thus the Elect is eminently a machine for purifying
the light devoured in the world. Indeed, he is the one and irreplaceable instrument of liberation in the entire living universe."[22] Yet he remains unper-
suaded that this ritual action possessed what he calls "sacramental efficacy" for
the Manichaeans. "Manichaeism remained profoundly true to the spirit of
Gnosis: it regarded consciousness and knowledge that transform the inner
man as the necessary and adequate conditions for redemption. The entire
church cult consists in fasting and prayer accompanied by the singing of
hymns."[23] Puech sees the disciplines principally as the expressive outcome of
the negative attitude toward the world conveyed by Mani's teachings. "Redemption is a problem of insight, solved 'objectively' by an act of the intellect.
Redemption is knowledge and knowledge is redemption."[24]

In Puech's reading of Manichaeism, "Redemption is a liberation based
solely on gnosis, which produces it, determines its course, provides its instru-

ments, and is its goal. In short, knowledge is the beginning, end, and meaning of redemption."[25] He not only identifies Manichaeism as a gnostic system, but goes so far as to characterize it as "Gnosticism of an intellectual type."[26] As for the effort of the ritual meal, Puech joins the company of those who see the establishment and maintenance of communal relations between the Elect and Auditor classes as its true meaning and function.[27] The ritual meal is never an integral part of the Manichaean systems modern researchers have reconstructed; at most it is an ancillary expression of community, or an enacted extension of Mani's worldview, taken—the embarrassed brevity of treatment strongly implies—one step too far.

The complete evidence, I contend, suggests the opposite conclusion: the ritual meal provides the essential meaning and function of the Manichaean community in its two classes, it is itself "the reference point for explaining or describing other areas of life."[28] Manichaeans belonged to a ritual community, not only identified as a community by their collective participation in the rite, but coming together into a community for the express purpose of performing it. Without the ritual meal, there would have been no Manichaean community. The two classes coexisted on the basis of this rite and this rite alone, without which the Elect truly would have disconnected utterly from the world and the Auditors would indeed have been a "mass of laypersons still engaged in ignorance and sin."[29]

Following in Puech's footsteps, Julien Ries declares, "There is no ritual properly speaking in the church of Mani," but only a "gnostic ritual" that transmits a body of knowledge as mysteries.[30] Ries constructs a fully Gnostic Manichaeism in which salvation involved purely psychological realignment on the part of the faithful.[31] Ritual had no place in this process; it was, in fact, pointedly rejected. "This religion of salvation is founded upon the knowledge of an ineffable mystery. Consequently, it is a dualist gnosis which rejects rites and rituals."[32]

In consonance with Ludwig Koenen, Ries sees Mani's break with the Elchasaites[33] not as a rejection of specific ritual practices in favor of others, but as a dismissal of ritual per se as a means of salvation.

> The controversy is presented as the scene of the progressive elaboration of salvation by gnosis. In the rejection of baptism, the opposition is not an opposition to water but to ritual. . . . To purification by the ritual of ablutions, Mani . . . opposes salvation by Gnosis because it leads to the separation of Light

from Darkness. . . . It is the ritual of ablution which is rejected in order to make room for the illumination by Gnosis.[34]

There is little place in such an interpretation for the subsequent establishment by Mani of a ritual system based upon the meal, as reported in the later pages of the Cologne Mani Codex and already foreshadowed in that document in the complaints first made against Mani by the Elchasaites. Jorunn Buckley has effectively countered the antiritual readings of the Cologne Mani Codex by Koenen and Ries by highlighting the ritual terms that control the entire conflict between Mani and the Elchasaites. The dispute is not of an antiritualist against a ritual tradition, but of a ritual reformer substituting a more efficacious rite for one he considers illegitimate and ineffective.[35]

Ries, like Puech, focuses on the ideology underlying Manichaean disciplines. Both authors are correct in directing attention to the central role of the Living Self, or the "world soul," in determining the Manichaean ethos. Ries states that "the foundation of the entire Manichaean ethic, expressed by the three signacula, is the doctrine of the world soul."[36] "It is on this mystery," he adds, "that the doctrine of the three signacula is grafted."[37] His choice of the word "grafted" is significant. He does not see the disciplines as constituting the practical component alongside the rationale of the Living Self in an integrated system. For him, the disciplines merely convey the outlook of Mani's worldview.

Yet when Ries sets forth the "gnostic truths" that distinguish Mani's message in the Cologne Mani Codex, he presents a list not of doctrines but of commandments:

> the anapausis or seal of the hands; the commandments, tas entolas; the proskynēsis before the celestial illuminators. Thus, the premier preaching has as its object the world soul and the seal of the hands, the ensemble of the comportment of the faithful and prayer. It is the seal of the hands which occupies the premier place.[38]

Koenen, too, acknowledges that "mention of the commandments of the savior in connection with gnosis is remarkable and, in comparison with other gnostics, seems to give the passage a particularly Manichaean ring."[39] Ries insists that the central point of Mani's demonstration to the Elchasaites is "the world soul and the anapausis tōn cheirōn: the rejection of ablutions, of agriculture, of the baking of bread, of the sale of vegetables, of the picking of fruit." For Ries, this means a denial of all practical means of salvation, and he concludes, "All of the discussion leads to one main conclusion: gnosis is the sole means of salvation."[40] In effect, Ries arrives at the same place as Puech and Lentz: nonaction is held up as the ultimate goal of Manichaean discipline, which is regarded as an entirely negative form of practice, an antiethos, as it were, identified solely by what it negates, basically all signs of life. In the words of Wolfgang Lentz, for the Elect "who stands in constant fear of any movement of his own body by which the elements of Light in the world might be hurt," the full mastery of the body "means no action at all, since through action the peace of the Paradise was disturbed, and since it can and will be restored only by paralyzing Darkness, the principle of action."[41] These authors see the goal of the Elect lifestyle as a kind of meditative quiescence, a removal from involvement in the world to the role of pure spectator.

The conclusion shared by these scholars amounts to a restatement of Augustine's polemical charge that the sole purpose of the alms-service is the support of the Elect in their otiose lifestyle. "The dualist doctrine based upon the world soul and the prohibition of work has need of an indispensable complement: namely, the obligation of the gift which permits those whom the CMC calls *latreus* and *dikaios*, the elect, to subsist."[42] Supposedly rejecting all rites, Mani establishes yet another rite: the ritual meal that makes use of the alms of the Auditors. Ries assimilates this apparent contradiction to his interpretation by carefully circumscribing the function of the Manichaean alms-economy. Among the four "victories" that served as the rationales for the alms-service discussed in chapter 5, Ries selects only one, the altruistic support of the Elect, as the true understanding of the practice. This sort of interpretation actively suppresses Manichaean exegesis in favor of a modern rationalist interpretation.

Ries's interpretation integrates the alms-service, but leaves aside the ritual meal that, for the Manichaeans, was the primary goal of the alms-service. Whereas ascetic elites of the Christian, Buddhist, and Manichaean traditions all received support through lay donations, and these alms could be characterized in all three cases as bestowing rewards upon the donors, only Manichaeism designated the alms for consumption solely within the context of a ritual sacrifice. But for Ries, Manichaean ritual is devoid of instrumentality: "[T]he liturgy orchestrates in a solemn and efficacious manner the dialogue of salvation." It is at best a dramatization and reminder of the themes of Manichaean discourse, and more probably simply an opportunity for the further enunciation of that discourse.[43]

With the axiom that Manichaeism "is a dualist gnosis which rejects rites and rituals," Ries is unable to make sense of the Manichaean ritual meal, and so, in his interpretation, there is no ritual meal. Instead, there is only the unfortunate necessity of compromising the Elects' disengagement from the world by sustenance supplied by the Auditors. Nowhere is the power of interpretive axioms more apparent than in Ries's conclusions. Despite his exemplary work of close readings and careful analysis of the sources that have enriched the field immeasurably, Ries selects from these sources only those elements that allow him to reaffirm the basic gnostic premise with which scholarship of the last century has approached the Manichaean tradition.

Ries is perfectly correct when he says that "the creation of the community of elect and catechumens appears to have been in Mani's mind at the moment when he quit the Elchasaites."[44] Mani had it in mind because of the necessity of dispersing roles in such a way that the ritual meal could be conducted. Sinners cannot eat correctly; eaters must not sin. This is Mani's axiom, which demands a division of labor, a screening of ritual from profanation, but not a rejection of ritual. His commandment to the Elect to eat, his rejection of isolated retreat as legitimate religious practice, his whole conception of the Living Self and how it percolates out of the mixed cosmos have no place in Ries's interpretation.

What seems to be missing from the received wisdom on Manichaeism is a full appreciation of how discipline and ritual operate together as a system that provides the historian with a visible Manichaean body in action as a historical agent.[45] The Manichaeans put into operation a plan of embodiment that recognized that "the body becomes a useful force only if it is both a productive body and a subjected body."[46] Foucault's language about a more recent episode in the production of "subjected and practiced bodies" works for the Manichaean case as well because of parallel divergences of these two power-knowledges from ascetic and moral disciplines that aim only at obedience and docility. Modern industrial society and ancient Manichaean community were both interested in "increases of utility" by which the body would become not just docile but efficient in the production of desired materials.[47] Quite naturally, from our own cultural locale we find it difficult to see that the Manichaeans produced anything at all. Yet the Manichaeans stand in history as a collectivity of individuals who committed the social, economic, political, and ideological forces at their disposal to this seemingly illusory enterprise.

Hans Schaeder is among a handful of researchers in this century who have been willing to take Manichaean rationales at face value.[48] For this reason, he was able to construct a powerful and coherent understanding of Mani's world.

> The structure of the world, the organization of nature, had for Mani a single interest; alongside the psychological-soteriological orientations of his thought, there ran independently a nature philosophy, and it is this which actually produced the connection and the unity of the system. . . . The soul was considered by him to be the one—the life force governing the cosmos and the human—of which the individual soul was only a part. . . . [I]n Mani's mind, the work of light-liberation, not only in the cosmos, but also in the human, is absolutely not symbolic, but an absolutely real process to be understood physically. The salvation of humans was not only considered as a psychic act, hence as an experience, but also as an event of nature. . . . The work of light-liberation is thus not an image of individual salvation projected into the cosmos, but in Mani's mind one is permitted rather to say the opposite, that this represents only a partial process of the real cosmic light-liberation.[49]

Thus, Schaeder endorses the earlier characterization of the Manichaean Elect by Edward Lehmann as a kind of "distillation apparatus," even though he acknowledges that the choice of words is "probably not excessively tasteful."

> For by it Lehmann has described perfectly correctly that he sees as the goal of the Manichaean ethic not only a purely spiritual, immanent purification process, but on the contrary the promotion of a completely concrete and general event of nature, namely the light-liberation. One misses a basic understanding of Mani if one separates the ground-laying of his ethic from his explanation of the world and nature: to him they lay precisely so close as to interpenetrate one other.[50]

Unfortunately, Schaeder himself fell away from this insight, partly as a result of exposure to the newly discovered Western Manichaean sources that he found to be more evocative of Hellenic philosophical traditions, partly as a consequence of shifts in his own thinking and interests.[51] In this way, he is an important forebear both of the tradition of interpretation embraced by Puech and Ries, as well as of the one carried forward by the present study.

Since normative Manichaean discourse explicitly enunciates an instrumental interpretation of its rites, and places those rites, especially the ritual meal, at the very center of Manichaean identity, what status should we give to the interpretation of Puech, Ries, and the constellation of other luminaries in the field? It is conceivable that individual Manichaeans at one time or another actually held views similar to those espoused by these scholars, and observed the rites with a private understanding of them different from that offered by the normative tradition. We actually have such a case in the Manichaean leader (archēgos) who, in Kephalaion 81, asks Mani's permission to abandon the angel-producing work of the ritual meal for solitary meditation. His reflections on Mani's teachings have led him to conclusions that do not conform to the normative system promoted in the community, and so weakens his enthusiasm about the practical application of those teachings in the life of the Manichaean community. He has come to the same conclusion as Puech and Ries: to act is to sin, so ascesis alone is the fulfillment of practice and rituals must be abandoned. Mani rejects the man's request, as well as his interpretation of the meaning of Manichaean doctrine, and Mani's words in doing so leave no room for doubt about the correct emic understanding of Manichaeism.

> The saying that you uttered, in that [is your answer, spoken] by your own mouth! "I know that this is a good thing that is achieved by virtue of these fasts . . . ," as if knowing that this thing is entirely beneficial. Then why do you ask exemption (paresis) from it? For in these words that you have uttered in my presence you make [. . .] as if you had not known anything true. Because if you had understood the truth and known the benefit, your heart would not have come after you to ask exemption from [the good].[52]

This "divine work," Mani says, must be done, and greater by far is "the glory and the victory and the good" of one who actively arranges and promotes the community practices "than that of the brother who turns his heart inward and keeps himself to himself, and edifies only himself."[53] Mani adds to his exhortation by reasserting that "your toil will be reckoned to your benefit,"[54] and promising that "you will go to this great [land] of rest."[55]

In holding such an interpretation at odds with the norm, individuals such as the *archēgos* would have been exercising a selective adherence, one that chooses to take some points of the tradition directly while reordering and redefining others. In short, they would have been adopting a *haerēsis* of Manichaeism. An etic interpretation such as that of Puech and Ries, which highlights certain doctrines at the expense of others favored by the normative tradition, and focuses on certain practices while neglecting others held to be essential by that tradition, is precisely such a *haerēsis*. By shifting the references of key statements to objects within our own range of reasonableness (the Elect are pious meditators rather than God digesters; the Auditors are altruistic—or duped—supporters of their saints, not pursuers of rebirth as plants to be chewed by the Elect), Puech and Ries have reconstructed a religion amenable to contemporary discourses; they have made a mystical philosophy from sources deriving from a ritual system.

What might be called the "Philonic reading"[56] of Manichaean practical systems by modern scholars is in part an inherent byproduct of the theoretical stance of the academic—that is, a consequence of the intention not to write a handbook of Manichaeism, but to provide an account of it in terms of modern discourse. Robert Campany argues in the case of ancient China, "The rites' opacity had made a *theory* about them both necessary and possible, and constructing a 'theory' about them meant giving an account of them from some point of view other than themselves, a stance already adumbrated in the very act of *writing a treatise*."[57] We moderns, likewise, must speak from outside Manichaeism in order to connect it with the realities of our world, in order to, in other words, "make sense" of what would otherwise be opaque to us. But, as Campany points out, in the attempt to make sense of ancient practices modern theories tend to overlook or set aside the theories of the ancients themselves, the very theories by which those who practiced the rites were supposed to "make sense" of them according to the normative canon of significance provided by the ritual tradition.

Mani himself, in developing his distinctive ritual system, was not operating on a historical *tabula rasa*, but appropriating, adapting, redefining, and interpreting antecedent rites of the ancient world.[58] The Manichaean tradition after Mani continued this process, and it was in this form that it had its impact in history. Even emic theorists such as Philo and Xunzi labored to provide problematized practices with new rationales that would allow the continuation of their respective ritual traditions. The etic interpreter, on the contrary, is involved not in the furtherance of practice, but in providing an account of it to those who wish to remain mere "spectators." Unfortunately, when the interpretation involves separating Manichaean religious practice from its moorings in the Manichaean universe, we must begin to wonder what we are spectators of. The resultant interpretive constructs often lack the ability to explain the choices and actions of Manichaeans in history. The Manichaean body in action, divorced from the perceived cosmos to which it was responding, becomes mute and meaningless, while the Manichaean dualist reality, with its elaborate cosmological and anthropological details, becomes mere literature.

THE EMERGENCE OF THE SOUL

A great deal can be learned from vocabulary and how cultures and religious traditions organize their terminology. In Eastern Manichaeism, the Iranian term "collection" (*'mwrdyšn*) is employed for both meditative solidification of identity within the individual Manichaean and the delivery and processing of alms-offerings in the sacred meal.[59] The relation between these two operations is complex, and cannot be resolved fully here. It can be said, however, that their relation certainly hinges on the intrinsic identity of the divine material of the Living Self dispersed in the world with that within the body of the Manichaean. This identity parallels that between the evil substance in food and that congenitally present in the body; several texts express concern about the contact and mutual reinforcement that occurs between them.[60] A similar process seems to be at work with the two sets of divine material.[61] For both of the latter, we can speak of separation, self-formation, and ascent.

Separation

Ephrem Syrus describes a homogeneous deity, gradually differentiated in response to evil.[62] The Coptic *Kephalaia* trace the multiple forms taken by an originally unified nature, promising an ultimate reunion. Thus the perfect Manichaean comes into conformity with his or her original *physis* or *ousia*, shedding all traces of differentiation. The Manichaean self emerges as "homomorphic" (*h'mcyhrg*) light;[63] "the nature (*hsing*) will be separated from the lightless, its name will be 'one form'—in this religion, this is called deliverance."[64] The Chinese *Hymnscroll* describes the perfected state of Manichaeans as "harmonious in mind";[65] "Every thought and reflection obtained and all intentions in mind / Are mutually shown and observed, and no suspicion and misunderstanding exist";[66] "Every one of them looks the same without exceptional appearance";[67] "All natures and forms are equal; and all places bear no differences."[68] Al-Biruni quotes Mani to the effect that the living bodies obtained in heaven "do not differ from each other in weakness and strength, in length and shortness, in form and beauty; they are like similar lamps."[69]

This unification and homogenization of the self corrects the condition of "mixture" in which ordinary humans find themselves. Originally, the Primordial Man was divested of five elements that became part of the constitutive matter of the cosmos. Contrary to interpretations that see in Manichaeism a form of spirit-matter dualism, the sources actually show a sweeping materialism in Manichaean discourse. Four divine elements go into the making of the human body, just as four dark elements do; both good and evil drives operate by means of respective fifth elements, "spirits" that course through the body. The contingency and impermanence of the body show that it is not a "real existence," but a temporary conglomeration of incongruous substances.[70] Ordinary humans, even Manichaean Auditors, do not experience *metempsychosis* at death, that is, their intact souls do not transmigrate to other bodies. Rather, the separable divine elements are reprocessed into new forms through "transfusion" *(metaggismos)*. The available evidence shows clearly that Manichaeans adhered to a traducian theory of the soul, whereby that which will constitute a soul in the individual is inherited biologically from that individual's parents, whose reproductive elements in turn derive from the food they eat.[71] Individual Manichaeans, like the Primordial Man, must "collect" their "limbs,"[72] that is, assemble separate identifiable traits into a complete "soul" or self.

Manichaean practices identify, mark, define, promote, circumscribe, and valorize particular traits of the human body, specific sensations and thoughts within human experience; these are "collected" as a unified self that, by its emergence from mixture with other, nonapproved traits and experiences, attains self-consciousness. As Ephrem reports, "[I]t has self-knowledge because it is collected together and fixed."[73] It "remembers" its identity, and the narration of its primordial division into pieces, each of which, by itself, has no self-awareness, but "slumbers in drunkenness." The Manichaean self is identified in its constituent parts amid the 140 myriad[74] or 840 myriad[75] demons that run amok in the unreformed body. The Manichaean "soul" or self does not possess an eternal or immutable identity; it is *made* by the processes of the faith, crafted in the metabolic fires, and forged as a unity from dispersed fragments of life. Manichaean discourse on the body is a chemical, elemental physiology. The soul is a byproduct—or rather the essential product—of metabolic processes. In saying this, the Manichaeans were very much in line with the leading medical thought of the day.[76] The great divide between science and faith has not occurred in Manichaean discourse; spiritual truths are also material truths here.

The Manichaean Elect must achieve separation of Light from Darkness within him- or herself to qualify for participation in the ritual meal, and must maintain that separation despite a flood of dark forces intruding into the body through food or the senses. Qualification for ritual service requires prerequisite changes in human physiology and psychology. This demand moves the Elect along the path toward individual salvation at the same time that it establishes the conditions for universal salvation.

Self-formation

As a conglomeration of substances, concentrated in sufficient quantity to cross the threshold to consciousness, the human soul possesses the potential to hold itself together and continue along a process of ever-increasing reunification. If it fails to hold on to that consciousness, or if it fails to find "the open gate" through which it can continue its ascent, that soul will, at death, fly apart once again into its separate components. It needs to find a form, a permanent cohesiveness that survives mortality, a "body" divested of the pollutants that undermine its unity and clarity. This is the need Mani proposes to resolve. He brings the true "commandments of the savior, [so that you] may redeem the soul from [annihilation] and destruction."[77] Salvation comes by means of establishing an integrity for the self, an identity beyond contingency.

The "person of the world" does not possess this integrity, because it is constituted of mixed elements. The demonic drive, Až, is "mixed into this body . . . (and) scans for what her concupiscenses and passions can provoke."[78] The "damaged vessel" scatters the mind, and is filled with spirits which "draw him hither and thither."[79] The buffeted divine identity within prays to the gods to "put my self in order *(grywm'n wyn'r'h)*."[80] Salvation requires that the body be trained, like a king's horse,[81] until it becomes a fully functioning instrument *(organon)*.[82]

The divine nature is dead and Christ resuscitates it. It is sick and he heals it. It is forgetful and he brings it to remembrance. It is foolish and he teaches it. It is disturbed and he makes it whole again. It is conquered and captive and he sets it free. It is in poverty and need, and he aids it. It has lost feeling and he quickens it. It is blinded and he illumines it. It is in pain and he restores it. It is iniquitous and by his precepts he corrects it. It is dishonored and he cleanses it. It is at war and he promises it peace. It is unbridled and he imposes the restraint of law. It is deformed and he reforms it. It is perverse and he puts it right. All these things, they tell us, are done by Christ not for something that was made by God and became distorted by sinning by its own free will, but for the very nature and substance of God, for something that is as God is.[83]

Manichaeism ascribes no fault to the soul prior to its awakening; it has no agency in actions performed when its constituent elements are still dispersed and subjugated within the body. Only when the soul is collected, and establishes dominion over the body, does it assume responsibility for action. This view obviously draws upon key Pauline themes also developed by the former Manichaean Augustine. But it is important to see the particular emphasis Manichaean authorities put upon this awakening as a birth. Still building on Pauline foundations, Mani and his North African successor Faustus describe the awakened self as coming into existence for the first time, as a new emergent in the mixed universe.

And how shall anyone tell me that our father Adam was made after the image of God, and in his likeness, and that he is like him who made him? How can it be said that all of us who have been begotten of him are like him? Yea, rather, on the contrary, have we not a great variety of forms, and do we not bear the impress of different countenances?[84]

Mani's attention to the plurality and dividedness of humanity, here placed into his mouth by an anti-Manichaean novelist, reflects the authentically Manichaean discourse about salvation as homogenization and reunification of the scattered sparks of light in the cosmos. So, Faustus adds,

The birth by which we are made male and female, Greeks and Jews, Scythians and Barbarians, is not the birth in which God effects the formation of man; but . . . the birth with which God has to do is that in which we lose the difference of nation and sex and condition, and become like him who is one, that is, Christ. . . . Man, then, is made by God not when from one he is divided into many, but when from many he becomes one. The division is in the first birth, or that of the body; union comes by the second, which is immaterial and divine.[85]

Manichaean anthropology consists largely of a *Listenwissenschaft* of the attributes of the perfected self, and their corresponding pollutants from the realm of evil. The *Sermon on the Light Nous*, in its various versions, provides our principal access to this science of the self. The twelve attributes known in Iranian as the "Authorities" *(šhrd'ryft)* link this text to the ritual meal via the "Authorities" hymns performed as part of the meal ceremony in Central Asia and China (the corresponding Western Manichaean hymns have not yet been identified). In the allegory of the Three Days central to the *Sermon's* organization, "the Second Day is the pure seed of the New Man; the Twelve Hours are the Twelve Virgins,[86] which Jesus the Splendor puts upon the soul[87] that is purified from oldness."[88] In the expanded Chinese version of the *Sermon*, the Twelve Virgins are further described as "the marvelous vestments of the victorious form of Jesus." "By means of these marvelous vestments, he adorns the interior nature and causes it never to lack them. Pulling it from above, he causes it to ascend and advance, and to be separated forever from the impure land."[89] These accounts refer to the reformation of the bodies of the Elect, their reorientation to the service of God in the form of a "New Man."[90]

The bulk of the *Sermon* is devoted to just this subject: the Mind of Light's victorious conquest of the body in the Elect. The Turkic version concludes: "These twelve hours unfold themselves and grow in the heart. And the (conditions) existing in the heart allow them to become visible outwardly." The Chinese version expands as follows: "These twelve great luminous hours, when entering into the five kingdoms (i.e., the five mentalities of divine substance within the human) cause to grow in each of them, in turn, a limitless light. Each of them successively manifests the fruits which are each limitless as well. These fruits are all manifested in the assembly of pure adepts." The connection, therefore, between the Twelve Authorities and the ritual meal, as expressed in the performance of the Twelve Authorities hymns at the meal, involves the necessity that the Elect be fit vehicles for transforming the divine substance in the food they consume at the meal. By manifesting the twelve virtues that indicate the complete reformation of their metabolism, the Elect reassure the Auditors that their alms-service is not rendered in vain.[91] The end of the *Sermon* contains an elaborated form of this idea, in which each of the twelve virtues (allegorically described as trees) cultivated within the Elect is displayed in five observable behaviors, together comprising a sixty-point comprehensive guide to the proper behavior of a true Elect.[92] In the expanded Chinese version, Mani says:

> It is necessary, O men and women of superior form and excellent wisdom, that each of you plants these trees in your pure heart, so that it causes them to prosper and grow. . . . Why must it be so? Because, O good people, it is by means of the fruits of these trees that you are able to free yourselves from the four hardships, and that all beings having bodies are delivered from life-and-death and, in a definitive manner, always victorious, abide in the realm of immutable felicity.[93]

In Manichaeism, then, the soul or self is formed by the *"gnosis* of separation," the *practical* knowledge of discerning and marking apart a self amid the flood of passions and drives of the human body.[94] The Manichaean ethos is a technique for investing the body with a self, a self whose Manichaean identity puts it in an effective relation with the salvational processes of the universe. By applying an external code of behaviors, Manichaeism crafts the exhibition of identity, and by narrating those behaviors with statements emplacing the human microcosm within a macrocosmic system of relations, it shapes as well the internal behaviors we call thoughts. Out of this complex of external and internal behaviors, the Manichaean self emerges in an embodied form.

It is difficult for a modern Western audience to equate discipline with liberation; our culture tends to valorize the individual in its idiosyncrasies and originalities. Rules, abstentions, self-effacements are regarded as dehumanizing. Even the Christian tradition, in some respects an unusually rule-bound and moralizing discourse, embraces a rhetoric that glorifies God's acceptance of the individual in his or her broken, unnormativized condition as a "sinner." Our cultural conditioning predisposes us to see everywhere selves like us. But to comprehend the historical manifestation of the Manichaean self,

> One has to dispense with the constituent subject . . . that's to say, to arrive at an analysis which can account for the constitution of the subject within a his-

torical framework. And this is what I would call genealogy, that is, a form of history which can account for the constitution of knowledges, discourses, domains of objects, etc., without having to make reference to a subject which is either transcendental in relation to the field of events or runs in its empty sameness throughout the course of history.[95]

This turn in our approach to the self in history would necessitate an understanding of how norms and codes actually delineate the subject in a given historical moment. Foucault articulates this point well.

We must cease once and for all to describe the effects of power in negative terms: it "excludes," it "represses," it "censors," it "abstracts," it "masks," it "conceals." In fact, power produces; it produces reality; it produces domains of objects and rituals of truth. The individual and the knowledge that may be gained of him belong to this production.[96]

In discussing how Manichaeans emerged from the discourses and practices promoted by the tradition, I am not speaking of a mere socialization of individuals into Manichaean life, but of the actual formation of what can be called the Manichaean soul. As Michel Foucault concludes on the basis of his own research into the formation of the modern Western "self,"

The individual is not to be conceived as a sort of elementary nucleus, a primitive atom, a multiple and inert material on which power comes to fasten or against which it happens to strike, and in so doing subdues or crushes individuals. In fact, it is already one of the prime effects of power that certain bodies, certain gestures, certain discourses, certain desires, come to be identified and constituted as individuals. The individual, that is, is not the vis-à-vis of power; it is, I believe, one of its prime effects. The individual is an effect of power, and at the same time, or precisely to the extent to which it is that effect, it is the element of its articulation. The individual which power has constituted is at the same time its vehicle.[97]

Overt adherence and public conformity to the Manichaean ethos marked participants as Manichaeans and created the conditions under which that identity would be transmitted and reproduced in succeeding generations. In the historically accessible past, this process is certainly in evidence.

Just as Foucault examined the historical formation of self suitable for the productive ends of modern industrial society, so I have tried to delineate the processes by which the Manichaean tradition formed a self fit for the productive ends of salvation. The metabolism of salvation operated within a body properly ordered and made amenable to its task by reformations and disciplines that changed its basic character and elevated a selected set of its given traits to the status of a core identity to be maintained and preserved against the onslaughts of contrary impulses. Foucault described his study as "a genealogy of the modern 'soul.'"

> It would be wrong to say that the soul is an illusion, or an ideological effect. On the contrary, it exists, it has a reality, it is produced permanently around, on, within the body by the functioning of a power that is exercised on those . . . one supervises, trains and corrects. . . . This is the historical reality of the soul, which . . . is born . . . out of methods of punishment, supervision and constraint.[98]

Manichaean disciplinary and ritual practices form an analogous system of constraint, proposing a particular form of embodiment and offering combined sets of rights and responsibilities ("roles") to those who want to accept the proposal. This assessment builds upon a pragmatist understanding of self-formation that needs to be reinjected into the discussion of what *real* processes Foucault's rhetoric redescribes in an evocative way.

It may be a mistake to stress the religious character of this system of practice, or to stipulate definitions of ascesis or ritual that set them apart from other forms of human practice. Talal Asad makes a similar point with respect to medieval Christian liturgical practices:

> In brief, it does not seem to me to make good sense to say that ritual behavior stands universally in opposition to behavior that is ordinary or pragmatic, any more than religion stands in contrast to reason or to (social) science. In various epochs and societies, the domains of life are variously articulated, and each of them articulates endeavors that are appropriate to it. How these articulations are constructed and policed, and what happens when they are changed . . . are all questions for anthropological inquiry. But unless we try to reconstruct in detail the historical conditions in which different projects and motivations are formed, we shall not make much headway in understanding agency.[99]

The historical effects of Manichaean practice occurred within the premediated field that the tradition proposed. The reality to which Manichaeans responded was one in which the self *did* have a divine pedigree, *did* grapple with contrary impulses, *could* emerge as a demarcated soul, and *could* attain to a promised salvation. That is, these are the truths that motivated the behavior we now identify historically as Manichaean. Our task is to give that behavior its place in history, not by replacing those truths with our own, but by placing those truths in a relation with our own precisely by means of understanding the generation of minds, selves, and societies in processes of human interaction—interaction mediated by local, specific, time-bound apprehensions of reality.

Returning to the dialogue in *Kephalaion 81* between Mani and the *archēgos* who wants to quit working in the ritual system, we hear Mani suggest that physical or psychological illness would be a legitimate reason to withdraw from the "divine work" for a time. But, he immediately adds, it is better to persevere, since the work itself helps solidify and reinforce the positive administration of the body. Obedience to the disciplines and service in the ritual actually perfects one's embodiment, so that in the end it can be said, "A divine work has come about, [your] body has been found safe for you [. . .] there being no blemish nor [destruction] nor pain for you."[100]

For Foucault, the "soul" inhabits the body and brings the individual into existence as "the effect and instrument of a political anatomy"; consequently, he declares, "the soul is the prison of the body."[101] But, for Mani, "He who sees himself outwardly, not seeing inwardly, is truly inferior and makes others inferior as well."[102] The soul arises from the body as a freeing of the constituent elements of potential selfhood from a seething mass of chaotic impulses. The invasion of further attributes from outside—the regime of the Mind of Light that conquers the body as described in the Manichaean literature represented by the *Sermon on the Light Nous* and its parallels—comes into contact with inherent properties awaiting the liberation of the conqueror, and the opportunity to emerge into a fully human identity.[103] That identity is not alienated from the cosmos but is intimately identified with the forces of life within the cosmos. Manichaeans erect walls between themselves and the world not just to flee its poison but also to restrain themselves from harmful action upon its goodness. Those walls of ascesis only serve to accentuate the single gate left open by which the world enters in and finds its path to the height. The Manichaean body functions as the perfected means of universal salvation and, in this function, builds up the power and integrity of the individual embodied soul also aspiring to that salvation.

Ascent

In the opening of his Gospel, Mani declares, "I have chosen the Elect, and I have shown a path to the height to those who ascend according to this truth."[104] Moreover, Jesus came in the body so that "he might ransom those enslaved from the powers, and set free their limbs from the subjection of the rebels and from the authority of those who keep guard, and that through it (i.e., the body) he might disclose the truth of its own knowledge, and in it open wide the door to those confined within."[105] Manichaean texts are replete with references to opening gates, forging paths, and freeing those confined. It is a striking element of the lexicon. "This is the road, this is the secret, this is the great commandment and gate of liberation (br mwxšyg)."[106] The unfortunate adherents of other religions, who "did not accomplish the work in their religion," receive the new dispensation of Mani's faith, "which will be for them the door of salvation."[107] The principal fault of the other religions lies in their defective practices of sacrifice and food ritual, for "there is no rest or open gate through which they (i.e., the offerings) emerge and find occasion to ascend to God." But in the two personas of the male and female Elect, who follow the "alms commandments," "they emerge from it and go to the God of truth . . . it becomes a door to them."[108]

According to the Coptic Manichaica, the Living Self strives for, and receives in the Elect, "breadth" or "spaciousness" (ouastn). Although the corresponding term in other languages cannot be identified with certainty, mwxš (from Sanskrit moksa) seems to be the closest equivalent in the Iranian material. Through the ritual meal, "a breadth exists for it, and it is healed in the Elect, in the psalms, prayers, and praises";[109] "that soul is released and it emerges from affliction to breadth."[110]

Part of the liberated self emerges as the vocalizations of the Elect;[111] but several sources speak of the Elect as depositories who somehow assimilate and store the divine substance.[112] In the latter case, especially, the fate of the soul-stuff of the sacred meal, and that of the individual Elect, coincide; but in either case the salvation of all life, both internal and external to the Manichaean, is interconnected.[113] A psalmist enjoins the Elect to "purify the light-self, so that it may save you";[114] "show a road to the light."[115] The practice of the ritual meal apparently opens and maintains a passage between heaven and earth, operative for the alms during an Elect's life, and utilized by the Elect's own self at death as a final ascent of liberation. In *Kephalaion 81*, Mani indicates that active participation in the ritual system forms a bond between the individual and the Light being liberated, with the result that the individual "will go to this great [land] of rest with [the] living children," and "[come] into a glory and [victory with] those on whom you set your heart; you strengthen[116] yourself by them *(aktajrak ajōw)*."[117] The *Ts'an-ching* describes the final liberation of an Elect at death in the following terms:

> If there is one from the pure Elect who is of the sort who assures the prosperity of the correct religion without superior, and until the end of life does not fall backwards, then after death that person's Old Man with the dark, non-luminous force of its mob of soldiers will fall into hell from which it will never come out. At the same moment, the beneficent light, rousing the pure kinsmen of its own luminous army, will go completely straight into the world of light. Definitively, this master will no longer be in fear and receives joy perpetually.[118]

It is clear from passages such as these that the Manichaean "soul" is a collectivity of divine elements, and that the final liberation of the individual Manichaean matches exactly the liberation of the Living Self that is collected in the alms-service and processed in the ritual meal. In *Kephalaion 2*, Mani identifies the five mentalities of the internal cosmos of the Manichaean self with five points of transmission for the liberated light in the external cosmos.[119] Just as rebellion of evil rises through these five mentalities if unchecked,[120] so the successful processing of the Living Self in the perfected bodies of the Elect passes through these mentalities, and emerges to pass through the corresponding stages of the macrocosm. These stages mark out the path "for the souls that ascend . . . together with the alms that the catechumens give, as they are purified in the [holy] church."[121]

In collecting and liberating the Living Self, the Manichaeans essentially are redeeming themselves from entanglement with the mixed world. Mani tells his disciples, "You yourselves must be purifiers and redeemers of your soul, which is established in every place, so that you [may be counted] to the company of the fathers of light."[122] The Manichaean who has attained gnosis declares, "The cross of light that gives life to the universe, I have known it and believed in it; for it is my dear soul, which nourishes every man, at which the blind are offended because they know it not."[123] This key point of the Manichaean worldview is missed in interpretations that imagine that salvation reaches its conclusion with the personal liberation of an ascetically quietist Elect. Recognizing one's true identity as a spark of the divine light does not in itself accomplish liberation. The prophets do not teach merely about the reality and existence of this divine presence, but also about "its cleansing and healing."[124] The salutary effects of Manichaean disciplines not only perfect the individual Elect body and keep it from harming the Living Self,[125] but also set the stage for the obligatory work of the religion to redeem the Living Self from the entire world.[126]

We lose the ability to "make sense" of the Manichaean system the moment we lose sight of the absolute identity of the individual and the collective soul. There is no individual salvation in Manichaeism, only the common "work of religion" involving solar and lunar orbits, ocean tides, and plant exhalations, as much as human activity. Humans are at the center of attention only insofar as they are a model of the larger cosmos and its operations. Salvation at the human scale of action cannot be effected by detachment and withdrawal, but only by active engagement—carefully circumscribed and rigorously ritualized—with the cosmos. The ritual meal provides the essential connection for that engagement to occur. The "commandments of the savior," the law brought by the apostle of light, encompass both disciplinary regimens and alimentary rites. For us it is heuristically useful to distinguish the two as separate phases or modes of practice. But for the Manichaeans they constituted a unified system: the approved, salvational behavior of the Manichaean body. When we look closely, Manichaean discourse about the soul and concern with its salvation turns out to be very much "a something about the body."

SEVEN

"EIN ETWAS AM LEIBE"

Seele ist nur ein Wort für ein Etwas am Leibe.
—Friedrich Nietzsche

Manichaeism is a truly peculiar religion, "constituted of elements unique in the history of ancient thought."[1] This study has sought to make sense of it on its own terms, within the confines of its own self-apprehension, with a minimum amount of heuristic gimmicks. But Manichaeism is also part of human history and culture, with antecedents, interactions, and lasting effects in the larger world. What can the Manichaean case tell us about the class of phenomena we moderns have committed ourselves to calling religion? What does it show concerning the strengths and weaknesses of our various methods for understanding religions? This final chapter attempts to apply Manichaean data to these larger issues in the study of religion, and to make explicit what I regard as the necessary approach to bridging the gap between the emic Manichaean world and the etic interpretive strategies of modern research.

PUTTING THINGS IN THEIR PLACE
Manichaean Rationales as Speech Acts

Scholars have frequently remarked upon the complexities and inconsistencies of Manichaean discourse, and have sought to sort out coherent accounts of Manichaean cosmogony, cosmology, anthropogony, and anthropology. This project of synthesis must contend with highly recalcitrant sources displaying a wide diversity of versions both between cultural areas and even within each region. Connected accounts are practically nonexistent, and in general Manichaean texts show a fondness for episodic retelling of the religion's fundamental narratives. The literary traditions of Western and Eastern Manichaeism appear to have developed all but independently of each other. All of these factors wreak havoc with efforts to place a set of established sacred narratives at the center of Manichaean identity. The systems of dispersion at work in Manichaean discourse must have operated on other than literary principles. I believe a large part of the answer to this troublesome literary tradition resides in classifying many of the examples at our disposal not as literature but as speech acts shaped by specific performative contexts.

Legomena, "things said" in a ritual context, do not follow the properties of ordinary discursive speech. Wade Wheelock comments on the peculiar "choppiness" of liturgical texts, the "oscillation" between "short editorial divisions" of discourse and the gestures and acts of the rite, the general lack of coherent argument or connected story in a ritual script, and the allusiveness of its references and ambiguous identity of its speaking voices.[2] Standing alone as texts, therefore, the things said in the performance of ritual do not possess the coherence of sermons, treatises, or myths. Part of the problem is simply that language does not bear the totality of significance within a rite.

> In ritual, the words spoken are not the only meaning-bearing elements. . . . [A]n examination of the words of the liturgy in isolation will reveal only part of the ritual's message. . . . The meaningful connecting link is often to be found only by looking to the "statement" being made in one of the nonverbal media.[3]

Ritual acts and the statements interspersed with them belong to a common set of behaviors that implement the accomplishment of the ritual. To make sense of such statements, therefore, "There must be a close examination of the complex set of relationships that hold between a ritual utterance and its context of participants, objects, actions, and other symbols."[4]

Rather than communicate novel information, many Manichaean ritual utterances possess the properties of *illocutions*, speech acts that actually do things by appealing to indigenous conventions of language, or established lexica of effective vocalizations. This aspect of speech was first defined by J. L.

Austin as "the performance of an act *in* saying something."[5] Manichaean hymns and other ritual statements act upon their listeners by ordering them to bow, stand, sit, pay attention, listen, rejoice, cry out, sing, pray, embrace, carry, and so on. Those assembled hear exhortations ("let us . . .") to do many of the same actions. The speakers, soloists, and choirs also declare that "I" or "we" perform a similar repertoire of ritual acts. The imperative and hortatory forms obviously constitute essential components of the rite itself, directing the ritual process; the declarative statements take the form of an autocommentary on the rite, placing the speaker at a particular juncture in the rite, as if telegraphing a description to a nonobserver. Some ritual scripts possess illocutions that are not spoken in the rite itself but provide the possessor of the script with instructions on the sequence of actions; how that sequence was to be governed in the actual performance is not made clear.

Other utterances scripted for performance in the ritualized contexts of Manichaean practice offer highly allusive references to objects, personages, and acts involved in the rite. Such statements cannot have been particularly effective in communicating novel information to those who heard them, but belong to a category of speech that "assumes detailed prior knowledge of the matter presented."[6] Manichaean hymns especially display such allusiveness, citing episodes of mythology or church history deemed relevant to the occasion in such a fashion that the modern researcher is unable to reconstruct a connected narrative. The performance of lists, such as the Manichaean pantheon or the *šhrd'ryft*, by sheer redundancy, may have served a more effective educational function.

The use of prestige language is also mentioned by Wheelock as a violation of the long-assumed communicative function of ritual language.[7] Evidence of hymns sung entirely in a foreign tongue is limited to Eastern Manichaeism: the Sogdians and Turks used hymns in Parthian and Middle Persian. The Chinese *Hymnscroll* also contains a few short verses in Iranian dialect. One also encounters stock phrases, such as *m'n'st'r hyrz'*, carried over into new languages. Their significance in a ritual context, however, was no doubt perfectly clear. Finally, in every region one finds technical terms introduced from languages representing earlier domains of proselytization; although etymologically mysterious in their new homes, these terms, too, must have possessed relatively clear significance in use. When recitations in prestige languages are employed, the meaning of the recitation must be looked for in its use and role within the rite.[8]

If ritual vocalizations are not primarily discursive, what is their function in the rite? Wheelock contends that ritual language differs from ordinary speech in that, whereas the latter responds to cues in the environment, ritual statements formulate the environment by declaring certain things to be so, certain identities to be present, certain effects to be achieved. In short, "ritual utterances serve both to engender a particular state of affairs, and at the same time express recognition of its reality."[9] In Meadian terms, then, one could say that the statements made in a ritual context structure or reiterate the environment to which the ritual relates as a normative response; they are a way of signaling within the context of a specific course of action.

> Because men have significant symbols they can hold on to stimuli (or indicate them) in their absence and can therefore commit themselves to selected . . . objects. . . . Through language men can command themselves, give to themselves the responses and the stimuli required for completing the process of adjustment.[10]

Ritual statements belong inseparably to the other actions of the ritual; they serve as what one might call icons: they are displayed, located, and responded to in the same way as a ritual implement, image, or role.[11] "Religious tenets are indeed symbols, functioning in very much the same ways as the concrete objects or actions that are more readily recognized as ritual symbols; and the acts of affirming, assenting to, or even adhering to, such tenets are ritual acts, like immolation, genuflexion, and so forth."[12] That is not to say that more extensive meanings are not associated with ritual symbols, or that the linguistic sense of ritual statements are not explained; but James Fernandez found among the Bwiti that the ability to reproduce expansive understandings declined rapidly after the initial instruction, as participants allow the "symbol" to become a "signal" limited to its function in the ritual context.[13] By connecting objects present, things done, and roles enacted with materials, actions, and personages not directly observed, the ritual speech act extends the reach of ritual action, and potentially elicits in the experience of the participant images of the larger domain of ritual effects.[14]

Ritual commands and declarations, of course, clearly occupy the speech act class, but other Manichaean texts should be seen in this light as well. The clearest case for reclassification can be made for the hymns, which do not give full accounts of Manichaean sacred narratives, but make allusions to them effective for an already informed audience. The inconsistencies between such compositions have been traditionally seen in terms of poetic license, with emphases shifting according to performative setting. Prose narratives, usually seen as instructional in nature, pose a more difficult problem, since their contradictions and multiple reformulations confound all attempts to acquire a fixed account. These too, I think, need to be explained in terms of their role vis-à-vis the practices for which they provided rationales. Rather than being sacred histories, the mastery of which answers existential questions, they are *historiolae*, the performance of which empower ritual solutions to existential problems.

The compositional category of *historiola* has been used for narrative passages incorporated into magical spells, and developed conceptually in this context definitively by David Frankfurter. He describes the *historiola* as "the performative transmission of power from a mythic realm articulated in narrative to the human present."[15] Such narratives "are not merely economical, instrumental speech like *voces magicae*, but stories told for their own sake, as gatherings of lore for the sake of some special need" (461). He finds that they do not necessarily make explicit reference to their ritual application. "The focal action or words may appear" in the narrative "as a past accomplishment," its application understood in context, so that the narrative "functions linguistically like a simile: '. . . thus, just like the accomplishment described, so also let it happen now'" (462). The *historiola* provides not only the rationale, but the "power" of the ritual act by linking it to an exalted precedent or to an analogous situation of successful action. "The *historiola*'s link between times is not as important as its link between a human dimension where action is open-ended and a mythic dimension where actions are completed and tensions have been resolved" (466). By connecting present ritual action with a divine paradigm in which the Primordial Man, for example, successfully frees himself from mixture with evil, the ritualist invokes the force of that archetypal success.

It is not essential to the role of the *historiola* that its recounting agree with a canonical version, or even any other version, of the sacred narrative it uses. It suffices that it alludes to recognizable figures of power in situations that can be associated with the project of the ritual. The search for a coherent ur-myth behind related *historiolae*, and containing all of the elements found in the variants, is thus a fruitless task. In many cases, Frankfurter contends, the "myths" we try to reconstruct as coherent narratives do not exist *except* as ritual librettos that are implicitly or explicitly oriented toward the ritual context and its goals. . . . That is to say, myths only exist in the form of ritual applications; the *historiolae* "are" the myths, rather than derivatives of them; and the "canonical" myths to which scholars . . . appeal are literary contrivances, masking the diversity and even incoherence of the actual traditions. (472–73)

Ritualists employ *historiolae* in a way that reflects a more expansive definition of sacred traditions which relies on "recognizability" in place of canonical fixity, and which is more concerned with efficacious application than scriptural verity (473). "The concept 'myth' therefore serves as a theoretical explanation of structural resemblances, links, and overall relationships among *historiolae*, liturgical recitations, texts, and other forms of mythical expression"; and the attested dispersion of narratives constitutes "the authoritative discourse of precedent in a given region at a certain time" (474).

The linkage of *historiola* to ritual context can be done in a number of ways, including analogy of situation (either in problem or solution, often made by an explicit "just as then . . . so now . . ."), conflation of mythic and contemporary presence (i.e., the figures of the narrative enter the present, or the present participants enter the narrative), and specific ritual precedent (i.e., an etiology of the rite, or of elements used in the rite) (469). Manichaean ritual statements provide examples of all of these applications, and the extended rationales offered as instruction to the community draw the same sort of connections time after time.[16]

By citing the sanctioning precedents for ritual acts as the latter were performed, Manichaean ritualists directed attention to the broader soteriological context to which these acts belonged. Such reiterated linkages between divine and human action constituted the native interpretation of what was being done and to what end it was directed. Through public recitation of, gestures of acknowledgment for, or attentive audition to such speech acts, Manichaeans displayed their adherence to the normative narration and placement of their religious practices. Internalized or not, these native interpretations were sustained by such adherence as the hallmarks of Manichaean identity.

The Manichaean Ritual Meal as an Instrumental Rite

The study of ritual is beset with a number of notorious problems, the most basic of which is the definition of the term itself. How do we distinguish, in a given culture, ritual acts from the many other kinds of acts that a population displays? That is, if we observe a number of different types of behavior, how do we identify those that are "ritual" behaviors purely on the basis of differentiation? We must be careful about imputing too much interpretive significance to an act being a ritual as opposed to belonging to some other heuristic category. Instead of asking, "How is it that *ritual* activities are seen or judged to be the appropriate thing to do?"[17] we should be asking, "Why this specific technique (whether we classify it as ritual or not) and not some other?" In other words, we must be careful not to predetermine our interpretations simply by choosing to call something a ritual.

The category of ritual presents such a threat of predetermination because of the history of the concept in modern Western thought. We are working still in the shadow of the tradition that identifies an act as a ritual when its emically instrumental purpose cannot be affirmed by etic standards of rationality, because it is not instrumental or effective in an overt, observable way. By starting from this standard of classification, we already constrain how the act can be interpreted. Either a ritual will be seen as an empty performance with no real effects, and therefore be considered as solely expressive, or else it will be seen to have real effects other than the instrumental ones emically associated with it, psychological or social ramifications of which the practitioners have no conscious intent.[18] *By definition*, a ritual does not produce real physical effects and is not instrumental in the way presented.

Because modern researchers have used ritual as one avenue of access to the cultural codes, values, and discourses of populations we study, we often make the mistake of thinking that communicating those very things is what ritual is for. Ritual obviously entails communicative acts, but

> to say that ritual is a mode of communication is surely not to say that it is interchangeable with other modes of communication. . . . It is, rather, to accept an expanded notion of communication, one that includes the achievement of effects through the transmission of information rather than through the application of matter and energy.[19]

Like communicative action, some ritual action operates by means of signaling, that is, its activity refers in an abbreviated fashion to a more extensive activity.[20] Julien Ries's understanding of Manichaean practices construes ritual as primarily communicative. But many specific ritual acts have no signaling properties. The consumption of the Manichaean ritual meal, although framed by signaling performances, does not itself operate through signaling, but by carrying through the act of eating as a technique which itself is supposed to have a salvational effect. Such a rite actually does operate "through the application of matter and energy, and not through information."[21] The fact that some of the ritual's activity takes place beyond immediate observation (that is, in the body or some other region to which human digestion is supposedly connected) entails no more symbolism for the participant or observer than the technique of agriculture, in which seeds are put out of sight for a time in expectation that they will yield food (and, of course, precisely this agricultural analogy is commonplace in the emic exposition of ritual behavior of many cultures). The point that the theories embedded in religious rationales are perfectly rational applications by analogy of directly observed physical laws, and not necessarily symbolic in some more attenuated way, has been demonstrated repeatedly and well in the work of Robin Horton.[22]

Those who seek to explain ritual in terms of its communicative function tend to overestimate the ongoing enrichment of knowledge in ritual participants. Maurice Bloch makes the point that ritual language represents a depleted, not heightened, form of communication.[23] Ritual language is highly redundant, from one performance to the next and even within a single ritual; the participant, therefore, is not exposed to novel information in the ritual context but to repetitive, canonized recitations. Communication is restricted and reduced to invariant formulae.[24] The effect of depleted communication is to focus semantic range into a carefully circumscribed set, to draw attention to specified significance at the expense of interpretive diversity.[25]

A second mistake made in the interpretive appeal to communicaton in ritual is a misunderstanding or misapplication of the ethological concept of "signaling" which focuses on content rather than function. Communication is action, and ethology has demonstrated that signaling is a part of social negotiation of role, status, power, and influence in behavior. Any linguistic or symbolic content can be appropriated, formalized, and employed as a signaling system, and the rise and fall of "ideologies" is as much determined by the success and failure of power groups employing them as the latter's success and failure is determined by the power and cogency of the sets of ideas they hold.

Ritual specialists possess, or are expected to possess, the full catalogue of exegetical knowledge culturally associated with the rites they perform or supervise. They do not always share this knowledge publicly, but may keep it as their own exclusive, empowering property. In situations that call for public exposition, however, ritual specialists have an obvious stake in the recognition and acceptance of their interpretations as the norm. Such situations do not necessarily entail education of the public in this knowledge; display and acknowledgment, rather, occupy center stage. Education and indoctrination come into play in a limited range of situations, all of which involve knowledge as rationale. When rituals are subject to rival interpretations that mark divisions within or between communities, for example, ritual specialists must defend their interpretations as the legitimate ones, and persuade their audience of the greater authority or congruity of their exegesis. They are as much defending their status as ritual specialists as they are supporting particular points of ideology.

Similarly, when ritual specialists have a stake in organizing the broader social life of the community (often in defense of the same community boundaries involved in the above situation, but also for the very simple purpose of perpetuating the ritual system through networks of support), particular interpretations can draw out ramifications of the ritual into that larger world, indicating to the community the entailments of ritual participation. In these contexts, knowledge performs a function in service of ritual (rather than vice versa) and has the character of a rationale. The "meanings" associated with ritual acts, roles and objects, are a set of implied signals that ritual specialists attempt to control and manipulate in support of the ritual process, and to invest in the minds and behaviors of the members of the community.

Any appeal to the ideas, feelings, or mental states of individuals in the interpretation of ritual comes up against the problem of the inaccessibility of these internal experiences to the researcher, and run afoul of Evans-Pritchard's notorious "if I were a horse" critique. I must agree with E. R. Leach when he says that "the anthropologist has absolutely no information about what is inwardly felt by any professed believer."[26] If this holds true of the anthropologist working with living subjects, moreover, it certainly must be the case as well of the historian working strictly from overt testimony. Many theories do not even presuppose the presence in any individual practitioner's mind of the complete belief system referenced by a rite; the researcher constructs the total belief system for the first time. What researchers describe as the "beliefs" of a population actually manifest themselves as statements and acts rather than concepts and attitudes.[27] These public gestures do not correlate univocally with a set of meanings held in the minds of those who employ them.[28] In ethnographic discourse, when a researcher says that a particular population "believes" X, she means that individuals within that population make statements avowing X. Ethnographers often make an extrapolation from the statements of individuals to a "belief" held by the whole population through typification, as a necessary expedient in talking about other cultures. Such an extrapolation is most justified when the statements are uttered in a formal context in which the whole population participates. In this case, the "belief" is something to which the population makes public assent, an icon to which they show allegiance, regardless of their individual understanding of or reservations about it.

The recent confluence of ritual studies with theories about self-formation has produced a new interpretation: the idea that ritual practice has real—"physical," if you will—effects on practitioners through the shaping of their habits of embodiment. Obviously, I am in greater sympathy with this theory than with the others, but it has its own share of weak points. In one of its better-known forms—Catherine Bell's *Ritual Theory, Ritual Practice*—the thesis amounts to a tautology: the function of ritual is to habituate individuals within a particular culture to the ways of doing ritual;[29] that is, ritualization is a process of sustaining ritualization.[30] In terms of embodiment, the body acquires "ritual mastery" and becomes a "ritualized body." It almost would seem that Bell has been led astray by the ambiguity of the English word *practice*, so that she conflates training for a ritual (learning and practicing its procedure) with performance of a ritual (the "official" enactment of it, the one that counts). Nevertheless, this theory does highlight key features of ritual otherwise neglected.

Bell points to "growing evidence that most symbolic action, even the basic symbols of a community's ritual life, can be very unclear to participants or interpreted by them in very dissimilar ways."[31] Yet research such as that of James Fernandez on the Bwiti cult shows that social solidarity is promoted by the mere assent to public symbols, regardless of the idiosyncratic meanings entertained by individuals.[32] Fernandez highlights the fact that, at an overt level, participation in a ritual involves "the acceptance of a certain set of signals and signs that give direction and orientation to [a particular] interaction permitting the coordination and co-existence of the various participants."[33] This suggests to Bell that "some level or degree of social consensus does not depend upon shared information or beliefs, and ritual need not be seen as a simple medium of communicating such information or beliefs."[34] Several studies have also demonstrated that the complete belief systems modern research retrieves have very limited if any distribution within the societies they supposedly serve. In many cases, they are the exclusive property of a very small specialist class, whereas knowledge of practical or ritual patterns is widely distributed.[35]

The maintenance of a ritual tradition such as that of the Manichaeans is accomplished by public performance and displayed assent, and does not necessarily entail or require community-wide conformity of belief. For one thing, we must be clear about what we mean by *belief*, a term whose meaning is at times restricted to discursive knowledge, and at other times extended to include any subjective experience. Tomas Gerholm astutely points out, "There is a 'correct' view as to how the rite should be performed and possibly also as to what it is supposed to achieve. But there is no correct *experience* of it."[36] Catherine Bell proposes that one of the special strengths of ritualized practices is that they "afford a great diversity of interpretation in exchange for little more than consent to the form of the activities."[37] Similarly, Roy Rappaport describes adherence to a ritual system as a public act of great social value. "Liturgical orders are public, and participation in them constitutes a public acceptance of a public order, regardless of the private state of belief. Acceptance is, thus, a fundamental social act, and it forms the basis for public orders which unknowable and volatile belief or conviction cannot."[38]

Social orders and ritual systems are maintained through public conformity, not through mental reflection. "It is the visible, explicit, public act of acceptance, and not the invisible, ambiguous, private sentiment that is socially and morally binding."[39] Edward Schieffelin likewise contends, "The performance is objectively (and socially) validated by the participants when they share its action . . . no matter what each person may individually think about it."[40] An individual who publicly avows adherence to a community or way of life has entered a social relation in which she assents to have her actions judged by the rules she has avowed, regardless of how she feels about those rules. The rules are reaffirmed and perpetuated by such avowals, even if no one adheres to them. At any point these standards can be reactivated as an embodied way of life, perhaps as part of a reform; they constitute the social icons that continue to be the touchstone against which the permutations of actual practice can be measured.[41]

Regardless of other motivations that may or may not be accessible to our gaze, the people who participate in a rite make a public investment in the relations presumed or the results promised by the rite's normative rationales. Participation comes at the price of mastering the approved performance of one's role in the rite. This public adherence and mastery of performance are essential elements of ritual behavior. Talal Asad makes this point perfectly:

> Ritual is therefore directed at the apt performance of what is prescribed, something that depends on intellectual and practical disciplines but does not itself require decoding. In other words, apt performance involves not symbols to be interpreted but abilities to be acquired according to rules that are sanctioned by those in authority: it presupposes no obscure meanings, but rather the formation of physical and linguistic skills. Rites as apt performance presuppose codes — in the regulative sense as opposed to the semantic — and people who evaluate and teach them.[42]

Manichaean identity is shaped in part by adherence to codes of ritual performance, by displaying the characteristic ritual acts of the Manichaean tradition as part of one's behavioral repertoire.

The danger to any interpretation that focuses on the construct of a "ritualized body" lies in its premature end of analysis.[43] To the "ritualized body" of any culture the further question must be asked: To what end is this body itself constructed and applied? A common answer heard is: social ends. Catherine Bell alludes to her belief that mastery of ritual techniques must have advantages in other sociocultural situations. "The specific strategies of ritualization," she says, "produce a ritualized social body, a body with the ability to deploy in the wider social context the schemes internalized in the ritualized environment."[44] But do ritual schemes have application outside the ritual setting, or are they specific to the effectiveness of what the ritual does? Bell simply presupposes that the behaviors cultivated in ritual settings are those needed for the general functioning of the society. Jonathan Z. Smith likewise sees ritual as "a means of performing the way things ought to be in conscious tension to the way things are," that is, as a mode of inculcating the ideal forms of ordinary social relations.[45] Certainly, rituals incorporate elements from social models: commensality, exchange, contract, appeal, gestures of deference; but they also frequently draw upon nonsocial sources of action-patterns: hunting, agriculture, cooking, manufacture, travel. Parallels between social structures and actions on the one hand and ritual structures and actions on the other have as much to do with the analogical application in ritual of models drawn from the larger human repertoire of action as they do with the shaping of profane behavior by sacred enactment.

The idea that a ritual is an end in itself, or an exercise for display purposes, rather than an instrumental means to the ends it purports, is abetted by lumping together rituals of personal transformation (initiation, passage, healing, purification) with rituals of external effect (sacrifice and various rites of cosmic maintenance, repair, or influence). It may be time to disassemble the monolithic category of ritual once and for all, since some theories and explanations are better suited to certain kinds of ritual than to others. In his ongoing seminar and publications on Manichaean practices, H.-C. Puech was most interested in the Manichaean rites of initiation as conveyers of gnostic truths; the ritual meal received much less attention, and its significance was absorbed into the dominant paradigm of communicative and transformative rites. More generally, in recent discussion of the "self-forming" character of ritual, preparatory rites and practices—Durkheim's "negative rites"—which often do focus on rendering the body of ritualists into a particular condition, frequently overshadow those ritual acts, or "positive rites," which the properly prepared body of a ritualist subsequently performs. Without this important distinction, ritual is seen merely as the verification and sanction of the purifications and transformations of the body by which the ritualist prepares for ritual participation. The ritualist literally prepares for nothing other than to be prepared.

The Latin term *sacrificium* seems to hold sway over the Western understanding of the essence of ritual action as "making sacred."[46] One needs to take account of what "making sacred" actually meant in the Latin culture that chose that term to convey its sense of ritual. It meant the ritual transference of an object from human to divine possession. Human participants are only "made sacred" in this sense in a discrete class of preparatory rites making them eligible for other ritual functions, or when rituals of initiation transfer them into a class that has special obligations in the cultus. They are not made sacred in the performance of *any* rite; rather, they must become sacred, or be rendered ritually "fit," by means of one practice or rite in order to perform other rites. Glossing this distinction implies that the techniques acquired in ritualized contexts have their end in social relations, or in personal transformations carried out within the rite, rather than in the instrumental force of the rites. The use made in modern ritual studies of "making sacred" in the sense of social endowment of special status on ordinary things as a mystified or misrecognized manufacture of the sacred category is an etic reapplication of the emic *sacrificium*.

So in the Manichaean case or any other, the questions to ask are: Why *this* ritualized body and not some other? Why *these* techniques, *these* disciplines? Why put a trained and prepared body to work in *this* ritual way rather than some other ritual or nonritual way? If ritualization is merely a mode of socialization, why would a Manichaean desocialize from a majority culture with inherent benefits and adopt an antisocial ethos full of social disadvantages? If its real end is to cultivate and reinforce social cohesion, why does it employ such arduous labors and such superfluous rationales when many easier means and less extraordinary discourses are readily available for this purpose? The first answer must be simply because these disciplines, these techniques, this ritualized body are believed to effect salvation, whereas the other alternatives do not. In other words, we must not neglect the Manichaeans' own explanatory affirmations as an important component of historical causality.

The modern researcher oscillates between disparaging ordinary believers for the mundane reasons they give for fulfilling their religious duties and seeking to recoup their religiosity by explaining the truly compelling (to the modern interpreter), if hidden, motives for their behavior. In the Manichaean case, or any other, we are tempted to reject a relatively straightforward cost-benefit analysis that they enunciate and to put in its place theories of elaborate and powerful social and psychological forces at work in their lives. Such general theories do nothing to explain the specific details of a particular religious tradition, but must reduce those details to accidental, arbitrary, and inessential accretions to more fundamental human relations. In our own, modern, academic way we are still trying to overcome difference, plurality, and behavioral anomaly and discover behind the complex, even chaotic manifestations of humanity a core of identity whose fixity provides us with a sense of what it is about us that transcends the individual and the individual's limitations and mortality. This was the Manichaeans' quest no less than ours.

NORMATIVE EMBODIMENT

The practices of members of the self-defined Manichaean community differ in certain carefully promoted ways from the behavior of nonmembers, and their distinctive practices identify individuals as Manichaeans. The Manichaean ethos, as a whole, partakes of what Catherine Bell calls ritualization. Bell deserves credit for focusing attention in the debate about defining ritual on how communities themselves possess systematic means of marking certain actions apart as "ritualized." Both the Manichaean disciplinary regimens and their alimentary rites fit Bell's category of "privileged acts" produced through the practice of ritualization, or being marked apart from ordinary action "by means of culturally and situationally relevant categories and nuances."[47] I do not mean to say that individuals who were Manichaeans lived totally ritualized lives; what I do mean to say is that those characteristic behaviors that identified individuals as Manichaeans were precisely ritualized behaviors. They were behaviors set apart, marked, identified, rendered significant, promoted in their noteworthiness.

> Ritualization is fundamentally a way of doing things to trigger the perception that these practices are distinct and the associations that they engender are special. . . . Hence, ritual acts must be understood within a semantic framework whereby the significance of an action is dependent upon its place and relationship within a context of all other ways of acting: what it echoes, what it inverts, what it alludes to, what it denies.[48]

The Manichaean tradition identifies all non-Manichaean behaviors as profane, even infernal. The Manichaean ethos is self-consciously presented as different from the ways of the world, a break with ordinary behavior, contrasted in every detail with corresponding acts of evil. The recognition of Manichaean identity as special, sacred, and salvational requires the constant shadow of the negated behaviors that one abandons in becoming a Manichaean.

Julien Ries has astutely pointed out, in the context of a conference devoted to the ontological and protological motivations of encratism, that such motivations are insufficient in the Manichaean case. In the latter, one must take into account equally soteriological and eschatological motivations.[49] In other words, Manichaean rationales for ascesis include particular goals toward which ascetic practice is directed, and in light of which the "fitness" achieved by disciplinary regimens is assessed. Manichaean ascesis is not primarily a re-action of abhorrence of, or flight from, what we are or have become, but a technique for achieving specific results within the limitations of what we are or have become—that is, the given, deficient conditions of "mixture." The hy-pertrophy of Manichaean disciplinary regimens so often commented upon, therefore, reflects not a *Weltabwendung*, but a heightened problematization of the world due to the ubiquitous presence in it of both an evil to be shunned and a good to be reverenced. Contrary to the cliché, the Manichaean tradition does not show itself to be the brainchild of "a wild anti-cosmicist and an en-emy of the body."[50]

The sharply delimited function of disciplinary regimens within the Mani-chaean tradition, which defined them as salvationally efficacious only insofar as they provided the conditions for the performance of the sacred meal rite, rules out the kind of role attributed to Manichaeism in the history of asceti-cism by Arthur Vööbus.[51] He contends that forms of Christian asceticism that display anticosmic, body-hating attitudes reflect the influence of a Mani-chaean worldview. His thesis is untenable not only because the Manichaean worldview does not conform to the anticosmic model, but also because Mani-chaean sources explicitly condemn precisely the kinds of solitary self-mortifi-cation Vööbus attributes to Manichaean influence. Because Manichaean dis-ciplinary regimens operate in reference to the daily ritual meal, solitary ascesis ruptures the rationales governing Manichaean practice and renders such asce-sis meaningless, pointless, and heretical.

In Augustine's rebuke of the supposed gluttony of the Manichaean Elect, another unexpected facet of Manichaean embodiment comes to our atten-tion, albeit with distinctly polemical coloring.[52] Contrary to the assumption that ascetics seek to reduce consumption to a minimum in order to purify themselves from the taint of the world, the Manichaean Elect exercise their disciplines in order to permit a more perfect consumption. Ephrem Syrus ex-presses his astonishment at the Manichaean project of metabolizing the whole world, and Augustine invokes the Manichaean slogan, "Purify all seeds!" Far from distancing themselves from contact with the mundane, the Elect enter into the most intimate contact possible with it as a duty and a sacred trust. Their disciplinary regimens do not establish barriers to this ritual contact, but prepare their bodies to undertake it. Thus it can be said that Manichaean as-ceticism does not attenuate exposure to the world so much as it reorders and ritualizes the circumstances in which that exposure will occur.

Manichaean authority promotes its own ascetic discourse as a rationale to legitimate and motivate behavior in the Manichaean community. The discourse cannot be understood as an end in itself, but must be examined in light of the practices that it seeks to institute and legitimate.[53] Discourse and practice are involved in a mutual construction in which both are essential factors, and in which neither can long survive the absence of the other.[54] The discourse and practice of Manichaean embodiment together produce a reality of their own, with its own built-in perspectives and motivations. Salvation is dependent upon the ability of the Elect to "succeed in digesting their dinner," as Augustine sarcastically puts it.[55] Manichaean physiological schemes are related closely, in fact, to the medical discourses of their contemporaries.[56] But the successful metabolism of the Living Self could only be achieved by surmounting the inherent resistances of bodily malfunction.

Western Manichaeans appropriated the Hellenistic discourse on *enkrateia* as a suitable vehicle for their bodily rationales. *Enkrateia* describes the regulation of the body in agonistic terms.

> This perception of the *hēdonai* and *epithumiai* as a formidable enemy force, and the correlative constitution of oneself as a vigilant adversary who confronts them, struggles against them, and tries to subdue them, is revealed in a whole series of expressions . . . : setting oneself against the pleasures and desires, not giving in to them, resisting their assaults, or on the contrary, letting oneself be overcome by them, defeating them or being defeated by them, being armed or equipped against them. It is also revealed in metaphors such as that of the battle that has to be fought against armed adversaries, or that of the acropolis-soul assaulted by a hostile band and needing a solid garrison for its defense.[57]

This discourse of spiritual combat made available images that could be appropriated and reinterpreted by specific religious programs, of which the Manichaean was one. Foucault points out that in its antecedent form in Hellenistic moral and medical tracts, the contrary forces are depicted as parts of a natural whole, which are to be arranged in a hierarchical order under the control of the virtuous properties of the self. The impulse to bad judgment and bad action, "however far removed it might be by nature from any conception of the soul, reason, or virtue, did not represent a different, ontologically alien power."[58]

It is tempting, therefore, to equate the Manichaean interpretation of this discourse with what Foucault calls "the Christian ethics of the flesh," whereby the adversarial forces become equated (so Foucault) with "the presence of the Other," which one desires to eradicate.[59] A close examination of Manichaean disciplinary rationales, however, shows that the fundamental reorientation of the body which those rationales describe involves a reversal of power hierarchies within the body as the interim solution to the passions. The latter do represent an alien power, but they are not eradicated from the body, indeed cannot be.[60] The passions remain, always threatening, literally, to rebel. Separation does occur—indeed the process of separation is precisely the gnosis Mani brings to the world—but is only finalized at the point of death, when the evil substance is discarded. Despite surface appearance, therefore, Manichaean ascetic discourse does not present a radical shift in the conceptualization of *enkrateia*. In Manichaeism, as in Hellenistic ethical discourse, "virtue was not conceived as a state of integrity, but as a relationship of domination, a relation of mastery."[61]

Enrollment in the Manichaean program of salvation is neither a Christian redemption nor a Gnostic liberation, but more on the order of a dietetic regimen. The Elect were never considered unassailably pure, and the Auditors, who constituted the all-important support network for the Elect, were instructed to certify the sanctity of the lifestyle of an Elect before offering him or her any alms. The Elect practitioner who failed to adhere to the strict ascetic regimen to which he or she was sworn would be deprived of food, and hence would face the unpleasant choice of penance, abandonment of the faith, or starvation. In this way, the Manichaean authorities crafted a tight network of interdependence and a set of checks on adherence to the regimen. Manichaean discourse provided the means for

a process in which the individual delimits that part of himself that will form the object of his moral practice, defines his position relative to the precept he will follow, and decides on a certain mode of being that will serve as his moral goal. And this requires him to act upon himself, to monitor, test, improve and transform himself.[62]

But this process was not left entirely to the determination of the individual; a network of coercive observations and approvals placed the process of self-formation in the midst of the Manichaean community.

Foucault's research into the modern development of the concept of the prison led him to conclude, "The exercise of discipline presupposes a mechanism that coerces by means of observation; an apparatus in which the techniques that make it possible to see induce effects of power, and in which, conversely, the means of coercion make those on whom they are applied clearly visible."[63] Manichaean discipline operated precisely upon such a mechanism of visibility. The Manichaean church possessed a hierarchical organizational structure that modern research tends to translate directly into a synonymous power structure. But in terms of the economy of the alms-service, power within the community was dispersed along a system of mutual observation in which higher hierarchical status placed its holder in greater visibility, and hence in greater subjectivity to the community's power. Isolated dissuasions of critical assessment of the Elect within Manichaean literature do not supersede the fundamental requirement, in terms of a donor's own salvation, to support only those Elect who conformed completely to the regimens. The Elect, too, had to be cautious about the source of their alms. This mutual scrutiny bound the community in a partnership the responsibilities of which could be flaunted by no one, "a network of relations from top to bottom, but also to a certain extent from bottom to top and laterally . . . supervisors, perpetually supervised."[64]

Despite the higher ritual status of the Manichaean Elect, the available data clearly shows the constraint placed upon them by the prerequisites of their ritual role. Catherine Bell similarly notes not only "how ritualization empowers those who more or less control the rite," but also "how their power is also limited and constrained," and "how ritualization depersonalizes authority, lodging the power of the specialist in an office or formal status, not in the person."[65] Close study of ritual specialists has shown that "the power to do the ritual correctly resides in the specialist's officially recognized or appointed status (office), not in the personhood or personality of the specialist. In this way, the institutionalized office can control, constrain, and pass judgment on a specialist."[66] The requirements of ritual fitness incumbent upon the Elect, in theory if not always in practice, severely restricted their ability to take material advantage of their status. They possessed the power of salvation or damnation over the Auditors only insofar as they themselves yielded to the requirements of their office, and only insofar as the Auditors granted to them a daily reaffirmation of their position as Elect.

Modern interpreters have adopted, with few signs of hesitation, the ancient polemical charge that the Manichaean Elect simply exploited the Auditors as a means of support. They have given little attention to the power dynamics of such exchange partnerships. In being instrumentalized, an Elect became a "field of merit" that served the specific salvational needs of Auditors;[67] failure to meet the criteria for filling that role rendered an Elect worthless and, consequently, alms-less. Elect status came with both privileges and responsibilities, and local circumstance probably determined how much the one outweighed the other. Manichaean values rejected both the encratite and the monk of Christian asceticism in favor of transient or semitransient lodgers always under the gaze of their Auditor hosts. As in a panopticon, "It is the fact of being constantly seen, of being able always to be seen, that maintains the disciplined individual in his subjection."[68] In such situations of disciplinary surveillance, pyramidal organization is not synonymous with pyramidal power; "it is the apparatus as a whole that produces 'power' and distributes individuals in this permanent and continuous field."[69]

By noting the relation of Manichaean disciplines to the ritual function it enabled, we are in a position to explain how ritual codes ramify into the larger life of the individual.[70] Rather than modify the general behavior of participants by means of "representation," Manichaean ritual placed direct behavioral requirements on the potential ritualist. The disciplinary regimens of both Elect and Auditor systematize the prerequisites of ritual participation. By a combination of the stringency of these prerequisites, and the daily occurrence of the ritual meal, the Manichaean ethos effectively fills the totality of behavioral opportunity. The Elect especially were constrained to a constant display of ritual aptitude. The Manichaean case can be compared with that of medieval Christian monastic disciplines as they appear in the assessment of Talal Asad. "It was not that the religious community repressed the self—on the contrary, it provided the discipline necessary for the construction of a certain kind of personality," one viewed as a necessary condition of salvation.[71]

Asad has studied the organization of conventionally prescribed emotions, sentiments, and virtues in the Christian tradition, including the liturgical program "for creating in its performers, by means of regulated practice, the 'mental and moral dispositions' appropriate to Christians."[72] He emphasizes the shared structuring force of ascetic disciplines and their coordinate rites in a manner consistent with my own position with respect to the corresponding practices of the Manichaean tradition.

The liturgy is not a species of enacted symbolism to be classified separately from activities defined as technical but is a practice among others essential to the acquisition of Christian virtues. In other words, the liturgy can be isolated only conceptually, for pedagogic reasons, not in practice, from the entire monastic program. . . . Each thing to be done was not only to be done aptly in itself, but done in order to make the self approximate more and more to a predefined model of excellence. The things prescribed, including liturgical services, had a place in the overall scheme of training the Christian self. In this conception, there could be no radical disjunction between outer behavior and inner motive, between social rituals and individual sentiments, between activities that are expressive and those that are technical (78).

Asad sees rituals as "disciplinary practices," as part of "programs for forming or reforming moral dispositions (that is, for organizing the physical and verbal practices that constitute the [in this case] virtuous Christian self)" (63). I maintain, however, that it is heuristically useful to distinguish between rites that are primarily disciplinary and self-constructing, and those that are technical operations whose performance is *made possible* by the conditioning of the operator by means of either the former kinds of rites or by disciplinary regimens. There remains an element of social-scientific reductionism in the idea that even instrumental rites are *really* about self-formation. An instrumental rite does not necessarily script a code of behavior to be followed at all times, but it may require adherence to such a code as the price of participation in a rite that will itself yield salvational results. While certain practices organize the self, rites such as the Manichaean sacred meal employ that self for instrumental effect.

Durkheim hypothesizes that ascetic disciplines arise historically from codes of ritual fitness. In his terms, these "negative rites" qualify a person to perform the "positive rites" in which contact with the divine takes place. The combination of these two varieties, not either alone, produces in the individual the normative embodiment that characterizes a member of the community. Asad demonstrates that this "organization of the soul" is a clearly recognized function of the Christian monastic-liturgical system (130). Likewise, Manichaeans explicitly describe their disciplines as a process of filtering the soul or self from the background noise of the total organism, creating the "New Man" capable of membership in the ritual community. These ancient traditions, without the benefit of modern social psychology or philosophy, anticipate the Foucauldian thesis, "The individual is not a pre-given entity which is seized on by the exercise of power. The individual, with his identity and characteristics, is the product of a relation of power exercised over bodies, multiplicities, movements, desires, forces."[73]

Through the social process of the Manichaean community, both the Elect and the Auditors learned the approved model of their respective roles in the cultus, and acquired the means to test any arising impulse in light of its favorable or unfavorable consequences within the community. In Meadian terms, they acquired a Manichaean "me." The individual "me" is "an importation from the field of social objects into an amorphous, unorganized field of what we call inner experience. Through the organization of this object, the self, this material is itself organized and brought under the control of the individual in the form of so-called self-consciousness."[74] Manichaean discourse focuses attention on particular experiences, bringing them into self-consciousness as manifestations either of the approved self or of the disapproved other with which the self is mixed.[75]

The normative embodiment promoted by Manichaean authority manifests itself in those who conform to it, and they in turn serve as models for others to emulate. As Mead explains, "The 'me' as the precipitate within me of a person who serves as a standard of reference for me is an evaluating moment serving the structuration of spontaneous impulses, as well as an element of my emerging self-image."[76] Individual Manichaeans potentially synthesize the specific examples of normative embodiment known to them into a "unitary self-image." "If this synthesis is successful, then there originates the 'self' as a unitary self-evaluation and orientation of action."[77] The Manichaean learns the significance of the implements, symbols, and terms of Manichaean practice by a process of adopting the "generalized habitual responses to them."[78] In the midst of the community, the individual is "subjected to a field of visibility," and as a consequence (potentially) "assumes responsibility for the constraints of power" by internalizing them.[79] In addressing this essential internalization process of self-formation, Peter Berger has commented as follows:

> If one imagines a totally socialized individual, each meaning objectively available in the social world would have its analogous meaning given subjectively within his own consciousness. Such total socialization is empirically non-existent and theoretically impossible, if only by reason of the biological variability of individuals.[80]

One should not, for this reason, dismiss the real effects of social self-formation and internalization, because obviously something is succeeding when a tradition is able to sustain itself.

> If socialization is not successful in internalizing at least the most important meanings of a given society, the latter becomes difficult to maintain as a viable enterprise. Specifically, such a society would not be in a position to establish a tradition that would ensure its persistence in time.[81]

The disciplinary template, which identifies approved and disapproved behaviors and impulses, operates in conjunction with a set of rationales that define the approved actions as intrinsic to the self or soul, and the disapproved actions as extrinsic and intrusive to that self.[82] Manichaean discourse provides the identifications needed to define a Manichaean self, and the disciplinary regimens supply the means to refine that self from the chaos of bodily experience by actively promoting those characteristics identified as of the self and suppressing those deemed to be not of the self. Adherence to the Manichaean code of life produces a body that manifests behaviors observable in other adherents, and therefore characteristic of a generalized Manichaean. The individual self, structured by a set of sanctioned physical and mental acts, comes into a degree of conformity with the ideal self that Manichaeism postulates.

According to Mead, the individual who enters into membership of a community must "take the attitudes of" or adopt the responses found among the members of the community

> towards the various phases or aspects of the common social activity or set of undertakings in which, as members of an organized society or social group, they are all engaged, and he must then, by generalizing these individual attitudes . . . act toward different social projects which at any given time it is carrying out, or toward the various larger phases of the general social process which constitutes its life and of which these projects are specific manifestations.[83]

Insofar as these responses constitute the self-consciousness of the individual, the latter has developed a Manichaean self.[84] The reorientation of the prior self, however defined, toward the authoritative models of the Manichaean tradition occurs in the process of practice, in the midst of the regimens and rites that offer, respectively, the means and ends of sanctioned selfhood.

This transformation occurs at the level of the Self as it is culturally typified and can potentially occur at the level of the individual ritual subject, insofar as the ritual subject is made to behave in a manner consistent with ritually displayed typifications of Self and is understood to experience Self in the terms of these typifications.[85]

The things said, as well as the things done, in ritualized contexts, create a situation potentially formative of a self, an identity for the participant. In the words of Wade Wheelock,

> The actual utterance of the words of the liturgy, which will include such very personal elements as expressions of attitudes and intentions, causes one to take on the identity of a cultural ideal. The formalized role is put into your mouth to speak and comes out as your own responsible perception of and involvement in the situation. The first person of the ritual text comes to life as the "I" or "we" of the participants who speak the liturgy and who then proceed to fashion around themselves a whole world made of language.[86]

While Wheelock's assessment stresses the role of ritual language, it can be extended generally to the total ritualized situation, in which roles are assumed as much in action as they are in speech. The two fields of performance reinforce each other, and together comprehend the external (physical) and internal (mental) behavior of the individual, guiding it toward the promoted models of perfection, shaping the expression of selfhood to a homogenous identity shared by all.

Manichaean normative embodiment establishes its regime in light of the specific ritual ends to which that embodiment is to be applied. By making those ritual ends the purview of an elite, Manichaeans explicitly disqualify the general population from participation. This explicit disqualification carries with it an implicit problematization of ordinary embodiment, whereby a process of normativizing the body becomes necessary as the disciplinary gateway to a ritual role. In its logic, "normalization operates through the creation of abnormalities which it then must treat and reform,"[87] that is, by identifying and drawing attention to certain specific traits of human behavior that impede ritual aptitude. The demand for a properly qualified body in the performance of a ritual is an example of power which, in conjunction with its directly implicated knowledge about what constitutes qualification, forms the starting point for a vast network of normativized bodies, objects, institutions, relations, and modes of discourse.

Manichaean embodiment, then, must be understood with reference to its utility. Manichaean disciplinary practices construct a body that "becomes a useful force only if it is both a productive body and a subjected body."[88] Subjection or "docility" alone is not enough, and in Manichaean discourse salvation is not attained by ascesis alone, by a stilling of the body to an ideal of absolute nonaction. Rather, the Manichaean "docile body" must be put to use. In this respect, Manichaean disciplines are similar to the industrial disciplines analyzed by Foucault and, like the latter, distinct from Christian asceticism, "whose function was to obtain renunciations rather than increases of utility" and which served as ends in themselves—direct approaches toward divinity— rather than preparations for other forms of utility.[89] In Manichaeism, as in the later industrial self-formation and training studied by Foucault, we see a conjunction of utility and conformity, "the formation of a relation that in the mechanism itself makes it more obedient as it becomes more useful, and conversely."[90] The force of such disciplined bodies is drawn away from random impulses and incoherent rebellions and directed toward specific aptitudes valorized by the community.[91] Discipline makes of the Manichaean body "an efficient machine."[92]

The "machinery" of the Manichaean body was able to process the raw material that entered it and refine from that material the "spiritual gold" of the Living Self. The disciplined life imposed on the Elect was based upon a conceptualization of the channels through which the *pneumatic* end-products of digestive purification were thought to flow.[93] In response to these natural channels, which could potentially thrust refined light or *pneuma* back into the mixture of the world, Mani imposed the fivefold rest, or *anapausis*, which was the precondition for the status of Elect and participation in the ritual meal. By these disciplines, the Manichaean Elect effectively blocked the detrimental channels of *pneumatic* emanation.[94] But in the case of the two remaining rests (those of the mind and mouth) the goal was purification rather than elimination. In this way, these two channels could still serve as pathways for the flow of the liberated Living Self, the victorious light, which departed from the body and proceeded to the celestial paradise. Indeed, Augustine and Ephrem specifically refer to meditations, prayers and psalms as the activity appropriate to the Elect and associated with the liberating activity of the ritual meal.[95]

The reparation, then, of the inherent pathology of the body and the maintenance of digestive salvation was dependent upon a regimen of life which at the same time formed the necessary prerequisite for the ritual salvation of the individual from the condition of human suffering in all its manifestations. Manichaean embodiment belies its traditional interpretation in terms of spirit-matter duality or a disdain for all things bodily, just as it fails to conform to a program for mystical ascent to divinity. In the Manichaean tradition, the concerns of the body, and issues of its perfectibility and control, are actually exalted into a paradigm for the structure of the entire cosmos and the course of salvation history. In the center of that cosmos, as in the vanguard of that history, stands the normatively embodied Manichaean Elect, constructed as agent, instrument, and locale of a salvational technique.

HISTORICAL REALITIES

In the Manichaean tradition, Mani is "the great hermeneut." While other prophets spoke in parables and symbols, he spoke plain simple words, explaining everything literally, leaving nothing in need of further interpretation. Manichaean discipline and ritual have their rationales clearly given, and do not conceal more abstract mysteries, are not themselves discourse in disguise. These are the facts of the tradition, testimonies that we flaunt at our own peril. There are a number of reasons why one might want to ignore them, to seize upon and transform the Manichaean tradition into something else, something more familiar, less bizarre. But whether from a charitable desire to put the best face on the other, or a defensive need to find confirmation of one's own world in the voices of the past, such endeavors will not truly bridge the emic-etic divide that constitutes the principal hurdle to humans' study of themselves.

The emic-etic gap is actually a problem in set theory. The set of acts (rites and disciplines) identified in Manichaean (emic) discourse, and that identified for the Manichaeans by academic (etic) discourse overlap to a large degree (the primary discrepancy being the internal phase of rites and disciplines, which etic analysis shifts to its rationales set). The set of rationales diverge, however, because the Manichaean universe in which its characteristic acts were conducted does not match the universe inhabited by the modern researcher. The latter, therefore, must try to identify the modern discourse that occupies the closest analogous position to Manichaean rationales in relation to the acts those rationales legitimate and contextualize. For much of Manichaean anthropological discourse, the modern analog is clearly physiology, just as for Manichaean cosmology the modern analog is physics. By their tendency to reject these identifications, modern scholars cloak their own culture's science in an illusion of objectivity and finality, mark it as something qualitatively different from the quasi-scientific discourses of other cultures, and fail to recognize its own mediation through perception, language, and modeling.

Like the charitable hermeneuts, I assume that what the Manichaeans said and did "makes sense," that there is a truth-conditional context in which they become comprehensible. Certainly, it made sense to them; but that is not good enough for our purposes. We need to find a way for it to make sense to us, situated where we are. Two ways in which this goal has been attempted so far have succeeded in producing Manichaeans that work for us, but these are not the Manichaeans of history. By proposing that Manichaean discourse is *metaphorical*, or by maintaining that it conveys a *misrecognition* of its social environment, we imply that their explicit claims are false. But Manichaean discourse in the form of the rationales reviewed in this study do have a truth-value, in fact they explain behavior, and they permit us to make sense of the historical Manichaeans.

Metaphor

As it is usually practiced, the interpretive process generates decisions about what is "appropriate" to a given discourse, and sets up a normative hermeneutic that treats as "metaphor"[96] any language that resists conventional discursive expectations. Modern Western scholars delineate discourses based largely on analogy with contemporary discursive boundaries that may have little or no correspondence with those of historically or culturally distinct populations, and which are not nearly as solid and clear even in our own culture as we like to believe.[97] After this ethnocentric determination, judgments of literal or metaphoric interpretation are made based upon it. Thus the statements of a medical text will be treated as literal, and the larger discourse on medicine is considered a literal treatment of the various objects and concepts involved.[98] Statements in a religious text, or which are part of a religious discourse, on the other hand, are thought to engage different objects and concepts than those found in the medical or philosophical discourses, and therefore are treated differently—that is, with a much greater propensity for metaphorization.

The logic of metaphorical or allegorical interpretation of utterances is dictated by the hermeneutics of charity: "When you encounter a proposition which, taken by itself or as it stands, is false, you try to find a way of reading it that will make it come out true."[99] By interpretation, we seek to be generous to the culturally other, removing his or her statements from the realm of an objective reality where we would regard them as incorrect or deficient to a domain of metaphor, symbolism, and poetry where statements are not about reality but affect. In this way, "the urge to see 'metaphors' is . . . ethnocentric insofar as it assimilates other peoples' 'facts' to our idea of 'meaningful fiction.'"[100]

> To regard other people's direct predications, including their myths, as metaphorical means that one does not believe in the facts of the manifest content . . . and yet would like to give the predications meaning, *and meaning only*, by making use of the manifest content. To think of metaphors means to rescue the belief in meaning, not the belief in things.[101]

Despite its claim to be cultural relativism, such an approach amounts to the very opposite; it glosses the differences between populations and presupposes shared categories of meaning and common discursive formations.[102] In the end, the hermeneutics of charity tends to become what Jonathan Z. Smith calls a "hermeneutic of recovery," an "exercise in cultural appropriation" that makes the other speak our own truths.[103]

Roger Keesing has warned against the opposite case, taking the conventional metaphor of others out of context and treating it literally when its own employers do not. He suggests as a safeguard against such misinterpretation a "relentless search for supporting evidence outside the realm of language,"[104] and the same method can and should be applied in either case. Manichaean disciplinary and ritual activities supply such supporting evidence. Scholars have only been able to metaphorize physical and physiological language in Manichaean sources by treating each utterance individually, or at most as a commonly employed trope, without acknowledging the set of relations that bind the individual utterances together into a universe of discourse, which in turn forms an integrated system with particular practices. The question of literality and metaphoricity involves the *relations* among the apparent statements and events themselves—that is, whether specific Manichaean utterances and claims have a direct or mediated relation to particular Manichaean practices.

Some researchers have promoted a theory of rituals as the enactment of metaphors. Keesing, for example, claims that "even if we were to find a ritual where, say, the living used fire or heated objects in order to induce the ancestors to do whatever it is they do, we could be seeing not the enactment of a folk theology of what ancestors do to effect changes in the world humans experience directly, but a dramatization of the metaphorized homology between source and target domains."[105] Whatever we *could* be seeing, if our concern is with the normative tradition, as it is in the present study, we need simply inquire of its authoritative sources how the ritual is interpreted by the tradition itself. In the Manichaean case, the tradition insists upon a literal interpretation of ritual acts. Our rejection of the normative interpretation would entail a coordinate rejection of the means by which the rite achieves its ends. A metaphorical ritual would produce only a metaphorical salvation. By negating the instrumental efficacy of the rite, we negate the promise of salvation attached directly to the rite.

In this way, academic interpretation of religions does not actually bracket questions of ultimate truth, as it often claims; it implicitly judges native views to be false.[106] It has been the program of the hermeneutical study of religion to "interpret" the utterances of subjects in order to find *behind* those utterances a meaning that makes sense by the standards of reason within academic circles and those found in the modern Western (but increasingly global) public that consumes academic discourse. There has been lively debate about *how* to interpret, the *tactics* of interpretation, but little reflection on the interpretive *strategy* itself. That strategy is a given, imbedded in the academic discourse, and to a degree necessitated by its role as mediator of the other to a wider audience being informed. I am not suggesting that we abandon such cultural translation; but I do think we need to examine very carefully whether or not we have been producing poor translations.

The seemingly well-intentioned program of the history of religions has been to presume in others a rationality like our own and to create a coherence for them on our own terms by applying the classification of metaphor to anything that does not fit our own sense of the real.[107] Unfortunately, this metaphorizing hermeneutic describes the other "within the language and rhetorical system shaped by the conqueror" and is "intended to project [the conqueror's] presence and ascendency."[108] In this way we not only violate the distinctive discursive formations of another culture, but also rupture that culture's entire epistemic universe. We thus appropriate the language of the other as a confirmation of our own paradigm and at the same time erase, marginalize, or misconstrue the other's paradigm within which the language was originally employed.

The hermeneutics of charity begins with very sound principles and important insights that I do not wish to slight. It is, for instance, the starting point for the simple (or not so simple) task of translation. One must assume that strings of utterances make sense and that we can somehow access that sense; this whole book is constructed on exactly such a premise. The fork in the road comes in determining the appropriate context in which to makes sense of the words before the reader. In the study of religions, the choice too often has been made of a rationalist interpretive code rather than a historicist one. The rationalist application of the hermeneutics of charity proceeds by "assigning truth conditions to alien sentences that make native speakers right when plausibly possible, according, of course, to our own view of what is right."[109] The hegemonic outcome of such an approach is that "[i]f we cannot find a way to interpret the utterances and other behaviour of a creature as revealing a set of beliefs largely consistent and true by our own standards, we have no reason to count that creature as rational, as having beliefs, or as saying anything at all."[110]

The rationalist application of the hermeneutics of charity makes the simple mistake of integrating a miscreant utterance into the wrong truth-conditional context. Both the intellectualist tradition in anthropology and the sociology of knowledge have performed journeyman work to point out and correct this mistake, sometimes with, sometimes without the benefit of concepts of human interaction formulated in the pragmatist tradition. Without these correctives, the hermeneutics of charity invariably produces confirmations of what is already held to be true, rather than radically different perspectives on reality. It "maximizes or optimizes agreement between the other and yourself," by following the principle that "you can understand only that with which you share a deep common accord."[111] By this standard, Manichaeism could only be understood by those who hear the screams of cut plants and have an inherent sense that God has need of their stomachs; or, failing such a connection, the Manichaeism that is understood is one in which such aspects are considered poetic ways of conveying more palatable truths.

For the metaphorical interpretive assumption to be true in a given case, the *action* of the other should reflect the presumed meaning (what the metaphor aims at) rather than the statement (the medium of the metaphor). When, however, the other acts as if the statement is understood literally, the

metaphorical interpretation is disproved, since, as Andras Sandor states unequivocally, "No metaphor occurs where none is recognized. . . . [T]here is no
such thing as an unconscious metaphor."[112] Because this dictate leaves a great
deal of religious data in a recalcitrant condition, ritual—the interpretive
spoiler—has been disparaged or marginalized, while mythology has been attended to largely in isolation from its performative context, as Jonathan Z.
Smith has noted.[113] What I would like to stress is that I am not suggesting that
we simply take a community's word for something; I am not arguing that we
surrender the ability to analyze and uncover unspoken aspects of religious
practice. But I am saying that when individuals within a community, and the
community in its collective persona, act in a way consistent with their own
claims, we have a historical causality in action.

We may very well "know" that the essence of life cannot be metabolized
and transmitted to heaven by ritual vocalizations, but in the Manichaean
world these processes do exist, because their discourses about reality define the
world in that way.[114] If we are to determine the character (locate the place and
role) of statements within a discourse, or analyze and determine the distinctive
relations among statements in a discourse, we must take the discourse on its
own terms, within its own *episteme*. Sandor has argued persuasively, "Predications should not be conceived as metaphoric whenever *it is acknowledged* that
they were not intended and not understood as metaphoric. . . . If certain people need no metaphoric transfer to make sense of their own predications, we
should not take refuge in such a transfer."[115] To deny the acknowledged intel-
ligibility of an utterance within its discourse "would only be a denial from the
perspective of another discourse."[116]

The Manichaeans would have been speaking metaphorically when they
said that "salvation is digestion" if they had taught that the point of salvation is
the separation of good from evil *as* digestion is the separation of nutriment
from excrement. This would have been the construction of an intelligible analogical model by a transference of statements from another discourse. But it is
quite another thing to have said, as the Manichaeans did, that salvation is the
product of digestion in the Elect, that digestion is actually the separation of
good from evil because both good and evil are material substances mixed together in our food, that pure digestion separates the good substance from the
evil substance and sets it free, that digestion produces not just nutriment for
the body but refines this still further into a conscious, divine exudation that

can be quantified.[117] This is no longer metaphor (or putting one thing in the terms of another); it is identification—it is enunciated as a direct description of reality.[118]

The contemporaneous critics of Manichaeism frequently note the absence of metaphoric or allegorical meaning in Manichaean statements. Simplicius reports:

> They mention some pillars, but they do not take them to mean "that which holds heaven and earth together," as they do not think it right to understand any of the things they say allegorically, but those (pillars) which are made of solid stone and carved, as one of their wise men informed me. . . . They fabricate certain marvels which are not worthy to be called myths. However, they do not use them as myths nor do they think that they have any other meaning but believe that all the things which they say are true (i.e., literal).[119]

The Manichaean *episteme* arranged its discourses in patterns as different from our own as they were from their own contemporaries, and its apprehension of the world came into conflict both with traditions we consider religious and with those we term scientific.[120] The Manichaeans knew full well what a metaphor was, and employed metaphors frequently in both poetry and prose. But their cosmology, anthropology, and soteriology also had concrete, literal statements that were not interpretively negotiable. "Since Mani was the Last Prophet, and had brought the final revelation to humankind, there was no place left for interpretation or exegesis of his message. Hence Manichaeans were asked to believe his apodictic sayings and mythical doctrines *au pied de la lettre*."[121] In fact it was a characteristic and notorious feature of Manichaean identity that the community was unable or unwilling to make their elaborate ideology palatable to outsiders by metaphorzing interpretation.

> The Manichaeans . . . when they abandon their material fancies, cease to be Manichaeans. . . . The divine mysteries which were taught figuratively in books from ancient times were kept for Manichaeus, who was to come last, to solve and demonstrate; and so after him no other teacher will come from God, *for he has said nothing in figures and parables, but . . . taught in plain, simple terms.* Therefore . . . the Manichaeans . . . have no interpretations to fall back on.[122]

These direct utterances grounded specific physical practices and, in fact, could only do so insofar as they were regarded as literal descriptions of reality.

Misrecognition

Theories of "misrecognition" or "mystification," ultimately deriving from Durkheim, continue to be a popular modern option for the interpretation of ritual.[123] It is axiomatic to all variations of this standpoint that those who perform rituals do not know the true nature of what they are doing, that is, that there is a reality involved in ritual behavior that only a modern Western scholar (or, at least, some cultural outsider) can perceive. Catherine Bell belongs to this tradition when she writes that ritualization

> is a way of acting that sees itself as *responding* to a place, event, force, problem, or tradition. It tends to see itself as the natural or appropriate thing to do in the circumstances. Ritualization does not see how it actively creates place, force, event, and tradition, how it redefines or generates the circumstances to which it is responding. It does not see how its own actions reorder and reinterpret the circumstances so as to afford the sense of a fit among the main spheres of experience—body, community, and cosmos. Ritualization sees its end, the rectification of a problematic. It does not see what it does in the process of realizing this end, its transformation of the problematic itself.[124]

"Misrecognition," then, implies that ritual agents are instinctively but unconsciously aware of the real problematic situations to which they are responding, but they are consciously aware of only the substitute, false or masking, problematics. Ritual resolutions of problematic situations work in ways their performers do not understand, but have hit upon by some Darwinian adaptation.[125] Native rationales are regarded as post hoc, arbitrary, and inessential. The universe that ritualists believe themselves to inhabit, and within which they act, is, according to those who embrace this interpretive strategy, fictitious and illusory.

The misrecognition theory can be challenged by observations that derive ultimately from the pragmatist analysis of G. H. Mead. The theory involves a positivist claim to perceive a true, unmediated reality (which, incidentally, cannot be perceived by other humans), and a consequent dismissal of the role of subjectivity in human behavior. In short, the misrecognition theory postulates a theory of human nature that makes the conscious brain superfluous to behavior. But against this theory I must reiterate that *fictitious and illusory universes, in the form of perceived environments, shape action*. If ritualists direct their attention to one situation while academics insist that another situation is the real one, we encounter a clash of perspectives in which one has objective priority for us, but the other—and only the other—has explanatory power in accounting for the behavior of the ritualist.[126] Noninstinctive, culturally transmitted behavior occurs in response to a perceived environment and requires attention and recognition to operate. It cannot be assimilated to the category of instinctive action or to the sphere of passive environmental effects.[127] Ritualists respond to the situation they construe, and one cannot argue that they in fact respond to a situation that is absent to them, one that has no means of eliciting their response. None of the postulators of misrecognition provide an adequate mechanism by which an individual both perceives and does not perceive a situation at the same time.[128] Hence, the miscrecognition theory of ritual commits a fundamental historical fallacy; namely, it fails to take into account that the totality of historical effects of ritual behavior have occurred *within* the field of so-called misrecognition, so that any other reality outside of that misrecognition is historically irrelevant.

Attempts to offer alternative interpretations of behavior by means of a postulated misrecognition also run afoul of the character of historical sources. The modern researcher cannot possibly claim, with any hope of assent, that the situation attested in historical sources is false, and another situation, unattested (because unperceived) by the historical actors concerned, is true. Some source must provide the evidentiary basis for historical reconstruction, or it becomes simply fiction. *If* such a theory was to work, it could only do so in ethnographic situations; historical situations are not amenable to such an approach. Historians have little chance to circumvent the biases of their sources, or to observe *anything* unobserved by those who produced those sources. Therefore, any proposition that what is testified to is a misrecognition of something else not attested rests entirely on *analogy* with contemporary ethnographic observations of populations and cultures. In other words, such a theory assumes an immutable human nature that not only universally misrecognizes, but misrecognizes the same particular object or situation in the same particular manner in every time and place. Such a claim must be demonstrated, not assumed; and the preponderance of evidence seems to be against it.

Finally, it can be said that theories of mystification and misrecognition only serve the purpose of trying to uncover immutable laws of human nature, and can never inform us of anything about particular communities at particular times. As a pragmatist, I have no confidence in the idea of static, immutable laws. But more important, as a historian I am interested not in the fact that humans act, but that they act in particular ways in certain circumstances at specific times; and it is the different ways that humans act that create culture and history. Humans constantly reorganize and repackage their biological and environmental givens into novel arrangements, and it is those arrangements, shaped by the perceived reality of a community, that form the material studied by the human sciences.

By no means do I wish to deny the operation of covert forces within communities, or the structuring of social life by biological, environmental, economic, and other factors that are not all mastered by a population at an explicit level. Instead, I want to safeguard humanly produced systems of practice from being dismissed as smoke and mirrors. Cultures arise and are maintained by a combination of intentional and unintentional factors, neither of which can be exalted as the only reality. John Hughes has made this point superbly:

> Thus, though the tribe may be engaged in a "rain dance" which for them is designed to produce rain, the anthropologist might claim that at the same time they are "reaffirming tribal norms." They may be "reaffirming tribal norms" without realising it, but they are not doing this instead of what they themselves say they are doing. They are doing both, one by way of the other.[129]

Beliefs shape human history not because they are objectively true, but because they are objectively assented to, not because they are assuredly the true motives of individuals, but because the true motives of individuals lead them to publicly invoke and act upon them. In the words of Alistair MacIntyre, "Actions which accord with the beliefs of an agent stand in need of no further explanations than do the beliefs themselves."[130]

Subjected Discourse

The ancient Babylonians watched gods cross their skies in such regular patterns and intervals that they were able to track and predict their movements.

Modern astronomers are able to use these ancient records to produce long-term models of movements of physical bodies without personalities or volition they call stars, planets, and comets. How is this possible? Certainly the Babylonians were simply wrong to think there were gods in their skies; how then can we make use of these erroneous texts to do hard science? This example may seem trite, but it cuts to the heart of the historical challenge of translation and understanding. G. H. Mead first introduced this very example in order to illustrate the concept of *subjective realities*.[131] His pragmatist explanation of how we incorporate the past into the present has had a second life in the guise of the Foucauldian category of *subjugated knowledges*.[132] In order to reconnect these two discussions to each other, I have coined the expression *subjected discourse* to refer to Mead and Foucault's common observation that past construals of things live on in a kind of marginal existence of humored obsolescence; they are understood primarily in their own idiosyncratic terms, but are recognized to be connected in an indirect way to the "true" objects of dominant discourse.

According to Mead's analysis of the phenomenal or human-perceived world, objective reality is that which possesses social consensus. When consensus changes, the old objective reality is displaced to the realm of the subjective.[133] We in the present retain memory of prior objective realities as subjective realities, and we account for them as prior, different, and implicitly inadequate perceptions corresponding to our own objective perceptions. These subjective realities help to account for the behavior of past people who held them to be objectively real. That is their historical explanatory power.

The mistake made by some engaged in the study of religions is the attempt to negate the characteristics of the realities that make them subjective in our world, and to recoup these realities as objective. This selective redefinition of past objective—now subjective—realities deprives them of their historical explanatory force by stripping them of the means by which they effected past actions. These means were precisely their compelling status as real perceptions of things, rather than poetic characterizations of things, or symbolic references to other things, or masks for other realities.

The whole history of science has presented the succession of one hypothesis after another; each hypothesis was rational, and, when it was embodied in experience, was a necessary order, but a succeeding hypothesis showed that it was but an alternative. To be sure, the evidence that the later hypothesis carried with it was something which was new from the standpoint of the old world. It is the natural assumption of the new situation that this new element was always there and, therefore, that the rational order of this hypothesis was at work with its necessity. But there can be no question that the new was new in the experience of the world into which it came. Metaphysically we assume that these experiences were subjective in so far as they excluded the presence of the element which appeared as novel, that these elements were actually present, and therefore the necessity which obtains with the new hypothesis was operative under the old hypothesis, though it was not recognized. . . . The possible alternative view is that each perspective is real in itself. It is physically real in the experiences that the individuals have who are there. These experiences are, then, hypothetically interpreted, and the judgment of reality is passed in so far as the hypotheses work.[134]

The objects of past cultures operated as indicators within systems of behaviors—directing attention, stimulating responses, evoking procedures. Their integration into such systems, indeed their emergence within such systems as the objects they were, gives them a significance only within the specific context in which they are construed to be real.[135] Whether or not they prove to be true according to our standards—in isolation, divorced from their operative context or displaced to another—is entirely trivial to the role they played in past human behavior.[136]

We understand nothing of religious behavior by grappling over whether gods, mystical experiences, possessions, visions, even healings, are true by some supposed objective or empirically verifiable standard. Religious behavior is determined in large part by perceptions and beliefs of what is true, and this religious behavior in turn impacts on other behaviors and spheres in society, economics, politics, art, and so on. We may reject the past perceived reality, but the effects of that perceived reality on objects we do take to be real is for us fact. Of course, even individual, idiosyncratic sets of perceptions impact on history, as is so readily apparent of late in the acts of lone sociopaths. The effect is correspondingly greater when a whole cosmos of self-understanding and action is successfully promoted into a system that reproduces itself in whole populations.

Suppose in analyzing the scriptural tradition of a religious community we discover that a key phrase has been mistranslated down through the centuries, and as a consequence a practice has been in force which the scripture, when correctly translated and understood, does not validate. We have made a discovery which now and in the future may alter the way religion is practiced, but has absolutely no bearing on what occurred in the past. If we look upon the newly discovered, "correct" reading as the true meaning of the passage, then we invalidate the historical practice of the religion based upon a mistranslation of it. If we somehow forget about this mistranslation in our excitement and zeal for our insight into truth, we will be unable to account for the strange and apparently groundless behavior of previous generations. Only by knowing what they knew, or knowing *as* they knew, can we make sense of their practice. We retain knowledge of the "better" reading, of course, but place their behavior in relation to the "worse" reading as its outcome in action. In this way, we succeed in taking subjected discourse into account in our later, broader construal of the world.[137]

Let's be honest about the place of these subjected discourses in our world. The consensus is against them, and so they are not objective realities. From our point of view, the lives of the Manichaeans, as of dozens of other religious communities in human history, were based upon erroneous understandings of how the cosmos worked, and what could be done about it. Our "real" world is quite different, and apparently has no room for Manichaeans. But consider the inspired creation of human ingenuity they built upon what we take to be error. Consider the labor of love, of compassion, of universal empathy they undertook, believing the world to be the sort of place where they could actually liberate the energies of life from pain, conflict, and death. If we could hang past cultures on the wall like paintings, Manichaeism would be a masterpiece. Subjected discourses make objective history, and if we are lucky the traces of that history are sufficient for us to get a taste of those alien worlds, and perhaps even find in them a perspective that challenges our own confident assumption that we live fully and completely in the really real. At the very least, they provide us with a view of how marvelously malleable the seemingly fixed facts of human reality have been.

And here's the twist. The ancient Greeks knew the world to be round; later medieval cosmography was assured that it was flat. Today, the medievally subjected discourse of Greek cosmography has become objective reality again. Who knows what similar surprises future history holds?

TABLE

OF TEXTUAL REFERENCES

Acts of Archelaus: See Hegemonius.

al-Biruni, *Athar-ul-Bakiya (Chronology of Ancient Nations):* For the English translation see Sachau 1879.

al-Biruni, *India:* Sachau 1888.

Alexander of Lycopolis: Horst and Mansfield 1974.

Augustine, *Confessiones:* Pine-Coffin 1961.

——, *Contra epistulam fundamenti:* Schaff 1983, 129–50.

——, *Contra Faustum:* Schaff 1983, 155–345.

——, *Contra Fortunatum:* Schaff 1983, 113–24.

——, *De duabus animabus:* Schaff 1983, 95–107.

——, *De haeresibus:* Müller 1956.

——, *De moribus manichaeorum:* Schaff 1983, 69–89.

——, *De natura boni:* Burleigh 1953, 326–48; Schaff 1983, 351–65.

——, *De utilitate credendum:* Burleigh 1953, 291–323

——, *De vera religionum:* Burleigh 1953, 225–83.

——, *Epistle 36 to Casulanus:* Parsons 1951.

——, *Epistle 236 to Deuterius:* Parsons 1956.

Ch 5554: Sundermann 1985.

Ch/U 6618: Le Coq 1922 (Nr. 29), 43; Zieme 1975 (Nr. 23), 54–55.

Ch/U 6814: Zieme 1975 (Nr. 12), 34–36.

Ch/U 6818: Zieme 1975 (Nr. 11), 33.

CMC: See Cologne Mani Codex.

Cologne Mani Codex: Koenen and Römer 1988.

Compendium: Chavannes and Pelliot 1913, 105–16; Haloun and Henning 1952.

Ephrem Syrus, *Against Mani*: Mitchell 1912, vol. 2; Reeves 1997 (selections).

——, *Hypatius*: Mitchell 1912, vol. 1; Reeves 1997 (selections).

Gy'n Wyfr's: See Sundermann 1997.

Hegemonius, *Acts of Archelaus*: Roberts and Donaldson 1987.

Homilies: Polotsky 1934.

Hymnscroll: Tsui Chi 1943.

Kephalaia: Böhlig 1966; Gardner 1995; Polotsky and Böhlig 1940.

Kephalaion: See *Kephalaia*.

M 1: Müller 1912a.

M 2.I: Andreas and Henning 1933, 301–6; Sundermann 1981, Text 1.

M 2.II: Andreas and Henning 1934, Text a.

M 7: Andreas and Henning 1934, Text g.

M 11: Waldschmidt and Lentz 1933, 556–57.

M 14: Waldschmidt and Lentz 1933, 547–48.

M 28.II: Andreas and Henning 1933, 312–18.

M 33: Andreas and Henning 1934, Text h.

M 35: Henning 1943, 71–72.

M 36: Andreas and Henning 1933, 323–26.

M 39: Andreas and Henning 1934, Text m.

M 42: Andreas and Henning 1934, Text i.

M 45: Sundermann 1973 (Text 26), 89–90.

M 47.II: Sundermann 1973 (Text 25), 86–89.

M 49.I: Sundermann 1981, Text 5.1.

M 74.I: Müller 1904, 75–77.

M 77: Andreas and Henning 1934, Text n.

M 83: Sundermann 1997.

M 95: Andreas and Henning 1933, 318–20.

M 101 + M 911: Henning 1943 (Text A), 56–65.

M 113: Henning 1936a (Text a), 41–42.

M 114: Henning 1936a (Text d), 46–47.

M 131: Henning 1936a (Text b), 42–45.

M 135: Henning 1945b.

M 139.II: Henning 1936a (Text f), 48–51.

M 174: Waldschmidt and Lentz 1933, 555–56.

M 177: Müller 1904, 88–90.

M 221: Sundermann 1973 (Text 36), 102–4.

M 259c: Morano 1982, 12; Sundermann 1997.

M 311: Müller 1904, 66–67.

M 388: Müller 1904, 28–29.

M 395 + M 5865: Henning 1936a (Text b), 43–44.

M 453c: Waldschmidt and Lentz 1933, 552.

M 454.I: Andreas and Henning 1934, Text q.

M 496a: Boyce 1960, 33.

M 529: Waldschmidt and Lentz 1933, 552.

M 546: Sundermann 1999.

M 549: Henning 1944, 142–43.

M 580: Sundermann 1973 (Text 37), 104–6.

M 680: Waldschmidt and Lentz 1926, 94–97.

M 722: Boyce 1952, 446–47.

M 729.I: Andreas and Henning 1933, 330–33.

M 731: Müller 1904, 32–33.

M 738: Waldschmidt and Lentz 1933, 561–62.

M 798a: Waldschmidt and Lentz 1933, 559–60.

M 801: Henning 1936a, 18–41.

M 1224: Gershevitch 1980a.

M 5779: Henning 1936a (Text c), 45–46 (as T II D 123).

M 5794.I: Andreas and Henning 1933, 295–97.

M 5794.II: Sundermann 1981.

M 5815: Andreas and Henning 1934, Text b.

M 6020: Henning 1965.

M 6062: Sundermann 1981.

M 6650: Waldschmidt and Lentz 1926, 115–16.

M 7420: Sundermann 1985a (Text b), 19–33.

M 7980–7984: Hutter 1992.

M 8251: Andreas and Henning 1933, 308–11.

MIK III 4974: BeDuhn 1999b, Nr. 36.

Monastery Scroll: Geng 1991.

an-Nadim, *Fihrist:* Dodge 1970.

Papyrus Rylands 469: Roberts 1938.

Pelliot Chinois 3049: Hamilton 1986 (Nr. 5), 37–53.

Pelliot Chinois 3072: Hamilton 1986 (Nr. 8), 63–66.

Pelliot Chinois 3407: Hamilton 1986 (Nr. 6), 55–56.

Pothi-Book: Clark 1982.

Psalm-Book: Allberry 1938a.

S 13 + S 9: Henning 1932, 214–28.

Šābuhragān: MacKenzie 1979, 1980.

Sermon on the Light Nous: Sundermann 1992.

Sermon on the Soul: Sundermann 1997.

So 10202: Morano 1982.

So 18220: Sundermann 1981, Text 3.2.

So 18221: Morano 1982.

T II D 119: Klimkeit and Schmidt-Glintzer 1984.

T II D 171: Le Coq 1911, 25–30.

T II D 173a: Le Coq 1911, 7–10.

T II D 173b,2: Le Coq 1922 (Nr. 6i), 11–12.

T II D 173c,1: Le Coq 1922 (Nr. 6ii), 12.

T II D 173d: Le Coq 1911, 15–17.

T II D 175,2.I: Le Coq 1922 (Nr. 13ii.I), 31.

T II D 178.I: Le Coq 1919, 12–13.

T II D 178.II: Le Coq 1922 (Nr. 12), 29–30.

Tebessa Codex: BeDuhn and Harrison 1997.

Theodore bar Konai, *Scholia*: Jackson 1932.

TM 148 + TM 165 + TM 177 + TM 183 + U 60: Le Coq 1922 (Nr. 20), 38.

TM 159: Le Coq 1922 (Nr. 17), 36.

TM 164 + TM 174: Le Coq 1922 (Nr. 27), 41–42.

TM 169: Le Coq 1922 (Nr. 21), 38–39.

TM 170: Le Coq 1922 (Nr. 22), 39.

TM 276: Bang and Gabain 1929, 411–22.

TM 298: Le Coq 1922 (Nr. 4), 9–10.

TM 351: Morano 1982, 10–34.

TM 393: Henning 1944.

TM 417: Le Coq 1922 (Nr. 15), 33–35.

TM 423: Klimkeit and Schmidt-Glintzer 1984.

TM 512: Le Coq 1922 (Nr. 11), 28–29.

TM 748 + TM 152 + TM 152a + TM 181a: Bang and Gabain 1928.

Ts'an-ching: Chavannes and Pelliot 1911.

U 52 (T II D 78j.I): Le Coq 1922 (Nr. 9x), 27.

U 196: Zieme 1975 (Nr. 13), 36–38.

U 197: Zieme 1975 (Nr. 13), 36–38.

U 198: Zieme 1975 (Nr. 13), 36–38

Xuāstuānīft: Asmussen 1965.

NOTES

PREFACE

1. Tardieu 1981 contains four chapters ("Mani," "The Books," "The Community," and "The Pantheon"), of which the chapter on the community covers the church hierarchy, the moral codes of the Elect and the Auditors, and the "liturgy" (solely on the Bema festival), but offers no account of salvation. More typical are works such as Widengren 1965, where the happy result of salvation is reported (the savior or Maiden of Light meets the soul of the dead with rewards and escorts it to the land of light) without any explanation of how it is achieved.

2. Decret 1974 offers an example of this approach, e.g., "By Revelation, the soul attains Illumination and, in this Light, it is restored again to the lost Kingdom" (92).

3. "The Historical Assessment of Speech Acts: Clarifications of Austin and Skinner for the Study of Religions," *Method and Theory in the Study of Religion* (forthcoming).

4. According to H.-C. Puech, "Manichaeism is the most perfect example which we are able to find of a religion of the gnostic type" (Puech 1972, 523). In opposing this claim, I must define what I take to be meant by the term "gnostic," which is notoriously fluid in its meaning from one scholar to the next. For the purposes of this book, I simply will use the definition offered by Puech himself, who states that "in all the gnoses . . . knowledge of the self and of God contains in itself the certitude of salvation" (Puech 1972, 554).

CHAPTER 1. OUT OF THE PAST

1. The best account is that of Ries 1988.

2. These include the anti-Manichaean corpus of Augustine of Hippo (late fourth and early fifth centuries), the *Panarion* of Epiphanius of Salamis (fourth century), the *Catecheses* of Cyril of Jerusalem (fourth century), the *Acta Archelai* of the otherwise unknown Hegemonius (early fourth century), and the anti-Manichaean treatises of Titus of Bostra and Serapion of Thmuis (both fourth century), as well as the work of the

Middle Platonist Alexander of Lycopolis against the Manichaeans (early fourth century).

3. E.g., Ephrem Syrus (fourth century), Theodore bar Konai (eighth century), and new manuscripts of Serapion of Thmuis and Titus of Bostra.

4. An-Nadim, *Fihrist ul-ulum* (tenth century) (Dodge 1970); al-Biruni, *Athar-ul-Bakiya* (Sachau 1879), and *India* (eleventh century) (Sachau 1888).

5. Chavannes and Pelliot 1913.

6. The discovery a decade earlier of our first western Manichaean document, the *Tebessa Codex* from Algeria, went almost unnoticed in the academic world, largely due to its extremely fragmentary condition. See BeDuhn and Harrison 1997.

7. Spiro 1982, 285.

8. *Kephalaion 154*; cf. M 5794.

9. Sundermann 1985a, Text b.

10. For an understanding of how institutional norms are cultivated and internalized in individual lives, the modern researcher can turn to the works of G. H. Mead, M. Foucault, and Peter Berger, among many others.

11. It is only against a background of conventions and norms that distinct, novel, or idiosyncratic speech and action can be identified. Without first outlining the context of speech or action—the assumptions and rules governing general behavior—we are in no position to identify development, innovation, or deviance. Hence the kind of study I am pursuing is foundational for any historical account that would focus on the historical development of Manichaeism.

12. This emphasis was first enunciated by G. H. Mead in *The Philosophy of the Present* (1932), and taken up by the historians G. J. Renier and Leon J. Goldstein, among others.

13. The category of "relic" or "trace" can include anything that is a product, existing in the present, of human action performed prior to the present, e.g., institutions, oral culture, social arrangements, literary texts, and monuments, as well as the material debris of everyday life.

14. I am speaking, of course, about the reconstruction of a particular historical moment, or of cultural or social arrangements as they operated at a particular time. The historian does have an advantage over his or her discrete sources in being able to see changes over time not visible to participants in those changes at any one particular time. The historian does not have access to any information not contained in the sources, but has the benefit of many sources reflecting different moments in time.

15. The one exception is Parthian, which is known almost exclusively through Manichaean materials. It is closely related to Middle Persian, however, and can be analyzed comparatively.

16. Skinner 1974, 115.

17. This highly abbreviated account of the historical application of the speech-act

theory of J. L. Austin and Q. Skinner is explained in detail in BeDuhn, "The Historical Assessment of Speech Acts: Clarifications of Austin and Skinner for the Study of Religions," *Method and Theory in the Study of Religion* (forthcoming).

18. Skinner demonstrates that one must distinguish between intention and motivation; illocution applies only to the former, not the latter (Skinner 1974, 113). "To ask and answer this question about the illocutionary force of the action is equivalent to asking about the . . . intentions in acting this way . . . this does not tell us the motives which prompted (and perhaps caused) the . . . behaviour" (114).

19. Campany 1992, 199. Subsequent page numbers appear in parentheses in the text.

20. Pike 1954 (1967).

21. Harris 1979, 32ff.

22. See Brian K. Smith 1987, 42–45.

23. See Smith 1968.

24. If, extrapolating from Campany's discussion of Xunzi, we say that "interpretation" of ritual "entails linking ritual events with the external 'meanings' to which they refer" (1992, 206), then interpretation properly so called involves identifying the traditionally proffered referents of ritual language, gesture, and objects. Since a ritual's referentiality is part of its canon, part of the script produced and sanctioned by the tradition, one could argue that no "meaning" outside of that canon constitutes a legitimate interpretation.

25. Smith 1982.

26. See the critique of subjectivist interpretation by Nagel 1963, 200–206.

27. Ibid., 203–4.

28. Sperber 1975, 44.

29. The construction of accounts of other cultures that are "reasonable" in this latter sense, in that they maintain the interrelationship of discourse and practice, and convey the distinct rationalities that discrete cultures possess, is characteristic of the so-called intellectualist tradition of social anthropology, which includes the work of E. E. Evans-Pritchard and R. Horton, and which derives in ways not always acknowledged from the earlier ruminations of Tylor and Levy-Bruhl.

30. Such "outsider" accounts are outside of the specifically Manichaean ethos, but share with that ethos the status of "insider" to the broader cultural and historical environment to which they belong. Their etic stance vis-à-vis the Manichaeans, therefore, is quite different from our own, and may have much more in common with the emic stance of the Manichaeans.

31. Durkheim promoted the idea that "social life should be explained, not by the notions of those who participate in it, but by more profound causes which are unperceived by consciousness" (*Revue Philosophique* 44 [1897]: 645–51). This approach, which constitutes one side of the fault line that runs through sociology and anthropol-

ogy, proceeds by disregarding the publicly asserted aims of individuals in society in order to focus upon the influences that they exert on each other as a result of social interaction regardless of intentions and declared plans of action.

32. "The view of beliefs and ideas as 'rationalisations' is one that is present in both
Marx and Durkheim. Both argued that in significant respects the members of society
do not know what they do and need to have the true causes of their actions revealed to
them by social science. Both agreed that the explanation of beliefs must be sought in
the nature of social reality; a reality which is, again for the members of society, mystified and concealed. . . . On this point, Weber's views directly opposed those of Marx
and Durkheim. For him people undoubtedly act on the basis of their beliefs and ideas,
and the ways in which they conduct themselves follow from the religious and political
conceptions to which they subscribe. Whether or not God exists does not matter, for
the fact is that people who believe that God does exist are likely to act in certain ways
because of their conviction that they are doing what God wants them to do. From the
point of view of the sociologist analyzing the way in which people's actions make up
and affect the organisation of society, the fact that people hold to and, to a greater or
lesser extent, act out the instructions of a religious doctrine will have a tangible impact
upon the patterns of their conduct and upon the organisation of the social arrangements in which they live. Thus, the sociologist who wishes to understand people's actions must take into account the beliefs and ideas to which those people are attached,
and seek to understand the way in which holding such beliefs and ideas leads them to
act" (Hughes, Martin, and Sharrock 1995, 90).

33. Natanson 1963, 281.

34. This point was developed in essence by Mead, and has been followed through
in different ways by Berger and Foucault.

35. It is "the daily work of the religion, which daily ascends from the whole election to the light vessels, and the gods commanding the vessels lead it up [and] send it
continually into Paradise" (Sundermann 1985a, Text b).

36. Augustine, *C. Faustum* 5.1.

37. See Lieu 1977; Lim 1989; Asmussen 1965.

38. The understanding of what is required to make a particular ethos "reasonable"
reflected here derives from the so-called intellectualist school of E. E. Evans-Pritchard
and the sociology of religion developed by Peter Berger.

CHAPTER 2. DISCIPLINARY REGIMENS

1. *CMC* 67.7–11.

2. Ephrem, *Hypatius* (Mitchell 1912), xliii.

3. Ephrem, *Hypatius* (Mitchell 1912), xciii–xciv.

4. An-Nadim, *Fihrist* (Dodge 1970), 795.

5. An-Nadim, *Fihrist* (Dodge 1970), 788–89.

6. *CMC* 35.2–7.

7. *Psalm-Book* 4.27.

8. *Psalm-Book* 24.18.

9. *Psalm-Book* 24.8–9, 25.27, 27.14, 30.19, 30.23–24, 31.14.

10. *Psalm-Book* 24.8–9.

11. *Psalm-Book* 38.5.

12. *Psalm-Book* 24.18–19; 25.27; 27.14; 30.19, 23–24; 31.14.

13. TM 159.R.3–4; TM 417.3–4; Ch/U 6618.19–21 (Zieme 1975).

14. TM 164/174.V.1ff.

15. For *tien-na-wu* (= *dinawar*), see Chavannes and Pelliot 1911, 554.

16. *Hymnscroll* 386.

17. *Hymnscroll* 342, 411–14.

18. E.g., Chavannes and Pelliot 1911, 582; *Hymnscroll* 136; and Chavannes and Pelliot 1913, 196 (Karabalgasun inscription).

19. The *Sung hui-yao* divides the Manichaean community into four groups: the *shih-che, t'ing-che, ku-p'o,* and *chai-chieh*; A. Forte has explained these epithets as male electi, male auditors, female electae, female auditors respectively (Forte 1973, 234–35; cf. Chavannes and Pelliot 1911, 585).

20. Augustine, *De haer.* 46.22–30.

21. See BeDuhn and Harrison 1997.

22. *Tebessa Codex*, col. 5.

23. *Tebessa Codex*, col. 8.

24. *Tebessa Codex*, col. 9.

25. *CMC* 92.14–93.2.

26. *Psalm-Book* 4.27–29.

27. *Homilies* 30.24–27.

28. *Homilies* 38.15–16.

29. *Homilies* 38.12–14.

30. An-Nadim, *Fihrist* (Dodge 1970), 788–89.

31. An-Nadim, *Fihrist* (Dodge 1970), 795–96.

32. *Psalm-Book* 25.27–29.

33. In M 801, a Middle Persian hymn speaks of "this flock *(rm)* and righteousness *('rd'yh),*" "all pure and holy brothers *(br'dr'n),*" "the virginal and holy sisters *(wx'ryyn),*" with their own assembly *(hnzmn)* and *mānīstān*," "all the Auditors *(nywš'g'n),* brothers and sisters *(br'dr'n 'wd wx'ryn),* from the east, west, north and south, who adhere to God-Light-Power-Wisdom." Later in the same hymn, the performer prays, "May (blessings) be arranged over the whole Holy Religion, especially over this place and (this) blessed assembly *(hnzmn),* over me and you, dearest brothers, holy virgin sisters, Auditors of good soul *(hw rw'n'n)."* The Parthian version of this hymn employs slightly different terminology: "the pure Righteous ones *('rd'w'n),* brothers (and) sisters *(br'dr'n*

wx'ryn), who in various places exist with their own flock *(crg)*, assembly *('njmn)* and *mānīstān*, protected and gathered by the right hand—i.e., the beloved elect-spirit—and also the devout Auditors *(ngwš'g'n)*, brothers and sisters, friends and children of health, who exist in every country, borderland and district, and who believe in God-Light-Power-Wisdom." Another hymn in the same book, the "Verses of the Joyful *(mhr 'yg s'dcn'n)*," line 449, contains the phrase *crg hnzmn u wcydg[yy]*, "flock, assembly, and election." Another hymn, the "Praise-hymn of the Throne *('pwrysn 'yg g'h)*," speaks of "the whole herd of light *(rm rwšn)* that you yourself have chosen through the spirit of truth." The Chinese *Hymnscroll* makes repeated use of the term "assembly" *(chung)* with reference to the Elect, in a variety of compounds including "assembly of the virtuous" *(shan-chung)*. Variants include *t'ou-chung* "assembly of disciples," and *seng-t'ou* "monk-disciples" (Chavannes and Pelliot 1913, 196).

34. Sundermann 1985, Text b, lines 71–78.

35. This Iranian term refers to the Manichaean alms-service and ritual meal complex.

36. *Pothi-Book* 226–31.

37. Ephrem Syrus, for example, tells us little about Manichaean disciplines in his *Hypatius*, apparently because he found them unremarkable. "For their works are like our works as their fast is like our fast, but their faith is not like our faith." Of course, Ephrem cannot allow this observation to stand alone, but draws appropriate polemical conclusions: "And, therefore, rather than being known by the fruit of their works they are distinguished by the fruit of their words. For their work is able to lead astray and (yet) appear as fine, for its bitterness is invisible; but their words cannot lead astray, for their blasphemies are evident" *(Hypatius* [Mitchell 1912], cxix).

38. An-Nadim speaks of "the sacred law which Mani brought and the ordinances which he ordained" *(Fihrist* [Dodge 1970], 789).

39. Al-Biruni identifies Mani's *Šābuhragān* as a source of regulations for Manichaean practice; he says that the book, which he valued for its reliable historical notations, "is used as a religious code" *(Athar-ul-Bakiya* [Sachau 1879], 121).

40. The Coptic *Kephalaia* are presented as the *ipsissima verba* of Mani, hence his authority sanctions the precepts contained in them. Likewise, the accounts contained in the Greek *Cologne Mani Codex* claim derivation from Mani himself, through his writings or the testimonies of his earliest disciples.

41. "Because of the arrival of the pure, divine Mani Buddha, the Elect *(dindar)* came into existence. And he delivered (to them) the pure religion *(nom)*. He delivered to them one command to abstain from harm (and) five precepts *(cxšapt)*" (TM 169.R.4–8).

42. Or: "and I will fix the methods of (attaining) wisdom and equanimity" (Robert Campany, personal communication).

43. *Compendium* (Haloun and Henning 1952), 192.

44. Augustine, *C. Faustum* 5.1.

45. *CMC* 79.21, 84.8–9, 91.20–21.

46. *Kephalaion 1*, 15.15–19.

47. Augustine, *C. Faustum* 30.4.

48. Cf. an-Nadim's report of the supernatural audition to Mani's father (*Fihrist* [Dodge 1970], 773–74).

49. An-Nadim, *Fihrist* (Dodge 1970), 788.

50. An-Nadim, *Fihrist* (Dodge 1970), 789.

51. Al-Biruni, *Athar-ul-Bakiya* (Sachau 1879), 190.

52. *Psalm-Book* 171.20–22.

53. TM 298; translation by Larry Clark (personal communication).

54. Or: "the fruit will testify (to it) in the three palaces" (Robert Campany, personal communication).

55. In addition to containing a few detailed treatments of these constructs, the surviving sources are replete with allusions to them, e.g., M 174: "through all injunctions and morals of righteousness, the five commandments of piety and the three seals."

56. The last phrase is restored: *'c [zn] dwr phryzym*, partly on analogy with the audition to Pateg reported in an-Nadim. Andreas and Henning originally reconstructed the line as *'c ["]dwr phryzym*, "we abstain from fire," which bears comparison with certain Indian ascetic practices.

57. M 2.I.V.i.8–14.

58. An-Nadim, *Fihrist* (Dodge 1970), 789; cf. the nearly identical combination of references in the Chinese *Hymnscroll* 414.

59. An-Nadim, *Fihrist* (Dodge 1970), 788.

60. Sims-Williams 1985, 576–77.

61. Augustine, *De mor. man.* 19.

62. Augustine, *De mor. man.* 27; he points to the Manichaeans' own scriptural authority for this regulation in Romans 14:21 (*De mor. man.* 31).

63. Augustine, *De mor. man.* 35 and 37, respectively.

64. Augustine, *De mor. man.* 39.

65. Cf. Augustine, *De haer.* 46.103–13, where he refers to these prohibitions explicitly.

66. Augustine, *De mor. man.* 47.

67. "You think that fruits and vegetables, when picked, stored, handled, cooked, and digested, are abandoned by the good" (Augustine, *De mor. man.* 47); "as you say, they are more and more deprived of goodness the longer they are kept after being separated from their mother earth" (*De mor. man.* 43).

68. Augustine, *De mor. man.* 51.

69. Augustine, *De mor. man.* 52.

70. Augustine, *De mor. man.* 55.

71. Augustine, *De mor. man.* 57.

72. "A certain compensation *(compensatio)* takes place, you say, when some part of what is taken from the fields is brought to the Elect and holy men to be purified" (Augustine, *De mor. man.* 60); "the injuries your Auditors inflict upon plants are expiated through the fruits which they bring to your church" (*De mor. man.* 61).

73. "But you say that in order that one be pardoned for the slaughter (of animals), the meat would have to be contributed as food, as is done in the case of fruits and vegetables, but that this is impossible since the Elect do not eat meat, and that, therefore, your Auditors must abstain from the killing of animals" (Augustine, *De mor. man.* 62).

74. Augustine, *De mor. man.* 65.

75. Augustine, *De mor. man.* 65. Augustine considers it axiomatic that "there is no marriage where action is taken to prevent motherhood."

76. *Psalm-Book* 115.28ff.

77. *Psalm-Book* 116.16–18.

78. *Psalm-Book* 116.13–15.

79. Cf. *Psalm-Book* 94.12.

80. *Kephalaion 80*, 192.6–15.

81. CMC 102.15–16.

82. CMC 5.3–8.

83. CMC 9.1ff.

84. M 174.I.R.5–10.

85. A fragmentary passage in M 101h, bearing the caption *nywš'g'n r'y*, "Concerning the Auditors," alludes to the "five commandments" *(pnz'ndrz)* and the "three seals" *(sh mw[hr])*, but the context is lacking.

86. TM 170.V.1ff.

87. *Pothi-Book*, 181–84. An isolated phrase from the fragmentary "Bilingual Hymn to Mani" (line 306) refers to "three pure commandments" *(üč arïg čxšapt)*.

88. Cf. *Xuāstuānīft* 15C.

89. *Hymnscroll* 392ff.

90. *Hymnscroll* 411ff.

91. Ries 1977, 1980, 1984, 1986a.

92. Ries 1977, 93.

93. Ibid., 93. Ries offers the brilliant insight that Mani's identification of his mission with the promise of the Paraclete from the Gospel of John, 16:8–10, stands as the cornerstone of the Manichaean regimen as *dikaiosynē* (Ries 1977, 95). This point holds true regardless of whether Mani identified himself, or his "Light Twin," as the Paraclete.

94. Ries 1986, 169. Ries claims that "this morality of three *signacula* presents specifically gnostic aspects: the liberation of light thanks to a vegetarian meal, a practice based upon the dogma of the luminous world soul imprisoned in matter" (Ries

1980, 121). The problem with such assertions is that we possess no such specific precepts, no such disciplinary models of "three seals," and certainly no such practice as the sacred meal in any material currently identified as Gnostic.

95. Ries 1977, 103.

96. Ries 1986a.

97. Yet Ries points out Augustine's addition of pure speech to the seal of the mouth, which is confirmed in *Kephalaion 85*, 211.3–19 (Ries 1977, 98).

98. Ries 1984, 1033.

99. Puech 1979, 276.

100. Ibid., 311.

101. Augustine, *De mor. man.* 18.65, 17.57, and 16.53, respectively.

102. Ries 1977, 102–3.

103. Puech cites several eastern sources as testimony to the Three Seals which are, in fact, only allusions to the pervasive "body, speech and mind" construct.

104. Sims-Williams 1985.

105. *Psalm-Book* 33.18–23. The purport of another Coptic passage cited by Sims-Williams is not altogether clear: "[Five are the] commandments which God gave to the five [ranks] which he appointed in his Church" (*Psalm-Book* 161.21–22). Its relevance in this context depends upon what the psalm means by the "five ranks," i.e., whether they include the Auditors or not. Of course, the correlation of commandments to ranks may be nothing more than a poetic device, and perhaps should not be held to such a rigid test.

106. M 801; M 174.I.R.7; M 101.162.

107. M 14.V.20–23; Sundermann 1981, Text 3.3, lines 485–90; Sims-Williams 1976, 48–51.

108. TM 169; *Pothi-Book,* 87–91.

109. An-Nadim, *Fihrist* (Dodge 1970), 788.

110. *Hymnscroll* 137.

111. Sims-Williams 1985, 573.

112. Sims-Williams's characterization is not particularly applicable to the Coptic form of the commandments, however, the first three of which are stated as prohibitions. The Arabic list, if Sims-Williams's identification is correct, is stated entirely as prohibitions.

113. An-Nadim, *Fihrist* (Dodge 1970), 788.

114. *Psalm-Book* 33.19–23.

115. TM 169.R.4–8.

116. *Hymnscroll* 137.

117. *Hymnscroll* 113, 246, and 258, respectively.

118. I have added numbers to the translation to direct the reader's attention to the specific phrases which correspond to the Five Commandments.

119. Cf. *kutlug čïgayim* in line 297, which is part of a confession passage.

120. *Pothi-Book*, 171–84.

121. Such an elaboration is alluded to as well in Sundermann 1981, Text 3.3, lines 485–90 ("five commandments [in] ten parts"), as indicated by Sims-Williams 1985, 574.

122. M 801.475–532. A Sogdian letter, charging violation of this precept by a female Elect of the Mihriyya faction, claims that she "took a hoe and dug up the earth, pound and cut medicinal herbs shamelessly with wood and metal . . . drew blood and washed the [wound] with water" (Henning 1936b, 16–17; cf. Sundermann 1984).

123. Mani (or Jesus) may be the subject of a passage with this theme, however it is to be interpreted: "He entrusted the commandments *(cxšapt)* and the seals *(tamga)* to his disciples, saying, 'Eat the flesh of the flawless, pure, *ymrax* (?) lamb, (but) do not break its bones'" (TM 170.V.1–6).

124. The Sogdian fragment M 113 preserves a complementary portion of this confession-rule: "[. . .] glory *(frn)* is wounded; daily going on its way, a portion is lost. For all this I speak: forgiveness!"

125. *dyncyhryft* translates literally as something like "religion-(con)formity," or "having the form *(cyhr)* of religion *(dyn)*."

126. M 113 complements this confession recital: "The third precept: religiously appropriate conduct, with its two sections—I cannot keep it correctly and fully! First: In great lewdness (I have not shrunk from) cutting down or planting trees (and) groves; I have not heeded the shoots of trees and the distress of the elements *(mrd'spnd'n)* on a spring morning; we (all, indeed) conspire with the belly to plant and sow a garden or a plot of land! Second: The masculine and feminine bodies [. . .]." A Sogdian letter charging the Manichaean leader Mīhr-pādār with violations of this precept states that he allowed a female doctor to tend to an infection, and that he seized the arm of a woman to break up a quarrel (Henning 1936b, 16–17; cf. Sundermann 1984).

127. A fragmentary Turkic text includes one of the specific rules connected to purity of the mouth: "This he said: 'You should not eat dried blood *(kurug kan)*'" (TM 169.V.6–7).

128. The surviving portions pertain to just those three of the Five Commandments which parallel the ideals of the Three Seals. One might be tempted to reconstruct the text differently than Henning, therefore, ascribing the three sections to the seals rather than the commandments, were it not for such complementary texts as M 113 and Sundermann 1981, Text 3.3.

129. For an allusion to the Five Commandments in a New Persian text, see Sundermann 1989, 358.

130. Ries 1984, 1034.

131. Sundermann 1985, Text b, lines 102–7.

132. Al-Biruni, *Athar-ul-Bakiya* (Sachau 1879), 190.

133. Vajda 1966, 121.

134. Pines 1966, 66.

135. Ephrem, *Hypatius* (Mitchell 1912), xxx (cf. Reeves 1997, 260).

136. Augustine, *C. Faustum* 5.1.

137. Augustine, *C. Faustum* 6.1.

138. Augustine, *C. Faustum* 6.4. This same restrictive "rest" from injuring the world could be, and often was, seen as a life of leisure. Diocletian condemns the *otia maxima* of the Manichaeans in his rescript against them (Ries 1986a, 177).

139. Augustine, *Epistle 236 to Deuterius* (Parsons 1956), 180.

140. Augustine, *De haer.* 46.114ff.

141. Augustine, *C. Faustum* 16.9.

142. Augustine, *De haer.* 46.103–13; cf. *C. Faustum* 16.31.

143. *Kephalaion 85*, 208.16–20.

144. *Kephalaion 85*, 209.1–211.3

145. *Kephalaion 38*, 97.24ff.

146. CMC 6.2–7.

147. CMC 12.1–6.

148. CMC 94.10–96.17.

149. Hegemonius, *Acts of Archelaus* 10, where water is said to "freeze" (*pēssei*) the soul. The Latin translator apparently could not fathom this statement, and decided on the more generic *vulnerat* by reading *plēssei* for *pēssei*. For the explanatory context of water potentially "freezing" the soul, see BeDuhn 1992.

150. Elsewhere he says that Manichaeans "abstain from eating ensouled things" (Horst and Mansfeld 1974, 94).

151. Ibid., 56–57.

152. LF 1465C (Lieu 1994, 251).

153. These are followed in turn by discussion of prayers and hymns, zeal, Monday precepts, and the daily ritual meal.

154. I am not sure how to interpret the absence of the forgiveness clause from this section, unless the last clause implies that no forgiveness is possible for these infractions. A section of M 801's "Praise Hymn of the Throne" invokes a related list, unfortunately incomplete, of incorporated attributes: "And from your glory, lord, and from the glory of all these, I beg, as a grace to all my limbs, that sense (*'y'dg'ryy*) may enter my heart (*dyl*), reason (*'y'sysn*) my intellect (*'wx*), thought (*'wsy*) my mind (*mnwhmyd*) and [. . .]."

155. Mani's own treatise on "The Closing of the Gates" (MP: *hrwbyšn 'y dr'n*, contained in the scripture *The Treasury of Life*) was apparently the authoritative treatment of this subject. The early Manichaean teacher Ammo employs it in his confrontation with the spirit Bagard in the legendary tale preserved in M 2. Although Mani's treatise is lost, Bagard's parabolic exposition of it to Ammo conveys its gist. "The gate of the

eyes which is deceived by vain sights is like a man who sees a mirage in the desert. A city, a tree, water and many other things that demon impostures, and kills him. Secondly, it is like a fort on a ridge to which enemies find no entrance. Then the enemies prepared a banquet (with) much song and tune. Those inside the fort desired to have a look. The enemies climbed up from behind and seized the fort. The gate of the ears is like that man who traveled on a secure road with much treasure. Then two thieves stood near (his) ear, (and) through pleasant discourse deceived (him); they lead (him) to a distant place and kill him, stealing his treasure. Secondly, it is like a beautiful maiden who is imprisoned in a fort. And a deceitful man [who] sang a sweet melody at the base of the wall, until that maiden died of sorrow. The gate of the scent-smelling nose is like an elephant when it desired the scent of flowers from a hill above a king's garden. In the night it fell from the hill and died" (M 2.I.V.i.34–ii.37). For another reference to "the closing of the five senses," see the New Persian text reconstructed from several fragments by Sundermann 1989.

156. Chavannes and Pelliot 1913; this translation from the Chinese by Robert F. Campany (personal communication).

157. Cf. *Tao Te Ching*, chap. 13: "The reason I have *great trouble (ta-huan)* is that I have a body. When I no longer have a body, what trouble have I?" (D. C. Lan, *Tao Te Ching* [London: Penguin, 1963], 69). I would like to thank Robert Campany for this reference.

158. Cf. *Lotus Sutra*, chap. 3 (H. Kern, *Saddharma-Pundartha, or the Lotus of the True Law* [New York: Dover, 1963], 72ff).

159. Chavannes and Pelliot 1913, 115; this translation from the Chinese by Robert F. Campany (personal communication).

160. The "five grades" = the totality of the community.

161. *Compendium* (Haloun and Henning 1952), 195–96.

162. *Hymnscroll* 246; translation by Robert F. Campany (personal communication). The instruction at the verse's end refers, as we shall see, to the purification of the five elements in the ritual meal.

163. *Hymnscroll* 258–59; translated by Robert F. Campany (personal communication).

164. Chavannes and Pelliot 1913, 269.

165. Quoted by Chih-p'an, *Fo-tsu tung-chi* (Lieu 1992, 290; Chavannes and Pelliot 1913, 330–39).

166. Chavannes and Pelliot 1913, 353–58.

167. Lieu 1992, 293.

168. Schaeder 1935, 79.

169. Sims-Williams 1985, 573.

170. M 1.266.

171. Sims-Williams 1985, 580–81.

172. *Xuāstuānīft*, 9A, 15C.

173. *Hymnscroll* 392. One should add to this a second allusion in stanza 414.

174. An-Nadim, *Fihrist* (Dodge 1970), 789.

175. "Since we have embraced the Ten Commandments, it has been necessary to embrace wholly three with the mouth, three with the mind, three with the hand, and one with the entire self."

176. The key passage reads: "Three with the Mind: one concerning the sophistry of false teachers, the second concerning the worship of idols, the third concerning lack of faith." Sims-Williams 1985, 580–81.

177. This reference to seven fast days per month does not conform with any other source, and may be a misstatement. Cf. al-Biruni, *Athar-ul-Bakiya* (Sachau 1879), 190: "fast during the seventh part of a lifetime."

178. Cf. al-Biruni, *Athar-ul-Bakiya* (Sachau 1879), 121: "Mani in his law has forbidden telling lies."

179. Cf. al-Biruni, *India* (Sachau 1888), 151.

180. An-Nadim, *Fihrist* (Dodge 1970), 789.

181. *Xuāstuānīft*, 6B.

182. No doubt it is the recalcitrance of the material, as much as its rhetorical form as a catalog of "sins," that prompts Sims-Williams, following Colpe and Asmussen, to relegate reference to this passage to a footnote (1985, 577 n. 39). Since all versions of the Ten Commandments are phrased as prohibitions of ten "sins," *Xuāstuānīft* 6A differs from them in no rhetorical respect, only in content. It is primarily the assumption that all the lists of Ten Commandments must agree in content that prevents the identification of this passage as one of them.

183. M 5794.II + M 6062.

184. The first in a hymn designated for "the penitential and prayer service for Auditors" (*Hymnscroll* 387ff.), the second in a "penitential prayer of the Auditor" (*Hymnscroll* 410ff.).

185. Al-Biruni, *Athar-ul-Bakiya* (Sachau 1879), 190.

186. Vajda 1966, 121.

187. *Kephalaion 91*, 228.6–7.

188. *Kephalaion 91*, 228.16–19.

189. *Kephalaion 91*, 228.22–229.20.

190. This meaning is suggested by Gardner 1995, 237.

191. That is, become electi / electae.

192. *Kephalaion 91*, 229.20–230.7.

193. *Kephalaion 91*, 230.20–30.

194. *Kephalaion 91*, 232.1–24.

195. *Kephalaion 91*, 232.31–233.1.

196. *Kephalaion 91*, 233.1–234.14. The Coptic *Homilies* also enjoin fasting (*nēstia:* 72.13, 19; 73.11) and other unspecified observances (*parateresis:* 72.8–9, 21).

197. Cf. *Kephalaion 91*, 231.5–11.

198. Ries maintains that the discipline of the Catechumens (*Kephalaion 80*, 192.27–193.22) constitutes a third "righteousness" alongside the two belonging to the Elect in this passage, but I cannot agree with his interpretation. Although the entire kephalaion is titled "The Commandments of Righteousness," only Elect are characterized as "righteous" (*dikaiosynē*)—indeed, this is their principal Iranian designation (*'rd'wyg*). The author of *Kephalaion 80* employs a different vocabulary when discussing Auditors: whereas Elect are made perfect in two "righteousnesses" (*dikaiosynē*), Auditors become perfect in two "characteristics" (*smat*). The two disciplines relate by analogy, not identity. This analogy includes the orientation, first noted by Ries (1977, 97), of the first set of practices to the self, the second (and third) toward the community.

199. *Kephalaion 80*, 192.29–193.11.

200. *Kephalaion 80*, 193.12–14.

201. *Kephalaion 80*, 193.15–16. We can understand this threefold division either as (1) fast/prayer/alms, (2) child, (3) building, or as (1) fast, (2) prayer, (3) alms (a. food, b. child, c. building).

202. *Kephalaion 80*, 193.20–21.

203. Augustine, *Epistle 236 to Deuterius* (Parsons 1956), 180.

204. Augustine, *C. Faustum* 20.23.

205. Augustine, *C. Faustum* 30.5.

206. Augustine, *C. Faustum* 16.31.

207. Augustine, *De mor. man.* 53. "They caution their same Auditors, furthermore, when they eat meat, not to kill the animals" (*De haer.* 46.130–32).

208. Augustine, *De mor. man.* 63.

209. Augustine, *De mor. man.* 61, 63.

210. Augustine, *De mor. man.* 60.

211. Augustine, *De mor. man.* 61.

212. Augustine, *De mor. man.* 62.

213. Augustine, *Epistle 236 to Deuterius* (Parsons 1956), 180.

214. Augustine, *Epistle 36 to Casulanus* (Parsons 1951), 161; in the Parsons translation, *auditoribus* is rendered ambiguously as "adherents."

215. Augustine, *C. Faustum* 15.7.

216. Augustine, *C. Faustum* 30.6. Cf. *De haer.* 46.135–41: "And if they make use of marriage, they should, however, avoid conception and birth to prevent the divine substance, which has entered into them through food, from being bound by chains of flesh in their offspring. For this is the way, indeed, they believe that souls come into all flesh, that is, through food and drink. Hence, without doubt, they condemn marriage

and forbid it as much as is in their power, since they forbid the propagation of offspring, the reason for marriage." It is worth noting that in all these passages Augustine offers as the grounds for his contrary position not biblical authority, but the norms of the Roman state and the civic institution of the marriage contract.

217. Augustine, *C. Faustum* 5.10.

218. Augustine, *De util. cred.* 3.

219. *Xuāstuānīft*, 3A–C.

220. "One: the two-legged humans; second: the four-legged creatures; third: the flying creatures; fourth: the water creatures; fifth: the terrestrial creatures that crawl on their bellies" (*Xuāstuānīft*, 5B).

221. *Xuāstuānīft*, 5C.

222. *Wusanti* is a loanword in Turkic from Sanskrit *uposatha*, a periodic observance of renunciate life by Buddhist laypeople.

223. *Xuāstuānīft*, 12A.

224. TM 148, TM 165, TM 177, TM 183 and U 60 (Tiα), R.1–12 of the reconstructed text; Le Coq 1922 (Nr. 20), 38.

225. *Hymnscroll* 392ff.

226. This is the Chinese form of the name of the Buddha Vairocana, and is employed here as an alternative name for the "Living Self."

227. The five elements that constitute the divine portion in the world, or the "Living Self," here match exactly the Syriac designation, the five *ziwane*.

228. *Hymnscroll* 411–14.

229. More specifically, M 177.R warns of the ill effects of consuming meat: "fourthly, the soul is sullied; fifthly, it increases lust; sixthly, that he becomes evil-mouthed; seventhly, that he (or: it) scandalizes many people; eighthly, the purification of the pious gifts is neglected; ninthly, the poor are left without alms." So even though vegetarianism was not required of Manichaean Auditors, it certainly had its advantages in the eyes of church authorities.

230. Henning 1945b, 469–70. Another Sogdian exhortation is equally wide-ranging: "You should hear the good salvation from the wise Elect who possesses the Right Law *(ršt' d'ty)* and Forgiveness *(prm'nty)*. . . . Never irritate the wise Elect. Furthermore, keep control . . . of treasure and wealth, honour your wife so that by your [. . .] they shall eat. . . . Keep also your horse well . . . do not be too greedy (?) so that you will not lead your soul *(rw'n)* to hell" (Henning 1945b, 480–82).

231. Puech 1979, 311.

232. In addition to outsider accounts that seem to confuse or conflate Elect and Auditor disciplines, some Manichaean texts also present problems of distinguishing references to one or the other class of adherent. Take for example the following psalm: "I have subdued desire. I have trodden upon the deceit of the [evil one]. I am a holy *enkratēs*. I have purified my God by my tongue. I have blessed his holy lights. I have

given rest to the power of God. I did not make my Lord be born in a womb defiled. I
scorned the treasures that perish. Give me thy treasures that perish not. I gathered in
all my members. I prayed, I sang, I gave alms. I served all thy holy ones. I clothed the
orphans. I closed not my door in the face of the holy. I fed the hungry, I gave drink to
the thirsty, I left father and mother and brother and sister. I became a stranger for thy
name's sake. I took up my cross, I followed thee. I left the things of the body for the
things of the spirit. I despised the glory of the world, because of thy glory that passes not
away" (*Psalm-Book* 175.10ff.). The reader here encounters characteristics of both
Manichaean classes. Perhaps the best solution is to posit a response structure (an-
tiphon) for this psalm, with Elect and Auditors singing in turn.

233. Foucault 1977a, 215–16.

234. "Power is not to be taken to be a phenomenon of one individual's consoli-
dated and homogeneous domination over others, or that of one group or class over others . . ., power . . . is not that which makes the difference between those who exclusively
possess and retain it, and those who do not have it and submit to it. Power must be analyzed as something which circulates, or rather as something which only functions in
the form of a chain" (Foucault 1980, 98). Foucault's key insight is that "individuals are
the vehicles of power, not its points of application"; and although he perhaps underes-
timates the ability of local institutions and even individuals to appropriate and consol-
idate power in coercive ways, he is right to draw attention to self-formation as an effect
of power, such that individuals "are always in the position of simultaneously undergo-
ing and exercising this power. They are not only its inert or consenting target; they are
always also the elements of its articulation" (Foucault 1980, 98).

235. "The exercise of discipline presupposes a mechanism that coerces by means
of observation; an apparatus in which the techniques that make it possible to see induce effects of power, and in which, conversely, the means of coercion make those on
whom they are applied clearly visible" (Foucault 1977a, 170–71).

236. Foucault 1977a, 170.

237. Foucault 1977a, 203.

238. Foucault 1980, 98.

Chapter 3. Disciplinary Rationales

1. Augustine, *C. Faustum* 15.5.

2. Augustine, *C. Faustum* 15.6.

3. Augustine, *C. epist. fund.* 25.

4. Asmussen 1965, 215.

5. *Kephalaion 112*, 268.19–27.

6. An-Nadim, *Fihrist* (Dodge 1970), 788.

7. Ephrem, *Hypatius* (Mitchell 1912), xciii–xciv.

8. Theodore bar Konai, *Scholia* (Jackson 1932), 252–53.

9. Theodore bar Konai, *Scholia* (Jackson 1932), 224–25. Similarly, an-Nadim states that the Primordial Man "took (the five elements) as armament": zephyr *(nasim)*, wind *(rih)*, light *(nur)*, water *(ma')*, and fire *(nar)* (*Fihrist* [Dodge 1970], 779).

10. An-Nadim, *Fihrist* (Dodge 1970), 779.

11. Ephrem, *Hypatius* (Mitchell 1912), xliv (cf. Reeves 1997, 236).

12. Ibid., lxxxv. This consumption of good by evil is depicted as a stratagem on the part of good. Ephrem quotes Mani to the effect that "the Primordial Man cast his five bright ones *(ziwane)* into the mouth of the sons of darkness, in order that, as a hunter, he might catch them with his [net]" (lxxix). Likewise, Theodore bar Konai says that "the Primordial Man with his five sons gave himself to the five sons of darkness as food, just as a man who has an enemy mixes a deadly poison in a kitchen and gives it to him" (*Scholia* [Jackson 1932], 226).

13. Ephrem, *Hypatius* (Mitchell 1912), xcvii (cf. Reeves 1997, 239–40).

14. Ephrem *Hypatius* (Mitchell 1912), xcix.

15. Ephrem, *Hypatius* (Mitchell 1912), lxxxiii.

16. Ephrem *Hypatius* (Mitchell 1912), xxx (cf. Reeves 1997, 260).

17. "The Apostles asked Jesus about the life of inanimate nature, whereupon he said, 'If that which is (originally) inanimate is separated from the living element with which it has been commingled, and appears alone by itself, it is again inanimate and is not capable of living, whilst the living element which has left it, retaining its vital energy unimpaired, never dies'" (Al-Biruni, *India* [Sachau 1888], 48).

18. An-Nadim, *Fihrist* (Dodge 1970), 787.

19. Ephrem, *Hypatius* (Mitchell 1912), lxxxiv.

20. Ephrem, *Hypatius* (Mitchell 1912), xciii.

21. Theodore bar Konai, *Scholia* (Jackson 1932), 226–28.

22. An-Nadim, *Fihrist* (Dodge 1970), 780–81.

23. In Theodore bar Konai, for example, the Living Spirit acts as demiurge (*Scholia* [Jackson 1932], 233ff.); but the same role is filled by the Primordial Man in an-Nadim (*Fihrist* [Dodge 1970], 781) and Ephrem Syrus (*Hypatius* [Mitchell 1912], xxxiii–xxxiv).

24. See, e.g., Ephrem, *Hypatius* (Mitchell 1912), xxxiv–xxxv. The sun and moon play a crucial role in transmitting the liberated light back to its proper home: "The moon is a vessel into whose midst the light is poured" (xli); "they greatly magnify and call it 'the ship of light which . . . bears away the burden of their refinings to the house of life'" (cxvi); and "they say, 'the moon receives the light which is refined, and during fifteen days draws it up and goes on emptying it out for another fifteen days'" (xxxvi). Moreover, "they say that the sun receives the light from the moon" (xxxviii); "and it is the sun that goes and comes every day on account of its purity to the house of life, as

they say" (xli). And elsewhere, "they say concerning the sun that it purifies from evil, because it goes and comes every day to the domain of the good one, which is a purification" (lxxxiv).

25. An-Nadim, *Fihrist* (Dodge 1970), 782.

26. *Kephalaion 61*.

27. Augustine, *C. Faustum* 2.3.

28. Augustine, *Epistle 236 to Deuterius* (Parsons 1956), 181. Cf. *De haer.* 46.42–51; *C. epist. fund.* 31.

29. Augustine, *Epistle 236 to Deuterius* (Parsons 1956), 181.

30. Augustine, *C. Faustum* 15.4.

31. Augustine, *De duab. anim.* 8. Cf. *C. Faustum* 22.2: "We also believe that the Holy Spirit, the third majesty, has his seat and his home in the whole circle of the atmosphere. By his influence and inpouring of the spirit, the earth conceives and brings forth the vulnerable Jesus who, as hanging from every tree, is the life and salvation of man."

32. Augustine, *De nat. boni* 44. Cf. *C. Faustum* 3.6: "you assert that in all men and beasts, in the seed of male and in the womb of female, in all conceptions on land or in water, an actual part of God and the divine nature is continually bound, and shut up, and contaminated, never to be wholly set free."

33. *Kephalaion 106*, 260.7–14.

34. *Kephalaion 60*, 151.28–32. Augustine reports of the Manichaeans, "You maintain that the fruit suffers when it is pulled from the tree, when it is cut and scraped, and cooked, and eaten. . . . One of your silly notions is that the tree weeps when the fruit is pulled" (*C. Faustum* 6.4).

35. "And regarding this beating and wounding of the Living Soul, Jesus is the one who reveals it. He also preaches about (the Living Soul) and its peace. He reveals about its cleansing and healing" (*Kephalaion 60*, 152.14–17).

36. *CMC* 7.2–5.

37. *CMC* 10.2–11.

38. *CMC* 12.1–6.

39. *CMC* 5.3–8.

40. Ries has surveyed these episodes, all part of Mani's speech before the Elchasaite sanhedrin: the revolt of water against the ablutions of Elchasai (*CMC* 94–95), the revolt of the earth against agriculture (96–97), the revolt of bread (97; cf. 91–92), the revolt of the vegetables against being taken to market (97–98), and the speaking palm tree (98) (Ries 1986a, 173).

41. *CMC* 97.3–10.

42. *Kephalaion 63*, 156.29–30.

43. Cf. *Psalm-Book* 121.32–33: "The trees and the fruits—in them is thy holy body, my lord Jesus."

44. *Kephalaion* 55, 135.17–21. The fact that the "Living Self" technically is not the offspring or emanation of this deity makes no difference to its identification as his "son" in this passage, since Manichaean discourse regularly interchanges deities and arranges them in new relationships with each other for immediate effect, rather than confining itself to a fixed pantheon.

45. Augustine, *C. Faustum* 2.4. A similar identification is found in Ephrem Syrus, *Hypatius* (Mitchell 1912), xc (cf. Reeves 1997, 239–40).

46. *Psalm-Book* 155.20–39.

47. *Kephalaion* 72, 177.6–178.23. In one Coptic psalm, the deity Call brings to the Primordial Man news of the triumph of light over darkness by means of the snare provided by the five elements consumed by evil: "Lo, we have laid waste the land of darkness: we are waiting for thee with the garland. We have bought the dens of the hungry ones, we took their land for five loaves" (*Psalm-Book* 201.23ff.).

48. *Kephalaion* 59.

49. *Kephalaion* 108.

50. Hegemonius, *Acts of Archelaus* 10; cf. *Kephalaion* 85.

51. Augustine, *C. Faustum* 20.11.

52. Augustine, *De mor. man.* 36.

53. Augustine, *C. Faustum* 6.8.

54. Augustine, *C. Faustum* 6.4.

55. *CMC* 23.7–11.

56. *Psalm-Book* 86.27–30.

57. *Psalm-Book* 86.31–32.

58. *Psalm-Book* 54.11ff.

59. Augustine, *De haer.* 46.114–32.

60. SC 164–75 (Lieu 1994, 246–48).

61. Hegemonius, *Acts of Archelaus* 10.

62. "A certain amount of the divine part escapes, so you maintain, when fruits and vegetables are picked, and it escapes when they are subjected to chopping, grinding or cooking, or even biting or chewing. It escapes, too, in every animal activity, whether the animal be carrying a load, exercising, working, or performing any other action. It escapes during our sleep while the process called digestion is being accomplished by the internal heat. Now, the divine nature, making its escape in all these ways, leaves behind only the worst filth, and it is out of this that flesh is formed through the act of sexual intercourse. However, the soul is produced from what is good, for although most of the good takes flight in the activities we have mentioned, not all of it does so. Accordingly, when the soul, too, has finally abandoned the flesh, what is left is nothing but utter filth, and, therefore, the souls of those who eat meat become defiled" (Augustine, *De mor. man.* 37).

63. M 33.I.V.i.1–ii.9.

64. Turkic Manichaean literature also includes recitations in which the adherent identifies him or herself with the light elements originally captured by evil in primordial time: "I was struck down in the battle which Ohrmizd (fought) in the former (time). Since then, (I was) rising, falling, dying, being born in the hands of the demon of lust. (Then) your god grabbed me (and lifted me) from the bowels of the earth" (*Pelliot Chinois* 3072.6–9). A less dramatic, "scientific" statement of this identification appears in a Sogdian fragment of the *Gy'n Wyfr's* (*Sermon on the Soul*), which states, "All souls *(rw'n)* and Fravashis *(prwrty)* are cut from these element-gods *(mrδ'sp'nt bgyšty)*; they are their seed" (Sundermann 1997, 87, line 112).

65. M 33.II.V.i.3–4.

66. M 33.II.V.ii.1–5.

67. M 2.II.R.i.22–23.

68. M 2.II.R.i.35–ii.9.

69. T II D 173a.

70. "Everyday, whenever we think evil thoughts, whenever we say sinful words that we should not say, whenever we do things that we should not do, by (these) evil deeds and sins we make our own souls suffer pain, and the light of the Five Gods which we eat daily goes to an evil land because our own soul acts according to its love for the demon of shameless greed and lust" (*Xuāstuānīft*, 15A–B).

71. *Hymnscroll* 245.

72. *Hymnscroll* 243.

73. *Hymnscroll* 256.

74. Ch/U 6814.V.2–5.

75. *Xuāstuānīft*, 3C. The *Xuāstuānīft's* emphasis on plants and animals and the seriousness with which it treats harm to them, finds dramatic expression and particularly compelling reinforcement in a vision of judgment of the dead: "It says: the deeds he has committed become visible. It says: the spirits of land and water will be distressed. It says: the spirits of grass and water will weep. It says: the spirits of shrubs and trees will howl. It says: the virtuous governor will appear as though in a mirror, holding the soul that has rejected the religion and weighing it in a scale. . . . His deeds which are transgressions will be examined. It says: the old female demon with disheveled hair will come and grab the souls that have rejected the religion, dragging them to the dark hell and pushing them in head downwards" (T II D 178.I.R.1–V.7).

76. Sundermann 1985b, 634.

77. Sundermann 1997, 75, line 12, emphasis added.

78. Sundermann 1991, 11.

79. *Xuāstuānīft*, 3B.

80. *Hymnscroll* 236–42.

81. *Hymnscroll* 250 and 253, respectively.

82. *Hymnscroll* 249, 252, and 250, respectively.

83. *Hymnscroll* 254.

84. *Hymnscroll* 244.

85. *Hymnscroll* 245–46.

86. *Hymnscroll* 258–59. In another part of the Chinese *Hymnscroll*, a hymn enunciates the Manichaean condemnation of meat-eating: "The living masses, who devour flesh, have bodies like graves / Or they are not unlike bottomless pits / Numerous kinds of animals are unjustly slaughtered / In order to supply the arms of the three venoms and six robbers / Deeply and clearly shut within are the Buddha-natures / Oppressed by afflictions and always made to suffer / Greed, lust, the fire of hunger and calamity / Torment them without a moment's pause" (104–5).

87. *Hymnscroll* 247.

88. *Hymnscroll* 255.

89. See chapter 6.

90. "They said: 'Where is the figure we caught sight of?' And Ashaklun, son of the king of darkness, said to the abortions: 'Give me your sons and your daughters and I shall make you a figure like the one you have seen.' They brought them and gave them to him. He ate the male ones and handed the female ones over to Nekbael, his companion. Nekbael and Ashaklun came together; Nekbael became pregnant and bore Ashaklun a son to whom she gave the name Adam. And she became pregnant and bore a daughter to whom she gave the name Hawwa" (Theodore bar Konai, *Scholia* [Jackson 1932], 248–49). An-Nadim's version is much more abbreviated: "Then one of those archons and the stars and urging, craving, passion, and guilt had sexual intercourse and from their intercourse there appeared the first man, who was Adam. What brought this to pass was (the intercourse of) the two archons, male and female. Then intercourse took place again, from which there appeared the beautiful woman who was Hawwa" (*Fihrist* [Dodge 1970], 783).

91. Theodore bar Konai, *Scholia* (Jackson 1932), 253–54; cf. an-Nadim, *Fihrist* (Dodge 1970), 783–84.

92. "This body with which we are clothed is of the same nature *(kyana)* as darkness, as they say, and this soul which is in us is of the same nature as the light" (Ephrem, *Hypatius* [Mitchell 1912], lxviii; cf. lxxxv). Elsewhere, Ephrem calls the body a "covering which is from the evil nature," while the soul is "from a pure root" (lxxi). Apart from the body, "all the souls are from one nature, and their nature is pure and beautiful" (cxi; cf. cviii).

93. Al-Biruni, *India* (Sachau 1888), 54–55.

94. Ephrem, *Hypatius* (Mitchell 1912), xc.

95. Vajda 1966, 17.

96. Ephrem, *Hypatius* (Mitchell 1912), cxviii.

97. Al-Biruni, *India* (Sachau 1888), 54–55.

98. Ephrem, *Hypatius* (Mitchell 1912), lxxi.

99. Ephrem, *Hypatius* (Mitchell 1912), ci.

100. Ephrem, *Hypatius* (Mitchell 1912), xxii (cf. Reeves 1997, 260).

101. Ephrem, *Hypatius* (Mitchell 1912), xliii (cf. Reeves 1997, 260–61).

102. Ephrem, *Against Mani* (Mitchell 1912), II.xcii.

103. Ephrem, *Hypatius* (Mitchell 1912), xxii. He asserts that "counsel and teaching are of no avail to counteract the poison in our bodies, nor are drugs and mixtures of any use for the evil which is in our souls" (xxviii).

104. Ephrem, *Against Mani* (Reeves 1997, 243–44; cf. Mitchell 1912, II.xcvi).

105. Al-Biruni, *India* (Sachau 1888), 39.

106. *Kephalaia 55* and 64.

107. *Kephalaia 57* and 64.

108. *Kephalaion 64*.

109. *Kephalaion 57*

110. Augustine, *De nat. boni* 46.

111. *Kephalaion 38*, 95.15–96.3.

112. *Kephalaia 38* and 70.

113. The body is divided, for example, into four "worlds," each inhabited by seven demons who are each assigned a particular spot on the body (*Kephalaion 70*, 172.30–173.20); this construct is followed by not one but two models assigning human anatomy to particular astrological signs (173.21–174.10, 174.17–175.2). In *Kephalaion 94*, Mani describes how the four divine elements within the physical body (the fifth divine element constitutes the "soul") "strip off" impure accretions as bodily effluvia: (1) fire → blood → wrath → rheum; (2) water → desire → bitterness → fever; (3) light → flesh → gloom → impudence; (4 is fragmentary) (239.16–26).

114. *Kephalaion 70*, 175.6–14.

115. *Kephalaion 70*, 175.16ff.

116. "If you consider the way in which the sons of men are begotten, you will find that the creator of man is not the Lord, but another being, who is also himself of an unbegotten nature, who has neither founder, nor creator, nor maker, but who, such as he is, has been produced by his own malice alone. In accordance with this, you men unite with your wives, which comes to you by the following occasion: When any one of you has satiated himself with meat or other food, then the impulse of concupiscence is incited, and in this way the enjoyment of engendering a son is increased; and this happens not from any virtue, nor from philosophy, nor from some other gift of intellect, but only from the satiety of food and lust and fornication. And how shall anyone tell me that our father Adam was made after the image of God, and in his likeness, and that he is like him who made him? How can it be said that all of us who have been begotten of him are like him? Yea, rather, on the contrary, have we not a great variety of

forms, and do we not bear the impress of different countenances?" (Hegemonius, *Acts of Archelaus* 16).

117. Augustine, *De haer.* 46.31–34.

118. Augustine, *De nat. boni* 45. Elsewhere, he gives the following account: "You say that flesh is composed of nothing but filth. For a certain amount of the divine part escapes . . . in every animal activity, whether the animal be carrying a load, exercising, working, or performing any other action. It escapes during our sleep while the process called digestion is being accomplished by the internal heat. Now, the divine nature, making its escape in all these ways, leaves behind only the worst filth, and it is out of this that flesh is formed through the act of sexual intercourse. However, the soul is produced from what is good, for although most of the good takes flight in the activities we have mentioned, not all of it does so" (*De mor. man.* 37; cf. *C. Faustum* 6.8).

119. Augustine complains that, "you seem to think that the worst charge you can make against flesh is that it is the dwelling place of dung" (*De mor. man.* 49).

120. Augustine, *C. Faustum* 20.15.

121. Augustine, *C. Faustum* 6.8; cf. *De duab. anim.* 1, 16.

122. Hegemonius, *Acts of Archelaus* 19.

123. Augustine, *De haer.* 46.184–91.

124. Augustine, *De duab. anim.* 18; cf. *C. Faustum* 19.24.

125. Augustine, *De nat. boni* 42.

126. Augustine, *De duab. anim.* 3.

127. In contrast to some forms of Gnosticism, Manichaeism does not teach that the soul is saved by its nature. See Hegemonius, *Acts of Archelaus* 28.

128. Augustine, *C. Faustum* 21.16.

129. Augustine, *C. Faustum* 6.5. Cf. *C. Faustum* 20.20: "You consider it a crime to kill animals, because you think that the souls of men pass into them."

130. "You do not give bread to the hungry, from fear of imprisoning in flesh the limb of your God" (Augustine, *C. Faustum* 15.7).

131. Augustine, *C. Faustum* 6.3.

132. Augustine, *De haer.* 46.135–41.

133. *Psalm-Book* 45.14–31. Cf. *Psalm-Book* 152.13–23: "Subdue the leader of the darkness who has seized me. The care of my poor body has made me drunk in its drunkenness. Its demolitions and constructions have taken my mind from me. Its plantings and its uprootings, they stir up trouble for me. Its fire, its lust, they trick me daily. Its begetting and destroying bind to me a recompense. Many are the labors that I suffered while I was in this dark house. Thou, therefore, my true light, enlighten me within. Set me up, for I have tumbled down, and help me with thee to the height. Be not far from me, O Physician that hast the medicines of life . . . do thou heal me of the grievous wound of lawlessness."

134. *Psalm-Book* 46.16–18.

135. *Psalm-Book* 47.10.

136. *CMC* 81.2–82.13.

137. *Kephalaion* 70.

138. See especially *Kephalaion* 38.

139. *Kephalaion* 70, 172.4–20.

140. *CMC* 83.20–85.3.

141. Koenen 1981, 741.

142. Buckley 1983 and 1986.

143. Buckley 1983, 333.

144. *CMC* 16.1–16.

145. *CMC* 22.1–15.

146. *CMC* 14.4–15.

147. See *Psalm-Book* 69.20–22, 107.24–25, and especially 149.22–25: "'What shall I do with this lion that roars at all times? What shall I do with this seven-headed serpent?' Take unto thyself fasting that thou mayest strangle this lion; lo, virginity, and kill this serpent."

148. *Psalm-Book* 172.3–4; cf. *Psalm-Book* 153.19–21, 167.54–55.

149. *Psalm-Book* 162.21–26.

150. *Kephalaion* 38, 96.13–27.

151. *Kephalaion* 38, 96.27–97.22.

152. In Latin Manichaeism, Christ seems to take over the role otherwise reserved for the Mind of Light. "The divine nature is dead and Christ resuscitates it. It is sick and he heals it. It is forgetful and he brings it to remembrance. It is foolish and he teaches it. It is disturbed and he makes it whole again. It is conquered and captive and he sets it free. It is in poverty and need, and he aids it. It has lost feeling and he quickens it. It is blinded and he illumines it. It is in pain and he restores it. It is iniquitous and by his precepts he corrects it. It is dishonored and he cleanses it. It is at war and he promises it peace. It is unbridled and he imposes the restraint of law. It is deformed and he reforms it. It is perverse and he puts it right. All these things, they tell us, are done by Christ not for something that was made by God and became distorted by sinning by its own free will, but for the very nature and substance of God, for something that is as God is" (Augustine, *De nat. boni* 41).

153. *Psalm-Book* 150.23–31.

154. *Kephalaion* 56, 141.14–142.26.

155. *Kephalaion* 56, 142.26–31.

156. *Kephalaion* 38, 100.1–6.

157. This is the conclusion to which Lentz, Puech, Ries, and Schaeder, among others, see the logic of the Manichaean worldview pointing.

158. *Kephalaion* 79.

159. *Kephalaion* 104.

160. *Kephalaion* 38, 97.24ff.

161. *Kephalaion* 38, 98.17–20.

162. *Kephalaion* 38, 99.2–8.

163. *Kephalaion* 38, 99.10–17.

164. *Psalm-Book* 224–25.

165. *Kephalaion* 100, 253.10–16.

166. *Psalm-Book* 54.3–4.

167. *Psalm-Book* 60.20–21.

168. *Psalm-Book* 51.8–10.

169. *Psalm-Book* 59.30–31; cf. 85.27–28: "your commandments I put upon me"; 93.14–15: "I made your commandments an armor for me."

170. Augustine, *C. Faustum* 5.10. Cf. *De haer.* 46.114ff.: "They believe that the souls of their Auditors are returned to the Elect, or by a happier short-cut to the food of their Elect so that, already purged, they would then not have to transmigrate *(revertantur)* into other bodies."

171. S 13 + S 9.R.i.1–ii.30.

172. Compare the similar telescoping in M 101b.V.1–10: " . . . bound [it in this corp]se, in bones, nerves, [flesh], veins and skin, and herself entered into it. Then it called upon the Righteous God, the sun and moon, the two flames given to hand (?), upon the elements *(mhr['spnd])*, trees and animals. Then the god [. . .] from time to time sent Šit[il, Zarathustra, B]uddha, Messi[ah as] apos[t]l[es]." For a more precise rendition of the Manichaean anthropogony, see the account from Mani's *Šābuhragān* preserved in M 7982–7984.

173. *Hymnscroll* 90–91.

174. *Ts'an-ching* (Chavannes and Pelliot 1911), 515.

175. *Ts'an-ching* (Chavannes and Pelliot 1911), 524–26.

176. *Ts'an-ching* (Chavannes and Pelliot 1911), 528–29.

177. *Ts'an-ching* (Chavannes and Pelliot 1911), 530–31.

178. *Hymnscroll* 19.

179. *Hymnscroll* 19–28

180. M 395 + M 5865.II.R.1–9; M 131.II.R.2–V.15 (Henning 1936, Text b).

181. *Hymnscroll* 49.

182. TM 298.R.9–V.7; this translation by Larry Clark (personal communication).

183. M 580.R.5–7.

184. Henning 1940, 64–65.

185. M 580.R.8–12.

186. M 580.V.1–8.

187. *Hymnscroll* 95.

188. *Hymnscroll* 117.

189. *Hymnscroll* 99.

190. M 722.R.2–9.

191. TM 276.1–7; this translation by Larry Clark (personal communication).

192. M 33.II.R.i.8–14.

193. M 7.I.V.i.12–15.

194. M 7.II.R.ii.15–20.

195. M 680.23.

196. The generic character of these prayers as scripts is indicated by the use of 'w'hman ("so-and-so") in place of a name at II.V.9.

197. M 39.

198. *Hymnscroll* 29–32.

199. *Wang-liang* is an archaic Chinese expression for a type of marauding spirit (Robert Campany, personal communication).

200. *Hymnscroll* 33.

201. *Hymnscroll* 36–38.

202. "The glory of the religion," that is, the Mind of Light.

203. TM 298.

204. M 7.I.R.ii.2–4.

205. M 7.II.R.i.1–ii.2.

206. "I am also the fertile soil of the Great Saint *(ta-sheng)* / On which have been grown the five poisonous trees by the devils / I only hope that the great hoe of religion, the sharp knife and sickle / Will hew down and cut, burn them out, and make me clean and pure / All the rest of the evil weeds and the thorny shrubs / Pray, destroy all of them with the fire of commandments / Let the fifteen sprouts thrive and bloom / Let the fifteen roots extend and luxuriate" (*Hymnscroll* 69–70).

207. *Pothi-Book*, 28–33.

208. *Hymnscroll* 9–11. Cf. *Hymnscroll* 55–59: "I wish only that you will stretch out your great compassionate hands / And caress my body of the three kinds of the pure religion / To remove and clear all bondages of the past kalpas / Cleansing away from my hair and body the dust and dirt of the past kalpas / Open my light-eyes of the religion nature *(fa-hsing)* . . . / Open my light-ears of the religion nature . . . / Open my light-mouth of the religion nature . . . / Open my light-hands of the religion nature . . . etc."

209. *Ts'an-ching* (Chavannes and Pelliot 1911), 535–36.

210. *Ts'an-ching* (Chavannes and Pelliot 1911), 537.

211. *Ts'an-ching* (Chavannes and Pelliot 1911), 541–42.

212. *Hymnscroll* 227–31.

213. T II D 171; this translation by Larry Clark (personal communication).

214. M 221.

215. M 311.V.10–13.

216. M 801.63.

217. *Hymnscroll* 234.

218. *Ts'an-ching* (Chavannes and Pelliot 1911), 554–55.

219. *Hymnscroll* 277–78.

220. *Hymnscroll* 284–87. Cf. 319: "In the world of light all the saints / Have an agile body, and suffer no fatigue and heaviness / Their wonderful bodies wander in many temples wherever they wish / Their intentions, when expressed and revealed, are unanimous"; 331–32: "All the saints are void of birth and death / And the killing devil of impermanence will not attack and hurt them / They do not commit adultery and have no dirty pregnancy / How can it be said they have mundane love? / That which damages the male and female bodies of men and women / Impermanence of birth and death, the fruits of lust and passion / From all these the world of extreme happiness is free / And the dwelling-places are clean and pure without distress and calamity."

221. Cf. *Hymnscroll* 312–14: "The wonderful shapes of those saints are precious and valuable / Naturally free from sickness and troubles, distresses and calamity / Mighty, always secure, never becoming feeble or old / Damaged by no maledictions, and always strong in body / Had not the Great Saint *(ta-sheng)* known their bodies and conditions / Who among mortals could calculate and describe them? / Their frames of diamond are beyond imagination and criticism / And their shapes and countenances, great or small, are only distinguished by the Saint / Complexions and forms of the saintly masses are very delicate and wonderful / Radiating great light limitless in extent."

222. *Hymnscroll* 314.

223. *Hymnscroll* 318.

224. *Hymnscroll* 320.

225. *Hymnscroll* 334.

226. *Hymnscroll* 336.

227. *Ts'an-ching* (Chavannes and Pelliot 1911), 551–53.

228. *Ts'an-ching* (Chavannes and Pelliot 1911), 568ff.

229. Julien Ries, for example, claims that "this morality of the three *signacula* presents specifically gnostic aspects" (Ries 1980, 121).

230. Ries 1986a, 175–76.

231. Koenen 1981.

232. Buckley 1983 and 1986.

233. Foucault 1977a, 155.

234. The key passage is often misconstrued as saying that washing food does no good since the body itself is impure, so that impurity is in the body, not in the food. But *CMC* 80ff. actually says that impurity is in both food and the body, that washing does neither any good because, by implication, both derive from the primordial mixture of light and darkness.

235. *Compendium* (Chavannes and Pelliot 1913), 114.

236. Ries 1986a, 174.

237. Foucault 1977a, 220.

238. Foucault 1980, 102.

239. Schaeder 1927, 81.

240. Ibid., 114.

241. Ibid., 81. Samuel Lieu also implies that making the strict discipline the responsibility only of the Elect somehow solves the practical difficulty of the ethic (1992, 27).

242. Hans-Joachim Klimkeit, for example, states that "two necessary prerequisites for the release of man's soul are redemptive knowledge about the soul's origin, and the observance of the ethical code that is derived from that knowledge. . . . Only one who can observe the commandments for the elect can hope for conditional salvation here and full salvation after death" (1993, 17).

243. Cf. Decret 1974, 112.

244. Durkheim 1915, 350. Subsequent page references appear in parentheses in the text.

245. Buckley 1986, 403–4, 409–10.

246. See Augustine, C. *Faustum* 20.3.

CHAPTER 4. ALIMENTARY RITES

1. M 11 speaks of the "good-souled Auditors" *(nywš'g'n [hwr]w'n'n)*, who are characterized as "the collectors *(hmb'r'g'n)* of the oppressed religion."

2. Al-Biruni, *Athar-ul-Bakiya* (Sachau 1879), 190.

3. Epistle of Sa'yus about the tithe (i.e., "the tenth"), Epistle of Sis about pledges, Epistle of Aba about alms, Epistle of Suhrab about the tithe, Epistle of Aqfid about the four tithes, Epistle of Yuhanna about the administration of charitable funds, Second Epistle of Maynaq about tithes and alms (An-Nadim, *Fihrist* [Dodge 1970], 799–801).

4. *CMC* 9.1ff.

5. *CMC* 35.1ff.

6. *CMC* 91.20–93.23.

7. *CMC* 123.4–13.

8. *CMC* 142.3–13. The reconstruction is hypothetical, but the general sense is clear. Based on the parallel account on prayer at 141.6–12, the "he" referred to is probably Pattikios.

9. A later reference to the meal appears in too fragmentary a context to yield further information, entailing only the isolated phrase *hē oiko[nomia tēs tr]ophēs* (*CMC* 150.6–7). This same expression appears in the Coptic Manichaica.

10. *CMC* 35.6–8.

11. *Psalm-Book* 221–22.

12. *Homilies* 28.10–12. This restoration follows a period of which the speaker says "I weep for my church. . . . I [weep] for my tables" (16.18–21).

13. *Homilies* 29.2–5.

14. *Kephalaion 79*, 191.31–192.3.

15. Augustine, *Epistle 36 to Casulanus* (Parsons 1951), 161; *Epistle 236 to Deuterius* (Parsons 1956), 180. See 1 Cor. 16:1–2.

16. *Psalm-Book* 222.19ff.

17. *Kephalaion 91*, 233.15–16.

18. *Kephalaion 80*, 192.29ff.

19. *Kephalaion 91*, 229.20ff. The obscure exchange between Mani and the representative of a "sect of the basket," reported in *Kephalaion 121*, provides the opportunity for one of Mani's elaborate analogies in support of the alms-service: "For as long as it hangs from the tree it shall not be called 'alms.' And you, too, as long as you are entangled in [the] universe you [shall not be] well called the son of the basket" (289.4–17). In the Coptic *Homilies*, the speaker prophecies the future golden age of the faith, when one will exclaim, "Behold, the alms-offering *(mntnae)* has been appointed, and those who [prepare] it *(net[chorch m]mas)*; behold, the fountain has been dug and the good tree planted in it." (*Homilies* 29.2–5). In that time, "[the] melody of psalms comes out in each city; the catechumens will be able to give alms greater than [. . .]" (27.30–32).

20. Augustine, *C. Faustum* 30.5.

21. Augustine, *De mor. man.* 57.

22. Augustine, *De haer.* 46.114–32.

23. Augustine, *De mor. man.* 60.

24. Augustine, *De mor. man.* 61. Greek polemical accounts touch upon more negative rationales for the alms-service. In the *Acts of Archelaus*, the character Turbo relates that "if one does not give a pious donation *(eusebeia)* to his Elect, he will be punished in *gehenna*, and will be translated *(metensomatoutai)* into the bodies of Catechumens, until he render many pious donations; and for this reason they offer to the Elect whatever is best in their food" (*Acts of Archelaus* 10). The Latin translator of the *Acts of Archelaus* inconsistently rendered the Greek technical term *eusebeia* in this passage. On the one hand, "if one does not give *eusebeia* to his elect" is rendered with *alimenta*; on the other hand, the clause "until he render many *eusebeia*" employs *misericordias*.

25. Augustine, *De haer.* 39. In *De mor. man.* 36, Augustine states more generically that "food prepared from fruits and vegetables is served to the holy men *(ad sanctos)*."

26. Augustine, *De mor. man.* 62.

27. Roberts 1938.

28. The author quotes from the "Apology" (lines 25–26; indeed, he coins the

characterization *hē pros ton arton auton apologia*, lines 27–28), and adds, "I have cited this in brief from the document of the madness of the Manichaeans that fell into my hands" (lines 29–30). This would be an odd, but not impossible, way to refer to the *Acts of Archelaus*, which did circulate in Egypt, though perhaps at a time subsequent to the letter's composition (late third / early fourth centuries). Cyril of Jerusalem, on the other hand, clearly employs the *Acts of Archelaus* as his source, but expands it, adding elements that further the impression of hypocrisy the "Apology" is used to convey.

29. Cyril's supplements to the prayer derive directly from the *Acts of Archelaus*, where immediately after the "Apology" Turbo adds, "For, as I remarked to you a little before, if anyone reaps, he will be reaped; and so, too, if anyone casts grain into the mill, he will be cast in himself in like manner, or if he kneads he will be kneaded, or if he bakes he will be baked" (*Acts of Archelaus* 10).

30. Augustine, *C. Fortunatum* 3.

31. Augustine, *Epistle 236 to Deuterius* (Parsons 1956), 180.

32. The ancient editor of *Kephalaion* 93 refers in the chapter title to the auditor who "makes a *prosphora* to the holy ones" (236.7–10), although in the body of the text the speaker "makes an alms-offering *(mntnae)*" (236.12–13). He thus employs a familiar term from Greco-Roman temple culture. The appropriation of the term *eusebeia* is comparable.

33. *Kephalaion* 87, 217.2–10.

34. *Kephalaion* 87, 217.11–13.

35. M 2.I.R.ii.12; M 28.II.V.ii.21; M 47.II.V.4; M 101.189, 192, 207; M 177.R.6, V.4; M 221.V.8, 11; M 8251.R.1.

36. Old Iranian: *urvan* + suff. *-akan*.

37. Henning 1939, 846–47. The "Great Inscription of Šapur" discussed in this article records the establishment of commemorative fires "for the soul" (*šm pwn* = *paδ ruvan*) of Šapur, his sons, etc.: "This I order that there shall be made day by day for our soul one lamb, etc." (cf. Henning 1954, 42–43).

38. Boyce 1968. She cites from the *Madigan*: 25.2–5; 34.3–6; 34.12–16; 35.7–9, 13–14, 16–17; cf. the *Pahlavi Rivayat Dadistan-i-denik*, chap. 24.

39. Bartholomae 1913, 369ff.

40. M 6020.5: *pd rw'n*; M 6020.12: *rw'n r'd*; M 74.I.V.9: *pd rw'n*; M 49.I.R.13: *rw'n r'y*; M 388.V.7: *cy d'dm pd rw'n*.

41. M 5815.180–83.

42. M 2.I.R.ii.8–12.

43. So 18220 (TM 389α).V.7ff.

44. Henning 1940, 63–67.

45. *Xuāstuānīft*, 11A.

46. This was first suggested by Asmussen 1965, 236, and is supported by the organizing structure of the *Xuāstuānīft* itself, which places this rule among daily obligations.

47. TM 276.69–77. Hans Schaeder called into question the reading *özüt aš-* ("soul meal"), and judged it to be a scribal error for *özüt iš-* ("soul-work"; Schaeder 1934, 19–24). But the parallel expression which Schaeder adduces appears as *özütlüg iš* (i.e., a true adjectival construct, "spiritual work," lines 86–87, 92–93), never as *özüt iš*; one would have to suppose, therefore, not one but two errors by the scribe of TM 276. That this is not the case can be confirmed not only by the appearance of *aš* elsewhere in the Turkic Manichaica (e.g., the *Monastery Scroll*), but also by the discovery of a corresponding expression *(trophē n.psychikos)* in Coptic sources.

48. With the limited amount of information available on Manichaeism at the time Bang and von Gabain first published this text, it is understandable that they construed the meal as a hitherto unknown sacrament for auditors: "Viel wichtiger aber als all diese Einsichten ist die Erkenntnis, der man sich nun wohl nicht mehr wird verschliessen dürfen, dass die Manichäer in der Tat auch für die einfachen 'Hörer' eine Art Abendmahl hatten . . . , denn der Ausdruck *üzüt aši* 'Seelen-Mahl,' zu dessen Genuss die neuen Bekenner Manis angefeuert werden (z.76), lässt unserer Meinung nach keine andere Auslegung mehr zu" (Bang and Gabain 1929, 412).

49. TM 276.85–94.

50. TM 148 + TM 165 + TM 177 + TM 183 + U 60 (T I α).R.10–12.

51. TM 512.V.8–10.

52. *Hymnscroll* 113.

53. E.g., *Hymnscroll* 253. A later stanza likewise utilizes the Chinese term for "donor" normally used to translate the Buddhist Sanskrit *dānapati* (*Hymnscroll* 354).

54. *Hymnscroll* 344.

55. T II D 175,2.I.V.2ff.

56. T II D 173b,2.R.2–6.

57. T II D 173b,2.V.1–7; this translation by Larry Clark (personal communication).

58. TM 148 + 165 + 177 + 183 + U 60 (T I α).

59. M 731.V.4ff.

60. TM 148 + 165 + 177 + 183 + U 60 (T I α).R.13–18.

61. *Xuāstuānīft*, 11B.

62. Cf. al-Biruni's reference to "one-tenth of their property" as the correct amount (*Athar-ul-Bakiya* [Sachau 1879], 190).

63. This fragment is from the same codex as a copy of the *Xuāstuānīft* and a hymn about the judgment of souls.

64. T II D 178.II.R.2–7. In another text we are told, "If one does not make a home

for the homeless, worthy *(arhat)* Elect, they say (that) they are placed in a pit of spikes.
. . . If one does not make food for the hungry, thirsty Elect [. . .]" (TM 512.R.9–12,
V.12–13).

65. Henning 1944, 142–43. Henning, while noting the similarity of this term to
the position of *'rw'n'g'n 'sp's'g* in the Manichaean hierarchy (whose duty was precisely
to oversee the alms-service), rejects for it an alms reference (143 n. 6).

66. Perhaps Auditors make a formal departure, such as that described at the time
when Mani bid farewell to his followers. The latter "pay homage" by kneeling *(nm'c
bwrd)*, to which Mani responds with a gesture of benediction *(pd drwd kyrd:* M
454.I.V.5–9; cf. Augustine, *Epistle 236 to Deuterius* [Parsons 1956], 180).

67. Lieu points out that this is a quote from the Confucian *Book of Rites: Li-chi
chu-shu* 2.22a (Lieu 1992, 289).

68. Lieu 1992, 288–89; Chavannes and Pelliot 1913, 343–45.

69. T II D 178.II.V.4–12.

70. *Hymnscroll* 168, 173. Both Tsui Chi and Schmidt-Glintzer gloss this rather
straightforward caption, the former with "A Gatha, being a list for the 'Collection of Offerings,'" the latter with "Gatha bei Empfang des Mahles." *Shou shih-tan chieh* translates simply as "Hymn *(chieh)* for collection *(shou)* of offerings *(shih-tan)*." Although
shih-tan is a conventional Chinese Buddhist term for "offerings" in general, its literal
meaning of "food and robe" may not be irrelevant in the Manichaean context.

71. M 546.V.1–6 (Sundermann 2000).

72. Sundermann 2000.

73. "We laud and praise Mani, the king of perfect wisdom / And the wonderful
precious body of light / We laud and praise all the law-protecting messengers of light /
And the broad and great compassionate fathers / May the teachers *(mu-she)* always
wander about without meeting obstacles / Wherever the bishops *(fu-tuo-tan)* come to
stay, may it be safe and calm / May the masters of the hall of law have increased joy and
happiness / May the Elect observing the commandments enhance the blessed strength
/ Inspire the clean and pure virgin girls to be industrious / And make all the Auditors to
be much-comprehending / May the holy assembly shelter and protect the halls of law
/ So that we be always at ease and free from cares and anxieties" *(Hymnscroll* 348–50).
This hymn appears to be related to the unpublished Iranian cantillated meal-hymn
preserved in M 360 and M 368, which reads: "Praise to the god Mar Mani. Obeisance
to the glory of the angels who protect the religion. May every Righteous One live se-
curely. May each Auditor be safe. May the angels receive the 'soul-work.'"

74. *Hymnscroll* 351.

75. *Hymnscroll* 352.

76. *Hymnscroll* 353.

77. *Hymnscroll* 354–55.

78. Gulácsi 1999, entry nrs. 36, 37, and 38. MIK III 4974 was first reproduced in

Le Coq 1923, as Tafel 7a (in Le Coq's edition, the old designation IB stands in the place of the modern MIK).

79. The illusion of a cross shape overlaying the disc is due to a blank area left when gold leafing used on the disc fell away from the page, as demonstrated by Gulácsi 2000.

80. Of course, the divine hand could be *lowering* an object to the Electus, or directly upon the Auditors, or holding it in front of the gaze of the Elect. The direction and exact nature of the action involved effects in only minor ways the relations entailed between the figures.

81. Gulácsi 2000.

82. Ebert 1994, 17.

83. In the latter case, those figures not in the familiar Elect uniform would be the deacons, servants, or assistants assigned to serve the Elect in the meal, rather than alms donors.

84. Other community acts depicted in the surviving fragments include the ritual meal (twice), instruction (twice), conversion (once), scribal work (once). If M 6290 shows a moment in the ritual meal rather than the alms service, then the meal would be depicted most often.

85. *Kephalaion 80*, 192.29–30; *Kephalaion 91*, 232.32–233.1; CMC 140ff.

86. The *Monastery Scroll* differentiates between *aš* "food" and *xuan* "meal" (from Iranian *xw'n*); the former term appears in the compounds *aš suvsuš* "food and drink" (31, 52) and *aš boguz* "food provisions" (45, 47) as well as independently, whereas *xuan* (51, 61) refers specifically to the ritual meal of the Elect. The food and drink for the Elect is to be equitable (28ff.), not unequal between the two *ančman* (43ff.); the preacher and the works-supervisor are jointly responsible for food distribution (43ff.), and the latter officer provides certain lay visitors with food from the *mānīstān's* holdings to be formally presented to the Elect at the ritual meal (28ff.).

87. M 580.R.8–12.

88. *Monastery Scroll* 26ff.

89. Augustine, *C. Faustum* 20.3.

90. Augustine, *C. Faustum* 20.3.

91. Ephrem, *Hypatius* (Mitchell 1912), xliii.

92. Ephrem, *Against Mani* (Mitchell 1912), II.xcvii.

93. Ephrem, *Hypatius* (Mitchell 1912), xxx.

94. Ephrem, *Hypatius* (Mitchell 1912), xxxi.

95. Ephrem, *Hypatius* (Mitchell 1912), xlii.

96. Ephrem, *Hypatius* (Mitchell 1912), xliii (cf. Reeves 1997, 260–61).

97. Ephrem, *Hypatius* (Mitchell 1912), xliv.

98. Ephrem, *Hypatius* (Mitchell 1912), xlii.

99. Ephrem, *Hypatius* (Mitchell 1912), xliv (cf. Reeves 1997, 236).

100. Al-Biruni, *Athar-ul-Bakiya* (Sachau 1879), 190.

101. Vajda 1966, 121.

102. De Blois 1999.

103. The fact that the Auditors do not have a prayer session corresponding to the second one of the Elect, and indeed complete their daily prayer obligations with the evening prayer, matches the evidence of other sources that the Auditors depart before the Elect partake of the meal.

104. This practice is known as "eating with *bāj*," and is considered an act of high piety typical for priests, but occasionally observed by laypeople as well. See Boyce 1989, 46.

105. *CMC* 87.18–88.7.

106. *CMC* 89.11–90.2.

107. *CMC* 91.20–93.23.

108. Later in the debate, Mani cites further hagiographical foundations from the Elchasaites' own lore, involving bread and vegetables that speak to their handlers (*CMC* 97.11–98.8). In one episode, a "baptist" named Sabbaios was carrying vegetables to a secular official when the produce objected: "Are you not righteous *(dikaios)*? Are you not pure *(katharos)*? Why do you carry us away to the fornicators?"

109. Augustine, *C. Fortunatum* 3.

110. Puech argues this interpretation persuasively (Puech 1972 and 1979).

111. *Homilies* 57.18–19.

112. *Kephalaion 115*, 279.16–18.

113. *Kephalaion 115*, 280.4–11.

114. Augustine, *C. Faustum* 6.4.

115. Augustine, *Epistle 236 to Deuterius* (Parsons 1956).

116. Augustine, *De mor. man.* 36.

117. *Kephalaion 85*, 213.7–12. Nils Arne Pedersen has argued that the topics referred to by Mani's interlocutor in this episode (particularly 211.5 and 211.24–26) constitute the content of recitations spoken over the alms (Pedersen 1996, 280). The situation under discussion, however, would seem to place those topics within the context of a sermon or private exhortation.

118. Augustine, *De mor. man.* 39.

119. Augustine, *C. Faustum* 6.4.

120. Augustine, *C. Faustum* 6.4.

121. Augustine, *De mor. man.* 52.

122. Augustine, *De mor. man.* 52.

123. Hegemonius, *Acts of Archelaus* 11.

124. *Psalm-Book* 162.21–163.32. Allberry makes what is for him an uncharacteristic error in translation when he renders *mntnae* here as "compassion," although throughout the rest of the *Psalm-Book* he correctly translates the term as "alms."

125. Chavannes and Pelliot 1911, 573–82.

126. *Compendium* (Chavannes and Pelliot 1913), 111–12.

127. Lieu 1992, 293.

128. Ibid., 298.

129. Chavannes and Pelliot, 1913, 269. Hung Mai, however, indicates a different time for the meal, saying, "Those who abide by their ascetic rules eat only one meal which they take in mid-day" (Lieu 1992, 290; Chavannes and Pelliot 1913, 330–39).

130. Geng 1991.

131. *Monastery Scroll* 25–28, 78–85.

132. The etymology of this phrase (undoubtedly made up of two loan words into Turkic) remains unclear, although Peter Zieme, in a paper delivered to the Manichaean Studies Group of the Society of Biblical Literature in 1998, has offered a possible derivation and route of transmission for it. My first inclination is to regard it as a designation for the dining hall. But Zieme treats it as a title for a specific rank within the Manichaean hierarchy.

133. *Monastery Scroll* 43–53; this translation by Larry Clark (personal communication).

134. *Monastery Scroll* 58–61; this translation by Larry Clark (personal communication).

135. On this subject, see BeDuhn 1999a.

136. This is Larry Clark's decipherment of *ekirär köpčük taš suv kelürüp buz suvï kilip* (personal communication).

137. It is possible that the latter two incipits are one long incipit, since no mark of punctuation separates them, in which case the third hymn is lost (or perhaps reciting the first hymn twice counts as two of the three hymn performances).

138. M 11.R.3: *'yn xw'n 'yg 'wzyxt'n* "this table of the pardoned ones" (with list of church ranks); M 801: *xw'n yzd'n* "divine table"; M 729.I.R.i.3: *xw'n ywjdhr* "holy table" (incorrectly translated in Andreas and Henning 1933, 330.18 and n.2); M 114.12: *xw'n . . . pš'x'rycyk 'frywn* "sit at the table . . . recite the after-meal benediction"; MIK III 4974. R.i.21: *xw'n 'y 'ry'm'n rwšn* "the table of Āryāmān-rōshan."

139. In the following translation, the Sogdian instructions are in italics.

140. M 5779 (T II D 123). Allberry suggested that the recto-verso sequence determined by Henning and followed above should be reversed (Allberry 1938b, 9 n. 31). Henning himself admitted the difficulty of establishing the original sequence (Henning 1936a, 45).

141. It is "the strength of the elements, this Living Self, the grandson of Zūrvān (i.e., the Father of Greatness) and son of Khōrmāzdā (i.e., the Primordial Man), the glory and food of the whole world, the [life] and soul of all living beings, that which for many myriads of years up to now has been scattered and dispersed everywhere on the earth and in the skies."

142. The meal is here specified as "this table of the pardoned ones *('wzyxt'n)*, mourners, grievers and sad ones." Appropriately to such a tone, the Manichaean community is called "the oppressed religion" *(dyn 'wyšt'ptg)*. After listing and characterizing each of the hierarchical and functional positions of the church, the text reaches the "good-souled Auditors" *(nywš'g'n [hwr]w'n'n)*, who are characterized as "the collectors *(hmb'r'g'n)* of the oppressed religion." M 36, also Middle Persian, belongs to the same genre as the preceding text. The speaker blesses the community rank by rank, making references to Elect-assemblies *(wcydgyycrg'n)* and *mānīstāns*, "dwelling-places of the gods, structures and abodes where Vahman-rōšn undertakes the desire for godliness *(q'm 'y yzdygyrdyy)"* (V.15–16). The "pure Elect" are called "radiant lambs, white-feathered doves, grievers mourning and sad over the highest self *(gryw bwrzyst)*, which is the son Āryāmān Yishō" (V.5–7).

143. M 729.I.R.i.2–6.

144. One hymn contained in the Chinese *Hymnscroll*, for example, uses the famous Manichaean slogan "purify all roots" *(ching chu-ken:* 259).

145. This sampling of allusions is taken from the incipits in M 1.392, 425, 426, 430, 440, and 444.

146. M 1.418, 427, 428.

147. M 1.398–403.

148. M 6650.R.18–V.2.

149. M 6650.V.3–6.

150. M 7.I.R.i.1ff.

151. M 7.I.R.ii.15–30.

152. M 7.I.V.i.15–18.

153. T II D 173c,1.R.1–V.9, here read and translated anew by Peter Zieme, who kindly drew my attention to it (personal communication).

154. Gulácsi 1999, entry nr. 32; Le Coq 1923, 54.

155. Ibid.

156. For the Zoroastrian antecedent of this feature, see BeDuhn 1999a.

157. Le Coq 1923, 54.

158. Jackson identified the contents of the bowl as flowers, based on the analogy with Zoroastrian offerings (Jackson 1929); cf. Le Coq: "eine goldene Schale mit weiss und gelblichen Blumen z. T. noch erkennbar ist" (Le Coq 1923, 54).

159. "Vor dem Tisch scheint noch ein Holzschemel oder dergl. gestanden zu haben" (Le Coq 1923, 54).

160. Ebert 1994, 18–19, with Figure 11; cf. Gulácsi 1999, entry nr. 33.

161. Pedersen 1996, 276–301.

162. The supposed suspension of the meal for weekly or special fasts is often stated in the scholarship as established fact, but it is debatable whether the Elect ever went a

day without performing their principal sacred duty. There may have been some regional variation in this matter.

163. I can find no basis in any source for Decret's assertion that there were two
meals per day (Decret 1974, 110–11).

164. Since Manichaean literature typically identifies its hymns, chants, prayers
and other recitations by their incipits, that is, the first word or words of the text, the correlation between the Zoroastrian *Yasna* and the Manichaean *nwyδm'* is that much
stronger.

165. *Monastery Scroll* 51.

166. On this subject, see BeDuhn 1999a.

167. *Homilies* 57.18–19.

168. *CMC* 91.20ff.

169. Greek and Coptic sources mention *boēthoi*, the *Monastery Scroll* speaks of
lay-deacons *(espasi)*, and the Chinese *Compendium* (Chavannes and Pelliot 1913),
112–13, states that "They employ only Auditors and do not keep either male or female
servants."

170. E.g., the Sogdian texts M 801 and M 139.II, the Coptic *Psalm-Book* 172, and
the Turkic fragment T II D 173c,1.

171. Hegemonius, *Acts of Archelaus* 11.

172. "This refining . . . goes out of the mouth" (Ephrem, *Hypatius* [Mitchell
1912], xliv); "they say that it is refined by prayer" (*Hypatius* [Mitchell 1912], xlii). "The
second (birth of food) is that which comes out of the person in voice and word"
(*Kephalaion* 104, 258.13–14). "A breadth exists for it, and it is healed in the Elect, in
the psalms, in prayers, in praises" (*Kephalaion* 93, 238.2–4). The "living soul" which
ascends from the meal becomes a spokesperson on behalf of the one in whose name
the food was offered (*Kephalaion* 115, 279.11–25). Cf. Augustine's references to orations and psalms (*De mor. man.* 36), and "exhalations" (*anhelaretur: C. Faustum* 5.10),
as vehicles for the ascending light. The same context perhaps can be given to the declaration at the end of Pelliot Chinois 3049: "Cause this prayer to enter into the palace
of the god Powerful."

173. The construct of the "Zwölf Herrschertümer" is well attested in Manichaean
sources, including Syriac (Theodore bar Konai; Jackson 1932, 241–42) and Coptic
(*Kephalaion 21*, 64.24ff.; *Kephalaion 4; Psalm-Book* 33.4, 36.29, 133–34, 138.65,
144.24, 220.3.), as well as Iranian, Turkic and Chinese. The basic form simply lists
twelve virtues, called variously "virgins," "authorities," or " wisdoms" (Theodore, M 14,
M 259c, M 453c, M 529, So 10202, So 18221, *Hymnscroll* 174–75). A slightly expanded version identifies each of these virtues with a god from the Manichaean pantheon (Pelliot Chinois 3049, U 52 [T II D 78j.I], *Hymnscroll* 174–75). Further expansion either adds epithets and praise to the divinities (M 798a), or correlates each virtue

with a specific position in the church, the occupants of which are said to be either like the associated divinity (MIK III 4974), or inspired to venerate it (M 738).

174. M 259c.V.2 preserves the single term *hw'bs['gyft]* from the hymn itself. V.3–5 read in full: *hnjft rwc [šhrd'ryft n'mg pd . . . s]wr, pd dw'd[ys bgp]whr šy'kt'[wy]*, "Finished is [the list of] the light [authorities for the reception of the] meal; in the twelve [God-]sons' remembrance" (Morano 1982, 12).

175. With this knowledge, we can look back at M 729.I, which bears a direct reference to "*this* holy table" in its first hymn, and see that its second hymn speaks of the "the triumphant lord, who arranged the twelve diadems of light upon (his) radiant helmet" (V.i.1–6), and provides a list of virtues, probably originally twelve but only nine remaining.

176. The "Twelve Authorities" hymns appear in the sources associated with (and in every case preceding) a hymn called "First Voice" after its incipit (Parthian *wcn hsyng*; Sogdian *wnγr pyrnmcyk*; Chinese *ch'u-Sheng tsan*). This hymn is attested in Parthian (M 259c, M 529), Sogdian (TM 351), and Turkic (Pelliot Chinois 3049 and 3407, and Ch/U 6818 verso); the Chinese *Hymnscroll* transliterates it from Parthian, and categorizes it as a *tsan i-shu*, a "praise of Jesus." It follows a *šhrd'ryft* hymn in M 259c, M 453c, M 529, PC 3049, and the *Hymnscroll*. Like the *šhrd'ryft* hymns, "First Voice" is essentially a list; also like them, it can be expanded by the association of each of its terms with a deity (as in Pelliot Chinois 3049.27–46 and 3407.1–15).

177. See BeDuhn 1999a.

178. Campany 1992, 214.

Chapter 5. Alimentary Rationales

1. *Kephalaion* 87, 217.2–13.

2. *Kephalaion* 115, 277.4–24.

3. Ephrem, *Hypatius* (Mitchell 1912), xxiv.

4. Ephrem, *Hypatius* (Mitchell 1912), xxxi.

5. Ephrem, *Hypatius* (Mitchell 1912), xliii.

6. Ephrem, *Hypatius* (Mitchell 1912), xxiii.

7. Ephrem, *Hypatius* (Mitchell 1912), xxxi (cf. Reeves 1997, 252). Ephrem suggests that the Manichaean appropriation of medical discourse is not consistent in this regard, for "if part of the poison which exists in fruits and roots is 'amassed and collected in us,' (and) if evil is all one, how is part of it in us conquered by 'a law and commandment,' and part conquered (only) by mixtures and drugs?" (*Hypatius* [Mitchell 1912], xxvii).

8. Ephrem, *Hypatius* (Mitchell 1912), xxvi (cf. Reeves 1997, 246).

9. Ephrem, *Against Mani* (Mitchell 1912), II.xcvi–xcvii (cf. Reeves 1997, 243–44). A few lines later, Ephrem remarks, "They also actually proclaim a refining

and cleansing of all rivers and sources and fountains . . . (of) fruits and produce and crops and vegetables" (*Against Mani* [Mitchell 1912], II.xcvii).

10. In Manichaean terminology, "righteousness" generally refers to the institution of the Elect, rather than to an abstract moral concept.

11. Cf. *Hypatius* (Mitchell 1912), xliv: "this refining . . . goes out of the mouth"; xlii: "it is refined by prayer."

12. An-Nadim, *Fihrist* (Dodge 1970), 782.

13. "But if the light is refined little by little and goes out, it is clear that it is a nature *(kyana)* which is dissolved and scattered. And so if the soul is of the same nature, how does it too not go out in the refining?" (Ephrem, *Hypatius* [Mitchell 1912], xxxi).

14. "And if they say that evil confined the soul within the body, in order to imprison it, why then did it not confine that light, which "is refined and departs," so that it could not escape?" (Ephrem, *Hypatius* [Mitchell 1912], xxxii; cf. Reeves 1997, 252–53).

15. Ephrem, *Hypatius* (Mitchell 1912), xxi.

16. Ephrem, *Hypatius* (Mitchell 1912), cix.

17. Ephrem, *Hypatius* (Mitchell 1912), ci.

18. Ephrem, *Hypatius* (Mitchell 1912), cxi.

19. Augustine, *De nat. boni* 44. Elsewhere, he says, "They think that the souls of men as well as of beasts are of the substance of God and are, in fact, pieces of God. They say that the good and true God fought with the tribe of darkness and left a part of himself mingled with the prince of darkness, and they assert that this part, spread over the world, defiled and bound, is purified by the food of their Elect and by the sun and moon, and whatever is left of that part of God which cannot be purified is bound in an everlasting bond at the end of the world" (Augustine, *Epistle 236 to Deuterius* [Parsons 1956], 181). Cf. also *De haer.* 46.42–51 and *C. epist. fund.* 31.

20. Augustine, *De haer.* 46.22–30.

21. Augustine, *De nat. boni* 45.

22. *CMC* 81.2–82.13. Similarly, in *Kephalaion 86*, Mani explains changing moods as reflecting the constituent properties of food, even after the body has been reformed by the Mind of Light and made into a "New Man." Sometimes when an Elect eats, "a troubled limb comes into him in the food *(trophē)* that he has eaten . . . or in the water that is drunk . . ., and wrath increases in him, and lust multiplies upon him, and gloom and sadness because of the meal of the bread that he eats and the water that he drinks, which fills the limbs, troubling his counsel . . . as they come into the body, [mixed] with these meals and they become blended also with the evil limbs of the body" (*Kephalaion 86*, 215.11–20). At other times, he adds, "you find the food that comes into you pure," with relatively little evil content. Then "those good limbs of the meal that come into you find you quiet, at rest, regulated, well in your behavior"

(*Kephalaion* 86, 216.1–3). "They become associates with the living souls that exist in you. Because of this, you find them quiet, in a rest, and they come out of you without disturbance; [and] they find you healthy in your body, your works also orderly, well established in their fashion . . . your soul lightweight to you, rising up in the manner of a bird" (*Kephalaion* 86, 216.7–13).

23. *CMC* 83.20–85.3.

24. Augustine, *De mor. man.* 36. Cf. *C. Faustum* 15.7: "You do not give bread to the hungry, from fear of imprisoning in flesh the limb of your God"; *Conf.* 3.10: "I was foolish enough to believe that we should show more kindness to the fruit of the earth than to mankind . . . . If a starving man, not a Manichaean, were to beg for a mouthful, they thought it a crime worthy of mortal punishment to give him one."

25. Augustine, *De mor. man.* 52.

26. Augustine, *De mor. man.* 50. Cf. Augustine, *De haer.* 46.135–41: "And if they make use of marriage, they should, however, avoid conception and birth to prevent the divine substance, which has entered into them through food, from being bound by chains of flesh in their offspring. For this is the way, indeed, they believe that souls come into all flesh, that is, through food and drink."

27. Augustine, *C. Faustum* 6.8.

28. "It escapes, too, in every animal activity, whether the animal be carrying a load, exercising, working, or performing any other action. It escapes during our sleep while the process called digestion is being accomplished by the internal heat. However, . . . although most of the good takes flight in the activities we have mentioned, not all of it does so" (Augustine, *De mor. man.* 37).

29. Augustine, *C. Faustum* 6.8.

30. *Psalm-Book* 172.15–20.

31. *Psalm-Book* 193.20–22.

32. Augustine, *C. Faustum* 2.5.

33. Augustine, *C. Faustum* 2.5. Cf. *C. Faustum* 20.11: "you maintain in regard to the vulnerable Jesus (*patibilem Jesum*)—who, as you say, is born from the earth, which has conceived by the power of the Holy Spirit—that he hangs in the shape of produce and fruit from every tree: so that, besides this pollution, he suffers additional defilement from the flesh of the countless animals that eat the fruit; except, indeed, the small amount that is purified by your aid."

34. Augustine, *C. Faustum* 20.13.

35. *Psalm-Book* 162.22–26.

36. *Psalm-Book* 162.31–163.13.

37. *Psalm-Book* 163.14–28.

38. *Psalm-Book* 163.29–30.

39. Vööbus 1958, 135.

40. *Kephalaion 84*, 211.24–26.

41. *Kephalaion 84*, 212.16–21. Likewise in *Kephalaion 81*, when a church leader with similar worries wants to withdraw into a private devotional practice similar to Christian eremeticism, Mani forbids it and commends the production of "angels" through the ritual meal as "divine work."

42. *Kephalaion 93*, 236.9–10.

43. *Kephalaion 93*, 236.23–27.

44. *Kephalaion 93*, 237.21–22.

45. *Kephalaion 93*, 238.3–4. Similarly in *Kephalaion 85*, an Elect concerned with the harm inflicted by Auditors treading up and down on the earth gathering alms hears from Mani that the Living Soul puts up with the necessary pain entailed in this ultimately rewarding "godly matter."

46. Augustine, *C. Faustum* 6.4.

47. Gardner translates this word as "rapture" (Gardner 1995, 263); while its general sense is clear, its technical meaning in this context is uncertain.

48. Gardner translates as "immeasurable" (Gardner 1995, 263); the phrase could also be interpreted as "without weight *(shi)*," i.e., "weightless."

49. Gardner translates this word as "springs forth" (Gardner 1995, 263); in either case, it refers to kinetic energy.

50. *Kephalaion 104*, 258.7–25.

51. *Kephalaion 87*, 217.11–20.

52. *Kephalaion 91*, 230.15–18.

53. Augustine, *Conf.* 3.10.

54. *Kephalaion 115*, 277.8–10.

55. *Kephalaion 79*, 191.16–19.

56. *Kephalaion 94*, 239.30–240.12.

57. *Kephalaion 114*, 269.19–270.24.

58. *Kephalaion 108*, 261.26–29.

59. *Kephalaion 81*.

60. *Kephalaion 122*, 292.9ff. "Now whenever any portion of the light is completely purified, it returns to the kingdom of God, to its own proper abode, as it were, on certain vessels, which are, according to them, the moon and the sun" (Augustine, *De haer.* 46.34–36).

61. M 801.754–764.

62. M 95.R.1–14.

63. M 95.V.1–16.

64. M 42.R.ii.11–16.

65. M 42.V.ii.6–14.

66. M 1.402.

67. M 1.437.

68. M 1.403, 423; cf. M 6650.R.5–6.

69. M 1.404.

70. M 1.405.

71. M 1.421.

72. M 1.443; cf. M 6650.V.12–13.

73. M 1.432, 441.

74. M 1.441, 442, 443.

75. Six of these parallels have yet to be published, but M 83 (M 1.396), M 33 (M 1.437), and M 7 (M 1.440) preserve hymns referred to in M 1, while M 6650, a hymn index like M 1, lists incipits matching M 1.399, 400, 402, 403, 406, 407, 408, 438.

76. M 33.R.ii.21ff.; the incipit is found in M 1.437.

77. M 7.I.V.i.25ff.

78. *Hymnscroll* 52.

79. *Hymnscroll* 236–42.

80. *Hymnscroll* 244.

81. *Xuāstuānīft*, 3.

82. T II D 173d.R.14–V.5; translation by Larry Clark (personal communication).

83. T II D 173d.V.5–20; translation by Larry Clark (personal communication).

84. M 35.24–26.

85. T II D 173c,1.R.1–V.9; translation by Peter Zieme (personal communication).

86. T II D 171.R.26–37.

87. M 6020.

88. M 6650.V.3–6.

89. M 454.I.R.7–11.

90. M 7; this song is mentioned in the indices M 1.440 and M 496a.R.2.

91. *Hymnscroll* 246.

92. In the Taisho edition, this is the same graph used in stanza 246 as "weigh," but with a speech radical in place of the latter's metal radical. Robert F. Campany conjectures an error here in the published edition, since the context seems to fit "weigh" better than "exposition" (personal communication).

93. *Hymnscroll* 249–54; translation by Robert F. Campany (personal communication).

94. M 6650.R.11–13 (= M 1.399).

95. M 6650.R.15–17 (= M 1.402).

96. M 6650.R.13–15; V.1–2.

97. M 6650.V.6–11 (= M 1.403).

98. M 7.I.R.ii.45ff.

99. M 7.R.i.5–8.

100. The terms are an-Nadim's, *Fihrist* (Dodge 1970), 791.

101. Al-Biruni, *Athar-ul-Bakiya* (Sachau 1879), 190.

102. *Kephalaion* 87, 217.20–25, reconstructing *jo[le]* in the last clause in place of

Polotsky-Böhlig's *jo[be]* (which Gardner follows in translating "through whom it shall be passed on" [Gardner 1995, 225]).

103. *Kephalaion* 87, 218.5–10.

104. *Kephalaion* 87, 218.27–30.

105. *Tebessa Codex*, col. 5.4–20.

106. *Tebessa Codex*, col. 4.6–14; cf. 16.14–19.

107. *Tebessa Codex*, col. 17.3–15.

108. Hegemonius, *Acts of Archelaus* 10.

109. Augustine, *C. Faustum* 6.8.

110. Augustine, *C. Faustum* 5.10. Cf. *De haer.* 46.114ff.: "They believe that the souls of their Auditors are returned to the Elect."

111. *Kephalaion* 88, 219.6–8, 10–12.

112. *Kephalaion* 88, 220.5–221.4.

113. M 101 + M 911.206–12. This is my own reconstruction of the very fragmentary passage. Compare the closely related parable in lines 258–62 of the same text: "One o[n the shore of] the sea, one on the bo[at. The one who is on] shore [to]ws that one who is o[n the boat]. The one who is on the boat [. . .] the sea."

114. T II D 173b,2.V.1ff.

115. MacKenzie 1979, 504–5.

116. Ibid., 506–9.

117. U 197.V.3–6 and U 196.V.2–4.

118. M 8251.R.1–16.

119. M 8251.R.16–V.19.

120. *Tebessa Codex*, col. 17.

121. Puech 1979, 267–68; for a similar opinion, cf. Ries 1986a, 181.

122. Schaeder 1935, 79.

123. Tardieu 1981, 88.

124. Klimkeit 1993, 21.

125. Augustine, *C. Faustum* 5.10.

126. Other social forces certainly impacted on this relationship in practice. The Elect could mean all sorts of things in the life of individual Manichaeans, not only in terms of the prestige of sponsoring "holy" persons, but also in terms of the complex dynamics involved when the Elect was a member of one's own family. This picture becomes even more complex in the Uygur realm, when the state weighed in with its support. I can only hope that someday we will have the kind of data to assess all of these factors, and to move beyond analysis of the normative system.

127. *Kephalaion* 115, 277.4–24.

128. *Kephalaion* 115, 271.13–20.

129. *Kephalaion* 115, 274.22–28.

130. *Kephalaion* 115, 277.4–24, quoted above.

131. *Kephalaion 115*, 279.7–8.

132. *Kephalaion 115*, 279.11–25.

133. *Kephalaion 115*, 279.26–30.

134. *Kephalaion 115*, 280.4–14.

135. M 177.V.1–16. The story recurs in M 45, where the focus is on the sinfulness of mourning the dead.

136. *Hymnscroll* 406–9.

137. *Kephalaion 115*, 271.8–9.

138. Whether technically it is the third or fourth of the "victories" that is missing is immaterial to this discussion. In either case, one of the four rationales is lost in a lacuna; cf. Gardner 1995, 282.

139. An-Nadim, *Fihrist* (Dodge 1970), 788.

140. *Kephalaion 90*, 224.8–9.

141. *Kephalaion 91*, 230.20–23.

142. *Kephalaion 91*, 230.14–20.

143. *Kephalaion 91*, 230.29–30.

144. *Kephalaion 91*, 233.16–234.14.

145. *Kephalaion 91*, 232.31–233.1.

146. *Psalm-Book* 95.26.

147. *Psalm-Book* 95.30–31.

148. *Psalm-Book* 97.3ff.

149. *Psalm-Book* 111.23–26.

150. *Kephalaion 93*, 238.27–28.

151. *Psalm-Book* 52.27.

152. *Psalm-Book* 87.16–24.

153. *Psalm-Book* 70.18–21.

154. *Psalm-Book* 54.3–4.

155. Hegemonius, *Acts of Archelaus* 10.

156. Augustine, *De haer.* 46.114–32.

157. Augustine, *De mor. man.* 60.

158. Augustine, *De mor. man.* 61.

159. Augustine, *C. Faustum* 5.10. He adds that "a man will not be received into the kingdom of God for the service of giving food to the saints, but because he . . . has himself been chewed and exhaled into heaven."

160. Augustine, *De haer.* 46.114ff.

161. M 454.I.R.5–11.

162. T II D 175,2.I.V.2–6. Cf. U 198.V.16 and U 196.R.1–5: "(May there be) good blessing, with joy and praise, for the providers who procure many perfect alms; may one be renowned for the collection of these, our entire light family!"

163. MacKenzie 1979, 506–9.

164. T II D 173b,2.R.1–V.7; translation by Larry Clark (personal communication).

165. T II D 178.II.R.2–7. This fragment is from the same codex as a copy of the *Xuāstuānīft*. Cf. M 6020: "The one who takes as much merit-food (*pwnw'r*) as a grain of mustard and is not able to redeem it," will suffer a long series of torments in hell. The Sogdian text M 139.II carries a similar warning about "those who eat unworthily."

166. M 221.

167. Another Middle Persian book contains part of the same parable: "The Auditor [who] gives ["soul-]work" is like a [poor] man who presents his daughter to the king; he attains to great honor" (M 101 + M 911.188–91). Even more fragmentary passages yield the following: (1) "The Auditor [is l]ike the b[ran]ch of a fruit[less tree . . .] and the Auditor [. . .] the fruit which [. . .] pious action" (214–20); (2) "The E[lect], the Auditor, and Vahman are like three brothers who were left property by (their) father: land, [. . .], seed. They become partners [. . .] they reap and [. . .]" (220–25); etc.

168. Boyce 1975, 179.

169. M 47.II.R.17–V.18. The story of the Pearl-Borer, deriving from popular Asian traditions, supplied the Manichaeans with another opportune parable about the importance of laboring for salvation. In the story, an owner of pearls hires a pearl-borer for a hundred dinars, but then assigns him other tasks. When the pearl-borer demands his wages, the owner refuses, since the pearls have yet to be bored. The two end up in court, where the judge informs the pearl owner: "You hired this man to do work, so why did you not order him to bore pearls? Why did you bid him play on the lute instead? The man's wages will have to be paid in full . . . give him another hundred gold dinars, and he shall then bore your pearls on another day." The text then explains that the pearl-owner is the soul, the pearl-borer the body, the hundred gold dinars a life of one hundred years, and the pearl-boring piety. If the soul does not direct the body to do works of piety, then the latter cannot be held accountable for the soul's situation. The soul will be forced to "re-hire" a body for another lifetime in order to accomplish what could have been completed in this lifetime (Henning 1945b, 465–69).

170. M 1224.R.1–16.

171. *Hymnscroll* 344.

172. M 1224.V.7–11. Gershevitch has argued persuasively that "the beauty of grain" is an aspect of the Living Self (Gershevitch 1980b).

173. *Hymnscroll* 247.

174. Spiro 1982, 286.

175. Ibid., 287.

176. Ibid., 410. Charges of "selfishness" made against religious elites overlook the ways in which these elites inherit the role not only of antecedent priesthoods, but also of antecedent objects of veneration. The rewards of serving the Elect correspond to those earned in other traditions by serving or directing worship to natural and manu-

factured symbols of divine presence which, even more than the Elect, do not respond in any overtly tangible way. The Elect embody the divine in a unique way, and are revered for this status. The benefits for this reverence and support accrue automatically, according to the laws governing the cosmos. Any personal response on the part of the Elect is superfluous.

177. *Kephalaion 87*, 217.2ff.

178. *Kephalaion 87*, 217.11–13.

179. *Kephalaion 91*, 229.20ff.

180. Jesus: CMC 91.20–93.23; *Tebessa Codex*, T II D 173b,2; TM 170; M 729.I.R.i.2–6; M 139.II; Zarathustra: M 42; M 95; the Buddha: M 1224.

181. In T II D 126, Mani says: "Thirdly, those earlier souls which did not accomplish the work in their religion will come to my religion, which will be for them the door of salvation."

182. Augustine, *De mor. man.* 57.

CHAPTER 6. THE LIBERATION OF THE EMBODIED SELF

1. Puech 1979, 261.

2. Lim 1989, 246 n. 59; cf. 242.

3. M 77; cf. M 722.R.2ff.; M 7.I.V.i.12ff.

4. *Kephalaion 91*.

5. Puech 1979, 311.

6. Puech 1972, 584.

7. Puech 1968, 292.

8. Wolfgang Lentz invokes the Nietzschean phrase "Verneinung des Willens zum Leben" in this context (1961, 106).

9. Puech 1968, 295.

10. Puech 1979, 276. "Abstinence, within the limits set by necessity for maintaining life, is the only means to redemption" (Puech 1968, 297). The Elect "are redeemed by virtue of their total asceticism" (Puech 1968, 309).

11. Puech 1968, 295; cf. Puech 1972, 585–86.

12. Lentz 1961, 106.

13. Lieu 1992, 27.

14. Sundermann 1995, 263. Nils Pedersen also states that "This meal is of crucial importance to the elect's salvation in so far as the elect's salvation is conditioned by their own participation in the work of salvation through the meal" (Pedersen 1996, 295). Nevertheless, he concludes this same sentence by saying, "but the conveyence itself of salvation from God to man appears to be linked to the revelation (of *gnosis*)." Later he reiterates, "The Manichees did not consider that they received salvation through their meal. The Manichee received his redeeming power in the form of the revealed γνῶσις" (299).

15. Puech 1968, 293.

16. An-Nadim, *Fihrist* (Dodge 1970), 787; *Psalm-Book* 54.8ff.; *Gy'n Wyfr's* (Sundermann 1997).

17. Ephrem, *Hypatius* (Mitchell 1912), xciii, cviii, cxi; *Psalm-Book* 155.20–39; *Kephalaion* 108; Gershevitch 1980b.

18. *Kephalaion* 81.

19. Contrary to Puech 1972, 607. In support of his interpretation of Manichaean discipline as mortification, Puech cites *Kephalaion* 79, 191.14–15, which speaks of subduing the *archontikē* within the body; he overlooks the subsequent passage which describes how the fast enables the metabolic processing of the alms. He also cites *Psalm-Book* 149.24, which speaks of strangling the lion within; but he does not weigh such language against the many surrounding passages which speak of setting up a new order within the body, enthroning a new ruler there to replace the slain "lion."

20. *Psalm-Book* 182.20ff.

21. E.g., Widengren 1965, 104; Decret 1974, 112–13; Lieu 1992, 28; Klimkeit 1993, 20.

22. Puech 1968, 296. Koenen, too, casually refers to the Elect's "obligation to separate the divine particles imprisoned in food and to liberate them by eating" (Koenen 1981, 745), without allowing this practice to displace *gnosis* from the center of his understanding of Manichaeism.

23. Puech 1968, 311.

24. Ibid., 265.

25. Ibid., 313–14. Similarly, Pedersen maintains that "the fundamental conveyence of life is the knowledge, γνῶσις, revealed by Mani which conveys salvation to man." On the other hand, he draws attention to the equal necessity of "observance of commandments" in the Manichaean scheme (Pedersen 1996, 295).

26. Puech 1968, 265.

27. Puech 1979, 267–68.

28. Campany 1992, 214.

29. Puech 1979, 261.

30. Ries 1986b, 281.

31. He describes a three-step process of salvation based on his reading of the Coptic sources: *tochme* "call" → *sotme* "hearing" → *saune* "knowledge" (Ries 1984, 1032–33).

32. Ries 1986a, 181.

33. *CMC* 80.18–85.12.

34. Ries 1992, 173. "Salvation does not come from the ritual baptism but from the gnostic message" (Ries 1986a, 176).

35. Buckley 1983 and 1986.

36. Ries 1986a, 178.

37. Ibid., 174. Cf. 179: "Upon the doctrine of the salvation of the world soul is grafted the three *signacula*."

38. Ries 1986a, 179–80.

39. Koenen 1981, 741. Cf. Pedersen 1996, 295.

40. Ries 1986a, 180. Cf. Pedersen 1996, 299.

41. Lentz 1961, 105.

42. Ries 1986a, 181.

43. Ries 1984, 1035.

44. Ries 1986a, 181.

45. Note how *Kephalaion 79*, in providing the rationales for pre- and post-meal fasting, combines disciplinary rationales with alimentary rationales.

46. Foucault 1977a, 26.

47. Foucault 1977a, 136–38.

48. Others include W. B. Henning (Henning 1965, 33–34) and Ilya Gershevitch (Gershevitch 1980b, 281–82), both philologists who perhaps for this very reason escaped the ascendent tropes of comparative religion.

49. Schaeder 1927, 124.

50. Ibid., 81n.

51. He later maintained of Manichaeism, "Its tendency went towards a purely spiritual worship in the form of the promulgation of teaching and preaching, of hymns and prayers, of diligent copying and decoration and artistic preparation of the holy scriptures" (Schaeder 1935, 80).

52. *Kephalaion 81*, 195.3–12, following very closely Gardner 1995, 202–5, for all of *Kephalaion 81*.

53. *Kephalaion 81*, 196.6–10.

54. *Kephalaion 81*, 196.26.

55. *Kephalaion 81*, 195.18.

56. This analogy was suggested to me by Luke Johnson (personal communication).

57. Campany 1992, 202.

58. On this subject, see BeDuhn 1999a.

59. M 6650.V.3–6; *Pothi-Book*, 28–33, 226–31.

60. E.g., T II D 173d. This contact occurs not only through ingestion, but also through the "gates" of the senses; see, e.g., M 801.

61. *Kephalaion 86*, 215.1–216.13.

62. Ephrem, *Hypatius* (Mitchell 1912), cxii.

63. M 2.II.20, 24.

64. *Compendium* (Haloun and Henning 1952), 194.

65. *Hymnscroll* 320.

66. *Hymnscroll* 318.

67. *Hymnscroll* 334.

68. *Hymnscroll* 336.

69. Al-Biruni, *India* (Sachau 1888), 39.

70. Al-Biruni, *India* (Sachau 1888), 54–55.

71. E.g., Augustine, *De mor. man.* 37, 50.

72. M 33.II.V.i.3–4.

73. Ephrem, *Hypatius* (Mitchell 1912), xxxii.

74. *Xuāstuānīft*, 1B.

75. *Kephalaion 70*, 175.6–14.

76. See BeDuhn 1992.

77. *CMC* 85.

78. M 801; cf. Augustine, C. *Faustum* 20.15.

79. *Kephalaion 38*.

80. M 680.23.

81. *CMC* 14.

82. *CMC* 22.

83. Augustine, *De nat. boni* 41.

84. Hegemonius, *Acts of Archelaus* 16.

85. Augustine, C. *Faustum* 24.

86. Chinese: "twelve luminous kings of secondary transformation."

87. Chinese: "luminous nature."

88. Sundermann 1992, line 40.

89. Chavannes and Pelliot 1911, 566–67. Elsewhere, the same text states, "The Second Day is the one wherein the Twelve—Authority, Wisdom, and the rest—are produced by transformation from the Beneficent Light" (543). The Turkic version says that they "emanate from the god Nom Qutï" (Klimkeit and Schmidt-Glintzer 1984, 86–87).

90. So, in terms of the allegory, "Day conquers, and defeats night . . . and then the majesties rule in their own authority: First Authority, second Wisdom, third Salvation, fourth Contentment . . ." (Sundermann 1992, line 44). Though the Parthian fragment breaks off, the Turkic and Chinese versions complete the list of the "Zwölf Herrschertümer" (Klimkeit and Schmidt-Glintzer 1984, 90–91; Chavannes and Pelliot 1911, 568–69).

91. Hence there is a clear, if as yet unexamined, relation between these manifestations of the "second day" and those of the "third day," of which the Chinese version says, "each time that the seven kinds of *mhr'spnd'n* enter into the body of a pure religious master, from the Beneficent Light this one receives the five generosities, and [these] twelve hours accomplish the complete day"; the Turkic version says of the third day that it "is itself the power of the Five Gods, which is freed daily from the body of the Elect." Cf. M 7.I.R.ii.15ff.: "Perfect every limb in the five, seven, and twelve."

92. Sundermann 1992, lines 45–79; Klimkeit and Schmidt-Glintzer 1984, 90–97; Chavannes and Pelliot 1911, 572–84; see Table 3.3.

93. Chavannes and Pelliot 1911, 584–85.

94. In the *Šābuhragān*, Mani speaks of "the knowledge of soul-gathering *(rw'n-cynyḥ)*" as the prerequisite for entering the religion (MacKenzie 1979, 520–21).

95. Foucault 1980, 117.

96. Foucault 1977a, 194.

97. Foucault 1980, 98. Foucault puts forward the hypothesis that "the individual is not a pre-given entity which is seized on by the exercise of power," but "is the product of a relation of power exercised over bodies, movements, desires, forces" (73–74).

98. Foucault 1977a, 29–30.

99. Asad 1993, 167.

100. *Kephalaion 81*, 195.21–23.

101. Foucault 1977a, 30.

102. M 801.

103. G. H. Mead speculates that a key facet of what has been called "religious experience" is the effect of this meeting of the individual "I" and the socially constructed "me," their (often transitory) fusion into a totally unproblematized self which manifests "the successful completion of the social process" (Mead 1934, 273–75).

104. *CMC* 67.7–11.

105. *CMC* 16.1–16.

106. M 39; cf. *Hymnscroll* 344.

107. M 5794.

108. *Kephalaion 87*, 217.11–20.

109. *Kephalaion 93*, 238.2–4.

110. *Kephalaion 115*, 279.18–19.

111. Ephrem, *Hypatius* (Mitchell 1912), xxlii, xxliv; *Kephalaion 104*.

112. The most detailed treatment (not necessarily duplicated in other regions) is *Kephalaion 114*, 269.17–270.24.

113. *Kephalaion 94*, 239.7–240.12.

114. M 7.I.R.i.5–8.

115. M 7.I.R.ii.15ff.

116. Or "confirm," "reinforce."

117. *Kephalaion 81*, 195.18–20.

118. Chavannes and Pelliot 1911, 554–55.

119. Consideration = the holy church; counsel = the pillar of glory; insight = the moon; thought = the sun; mind = the aeons of light.

120. *Kephalaion 38*.

121. *Kephalaion 2*, 20.3–4.

122. *Kephalaion 26*, 77.17–20.

123. *Psalm-Book* 86.27–30.

124. *Kephalaion 60*, 152.14–17.

125. The first and fourth of the "great works" accomplished by fasting in *Kephalaion 79*.

126. The second and third of the "great works" accomplished by fasting in *Kephalaion 79*.

Chapter 7. "Ein Etwas am Leibe"

1. Ries 1985, 687 (conference discussion).

2. Wheelock 1982, 50.

3. Ibid., 51.

4. Ibid.

5. Austin 1975, 99–100.

6. Wheelock 1982, 56.

7. Ibid., 57.

8. It serves as what Fernandez calls a "social signal," whose significance "lies in the action it stimulates, the orientation of behavior made to it in the process of interaction in the social situation in which it belongs" (Fernandez 1965, 917). The background to such a concept is, of course, Mead's theory of signaling.

9. Wheelock 1982, 58.

10. Miller 1973, 152.

11. Cf. Fernandez 1965, 911: "Symbols which are elaborately expressive for some . . . are simply *situation referential* for others—that is, insofar as they are signaled out for attention they refer back to the ritual itself out of which they sprang rather than to meanings beyond ritual activity . . . simply clues to the conduct of ritual activity rather than expressive of cultural dimensions associated with but beyond that activity."

12. Southwold 1979, 635.

13. Fernandez 1965, 919.

14. As images, they are "objects in experience" with the same epistemological presence as "mountains and chairs" perceived by means of the same sensory apparatus (Mead 1964, 242). Wheelock, however, does not adopt this pragmatist interpretation of the situation (see esp. Wheelock 1982, 61).

15. Frankfurter 1995, 464. Subsequent pages references appear in parentheses in the text.

16. The exposition of Manichaean ritual processes in the Coptic *Kephalaia*, for example, amounts to little more than a detailed analogizing of present acts and operations to primordial deeds and accomplishments.

17. Bell 1992, 115.

18. See the very helpful discussion in Williams and Boyd 1993, 5–11.

19. Rappaport 1979, 178–79.

20. The signaling process accomplishes its effect in the recipient of the signal by eliciting from the recipient a voluntary adjustment to the action referred to by the signal. This "canalization" of direct action upon another into a signaling of that action to the other has the adaptive benefit of curtailing physical coercion between individuals and of abbreviating and regularizing social negotiation of relationships and behavior. The transformation of behavior into formalized patterns, according to the ethologist Julian Huxley, is "the adaptive . . . canalization of emotionally motivated behavior, under the teleonomic pressure of natural selection" (Huxley 1966, 250). Ritualization thus serves "to secure more effective communication ('signaling') function, reduction of intra-group damage, or better intra-group bonding" (258, 266). The rather broad scope given to ritualization by ethology, which correctly finds such processes in other animals besides humans, apparently includes all socially mediated signaling, or what G. H. Mead calls "gesture." Such an inclusive definition fails to distinguish ritual action adequately from other forms of communication or social behavior in general. Jack Goody raises this objection, pointing out that "routinisation, regularisation, repetition, lie at the basis of social life itself" (Goody 1977, 28). Ritual in the narrower sense, the sense usually meant in the study of religions, certainly is involved in the regularization of certain acts, and insofar as it operates by means of the formal properties of signaling, it presupposes a recipient of the signal from which the signaler desires an adjustment or response.

21. Using the language of Rappaport 1979, 179.

22. See, e.g., Horton 1964 and 1967.

23. Bloch 1974, 55–81.

24. "The language of ritual is most often a fixed and known text repeated verbatim for each performance, and the constituents of the immediate ritual setting, to which the language of the liturgy will make frequent reference, are generally standardized and thus familiar to the participants, not needing any verbal explication. Therefore, practically every utterance of a ritual is superfluous from the perspective of ordinary conversational principles" (Wheelock 1982, 56).

25. See Schieffelin 1985, 708–709.

26. Leach 1968, 655.

27. See Southwold 1979.

28. Edward Schieffelin makes the astute point that "unless there is some kind of exegetical supervision of both performance and interpretation by guardians of orthodoxy, the performance is bound to mean different things to different people. In the absence of any exegetical canon one might even argue there was no single 'correct' or 'right' meaning for a ritual at all" (Schieffelin 1985, 722).

29. "The implicit dynamic and 'end' of ritualization—that which it does not see itself doing—can be said to be the production of a 'ritualized body'" (Bell 1992, 98). Ritual "temporally structures a space-time environment through a series of physical movements . . . , thereby producing an arena which, by its molding of the actors, both

validates and extends the schemes they are internalizing" (109).

30. "Essential to ritualization is the circular production of a ritualized body which in turn produces ritualized practices" (ibid., 93).

31. Bell 1992, 183.

32. Fernandez 1965; Catherine Bell reports similar findings by other researchers (Bell 1992, 183 n. 60).

33. Fernandez 1965, 913.

34. Bell 1992, 183. The same point is demonstrated in detail with respect to Burmese Buddhism in Spiro 1982.

35. See Converse 1964; Fernandez 1965.

36. Gerholm 1988, 195.

37. Bell 1992, 186.

38. Rappaport 1979, 194.

39. Ibid., 195.

40. Schieffelin 1985, 722.

41. Rappaport 1979, 195–197.

42. Asad 1993, 62.

43. In the words of Ron Williams and James Boyd, it is in danger of "the mistake of treating a means as an end" (Williams and Boyd 1993, 44).

44. Bell 1992, 107. Bell claims that the "sense of ritual exists as an implicit variety of schemes whose deployment works to produce sociocultural situations that the ritualized body can dominate in some way" (130).

45. Jonathan Z. Smith 1987, 109.

46. This is the principal weakness of the otherwise very important essay on sacrifice by Hubert and Mauss: "The sacrificer—and . . . the object of sacrifice . . . —is not invested with any sacred character before the sacrifice. Sacrifice, therefore, has the function of imparting it to him" (Hubert and Mauss 1981, 51).

47. Bell 1992, 205.

48. Ibid., 220.

49. Ries 1985.

50. Bianchi 1983, 39.

51. Vööbus 1958.

52. Augustine, *De mor. man.* 52.

53. "Discursive practices are not purely and simply ways of producing discourse. They are embodied in technical processes, in institutions, in patterns for general behavior, in forms for transmission and diffusion, and in pedagogical forms which, at once, impose and maintain them" (Foucault 1977b, 200).

54. According to Foucault, a discourse's "role among non-discursive practices" is not "extrinsic to its unity, its characterization, and the laws of its formation," but is one of its "formative elements" (Foucault 1972, 67–68).

55. *C. Faustum* 2.5.

56. See BeDuhn 1992.

57. Foucault 1985, 66–67.

58. Ibid., 68.

59. Ibid.

60. CMC 80ff.

61. Foucault 1985, 70.

62. Ibid., 28.

63. Foucault 1977a, 170–71.

64. Foucault 1977a, 176–77.

65. Bell 1992, 211.

66. Ibid., 134; cf. 212.

67. Cf. Spiro 1982, 409ff. Spiro reports of the Buddhist case that in Burma even monks in violation of the regulations receive alms. In Buddhism, however, alms are simply food, and merit comes not from what the donor does for the food, but for the monk. In Manichaeism the divine status of the food creates a different set of concerns relative to the merit of donation.

68. Foucault 1977a, 187.

69. Ibid., 177.

70. The claim that socialization to a particular way of life occurs within ritual performance itself (e.g., Geertz 1973, 112) does not take account of the apparent disjunction between the kind of fully scripted series of acts that constitute a ritual, and the more loosely structured ethos of nonritual action. Moreover, the actual performance of ritual occupies a very limited portion of a Manichaean's total behavior. Adherents, both Elect and lay, are not expected to constantly perform ritual acts, but to do so periodically. Citing similar periodizations of ritual in other cases, Jonathan Z. Smith and others have proposed that ritual performance reimpresses upon the adherent a code of behavior that decays during nonritual time, and in this way maintains socialization to a particular ethos. Neither of these theories gives due attention to the direct ways that ritual codes ramify into nonritual action through the aptitudes they require for participation.

71. Asad 1993, 114. Subsequent page references are in parentheses in the text.

72. Ibid., 134ff. He follows out some of the implications of Foucault's intuitions; see esp. Foucault 1977a, 161–62.

73. Foucault 1980, 73–74.

74. Mead 1964, 140. It is important to note that the "amorphous, unorganized field of . . . inner experience" arises from particular insurmountable problems that show the previous self of the individual to be inadequate. Hence, this is Mead's account of conversion.

75. Bruce Kapferer has conducted a similar investigation in Meadian terms of rites

of exorcism, which share many discursive elements with the Manichaean analysis of the constituents of human identity (Kapferer 1979).

76. Joas 1985, 118.

77. Ibid., 119.

78. Mead 1964, 129. The "meaning" of these objects are "the consciousness of attitudes, of muscular tensions and the feels of readiness to act in the presence of certain stimulations" within the behavioral repertoire of the individual.

79. Foucault 1977a, 203.

80. Berger 1967, 15.

81. Ibid., 15–16.

82. A unitary experience of the body or the self emerges through socialization, and although the acquisition of such a perception of what is self and what is other occurs in early childhood, the process must recur in any fundamental reformation of the self. One learns the parameters of her body again as it becomes a redefined object for her upon conversion to a new perspective on it. See Joas 1985, 159.

83. Mead 1934, 154–55.

84. Cf. Foucault 1977a, 166, 170.

85. Kapferer 1979, 130.

86. Wheelock 1982, 65.

87. Dreyfus and Rabinow 1983, 196.

88. Foucault 1977a, 26.

89. Ibid., 137.

90. Ibid.

91. "In the correct use of the body . . . nothing must remain idle or useless; everything must be called upon to form the support of the act required. A well-disciplined body forms the operational context of the slightest gesture" (ibid., 152).

92. Ibid., 164. This etic analogy has already been applied to the Manichaean Elect several times, most compellingly by Puech 1968.

93. These channels are set forth in *Kephalaion 104*.

94. The vow of poverty precluded the production of offspring who were considered a burdensome and mundane involvement as well as a re-entrapment of life; the vow of chastity eliminated the exudation of lustful energies; noninjury entailed the cessation of all harmful action and, indeed, the expending of energies in mundane labor of any kind.

95. Augustine, *De mor. man.* 36; Ephrem Syrus, *Hypatius* (Mitchell 1912), xxvii.

96. Metaphor can be defined as "a structural mapping from one domain of subject matter (the source domain) to another (the target domain)" (Lakoff 1986, 294). Understanding an utterance that employs metaphor requires a recognition of the transference from the source to the target domain, regardless of whether that transference is novel or conventional. When metaphors become conventional the source domain re-

cedes from notice but the transferred character of the metaphor is no less recognized from its context of use. Not to recognize the contextual demand for metaphorization would result in dramatic misunderstanding. The conventionalization of metaphorical speech is a process of habituation over time and does not affect the requirements of metaphor production, namely, that "metaphoric predications cannot be *produced* and *noticed* unconsciously" (Sandor 1986, 112, emphasis added). "We speak of metaphor when we think or feel that an identification or predication in question cannot be literal, direct, because it is contrary to our experience and/or logic. . . . The very same verbal form (or visual presentation) may constitute a direct or a metaphorical predication according to one's beliefs" (101).

97. See Foucault 1972, 22.

98. Except for particular statements of analogy or comparison, which will be marked by clear linguistic indicators, and the imbedded metaphors of conventional speech.

99. Bruns 1987, 640.

100. Sandor 1986, 101–2.

101. Ibid., 114.

102. "We universalize in the name of metaphor, forcing our own way of thinking, our logic, on others" (ibid., 102).

103. Jonathan Z. Smith 1987, 101–2.

104. Keesing 1985, 212.

105. Ibid., 211.

106. To borrow a phrase from Kurt Rudolph, the study of religions is "implicitly ideological-critical."

107. Ascription of metaphor is dependent upon two interpretive determinations: "not to accept literal meaning and not to accept absurdity or inanity" (Sandor 1986, 108). This determination stands behind Decret's interpretation of Manichaeism, since he insists that, "to receive the Message of Mani in the literal sense is to condemn it to being the 'vain fable' of which Augustine speaks, for it is to refuse to understand it in its authentic signification" (Decret 1974, 80).

108. Burshatin 1984, 212.

109. Davidson 1984, 137.

110. Ibid., 137. In the characterization of Robert Feleppa, "The interpreter must take the subject's beliefs as being both about, and caused by, objects or states of affairs as the interpreter sees them" (Feleppa 1990, 106–7).

111. Bruns 1987, 642.

112. Sandor 1986, 103; for supporting arguments, see 111ff. By metaphor in this context Sandor means active, not conventionalized, metaphorical utterance. Nothing in my presentation should be regarded as a rejection of the Lakoff-Johnson hypothesis about the ways in which languages expand into new experiential domains by

metaphorical application of pre-existing vocabularies. An analysis of Manichaean discourse in these terms must await future study.

113. According to Smith, in the study of ritual "that which was 'other' remained obdurately so and, hence, was perceived to be bereft of all value. The 'other' displayed in ritual could not be appropriated as could myth and was therefore shown the reverse face of imperialism: subjection or, more likely, extirpation" (Jonathan Z. Smith 1987, 102). Ritual can also be extirpated more subtly, simply by being ignored.

114. "A universe of discourse is . . . conditioned by . . . the assumption of the reality of the universe in which the discourse takes place. Mutual acknowledgment of that supposition is the condition of meaningful or intelligible discourse. The condition of the meaningfulness of an assertion or proposition is, then, *not* that certain entities about which the assertion is made exist, in the sense of being empirically verifiable, but that the universe of discourse in which these entities have their existence is mutually acknowledged" (Urban 1939, 201).

115. Sandor 1986, 112.

116. Shibles 1971, 56.

117. According to *Kephalaion 81*, the digestive fast produces precisely seven angels per person per day.

118. In his analysis of discursive formations, Foucault recognizes the distinction between these two modes of enunciation, metaphors in what he calls the "field of concomitance," and the "field of presence" including "all statements . . . taken up in a discourse, acknowledged to be truthful, involving exact description, well-founded reasoning, or necessary presupposition" (Foucault 1972, 57).

119. *In Epictetum Encheiridion* 27:71,44–72,15, quoted in Lieu 1992, 31. Cf. Alexander of Lycopolis: "Their stories are undoubtedly of the same sort (as those of the Greek myths) since they describe a regular war of *hyle* against God, but they do not even mean this allegorically, as e.g., Homer did, who, in his *Iliad*, describes Zeus' pleasure on account of the war of the gods against each other, thereby hinting at the fact that the universe is constructed out of unequal elements, which are fitted together and both victorious and vincible" (Horst and Mansfeld 1974, 70); cf. also Augustine, C. *Faustum* 16, 26. On this polemical response, see esp. Lieu 1985.

120. *Xuāstuānīft* 2C; Ephrem Syrus, *Hypatius* (Mitchell 1912), xxii–xxiii; cf. Ferrari 1973; Lieu 1985, 449–54.

121. Stroumsa and Stroumsa 1988, 40.

122. Augustine, C. *epist. fund.* 23, my italics.

123. Although Catherine Bell insists that misrecognition is a concept distinct from Durkheimian mystification (Bell 1992, 108), the two theories have enough in common to be treated together. For Durkheim, mystification obscures the real ends of action from those involved in it. For Bell, misrecognition allows actors to see a generic end for which they are striving, "an intent to order, rectify, or transform a particular situation,"

but does not allow actors to be cognizant of how they are actually reaching those ends; they misrecognize the means (108).

124. Ibid., 109.

125. Actually, in Bell's version of this theory, rituals effect no real change in the situation at all; they merely adjust individuals to it by substituting a comprehensible problematic for an incomprehensible one. "We can say that practice sees what it intends to accomplish, but it does not see the strategies it uses to produce what it actually does accomplish, a new situation . . . the effectiveness of practice is *not* the resolution of the problematic to which it addresses itself but a complete change in the terms of the problematic, a change it does not see itself make" (ibid., 87–88).

126. James Lett has leveled a damning criticism of the whole project of etic descriptions of indigeneous mental systems necessarily entailed in theories of mystification or misrecognition, that is, the proposition that researchers "know more about what is in other people's minds than they do." In brief, if an etic description corresponds to what the insiders recognize in themselves, then it is in fact an emic description; if it does not so correspond, "then in what sense can that description claim to pertain to their thoughts? As scientists, we are either describing *their* thoughts, or we are not; if we are, then the domain of inquiry is emic, but if we are not, then the domain of inquiry may be etic, but the resulting description pertains to our thoughts, and not to theirs" (Lett 1990, 136).

127. E.g., climatic, viral, nutritional, or toxic elements of the environment, accident, violence, etc.

128. The properties of a specific problematic situation elicit what is deemed by that situation's perceiver to be an appropriate response; if the individual has misconstrued the situation, the response will fail, or at best succeed only by accident or coincidence, unless one proposes a Darwinian model which would claim that over the course of human evolution particular ways of responding proved effective (or at least not detrimental) in a set of situations which elicit from humans generally a particular cue of recognition. The latter could be called "the religious cue," or even "the numinous," and would be a case of coincident marking (as in nature a particular color becomes associated with a food source—the animal is cued to respond to a color, though it is the organic content coincident in many cases with that color that makes the response an effective one).

129. Hughes 1980, 111.

130. MacIntyre 1971, 255.

131. See Mead 1938, 60–62.

132. See Foucault 1980, 82.

133. "Thus as we look back the same world was there existing for a narrower experience, in a form which to wider experience possesses reality only for that narrower experience, from our standpoint only as an idea" (Mead 1938, 40; cf. Mead 1932, 171ff.).

134. Mead 1938, 613–14.

135. This property of emic aprehensions of reality, which makes etic reconfiguration unfelicitous for explanation, is called "referential opacity" by Robert Feleppa (Feleppa 1990, 112).

136. See Dretske 1988, 79–107, for a precise, compelling account of how beliefs function as causes in systems of behavior.

137. Mead proposed that historians formalize what is already our instinctive tactic of translation, that is, the subsuming of past worldviews into modern accounts by observations of equivalence, by a "system of transformations." The mind is able to bring conflicting realities under control by symbols, with a suspension of response or affirmation of them, manipulating them just as one ordinarily spins out scenarios before acting upon the one of choice (Mead 1932, 79ff.). Mead contends that two contradictory realities "are both real for a mind that can occupy in passage both systems" (82). The basic idea of rejecting the competition of realities in favor of the application of rules of equivalence has recently been taken up in Wallis and Bruce 1986.

BIBLIOGRAPHY

Allberry, C.R.C. 1938a. *A Manichaean Psalm-Book, Part II*. Stuttgart: W. Kohlhammer Verlag.

———. 1938b. Das Manichäische Bema-Fest. ZNW 37:2–10.

Andreas, F. C., and W. B. Henning. 1933. Mitteliranische Manichaica aus Chinesisch-Turkestan, II. SPAW 292–363.

———. 1934. Mitteliranische Manichaica aus Chinesisch-Turkestan, III. SPAW 846–912.

Asad, Talal. 1993. *Genealogies of Religion*. Baltimore: Johns Hopkins University Press.

Asmussen, Jes P. 1965. *Xuāstuānīft: Studies in Manichaeism*. Copenhagen: Prostant apud Munksgaard.

Austin, J. L. 1975. *How to Do Things with Words*. Cambridge: Harvard University Press.

Baldwin, John D. 1986. *George Herbert Mead: A Unifying Theory for Sociology*. Beverly Hills, Calif.: Sage.

Bang, Willi. 1931. Manichäische Erzähler. *Le Muséon* 44:1–36.

Bang, W., and A. von Gabain. 1928. Ein uigurisches Fragment über den manichäischen Windgott. *Ungarische Jahrbücher* 8:248–56.

———. 1929. Türkische Turfan-Texte, II. Manichaica. SPAW 411–30.

Bartholomae, Christian. 1913. Mitteliranische Studien IV. *Wiener Zeitschrift für die Kunde des Morgenlandes* 27:347–74.

———. 1961. *Altiranisches Wörterbuch*. Berlin: W. de Gruyter Verlag.

BeDuhn, Jason D. 1992. A Regimen for Salvation: Medical Models in Manichaean Asceticism. *Semeia* 58:109–34.

———. 1999a. Eucharist or Yasna? Antecedents of Manichaean Food Ritual. In *Studia Manichaica. IV. International Congress zum Manichäismus, 14.–18. Juli 1997*, edited by R. E. Emmerick, W. Sundermann, and P. Zieme. Berlin: Akademie Verlag.

———. 1999b. Middle Iranian and Turkic Texts Associated with Manichaean Art from Turfan. In *Medieval Manichaean Art in Berlin Collections*, edited by Z. Gulácsi. Turnhout: Brepols.

———. 2000. The Historical Assessment of Speech Acts: Clarifications of Austin and Skinner for the Study of Religions. *Method and Theory in the Study of Religion* (forthcoming).

———. 2000. The Metabolism of Salvation: Manichaean Concepts of Human Physiology. In *The Light and the Darkness: Studies in Manichaeism and Its World*, edited by P. Mirecki and J. BeDuhn. Leiden: E. J. Brill, forthcoming.

BeDuhn, J. D., and G. Harrison. 1997. The *Tebessa Codex*: A Manichaean Treatise on Biblical Exegesis and Church Order. In *Emerging from Darkness: Studies in the Recovery of Manichaean Sources*, edited by P. Mirecki and J. D. BeDuhn, 33–87. Leiden: E. J. Brill.

Bell, Catherine. 1992. *Ritual Theory, Ritual Practice*. Oxford: Oxford University Press.

Berger, Peter. 1967. *The Sacred Canopy: Elements of a Sociological Theory of Religion*. New York: Doubleday.

Bianchi, Ugo. 1983. Some Reflections on the Greek Origin of Gnostic Ontology and the Christian Origin of the Gnostic Savior. In *New Testament and Gnosis*, edited by A.H.B. Logan and A.J.M. Wedderburn, 38–45. Edinburgh: T. & T. Clark.

Bloch, Maurice. 1974. Symbols, Song, Dance, and Features of Articulation. *European Journal of Sociology* 15:55–81.

Böhlig, A. 1966. *Kephalaia. Zweite Hälfte*. Stuttgart: W. Kohlhammer.

Boyce, Mary. 1952. Some Parthian Abecedarian Hymns. *BSOAS* 14:435–50.

———. 1960. *A Catalogue of the Iranian Manuscripts in Manichaean Script in the German Turfan Collection*. Berlin: Akademie Verlag.

———. 1962. On Mithra in the Manichaean Pantheon. In *A Locust's Leg*, 44–54. London: Percy Lund, Humphries.

———. 1966. Ataš-zohr and Ab-zohr. *JRAS* 100–118.

———. 1968. The Pious Foundations of the Zoroastrians. *BSOAS* 31:270–89.

———. 1975. *A Reader in Manichaean Middle Persian and Parthian*. Leiden: E. J. Brill.

———. 1989. *A Persian Stronghold of Zorastrianism*. Lanham, Md.: University Press of America.

Bruns, Gerald L. 1987. Midrash and Allegory: The Beginnings of Scriptural Interpretation. In *The Literary Guide to the Bible*, edited by Robert Alter and Frank Kermode, 625–46. Cambridge: Harvard University Press.

Buckley, Jorunn J. 1983. Mani's Opposition to the Elchasaites: A Question of Ritual.

In *Traditions in Contact and Change*, edited by P. Slater and D. Wiebe, 323–36, 713–15. Waterloo: Wilfred Laurier University Press.

——. 1986. Tools and Tasks—Elchasaite and Manichaean Purification Rituals. *Journal of Religion* 66:399–411.

Burkitt, F. C. 1925. *The Religion of the Manichees*. Cambridge: Cambridge University Press.

Burleigh, J.H.S. 1953. *Augustine: Earlier Writings*. Philadelphia: Westminster.

Burshatin, Israel. 1984. Power, Discourse, and Metaphor in the *Abencerraje*. *MLN* 99:195–213.

Campany, Robert F. 1992. Xunzi and Durkheim as Theorists of Ritual Practice. In *Discourse and Practice*, edited by F. Reynolds and D. Tracy, 197–231. Albany: State University of New York Press.

Chavannes, Éduard, and Paul Pelliot. 1911. Un traité manichéen retrouvé en chine. *Journal asiatique* 499–617.

——. 1913. Un traité manichéen retrouvé en Chine, II. *Journal asiatique* 99–199, 261–394.

Chidester, D. 1986. Michel Foucault and the Study of Religion. *RSR* 12:1–9.

Clark, Larry V. 1982. The Manichaean Turkic *Pothi-Book*. *Altorientalische Forschungen* 9:145–218.

Converse, Philip. 1964. The Nature of Belief Systems in Mass Publics. In *Ideology and Discontent*, edited by D. Apter, 206–61. New York: Free Press.

Davidson, D. 1984. *Inquiries into Truth and Interpretation*. Oxford: Clarendon.

De Blois, F. 1999. The Manichaean Daily Prayers: In *Studia Manichaica. IV. Internationaler Kongress zum Manichäsmus 14.–18. Juli 1997*, edited by R. E. Emmerick, W. Sundermann, and P. Zieme. Berlin: Akademie Verlag.

Decret, François. 1970. *Aspects du Manichéisme dans l'Afrique Romaine*. Paris: Études Augustiniennes.

——. 1974. *Mani et la tradition manichéenne*. Bourges: Tardy Quercy Auvergne.

——. 1978. *L'Afrique Manichéenne*. Paris: Études Augustiniennes.

Dodge, Bayard. 1970. *The Fihrist of al-Nadim*. New York: Columbia University Press.

Dretske, Fred. 1988. *Explaining Behavior: Reasons in a World of Causes*. Cambridge: MIT Press.

Dreyfus, H. L., and P. Rabinow. 1983. *Michel Foucault, Beyond Structuralism and Hermeneutics*, 2nd ed. Chicago: University of Chicago Press.

Drijvers, Hans. 1984. Conflict and Alliance in Manichaeism. In *Struggles of the Gods*, 99–124. The Hague: Mouton.

Durkheim, Émile. 1915. *The Elementary Forms of the Religious Life*. London: Allen and Unwin.

Ebert, Jorinde. 1994. Darstellungen der Passion Manis in bekannten und unbekannten Bildfragmenten des Bema-Fests aus der Turfan-Sammlung. In *Memoriae Munusculum: Gedankband für Annemarie v. Gabain*, edited by K. Röhrborn and W. Veenker, 1–28. Wiesbaden: Otto Harrassowitz.

Feleppa, Robert. 1990. Emic Analysis and the Limits of Cognitive Diversity. In *Emics and Etics: The Insider/Outsider Debate*, edited by Thomas N. Headland et al., 100–119. London: Sage.

Fernandez, James W. 1965. Symbolic Consensus in a Fang Reformative Cult. *American Anthropologist* 67:902–29.

Ferrari, Leo C. 1973. Astronomy and Augustine's Break with the Manichees. *REA* 19:263–76.

Forte, A. 1973. Deux études sur le manichéisme chinois. *T'oung Pao* 59:234–35.

Foucault, Michel. 1972. *The Archaeology of Knowledge*. New York: Pantheon.

———. 1977a. *Discipline and Punish*. New York: Pantheon.

———. 1977b. *Language, Counter-Memory, Practice*. Ithaca, N.Y.: Cornell University Press.

———. 1980. *Power/Knowledge*. New York: Random House.

———. 1985. *The Use of Pleasure*. New York: Random House.

Frankfurter, David. 1995. Narrating Power: The Theory and Practice of the Magical *Historiola* in Ritual Spells. In *Ancient Magic and Ritual Power*, edited by M. Meyer and P. Mirecki, 457–76. Leiden: E. J. Brill.

Gardner, Iain. 1995. *The Kephalaia of the Teacher*. Leiden: E. J. Brill.

Geertz, Clifford. 1973. Religion as a Cultural System. In *The Interpretation of Cultures*, 87–125. New York: Basic Books.

Geng Shimin. 1991. Notes on an Ancient Uighur Official Decree Issued to a Manichaean Monastery. *Central Asiatic Journal* 35:209–30.

Gerholm, Tomas. 1988. On Ritual: A Postmodernist View. *Ethos* 53:190–203.

Gershevitch, Ilya. 1954. *A Grammar of Manichaean Sogdian*. Oxford: Oxford University Press.

———. 1980a. The Bactrian Fragment in Manichaean Script. *Acta Orientalia Hungaricae* 28:273–80.

———. 1980b. Beauty as the Living Soul in Iranian Manichaeism. *Acta Orientalia Hungaricae* 28:281–88.

Goody, Jack. 1977. Against "Ritual": Loosely Structured Thoughts on a Loosely Defined Topic. In *Secular Ritual,* edited by S. F. Moore and B. G. Myerhoff, 25–35. Amsterdam: Van Gorcum.

Gulácsi, Z. 1999. *Medieval Manichaean Art in Berlin Collections.* Turnhout: Brepols.

———. 2000. Reconstructing Manichaean Book Paintings through the Technique of Their Makers. In *The Light and the Darkness: Studies in Manichaeism and Its World,* edited by P. Mirecki and J. BeDuhn. Leiden: E. J. Brill, forthcoming.

Haloun, G., and W. B. Henning. 1952. The Compendium of the Doctrines and Styles of the Teaching of Mani, the Buddha of Light. *Asia Major* (n.s.) 3:184–212.

Hamilton, James. 1986. *Manuscrits ouïgours du IXe–Xe siècle de Touen-Houang.* Paris: Peeters Press.

Harris, Marvin. 1979. *Cultural Materialism.* New York: Random House.

Henning, W. B. 1932. Ein manichäischer kosmogonischer Hymnus. *NGGW* 214–28.

———. 1936a. *Ein manichäisches Bet- und Beichtbuch* (APAW 1936, phil.-hist. Kl., Nr. 10).

———. 1936b. Neue Materialen zur Geschichte des Manichäismus. *ZDMG* 90:1–18.

———. 1936c. Soghdische Miszellen. *BSOS* 8:583–99.

———. 1937. A List of Middle-Persian and Parthian Words. *BSOS* 9:79–92.

———. 1939. The Great Inscription of Šapur I. *BSOS* 9:823–50.

———. 1940. *Sogdica.* London: James G. Forlong Fund.

———. 1943. The Book of the Giants. *BSOAS* 11:52–74.

———. 1944. The Murder of the Magi. *JRAS* 133–44.

———. 1945a. The Manichaean Fasts. *JRAS* 146–64.

———. 1945b. Sogdian Tales. *BSOAS* 11:465–87.

———. 1954. Notes on the Great Inscription of Šapur I. In *Jackson Memorial Volume.* Bombay.

———. 1965. A Grain of Mustard. *AION* 50:29–47.

Horst, P. W. van der, and J. Mansfeld. 1974. *An Alexandrian Platonist against Dualism: Alexander of Lycopolis' Treatise "Critique of the Doctrines of Manichaeus."* Leiden: E. J. Brill.

Horton, Robin. 1964. Ritual Man in Africa. *Africa* 34, no. 2.

———. 1967. African Traditional Thought and Western Science. *Africa* 37: 50–71, 155–87.

Hubert, H., and M. Mauss. 1981. *Sacrifice: Its Nature and Functions.* Chicago: University of Chicago Press.

Hughes, John. 1980. *The Philosophy of Social Research.* London: Longman.

Hughes, John A., Peter J. Martin, and W. W. Sharrock. 1995. *Understanding Classical Sociology: Marx, Weber, Durkheim.* London: Sage.

Hutter, Manfred. 1992. *Manis kosmogonische Šābuhragān-Texte*. Wiesbaden: Otto Harrassowitz.

Huxley, Julian. 1966. A Discussion on Ritualization of Behavior in Animals and Man. *Philosophical Transactions of the Royal Society of London*. Series B, 251: 247–526.

Jackson, A.V.W. 1929. On Turfan Pahlavi *Miyazdagtacih*, as Designating a Manichaean Ceremonial Offering. *JAOS* 49:34–39.

———. 1932. *Researches in Manichaeism with Special Reference to the Turfan Fragments*. New York: Columbia University Press.

Joas, Hans. 1985. *G. H. Mead: A Contemporary Re-examination of His Thought*. Cambridge: MIT Press.

Kang, W. 1976. *G. H. Mead's Concept of Rationality: A Study of the Use of Symbols and Other Implements*. The Hague: Mouton.

Kapferer, Bruce. 1979. Mind, Self, and Other in Demonic Illness: The Negation and Reconstruction of Self. *American Ethnologist* 6:110–33.

Keesing, Roger. 1985. Conventional Metaphors and Anthropological Metaphysics: The Problematic of Cultural Translation. *Journal of Anthropological Research* 41:201–17.

Klimkeit, H.-J. 1982. Manichaean Kingship: Gnosis at Home in the World. *Numen* 29:17–32.

———. 1993. *Gnosis on the Silk Road: Gnostic Parables, Hymns and Prayers from Central Asia*. San Francisco: HarperCollins.

Klimkeit, H.-J., and H. Schmidt-Glintzer. 1984. Die türkischen Parallelen zum chinesisch-manichäischen Traktat. *Zentralasiatische Studien* 17:82–117.

Koenen, Ludwig. 1981. From Baptism to the Gnosis of Manichaeism. In *The Rediscovery of Gnosticism*, edited by B. Layton, 734–56. Leiden: E. J. Brill.

———. 1983. Manichäische Mission und Klöster in Ägypten. In *Das Römisch-Byzantinische Ägypten*, 93–108. Mainz am Rhein: P. von Zabern.

Koenen, L., and C. Römer. 1988. *Der Kölner Mani-Kodex*. Opladen: Westdeutscher Verlag.

Lakoff, G. 1986. The Meaning of Literal. *Metaphor and Symbolic Activity* 1:291–96.

Leach, E. R. 1968. Virgin Birth (letter). *Man* (n.s.) 3:655.

Le Coq, Albert von. 1911. *Türkische Manichaica aus Chotscho, I* (APAW 1911, phil.-hist. Kl., Nr. 6).

———. 1919. *Türkische Manichaica aus Chotscho, II* (APAW 1919, phil.-hist. Kl., Nr. 3).

———. 1922. *Türkische Manichaica aus Chotscho, III* (APAW 1922, phil.-hist. Kl., Nr. 2).

———. 1923. *Die buddhistische Spätantike in Mittelasien, II: Die manichäischen Miniaturen.* Graz: Akademische Druck- u. Verlagsanstalt.

Lentz, Wolfgang. 1961. What Is the Manichaean Nous? *Ural-Altäische Jahrbücher* 33:101–6.

Lett, James. 1990. Emics and Etics: Notes on the Epistemology of Anthropology. In *Emics and Etics: The Insider/Outsider Debate,* edited by Thomas N. Headland et al., 127–42. London: Sage.

Lieu, Samuel N. C. 1977. A Lapsed Chinese Manichaean's Correspondence with a Confucian Official in the Late Sung Dynasty (1265). *Bulletin of the John Rylands University Library of Manchester* 59:397–425.

———. 1981. Precept and Practice in Manichaean Monasticism. *JTS* 32:153–73.

———. 1985. Some Themes in Later Roman Anti-Manichaean Polemics, I. *Bulletin of the John Rylands University Library of Manchester* 68:434–72.

———. 1992. *Manichaeism in the Later Roman Empire and Medieval China.* 2nd ed. Tübingen: Mohr.

———. 1994. *Manichaeism in Mesopotamia and the Roman East.* Leiden: E. J. Brill.

Lim, R. 1989. Unity and Diversity among Western Manichaeans: A Reconsideration of Mani's *sancta ecclesia. REA* 35:231–50.

MacIntyre, Alistair. 1971. *Against the Self-Images of the Age.* New York: Schocken.

MacKenzie, D. N. 1976. *The Buddhist Sogdian Texts of the British Library.* Leiden: E. J. Brill.

———. 1979. Mani's *Šābuhragān. BSOAS* 42:500–534.

———. 1980. Mani's *Šābuhragān*—II. *BSOAS* 43:288–310.

Mead, G. H. 1932. *The Philosophy of the Present.* Chicago: University of Chicago Press.

———. 1934. *Mind, Self, Society.* Chicago: University of Chicago Press.

———. 1938. *The Philosophy of the Act.* Chicago: University of Chicago Press.

———. 1964. *Selected Writings.* Chicago: University of Chicago Press.

Miller, David L. 1973. *George Herbert Mead: Self, Language, and the World.* Austin: University of Texas Press.

Mitchell, C.W.S. 1912. *S. Ephraim's Prose Refutations of Mani, Marcion and Bardaisan.* 2 vols. London: Williams and Norgate.

Morano, Enrico. 1982. The Sogdian Hymns of of the *Stellung Jesu. East and West* 32:9–43.

Moriyasu Takao. 1991. *A Study on the History of Uighur Manichaeism: Research on some Manichaean meterials and their historical background.* Osaka: Osaka University Press.

Müller, F.W.K. 1904. *Handschriften-Reste in Estrangelo-Schrift aus Turfan, Chinesisch-Turkistan. II. Teil (APAW* 1904, phil.-hist. Kl., Nr. 2).

———. 1912a. *Ein Doppelblatt aus einem manichäischen Hymnenbuch (Mahrnâmag) (APAW* 1912, phil.-hist. Kl., Nr. 5).

———. 1912b. *Soghdische Texte I (APAW* 1912, phil.-hist. Kl., Nr. 2).

Müller, Liguori. 1956. *The De Haeresibus of Saint Augustine.* Washington, D.C.: Catholic University Press.

Nagel, Ernest. 1963. Problems of Concept and Theory Formation in the Social Sciences. In *Philosophy of the Social Sciences: A Reader,* edited by Maurice Natanson, 189–209. New York: Random House.

Natanson, Maurice, ed. 1963. *Philosophy of the Social Sciences: A Reader.* New York: Random House.

Parsons, Wilfrid. 1951. *Saint Augustine. Letters, Volume 1 (1–82).* New York: Fathers of the Church.

———. 1956. *Saint Augustine. Letters, Volume 5 (204–270).* New York: Fathers of the Church.

Pedersen, Nils Arne. 1996. *Studies in the Sermon on the Great War.* Aarhus: Aarhus University Press.

Pike, K. L. 1954 (1967). *Language in Relation to a Unified Theory of the Structure of Human Behavior.* The Hague: Mouton.

Pine-Coffin, R. S. 1961. *Saint Augustine. Confessions.* Harmondsworth: Penguin.

Pines, Shlomo. 1966. *The Jewish Christians of the Early Centuries of Christianity according to a New Source.* Jerusalem: Academy of Sciences and Humanities.

Polotsky, H. J. 1934. *Manichäische Homilien.* Stuttgart: W. Kohlhammer Verlag.

Polotsky, H. J., and A. Böhlig. 1940. *Kephalaia.* Stuttgart: W. Kohlhammer Verlag.

Puech, H.-C. 1949. *Le Manichéisme. Son Fondateur—Sa Doctrine.* Paris: S.A.E.P.

———. 1968. The Concept of Redemption in Manichaeism. In *The Mystic Vision,* edited by J. Campbell, 247–314. Princeton: Princeton University Press.

———. 1972. Le Manichéisme. *Histoire des Religions, II,* Encyclopédie de la Pléiade, 523–645. Belgium: Éditions Gallimard.

———. 1979. *Sur le Manichéisme et autres essais.* Paris: Flammarion.

Rappaport, Roy A. 1979. The Obvious Aspects of Ritual. In *Ecology, Meaning, and Religion,* 173–222. Richmond: North Atlantic.

Reeves, John C. 1997. Manichaean Citations from the *Prose Refutations* of Ephrem. In *Emerging from Darkness: Studies in the Recovery of Manichaean Sources,* edited by P. Mirecki and J. D. BeDuhn, 217–88. Leiden: E. J. Brill.

Renier, G. J. 1950. *History: Its Purpose and Method.* New York: Harper and Row.

Ries, Julien. 1977. Commandments de la justice et vie missionaire dans l'Église de Mani. In *Gnosis and Gnosticism*, edited by M. Krause, 93–106. Leiden: E. J. Brill.

———. 1980. Á propos de la vie religieuse et missionaire des élus manichéens. In *Gnosticisme et Monde Hellenistique*, edited by J. Ries and J.-M. Sevrin, 120–22. Louvain-la-Neuve: Centre d'Histoire des Religions.

———. 1984. Manichéisme. In *Dictionnaire des Religions*, edited by P. Poupard et al., 1030–36. Paris: Universitaires de France.

———. 1985. L'*Enkrateia* et les motivations dans les *Kephalaia* Coptes de Medinet Madi. In *La Tradizione dell'Enkrateia: Motivazioni Ontologiche e Protologiche*, edited by Ugo Bianchi, 369–83. Rome: Edizioni dell'Ateneo.

———. 1986a. La doctrine de l'âme du monde et des trois sceaux dans la contraversé de Mani avec les Elchasaites. In *Codex Manichaicus Coloniensis*, edited by L. Cirillo and A. Roselli, 169–81. Consenza: Marra editore.

———. 1986b. Sacré, Sainteté et Salut Gnostique dans la Liturgie Manichéenne Copte. In *L'Expression du Sacré dans les Grandes Religions*, 3:257–88. Louvain-la-Neuve: Centre d'Histoire des Religions.

———. 1988. *Les Études Manichéennes*. Louvain-la-Neuve: Centre d'Histoire des Religions.

———. 1992. Le Codex de Cologne et les débuts de l'enseignement de Mani. In *Studia Manichaica*, edited by G. Weissner and H.-J. Klimkeit, 167–80. Wiesbaden: Otto Harrassowitz.

Roberts, Alexander, and James Donaldson, eds. 1987. *The Ante-Nicene Fathers*, vol. 6. Grand Rapids, Mich.: Eerdmans.

Roberts, C. H. 1938. *Catalogue of the Greek and Latin Papyri in the John Rylands Library, Manchester, 3: Theological and Literary Texts (Nos. 457–551)*. Manchester: John Rylands University Press.

Rudolph, Kurt. 1985. The Foundations of the History of Religions and Its Future Task. In *History of Religions: Retrospect and Prospect*, ed. Joseph M. Kitagawa, 105–20. New York: Macmillan.

———. 1992. Stand und Aufgaben der Manichäismusforschung. Einige Überlegungen. In *Studia Manichaica*, edited by G. Weissner and H.-J. Klimkeit, 1–18. Wiesbaden: Otto Harrassowitz.

Sachau, Eduard. 1879. *The Chronology of Ancient Nations*. London: William H. Allen.

———. 1888. *Alberuni's India*. London: K. Paul, Trench, Trubner.

Sandor, Andras. 1986. Metaphor and Belief. *Journal of Anthropological Research* 42:101–22.

Schaeder, Hans. 1927. Urform und Fortbildung des Manichäischen Systems. *Vorträge der Bibliothek Warburg* 1924–25:65–157.

———. 1934. *Iranica* (AGWG, 3.10).

———. 1935. Manichäismus und spätantike Religion. *Zeitschrift für Missionkunde und Religionswissenschaft* 50:65–85.

Schaff, Philip, ed. 1983. *Nicene and Post-Nicene Fathers,* vol. 4. Grand Rapids, Mich.: Eerdmans.

Schieffelin, Edward. 1985. Performance and the Cultural Construction of Reality. *American Ethnologist* 12:707–24.

Shibles, Warren. 1971. *An Analysis of Metaphor in the Light of W. M. Urban's Theories.* The Hague: Mouton.

Sims-Williams, Nicholas. 1976. The Sogdian Fragments of the British Library. *Indo-Iranian Journal* 18:43–74.

———. 1985. The Manichaean Commandments: A Survey of the Sources. In *Papers in Honour of Professor Mary Boyce* (Acta Iranica 25), 573–82. Leiden: E. J. Brill.

Skinner, Quentin. 1974. "Social Meaning" and the Explanation of Social Action. In *The Philosophy of History,* edited by P. Gardiner. Oxford: Oxford University Press.

Smith, Brian K. 1987. Exorcising the Transcendent: Strategies for Defining Hinduism and Religion. *History of Religions* 27:32–55.

———. 1989. *Reflections on Resemblance, Ritual, and Religion.* Oxford: Oxford University Press.

Smith, Jonathan Z. 1982. Sacred Persistence: Toward a Redescription of Canon. In *Imagining Religion,* 36–52. Chicago: University of Chicago Press.

———. 1987. *To Take Place: Toward Theory in Ritual.* Chicago: University of Chicago Press.

Smith, Morton. 1968. Historical Method in the Study of Religion. In *On Method in the History of Religions,* edited by James Helfer, 8–16. Middletown, Conn.: Wesleyan University Press.

Southwold, Martin. 1979. Religious Belief. *Man* 14:628–44.

Sperber, Dan. 1975. *Rethinking Symbolism.* Cambridge: Cambridge University Press.

Spiro, Melford. 1982. *Buddhism and Society.* 2d ed. Berkeley: University of California Press.

Stroumsa, G. 1982. Monachisme et Marranisme chez les Manichéens d'Egypte. *Numen* 29:184–201.

———. 1984. *Another Seed.* Leiden: E. J. Brill.

Stroumsa, S., and G. Stroumsa. 1988. Aspects of Anti-Manichaean Polemics in Late Antiquity and under Early Islam. *HTR* 81:49–72.

Sundermann, Werner. 1973. *Mittelpersische und parthische kosmogonische und Para-*
beltexte der Manichäer. Berliner Turfantexte 4. Berlin: Akademie Verlag.

———. 1978. Some More Remarks on Mithra in the Manichaean Pantheon. *Acta Iran-*
ica 17:485–99.

———. 1981. *Mitteliranische Manichäische Texte Kirchengeschichtlichen Inhalts*.
Berliner Turfantexte 11. Berlin: Akademie Verlag.

———. 1983. Der chinesische Traité manichéen und der parthische Sermon vom
Lichtnous. *Altorientalische Forschungen* 10:231–42.

———. 1984. Probleme der Interpretation des manichäisch-soghdischer Briefe. In
From Hecataeus to al-Huwarizmi, edited by J. Harmatta, 289–316. Budapest:
Akadémia Kiadó.

———. 1985a. *Ein manichäisch-soghdisches Parabelbuch*. Berlin: Akademie-Verlag.

———. 1985b. Der Gōwišn ī Grīw Zīndag-Zyklus. In *Papers in Honour of Professor*
Mary Boyce (*Acta Iranica* 25), 629–50. Leiden: E. J. Brill.

———. 1989. Ein manichäischer Bekenntnistext in neupersischer Sprache. In *Études*
Irano-Aryennes offertes à Gilbert Lazard, edited by C.-H. De Fouchécour and
Ph. Gignoux, 355–65. Paris: Association pour l'avancement des études irani-
ennes.

———. 1991. *Der Sermon von der Seele: ein Literaturwerk des östlichen Manichäismus*.
Opladen: Westdeutscher Verlag.

———. 1992. *Die Sermon vom Licht-Nous*. Berliner Turfantexte 17. Berlin: Akademie
Verlag.

———. 1995. Who is the Light-Noῦς and What Does He Do? In *The Manichaean*
Noῦς: *Proceedings of the International Symposium organized in Louvain from*
31 July to 3 August 1991, edited by A. van Tongerloo and J. van Oort, 255–65.
Louvain: IAMS-BCMS-CHR.

———. 1997. *Die Sermon von der Seele*. Berliner Turfantexte 19. Turnhout: Brepols.

———. 2000. A Manichaean Liturgical Instruction on the Act of Almsgiving. In *The*
Light and the Darkness: Studies in Manichaeism and Its World, edited by P.
Mirecki and J. BeDuhn. Leiden: E. J. Brill, forthcoming.

Tardieu, Michel. 1981. *Le Manichéisme*. Paris: Universitaires de France.

———. 1987. Principes de l'Exégèse Manichéenne du Nouveau Testament. In *Les rè-*
gles de l'interprétation, edited by M. Tardieu, 123–28. Paris: Cerf.

Thorp, J. P. 1983. Sacramental Food Transactions among South Asian Muslims and
Hindus. In *Traditions in Contact and Change*, edited by P. Slater and D.
Wiebe, 481–502. Waterloo: Wilfred Laurier University Press.

Tongerloo, Aloïs van. 1982. La Structure de la communauté manichéenne dans le

Turkestan Chinois à la Lumière des emprunts moyen-Iraniens en Ouigour. *Central Asiatic Journal* 26:262–87.

Tsui Chi. 1943. Mo Ni Chiao Hsia Pu Tsan, The Lower (Second?) Section of the Manichaean Hymns. *Bulletin of the School of Oriental and African Studies* 11:174–219. English translation of *Hymnscroll: Taishō Shinshū Daizōkyō*, vol. 54, Text 2140, 1270–79 (Tokyo, 1922–33).

Urban, W. M. 1939. *Language and Reality*. London: Allen and Unwin.

Utas, Bo. 1985. Manistan and Xanaqah. In *Papers in Honour of Professor Mary Boyce*, 655–64. Leiden: E. J. Brill.

Vajda, Georges. 1966. Le témoignage d'al-Maturidi sur la doctrine des Manichéens, des Daysanites et des Marcionites. *Arabica, Revue d'Études Arabes* 13:1–38, 113–28.

Vööbus, Arthur. 1958. *A History of Asceticism in the Syrian Orient*. Louvain: CSCO.

Waldschmidt, E., and W. Lentz. 1926. *Die Stellung Jesu im Manichäismus* (APAW 1926, phil.-hist. Kl., Nr. 4).

———. 1933. Manichäische Dogmatik aus chinesischen und iranischen Texten. *SPAW* 480–607.

Wallis, Roy, and Steve Bruce. 1986. *Sociological Theory, Religion and Collective Action*. Belfast: Queen's University Press.

Wheelock, Wade. 1982. The Problem of Ritual Language: From Information to Situation. *JAAR* 50:49–71.

Widengren, Geo. 1965. *Mani and Manichaeism*. London: Weidenfeld and Nicolson.

Williams, Ron G., and James W. Boyd. 1993. *Ritual Art and Knowledge: Aesthetic Theory and Zoroastrian Ritual*. Columbia: University of South Carolina Press.

Zieme, Peter. 1975. *Manichäisch-türkische Texte*. Berliner Turfantexte 5. Berlin: Akademie Verlag.

INDEX